P9-AOG-007

MIND
BODY
SPIRIT

For Vivienne, sister and seeker of the heart

THIS IS A CARLTON BOOK

Design copyright © 2001 Carlton Books Limited
Text copyright © 2001 Jane Alexander

This edition published by
Carlton Books Limited 2001
20 Mortimer Street, London W1T 3JW

A CIP catalogue record for this book is available from
the British Library
ISBN 1 84222 267 8

Printed and bound in Dubai

EDITORIAL MANAGER: *Venetia Penfold*
ART DIRECTOR: *Penny Stock*
SENIOR ART EDITOR: *Barbara Zuñiga*
COMMISSIONING EDITOR: *Zia Mattocks*
EDITOR: *Siobhán O'Connor*
DESIGN: *Balley Design Associates*
PRODUCTION MANAGER: *Garry Lewis*

MIND
BODY
SPIRIT

A COMPLETE GUIDE TO HOLISTIC THERAPIES
FOR MAINTAINING OPTIMUM HEALTH AND WELLBEING

JANE ALEXANDER

CARLTON
BOOKS

contents

introduction

Life is for living, so why aren't you living life to the full? In today's frenetic, stress-filled world,

it's all too easy to let life pass you by. Most of us feel life is a struggle: a battle to get fit and

healthy, a fight to meet deadlines and pay the bills. Our relationships with our own selves can

be less than congenial; our relationships with others are often fraught. Few of us even think

about our relationship with the spiritual world – we simply don't have the time.

Yet all the information we need to lead healthier, happier, more fulfilled lives is ours

for the taking. The fields of natural healing, mind–body medicine, psychology and spiritual

understanding offer many paths to a vital yet peaceful life. Unfortunately we can often

become overwhelmed by the sheer choice.

There are literally hundreds of different therapies and teachings all promising to heal your

body, mind and soul in some way. Which should you choose? Where do you start? The choice

can be bewildering. Fortunately, the answers lie within the pages of one book – this one.

The aim of *Mind Body Spirit* is to provide a simple, straightforward, friendly guide through

the maze of holistic living. We have done all the hard work for you, picking out the nuggets

of sheer gold amid the tomes of heavy theory and complex philosophy. As you work your way

through this clear and concise book, you will readily learn how to incorporate natural health,

emotional healing and spirituality into everyday life. There is no preaching or dictating in these

pages; you are merely presented with useful, effective information and techniques that really

work. Encyclopedic in scope, *Mind Body Spirit* offers a manual for twenty-first century living,

a guide to living your life to the full – each and every day.

how to use this book

How you use this book is entirely up to you. There is a lot of information here – probably way too much for any one person to incorporate into their life! You most certainly *can* read it through from start to finish, but I suspect that most people will find they want to dip in and out. That's fine. Most chapters will stand quite happily alone. You can let your intuition do the deciding – flick through the contents and see what grabs your attention. Or, if you really want to let your unconscious mind choose what it needs, close your eyes and flick through the pages until you feel drawn to stop. Open your eyes and see where you've landed. You may well be surprised to find how relevant the page is to you.

taking responsibility

I firmly believe that the most important thing any of us can do is to take responsibility for our lives. Once we decide that we have the power to change, almost anything can happen.

In the past, it has been common for many of us to hand over responsibility for our health, emotional wellbeing and spiritual lives to other people: to doctors and hospitals; to teachers and therapists; to priests and ministers. We have relied heavily on the opinions and thoughts of other people; we have looked to newspapers, television and society for approval. Yet, when you decide that *you* are in charge of your destiny, it is almost as if a quantum leap occurs and absolutely everything is open to change.

Rest assured, you don't have to go out and make major changes overnight. Even the tiniest shift can create ripples. Adjust your diet a little, start to exercise, practise a ritual, say a prayer and you will have begun a process that almost inevitably leads to other changes. People can and do heal themselves – so can you. You can also develop new ways of living and loving, so that your relationships become more fulfilling and exciting. Work need not be a drag and a duty. Your spirit can be allowed to soar.

when to seek professional help

This book offers plenty of suggestions for leading healthier, happier lives. Yet it cannot work miracles. There are times when you will need expert help. Although I have included numerous self-help tips and do-it-yourself techniques, I would strongly recommend that, if you are drawn to a particular therapy or practice, you seek out an experienced, well-qualified practitioner. Unfortunately, there is still little or no regulation governing natural health therapies. Hence, a large resource section has been supplied at the end of this book, which lists reputable organizations through which you should be able to get in touch with your nearest qualified practitioner (see page 153).

If you have any serious medical concerns or ailments, you must always see your primary care doctor. Of course, there is nothing to stop you using the advice given in this book, but it is imperative that you have standard medical care as well. If you feel that your psychological state is precarious – if, for example, you feel suicidal, are suffering from chronic depression, are psychotic or have severe mental health problems – you need to see an experienced physician or psychiatrist. Also, be aware that many of the exercises in this book are designed to shift emotions and, in the process, they may bring past traumas or difficulties to the surface. If you know that you have painful events in your past, any abuse or trauma for example, it is advisable to work alongside a well-qualified psychotherapist who can help you through any tough times.

fundamental principles

The whole field of mind, body, spirit is vast: there are so many therapies from which to choose; so many traditions; so much advice. Sometimes, it can be difficult to know where to start. In this section of the book, we will be looking at some of the cornerstones of holistic health and living.

Many people find that the best way to get started on the mind, body, spirit path is through one of the major systems of holistic healthcare. Systems such as ayurveda, the Indian mind–body medicine, and traditional Chinese medicine cover all the basic, fundamental principles. If you choose to consult a practitioner of one of these venerable traditions, you will learn about the benefits of good nutrition, good exercise, good breathing and how to cultivate a healthy mind and spirit.

In fact, much of the knowledge of holistic living today comes from the wisdom of the ancients. Most of the great civilizations of the ancient world possessed sophisticated knowledge which has generally been overlooked by modern culture. Ayurveda and traditional Chinese medicine are incredibly ancient – some say more than 5,000 years old. Other systems – such as the Tibetan, Middle Eastern, Mongolian, Hawaiian huna, Native American and so forth – are equally venerable.

These ancient cultures hold many of the key concepts for natural health. For centuries, the people of these cultures have known about the vital energy that circulates through the body. The Chinese called this energy *qi* or *chi*, the Indians called it *prana*; the Sufis, *qawa*. They mapped it clearly and understood that, if the energy were flowing smoothly, good health would follow.

Equally, they understood that mind and body are intrinsically linked. If you make changes to your mind-set, to the way you see the world, your body may undergo quite extraordinary changes. Not only that, but they also believed that by changing the body, shifting posture, realigning joints, releasing tension in muscles and fascia, you may experience profound psychological changes.

This part of the book will introduce you to the basic tenets of energy healing. You will also learn how to start healing yourself – using your own energy channelled through your hands. It's an exciting adventure, so let's get started ...

AYURVEDA

AYURVEDA IS THE OLDEST SYSTEM OF MEDICINE ON EARTH. ITS PRINCIPLES ARE SAID TO HAVE BEEN PASSED DOWN TO HUMANKIND FROM A CHAIN OF GODS LEADING BACK TO BRAHMA, FATHER OF ALL GODS. IT HAS BEEN CALLED THE 'MOTHER OF MEDICINE' AND IS GENERALLY ACCEPTED TO BE THE FORERUNNER OF ALL THE GREAT HEALING SYSTEMS OF THE WORLD.

Written texts show that the ayurvedic medicine practised from about 1500 BC to AD 500 was incredibly advanced, with detailed knowledge of pediatrics, psychiatry, surgery, geriatrics, toxicology, general medicine and other specialties. However, invasions disrupted its teaching and, when the British introduced Western medicine to India, ayurveda became unfashionable and almost disappeared entirely. It was saved, however, by the intervention of Mahatma Gandhi who opened the first new ayurvedic college in 1921.

The fundamental aim of ayurveda is to attain perfect health and wellbeing. The ancient texts say that the human lifespan should be around 100 years – and that all those years should be lived in total health, both physical and mental. The ayurvedic practitioner is therefore looking to balance the body and mind, to ferret out health problems before they happen or to nip them in the bud before they do any real harm. Unfortunately, illnesses (and the shortening of life) are caused by many factors: constant stress; irregular meals; eating the wrong kind of food; taking the wrong medication; living an unhealthy lifestyle; having bad body posture; breathing in polluted air; allowing microorganisms to enter the body; becoming injured; not digesting food properly and even indulging in too much sexual activity!

So, an ayurvedic practitioner's job is pretty complex, to put it mildly. However, ayurveda does produce remarkable results with even the tiniest adjustment: changing your diet or readjusting your working times can have surprising effects on your health. Even if you do decide that the complete ayurvedic package is too much to take en masse, it would still be well worth investigating some of its principles.

Ayurvedic philosophy is incredibly intricate and takes years of study to begin to comprehend. Put at its simplest, it teaches that each atom consists of five elements: its weight comes from earth, its cohesion from water, its energy from fire and its motion from air, while the space between its particles is composed of ether. Under this principle, the entire human body is composed of the five elements and it is thought that an excess of one or more elements can be the cause of imbalance and hence lead to illness.

the doshas

Over the centuries, a kind of shorthand for working out imbalances evolved within ayurveda – the three *doshas*, or bioenergies, which are various combinations of the five elements. *Vata* is a combination of ether and air; *pitta* of fire with water; *kapha* of water and earth. In an ideal state, we would have all three doshas in perfect balance, but this is rare. Most of us have one or perhaps two which outweigh the others. The overall aim of ayurvedic medicine is to balance the doshas to restore health.

Your predominating dosha can be detected by a series of physical and emotional characteristics. For example, vata people are usually thin, agile, quick-thinking and restless; pitta people tend to be of medium build, competitive and make good leaders; kapha people are larger framed and are more placid in nature, possessing great reserves of strength and endurance. The aim of the practitioner is to coax all the elements into perfect balance so perfect health can follow. However complex the theory, the advice is very practical and down-to-earth. The ayurvedic practitioner seeks to balance the body, using primarily a combination of lifestyle advice, diet, exercise and herbal medicines. Massage, manipulation, marma therapy (similar to acupressure), neurotherapy, aromatherapy and sound therapy are also used. Yoga, meditation and deep breathing are highly recommended.

OPPOSITE IN AYURVEDIC PRACTICE, EVERYTHING IN LIFE (INCLUDING OURSELVES) IS COMPOSED OF A COMBINATION OF FIVE BASIC ELEMENTS: ETHER, AIR, WATER, FIRE AND EARTH. AYURVEDA TEACHES THAT KEEPING THESE ELEMENTS IN BALANCE AND IN HARMONY LEADS TO NOT ONLY PHYSICAL, BUT ALSO MENTAL, HEALTH AND WELLBEING.

how to find your ayurvedic type

As we've already seen, we each contain within us the three doshas: *vata*, *pitta* and *kapha*. The dosha that dominates within our bodies gives rise to our *prakruti*, or body–mind type – the basic force that affects everything about us, from our shape and weight to our predisposition to different illnesses. Our prakruti will influence the kind of foods we should eat; the exercise we should take; even the kind of holiday we should enjoy.

Discovering your prakruti is really quite simple – just answer the questions opposite, ticking the answers which most apply to you.

Vata – air and space. Vata people eat little, usually preferring sweet, sour and salty foods, and they tend to be thin. Vatas are active, talkative and do not sleep much; their short-term memories are stronger than their long-term memories and they are often emotionally insecure. Vata elements are responsible for body motion, respiration, sensory impulses, autonomic mind function, circulation, separating digested from undigested food, regulation of menses and the passage of body fluids.

Pitta – fire. People dominated by the pitta element tend to become hot and sweaty easily, and have colour in their skin. They have strong appetites for spicy, sweet and bitter foods. Pittas are articulate and precise, and have strong memories; they can become fiercely angry and emotionally intense. The pitta element is responsible for vision, digestion, heat production, immunity, metabolism, the colour of the skin, organs and body fluids, appetite, thirst, suppleness and intellectual thought.

Kapha – earth and water. Kaphas tend to be large framed, stable and patient. They learn slowly, but have a good long-term memory. Kapha people sleep a lot and tend to be affectionate and emotionally secure. The kapha elements are responsible for maintaining the oiliness of the body and organs, general physical stability, virility, strength and the fluidity of muscular and joint movement.

YOUR BODY

1. What were you like as a child?
a) Small and thin
b) Average
c) Large and plump

2. What is your build now?
a) Thin build with light bones and prominent joints
b) Medium build and bone structure
c) Large-boned, quite heavy and dense in build

3. Do you put on weight?
a) Hardly ever
b) Both easily gain and easily lose weight
c) Find it hard to lose weight

4. What is your skin like?
a) Dry and delicate
b) Soft, maybe ruddy or freckled
c) Thick and oily

5. What kind of appetite do you have?
a) Irregular. You often snack or nibble, and can't finish a large meal
b) Good. You hate to skip meals and feel rotten if you do
c) Healthy. You like your food, but can miss meals without any ill effects

6. How do you walk?
a) Quickly, lightly – always in a hurry
b) Medium pace, determined and purposeful
c) Slowly, steadily and calmly

7. How do you sleep?
a) Lightly, with sleep often interrupted. You may suffer from insomnia
b) Regularly and soundly
c) Heavily and for a long time. You often oversleep or feel drowsy in the day

8. What kind of illnesses are you prone to?
a) Sharp pains, headaches, eczema, dry rashes, nervous disorders, gas or constipation
b) Rashes and allergies, inflammation, heartburn, ulcers, acidity, feverish complaints
c) Fluid retention, excess mucus, bronchitis, sinus problems, asthma, congestion

YOUR MIND AND EMOTIONS

1. What is your basic personality?
a) Enthusiastic, outgoing, talkative
b) Strong-minded and purposeful
c) Calm, placid and good-natured

2. What are you like at work?
a) Quick, imaginative and alert – you are a creative thinker. You hate rigid routine or discipline
b) Efficient, a natural leader. You like well-planned routines and tend to be a perfectionist
c) Calm and organized. You enjoy a regular routine and keep projects running along smoothly

3. How do you react to stress?
a) You become anxious and nervous
b) You become angry or irritable
c) You try to avoid it at all costs

4. How do you dream?
a) Frequently, but you often can't remember dreams on waking

b) Vividly, often in colour. You find it easy to remember your dreams

c) You only remember highly significant or clear dreams

5. How is your sex life?

a) It fluctuates – sometimes you love it, sometimes you aren't interested. You have an active fantasy life

b) Pretty average sex drive

c) You take a while to 'warm up', but then have intense sex – you love it and have great stamina

6. Do you save or spend money?

a) Spend it! You're an impulse buyer with a huge credit-card bill

b) Sensibly spend. You buy useful and classic items

c) Save. You always have enough money to get by

7. What is your memory like?

a) Quick to learn, quick to forget

b) Generally quite good

c) You take a while to learn, but your memory is excellent

8. How would you describe your lifestyle?

a) Erratic, always changing

b) Busy with plenty of plans – you achieve a lot

c) Steady and regular – you may feel rather stuck in a rut

ASSESSING YOUR SCORE

Simply add up the number of a's, b's and c's you have ticked. Predominantly a's means you are mostly a vata type; b's indicate pitta and c's indicate kapha. You may find two scores are equal or very close – it's common to be a combination. Some rare people possess all three doshas equally. Now turn the page to discover what your score means for your health and wellbeing.

While all of these are gentle, non-invasive treatments, some ayurvedic physicians perform quite brutal techniques as well. The deep-cleansing process known as *panchakarma* can include therapeutic vomiting, enemas and purging. Nasal cleansing can be administered and, in cases of blood disorders, blood-letting is sometimes performed.

Ayurveda can be a tough therapy to take because, to achieve the best results, you do need to be totally dedicated to following the lifestyle and diet guidance. However, many Westerners are not willing to get up at 5 am, for example, or eat their main meal at lunchtime as advised. Practitioners and physicians vary in their insistence on rigidly following the rules: some are very dogmatic; others accept that ayurvedic routines can be difficult to adhere to in a Western lifestyle and more and more practitioners are adapting their cures for Western sensibilities. In addition, although ayurveda is considered an 'alternative' therapy, it can be (and often is) used alongside Western treatments.

There is little doubt that, in the hands of an experienced practitioner, ayurveda can achieve wonderful (some would say miraculous) results. At present, a number of research projects are being conducted to try to discover how these cures take place and to investigate the properties of several ayurvedic herbs and herbal preparations. Preliminary studies by the (American) National Cancer Institute research project indicate that one herb, *Semicarpus anacardium*, may inhibit the growth of certain cancers. Meanwhile, a compound of herbs called *maharishi amrit kalash* has been found to possess anticarcinogenic and antineoplastic properties – the compound appears to both prevent the start of cancer and decrease the size of existing tumours. A series of experiments carried out at South Dakota State University and the Ohio State University College of Medicine indicates that it 'may have great value in the prevention and treatment of cancer'.

what can ayurveda help?

- Digestive problems such as stomach ulcers, chronic gastritis, acid indigestion, heartburn, constipation and flatulence benefit from ayurveda.
- Gynaecological problems such as menstrual and menopausal difficulties can be helped.
- Ayurveda helps with weight problems such as weight loss and weight gain.
- Skin complaints such as eczema, dermatitis, psoriasis and acne can be improved.
- Allergic conditions such as asthma, hayfever and sinus problems respond well.
- Problems with joints such as chronic pain, muscle tension, sciatica, rheumatism, arthritis and osteoporosis can be alleviated.
- It can help psychosomatic illnesses such as sleep disturbances, migraine and tension headaches, depression and anxiety attacks.
- Heart and blood-circulation problems such as angina, high blood pressure, palpitations and an irregular pulse can be treated.
- Some physicians have also treated conditions such as cancer, multiple sclerosis and myalgic encephalomyalitis (ME) with success – and there is research into HIV/AIDS.
- Ayurveda helps with addictions such as those to alcohol, smoking and drugs.

what can I expect from a session?

WHERE WILL I HAVE THE TREATMENT?

You will be lying on a special massage couch for massage and marma therapy. You will sit in a chair for consultations.

WILL I BE CLOTHED?

It depends. You will generally be completely naked for massage and fully clothed for other treatments.

WHAT HAPPENS?

A session will always begin with pulse diagnosis. The taking of pulses is an exact science – pulses are read in 12 positions. Practitioners will also want to know about your urine and stools, how you sleep, what you eat, how you think and feel. They will probably examine your eyes and your tongue, and they will also be watching how you talk and move.

After diagnosis comes treatment – and the range of treatments is vast. Without doubt, however, you will be given guidelines for healthy living and instructed in the diet that will soothe and counter imbalances in your body type. Ayurveda teaches that what is food for one person could be poison for another: your diet will be tailored precisely for your body type. Herbs are often prescribed. So, too, are yoga exercises and pranayama (breathing) exercises. If necessary, you will be prescribed marma therapy (see pages 22–3) or any one of the incredible range of massage therapies.

WILL IT HURT?

Marma therapy can be particularly painful. However, the other massage therapies don't generally hurt.

WILL ANYTHING STRANGE HAPPEN?

Ayurveda often feels very strange to Westerners. The massage therapies are quite unusual – you may find yourself being bathed in a continuous stream of warm oil, or having rings placed around your closed eyes while warm oil is poured over them. The enemas can take some getting used to as well.

WILL I BE GIVEN ANYTHING TO TAKE?

You may well be given herbal preparations. Your diet will often be modified or changed. Some practitioners recommend bastis (herbal enemas). And sometimes you might be asked to take ghee (clarified butter).

IS THERE ANY HOMEWORK?

Yes, there's plenty. Ayurveda teaches a whole system of lifestyle, so expect to be asked to adjust your eating, sleeping and working patterns; start or continue exercising; and perhaps to do yoga or breathing exercises as well.

balancing the doshas

Now you know which is your predominant dosha, you can learn how to balance it. Ayurveda is incredibly practical – there is not necessarily any need to take herbs or undergo complicated treatments; the first step is to make very simple changes in your everyday life.

balancing vata

- Above all else, you need regularity in your life. You will find this difficult, but do try because it will give you a far more steady and balanced output of energy. You will be able to keep going for far longer, rather than continue your usual pattern of expending masses of energy in short bursts, followed by periods of complete collapse.
- Make yourself eat your meals regularly, at the same time each day. Always sit down for your food – eating on the run or snatching snacks will aggravate vata very quickly.
- Try to go to bed at the same time each night and get up at the same time each morning. Going to bed early (about 10 pm is ideal) will make you less anxious and agitated.
- Learn to recognize when you are going into overdrive and consciously slow down. Meditation, yoga, chi kung or autogenic training could really help you.
- You love fast, high-energy sports and activities, but, to balance vata, you should try something more calming and lower in impact. Again yoga is great. So, too, is tai chi. If you always run or do high-impact aerobics, lessen the pace and try hill-walking or low-impact aerobics. Take a regular amount of steady exercise throughout the week, rather than doing nothing all week and then exhausting yourself with a two-hour squash marathon at the weekend.
- Try to avoid loud music, flashing lights and computer games. Calm, gentle, creative pursuits may sound boring to your swift brain, but taking up painting or tapestry could be just what you need. Cultivate the fine art of doing nothing.
- If you're going on holiday, resist the urge to book the 'learn a different sport each day' or 'seven locations in five days' type break. Instead, pick a beautiful spot and stay there. Give yourself sun, warmth and relaxation.
- Follow the vata-calming diet (see the guidelines on pages 18–19). Never eat very dry food, frozen foods or leftovers.

- Keep warm. Vata needs warmth in all senses – physical and spiritual. Place yourself in a safe, warm, caring environment. Saunas and steam rooms are wonderful for vata.
- Learn to express your feelings. Vatas often suppress their feelings, which aggravates their dosha.
- Get enough sleep. Vatas should avoid late nights and particularly shun jobs that involve night shifts.

balancing pitta

- Keep cool. Avoid extreme heat, stay out of very hot sun and keep clear of steam rooms and saunas (although you probably adore them). After a warm bath or shower, finish off with a cool rinse. Get out in the open air as much as you can, but, if it's hot, keep cool in the shade.
- You're normally highly organized, so introduce a little spontaneity into your life. Be careful you don't become too goal-oriented, too focused on objectives and nothing else. Try taking a walk 'just for the hell of it' or just sitting in the garden and gazing out of the window. Simply muse rather than doing something – very therapeutic for pitta.
- You will thrive on challenge, hate being bored and love competition. Obviously, it is important not to get bored, but don't take on too much or challenge yourself too far. Be very careful you don't end up sacrificing everything just to win.

LEFT EXERCISE IS ESSENTIAL FOR BALANCING ALL THE DOSHAS. YOGA IS AN IDEAL CHOICE, AS IT SUITS ALL TYPES AND SO WILL BENEFIT YOU WHETHER YOU ARE VATA, PITTA OR KAPHA.

- You can easily take sport too seriously and be far too competitive. Balance this by taking up non-competitive activities as well, such as yoga, walking or Pilates. Do things for sheer fun. Water sports are calming and soothing for pitta and, of course, winter sports in the snow and ice will cool your fire.
- Pittas should watch their diet with great care (see the guidelines on page 19). Avoid, or at the very least cut right down on, oily and greasy foods, caffeine, salt, red meat, alcohol and highly spiced foods (things you will love).

balancing kapha

- Let go. Kaphas are great hoarders. You hold on to things – even weight, people and emotions. Loosen up and allow yourself to trust a little, to release anything you are holding on to too tightly. Trust there will always be enough.
- Allow change, unpredictability and excitement into your life. Kaphas love routine and feel safe and secure when everything stays the same, but taking the odd chance or allowing the pulse rate to speed up a little from time to time will give you a good energy boost.
- Vary the route you take to work; shift the furniture around in your office or home; if you always have a drink at 6 pm, go for a walk instead.
- Kaphas love to sit doing nothing in particular (Winnie the Pooh is a typical kapha!). To balance your dosha, you need to get your system moving, to give it a shake-up. Take on new activities and challenges that will stimulate you both physically and mentally. Try a new sport or night class, or see a different film to the kind you usually watch.
- Keep your activities varied: if you normally do aerobics, do step or circuits instead. Keep changing your routine in the gym or take a different route each time you jog.
- On holiday, kaphas are the ones whose idea of fun is flopping onto a sun lounger in the morning and being prized from it come dusk. To stimulate kapha, choose a touring holiday or an activity break.
- Follow the kapha diet on page 19. Avoid iced food and drinks; cut right down on sweet things and make sure you don't eat too much bread. Dairy produce will aggravate kapha – it produces mucus (a particular problem for the kapha type). Wheat can be a problem, too. Heavy, starchy foods are really unsuitable for kapha.

ayurvedic eating

Food is medicine, according to ayurveda. If you eat the right foods, your body will automatically start to heal. Again, the philosophy is very complex, but, put simply, food possesses three basic qualities:

LIGHT (known as *satvic*): said to bring the psyche into a state of harmony. Foods with light qualities include vegetables and fruits, nuts, honey, milk and dairy produce, wheat, rice and rye. You should aim to make up most of your diet with foods with a light quality.

PASSIONATE (known as *rajastic*): said to stimulate the sensuality of the person, increasing motivation, ambition, jealousy, egotism. Foods with passionate qualities include all highly spiced, sour, salty, hot and dry foods, plus wine and beer, tea and coffee. You need a certain amount of these foods to sustain you in a tough world, but don't overdo them.

SLUGGISH (known as *tamasic*): foods with a sluggish quality increase pessimism, ignorance, greed, laziness, stinginess and feelings of inferiority. Some ayurvedic texts even go so far as to say they will seduce people into crime. Foods with a sluggish quality include all highly processed foods (canned, dried, frozen and 'quick' or convenience foods), peanuts, leftovers and overcooked food, strong alcoholic drinks and all meat and meat products. Naturally, it is advisable to avoid these as much as possible.

Food is also classified into six 'tastes' and six characteristics. The six tastes are: sweet, sour, salty, pungent (many spices and herbs come into this category), bitter (i.e. rhubarb, many greens) and astringent (certain vegetables and pulses).

The characteristics are: heavy or light (e.g. beef is heavy, while chicken is light; full-fat cheese is heavy, while low-fat cottage cheese is light); oily or dry (e.g. milk is oily, honey is dry); and hot or cold (in essence, rather than temperature – i.e. pepper is hot, while mint is cold). You should generally aim to include all of the six tastes in your diet, but avoid the characteristics that are known particularly to aggravate your predominating dosha (see the guidelines on pages 18–19).

the ten rules of healthy eating

1 Allow plenty of time to prepare and eat your food. Eat in a relaxed, congenial atmosphere and concentrate on what you're eating – don't read a book or watch television while having your meal. Always sit down to eat and take the time to savour your food.

2 The foods you eat should be attractive and wholesome – both to your taste buds and your eyes. Always prepare your table with care: use a fresh tablecloth and have fresh flowers or perhaps a candle as a centrepiece.

3 Try to eat at the same time each day. Be mindful of what you eat and be aware of your appetite – stop when you are not quite full. Never eat to excess. Eat your food slowly and chew each mouthful thoroughly, paying attention to the texture and taste of the food.

4 Always make sure you have digested your last meal before eating another. Generally, you should allow 3 to 6 hours between meals. Don't eat if you are not hungry.

5 Avoid ice-cold drinks – particularly around and with meals. Drink hot or warm water with your meals instead. If you want to eat or drink anything cold (such as ice cream), do so between meals – or warm your stomach with a cup of ginger tea beforehand, if you are having something cold.

6 Ideally, the bulk (if not all) of your diet should come from organic, locally produced, seasonal food. The majority of your meal should consist of warm, freshly prepared food, which is easier to digest.

7 Make lunch, the midday meal, the main meal of the day. Your digestion functions best between noon and 1 pm.

8 The digestive fire, known as *agni*, is low by evening, so make your evening meal small and easily digested. Avoid heavy dairy produce, animal protein and raw, cold foods at this time, as they are more difficult to digest.

9 Don't race off after your meal. Allow yourself a few minutes of calm relaxation. Relax, sit quietly and give thanks for your food. Take a gentle walk if you can, to aid digestion.

10 Notice how you feel after each meal. Become aware of what foods your body likes and doesn't like. What do certain foods do for your energy levels? Do any make your heart race or make you feel breathless, uncomfortable or bloated? Be guided by your body when it comes to your food choices.

diet & the doshas

Food is one of the prime ways we can balance the doshas. These are the foods that balance or soothe your main dosha.

FOODS TO SOOTHE VATA

People who are predominantly vata should ensure that, above all, they eat at regular times in a calm, relaxed atmosphere. Their diet should be warming and nourishing, with plenty of salty, sour and sweet tastes. So, boost the following in your diet:

- dairy produce – milk, cream, cheese, butter, yogurt, ghee (clarified butter)
- natural sweeteners – honey, cane sugar, maple syrup
- all types of nuts and seeds – but in small amounts
- chicken, duck, fish, turkey, seafood
- eggs
- sesame oil
- wheat and rice, cooked oats
- sweet, ripe fruits: bananas, apricots, mango, melon, pineapple, papaya, peaches, berries, figs etc.
- vegetables cooked with a little added ghee: garlic and onions, asparagus, beetroot, carrots, cucumber, sweet potato, green beans. In moderation: potatoes, peas, spinach, courgettes (zucchini), tomatoes, celery

18

- pulses (eat only in moderation): aduki beans (very occasionally), red lentils, black lentils (very occasionally), mung beans
- herbs: those with sweet and warming tastes such as basil, marjoram, coriander (cilantro), fennel, bay leaves, oregano, sage, tarragon, thyme
- spices: again, sweet and warming spices such as liquorice, mace, caraway, cardamom, cloves, cumin, cinnamon (shown opposite), ginger, mustard, black pepper, nutmeg (below)

FOODS TO SOOTHE PITTA

Pitta is hot and so pitta people need to cool themselves down. Anything that makes you hot – such as salt, hot and pungent spices and seasonings, and oil – should be avoided. Bitter and astringent tastes are useful for pitta. Pittas should aim for calm mealtimes, too – stress often causes them to miss meals or eat on the run.

These are the foods which particularly suit pittas:

- unsalted butter, ghee, milk, ice cream, cottage cheese
- almost all kinds of pulses and legumes, except for black and red lentils

- barley, cooked oats, wheat, white rice
- poultry, rabbit, fish (freshwater, in moderation)
- egg (but just the whites)
- all sweeteners except honey and molasses
- vegetables: asparagus, cucumber, broccoli, Brussels sprouts, cabbage, celery, green beans, all green leafy vegetables, mushrooms, potatoes, sweet peppers, courgettes (zucchini), bean sprouts, chicory
- ripe, sweet fruits: apples, coconut, figs, grapes, mangoes, cherries (but they must be sweet, rather than the sour varieties), raisins, prunes, lemons, oranges
- sunflower and pumpkin seeds
- coconut
- spices: cardamom, coriander (cilantro), cinnamon, saffron, ginger, turmeric, black pepper (in small amounts)
- herbs: dill, fennel, mint

FOODS TO SOOTHE KAPHA

Kapha people should aim for a light, dry, hot diet. Anything heavy, fatty or cold will weigh kapha down and make you sluggish and more prone than usual to putting on weight (a perennial kapha problem). Aim for low-fat, spicy, lightly cooked meals.

These foods will help balance your constitution if you are predominantly kapha:

- skimmed milk (or goat's milk), buttermilk, ghee (in small quantities only)
- all pulses except lentils, kidney beans and soya beans
- poultry, prawns (shrimp), game (in small, seasonal quantities only)
- sunflower and pumpkin seeds
- raw honey
- small amounts of oils and fat: ghee, almond oil, corn, sunflower oil
- barley, buckwheat, corn, maize, millet, rye, white rice (small quantities)
- most vegetables except cucumber, tomatoes, courgettes (zucchini), pumpkin, squash and olives
- fruit: apples, pears, pomegranates, cranberries, dates, figs, dried fruits
- herbs: all and plenty
- spices: all and plenty, especially ginger, coriander (cilantro), cloves, black pepper, turmeric, cardamom, cinnamon

rules for a healthy lifestyle

- Get up between 4 am and 6 am! Ideally, you should have between 6 and 8 hours of sleep (but no more). Ayurveda teaches that the habit of going to bed late and sleeping in late can lead to all sorts of complaints, from digestive disorders to headaches and eye problems.
- Urinate first thing after rising. If it's difficult, drink a glass of water or herbal tea (not coffee). Next, attend to mouth hygiene: brush your teeth, clean your tongue and gargle with cold water. Rinse your eyes with cool water. Remember to trim fingernails and toenails every fifth day.
- Exercise. A long, fast walk, swimming or yoga is ideal.
- Massage after exercise reduces fat and removes dead skin. Rub oil into your entire body and then take a warm (body-temperature) bath to revitalize your body and stimulate your energy levels.
- As you leave the bath, dry and put on a little natural perfume. Dress in loose, comfortable, clean clothing.
- Take a few minutes for meditation, prayer or simply thinking about beautiful things.
- Then (at last) have breakfast. Breakfast should be eaten before 9 am. (No wonder you need an early start!)
- Lunch should be at least 3 hours later than breakfast – around 1 pm is fine. It should be the largest meal of the day, as this is when your body can most easily digest food.
- Dinner should be eaten no later than 9 pm – 6 pm is ideal. This meal should be quite light.
- You should aim to be in bed by 10 pm and asleep no later than 11 pm. If you are awake later, your body will move into a different dosha and you will find it even harder to fall asleep. Keep a window open in your bedroom – air should circulate freely. Sleep on the right side to promote digestion and have your head pointing either to the east or to the west. Do not share your room with animals.
- Sex is a strong part of ayurveda and is recommended in unrestricted amounts in winter. In spring and autumn, it is recommended no more than three times a week, while, in summer, according to the texts, you should only have sex two or three times a month.

shirodhara

Shirodhara is one of a series of remarkable body treatments which form an essential part of ayurveda. It is an incredibly simple treatment: you lie down on a couch and a needle-thin stream of herbal oil, heated to a specific temperature, is poured continuously over the forehead. This usually lasts between half an hour and an hour, and is highly effective for balancing and settling vata disorders such as insomnia, anxiety and worry. It settles the mind and profoundly relaxes the central nervous system, giving the effect of a deep, silent meditative state. Best of all, shirodhara feels blissful.

There are a host of other ayurvedic massage techniques that might be prescribed for you:

abhyanga

This is an incredibly relaxing massage which helps the body to release toxins. It is performed by two people working in perfect synchronization. There are three types of basic abhyanga, depending on your ayurvedic type – they vary in depth and speed of stroke, and in the type of oil used.

vishesh

A firm, squeezing massage, designed to remove deep-rooted toxins, vishesh is quite a tough massage. It is particularly suitable for strong kapha people.

garshan

This is a brisk, enlivening massage using raw silk gloves to create friction and static electricity on the surface of the skin. Garshan is very useful for weight loss.

pizzichilli

This is known as the Royal Treatment and was once the preserve of Indian royalty. Literally gallons of warm oil are poured over the body, while two therapists gently massage in the oil. Pizzichilli relieves deep-seated aches and pains, and increases flexibility of the joints.

OPPOSITE SHIRODHARA IS ONE OF THE MOST SOOTHING OF ALL AYURVEDIC TREATMENTS. A STEADY, VERY FINE STREAM OF WARM HERBAL OIL IS POURED ONTO THE THIRD EYE POSITION ON THE FOREHEAD.

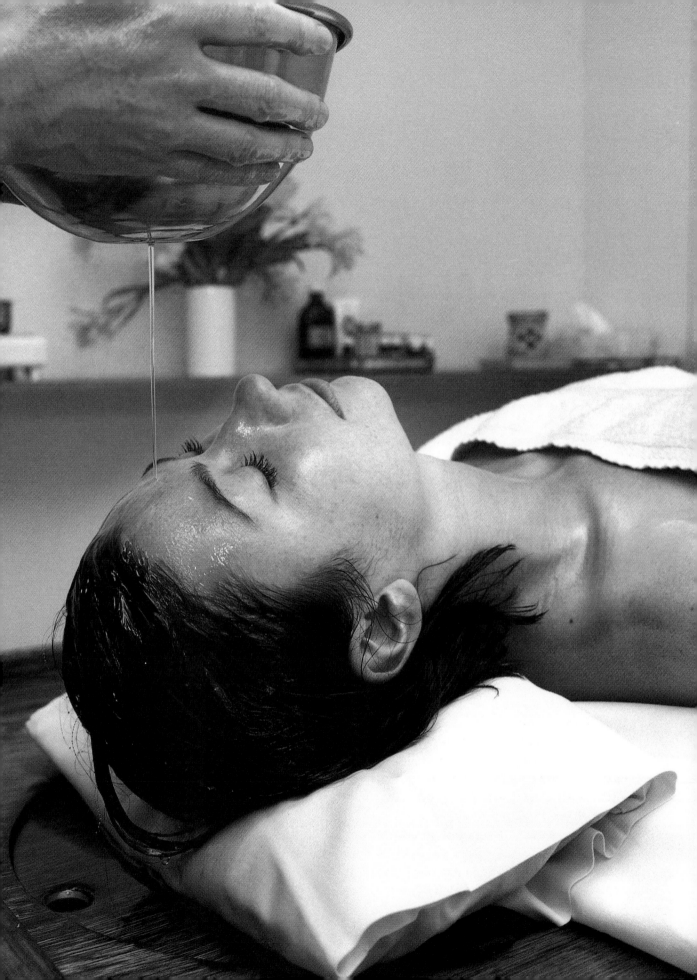

marma therapy

Anyone who wants to live long, appear young and remain in perfect health should look to their marmas. Here in the West, few people have even heard of the word marma, yet, to an Indian ayurvedic physician, the marmas are the key to health, emotional security, longevity and beauty – even life itself. The marmas are like the junction boxes of the body, 107 points or areas where nerves and muscles meet. While they stay uncongested, you will remain healthy and happy. If they become clogged or unbalanced, you could find your confidence failing alongside your health; both emotions and physiological functions become impaired if your marma points are out of alignment.

Ancient ayurvedic texts describe the marmas in precise detail. Centuries of observation had taught the ayurvedic surgeons that, if certain marmas were cut or damaged, death, disability, loss of function or pain would ensue.

Although they sound, at first hearing, very similar to the Chinese acupuncture points, the marmas differ in significant ways. They are connected directly with the nervous system, linking the body with the brain; they also lie deeper in the body than the acupuncture points and many cover an area of the body, rather than just a tiny point.

The reason why the marmas are so crucial is that they provide the links between body and mind. If the marma points are blocked, the nervous system cannot send clear messages to the brain. If there is a problem in the body, the alarm message sent from the body might simply not be able to get through. Not realizing anything is wrong, the brain would fail to mobilize the body's rescue forces to sort out the problem. The result would be that we fall ill.

Unfortunately, modern life is not easy on the marmas. We eat the wrong kind of diet, we don't exercise enough, we ingest and inhale vast quantities of pollutants and expose ourselves to a bombardment of stress almost every day of our lives. Although the marmas valiantly try to deal with the combined debris these abuses create, they often become overloaded and congested. It is easy to see why ayurvedic practitioners believe it is so important to keep your marmas in optimum condition for not only your physical, but also your emotional, wellbeing.

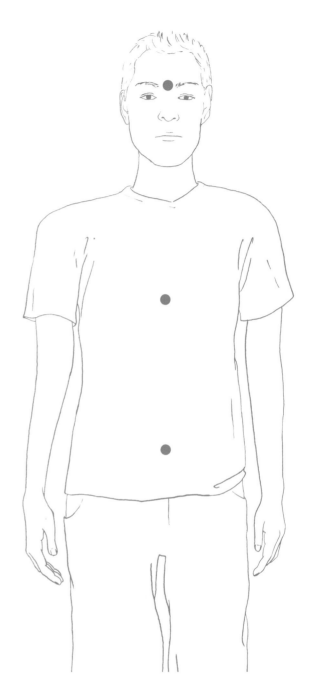

ABOVE THE MARMA POINTS ARE LIKE THE JUNCTION BOXES OF THE BODY. KEEPING THE MARMA POINTS UNCONGESTED IS VITAL TO OUR GOOD HEALTH AND WELLBEING.

ACCORDING TO AYURVEDA, THEY ARE THE KEY TO HEALTH, LONGEVITY, EMOTIONAL WELFARE AND BEAUTY, AS THEY PROVIDE THE LINKS BETWEEN BODY AND MIND.

what can marma therapy help?

- Marma therapy can have a beneficial effect on a wide variety of conditions. It is ideal for conditions which seem to have no physiological cause – vague aches and pains, and so-called psychosomatic conditions.
- It is deeply detoxifying and so therefore can help to treat conditions such as rheumatism and arthritis, weight problems, headaches and migraine.
- Patients report not just physiological improvements, but emotional benefits as well. Confidence is usually boosted. Anxiety, depression, fear and stress usually diminish.
- Marma therapy can be wonderful for low energy states and general weakness and fatigue.

what can I expect from a session?

WHERE WILL I HAVE THE SESSION?

You will be lying on a couch or on the floor.

WILL I BE CLOTHED?

Yes, you will remain fully clothed.

WHAT HAPPENS?

Marma therapy works by the therapist manually stimulating the marma points with either direct pressure or insistent massage. Before treatment, the practitioner will take your pulses and ask to see your tongue. You will then be asked to lie down on the couch or floor.

Marma therapy is certainly no feel-good massage: some points are very tender and the touch is very hard. You may also find the practitioner shaking your limbs or giving a sharp slap to the soles of the feet. Sometimes, he or she will measure your limbs to check on imbalances.

For the final stage of the treatment, a light oil may be used to rub up and down either side of the spine.

WILL IT HURT?

Yes, quite possibly. Some people may even find the touch too harsh to tolerate.

WILL ANYTHING STRANGE HAPPEN?

You may feel the blockages as the practitioner works on them – like bubbles under the skin.

WILL I BE GIVEN ANYTHING TO TAKE?

No, medication is not part of the treatment.

IS THERE ANY HOMEWORK?

Yes, you may well be given adjustments to make in your lifestyle and particularly in your diet.

tuning up the marmas – home techniques

Fortunately, there are plenty of simple do-it-yourself techniques for keeping your marmas clear which you can practise without the aid of a therapist.

- The marmas can be activated and toned through yoga. Try to practise at least a few yoga postures every day – they stretch the marma points. The Salutation to the Sun series of postures is an ideal toning routine for the marmas. Gentle exercise such as walking and swimming can help, too.
- A cluster of important marma points can be found on the soles of the feet. Giving your feet a gentle foot massage with sesame oil for 3 to 5 minutes a day will be highly beneficial. If you do this just before bedtime, it will soothe the nervous system and help you get a restful night's sleep. Allow your bowl of sesame oil to sit on a radiator or in a *bain-marie* for a while to warm. Take your time and slowly massage each part of the foot with a gentle, circular motion.
- There are three major marma points which should be gently massaged every day. Use a light, circular motion, taking a few minutes at each site.

  There is a head marma situated between the eyebrows, extending to the centre of the forehead. Gently massaging this area while your eyes are closed is good for relieving anxiety, headaches and mental strain. It will also help you to sleep well at night.

  The heart marma is located just below the sternum, where the rib cage ends, and massaging the heart marma will help settle upset emotions.

  Massaging the marma point on the lower abdomen, about 10 cm (4 in) below the navel, will help the intestinal tract and ease constipation and gas.
- Make sure your diet is as good as possible (see the guide to ayurvedic eating on pages 17–19). If possible, choose organic wholefoods low in acid and avoid processed or highly refined foods, all of which can clog the marmas. In addition, all meals should be eaten slowly and calmly at regular times: snacking between meals is forbidden, as the food will not digest properly and waste will be dumped at the marma points.

neurotherapy

Practitioners of neurotherapy believe they can cure most of our problems by walking all over us – literally. In India, where the therapy originated, film stars, politicians and government ministers are ignoring orthodox Western medicine in favour of neurotherapy, drawn by tales of amazing cures. It may sound bizarre, but the entire therapy has been very precisely analysed and researched; it is based on a deep understanding of physiology and anatomy.

Unlike many alternative traditions, neurotherapy is refreshingly down-to-earth. Although their field is rooted in the ancient system of ayurveda, neurotherapists tend to talk in language that any medical doctor would recognize and understand, and even use themselves: of hormones and enzymes; blood cholesterol levels and peptides; glands and nerve reflexes. Neurotherapy acts through the body's nadis or nerve channels directly on the organs and glands, fine-tuning the biochemical balance of the body.

Therapists don't seek a quick fix; they are like genealogists of the body, not content until they have ferreted back to the great-great-grandparent of your symptoms. Take the case of rheumatoid arthritis, for example. This causes the joints to become inflamed and eventually degenerate because of an accumulation of poisonous acids in them. The root cause, however, may well lie further afield: the pancreas might not be producing sufficient alkaline salts to neutralize the acidic foods coming from the stomach, for instance. The intestines cannot then properly digest the food and the excretory system cannot properly get rid of the acids. The subsequent malfunctioning of the endocrine glands can then cause problems in the auto-immune system.

While Western doctors would tend to prescribe drugs to ease the symptoms, neurotherapists assert that, instead of giving the body synthetic medicine, they can stimulate the body to produce the biochemicals it needs by itself.

This is where the feet come in. Pressure is placed on various parts of the body (either the organ or gland itself, or on the connecting nerves), using the insteps of the feet to provide a kind of suction effect. Rhythmic pressure on the precise spot will apparently stimulate the ailing organ or underproductive gland.

what can neurotherapy help?

- Digestive disorders (irritable bowel syndrome, gastritis, gallstones, colitis etc.) can be alleviated.
- Back problems (injuries, spondilytis etc.) respond well.
- It is good for hormonal imbalances (such as premenstrual syndrome, menopausal problems, thyroid problems and pituitary malfunctioning).
- Some people have found neurotherapy very helpful following a stroke and it has also had beneficial effects on multiple sclerosis, arthritis, cerebral palsy and Down's syndrome.
- Enthusiasts have found they have lost weight and conquered insomnia. They even say it can cure psychiatric illness.
- Some people should avoid neurotherapy: it cannot be used on hernias (other than hiatus hernias); people with pacemakers cannot be treated; and nor can it be used if someone has undergone a hip replacement.

what can I expect from a session?

WHERE WILL I HAVE THE TREATMENT?

You will be lying on the floor between two chairs.

WILL I BE CLOTHED?

Yes, you remain fully clothed throughout.

WHAT HAPPENS?

Neurotherapy sessions are surprisingly short and sweet. In India, practitioners can treat up to 90 patients in one day. In the West, the initial consultation takes an hour with follow-up treatments lasting just 30 minutes. The first appointment is taken up almost entirely with completing a detailed questionnaire. In particular, the therapist needs to know about any drugs that are being taken; as neurotherapy works directly on the glands, its results are often instantaneous and powerful.

You will then be asked to lie down, fully clothed, on a thick towel on the floor, with a rolled-up towel positioned under your knees for support.

Two chairs are placed on either side of your body, close to your hips. The practitioner then feels your abdomen, pressing firmly under the ribcage. This process (known as *nabi diagnosis*, similar to the hara diagnosis used in shiatsu) has been practised in India for thousands of years and is held to be highly precise. Balancing his or her weight on the chairs, the therapist places his or her feet on the inside of your thighs and gently rocks from side to side. This process is then repeated several times before you are asked to get up.

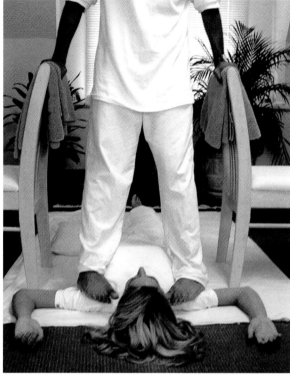

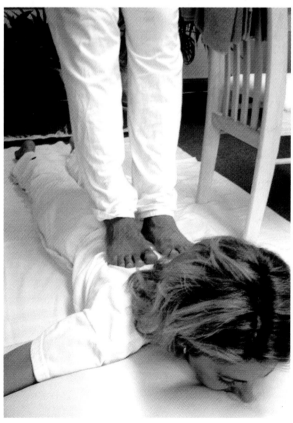

WILL IT HURT?

No. Surprisingly, neurotherapy is not at all painful.

WILL ANYTHING STRANGE HAPPEN?

Within minutes, you may well notice changes such as tenderness in the lymph glands.

WILL I BE GIVEN ANYTHING TO TAKE?

Neurotherapy does not use herbs or supplements, but neurotherapists will often recommend particular diets or certain foods to help heal conditions.

IS THERE ANY HOMEWORK?

Although the results can be swift and strong, you are still expected to put in some hard work towards leading a healthier life. Imbalances in the endocrine system most frequently occur because of the way we live and our bad habits. As a result, practitioners frequently teach patients how to breathe fully and properly, and will often demand dietary changes.

ABOVE NEUROTHERAPY MAY LOOK A LITTLE OFFPUTTING, BUT IN FACT THE SENSATION OF BEING 'WALKED OVER' IS EXCEEDINGLY PLEASANT – AND HAS HIGHLY BENEFICIAL RESULTS.

THROUGH PLACING PRESSURE ON VARIOUS PARTS OF THE BODY USING THE INSTEP OF THE FEET, THERAPISTS STIMULATE THE AILING ORGAN OR UNDER-PRODUCTIVE GLAND.

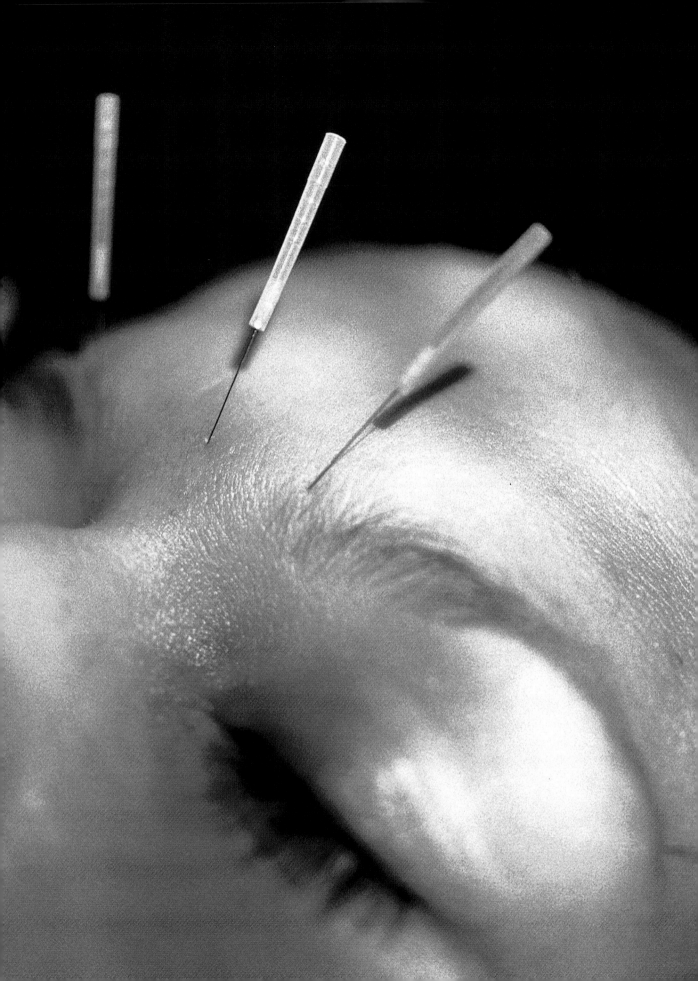

CHINESE MEDICINE

In the old days in China, you paid your doctor while you were well and stopped paying him when you fell ill. Can you imagine a modern Western physician daring to launch such a scheme? Practitioners of traditional Chinese medicine had no such fears: their system of preventative medicine worked superlatively.

Patients were taught a combination of good diet, good exercise and good breathing technique. If a patient *did* fall sick, there were powerful ways to bring him or her back to health: acupuncture, herbalism and massage. Sickness was simply not a way of life – surely a tempting enough reason to investigate this incredible holistic system of healing.

Nowadays, in the West, we generally use only a small part of traditional Chinese medicine. Many people practise solely acupuncture; others purely herbalism. Both can have powerful effects on their own, but, if you really want to use this therapy in its most potent form, seek out a practitioner who can counsel you on all aspects of the Chinese way to health. Once you are eating, exercising and breathing properly, you shouldn't need more than a quarterly check-up and perhaps the odd tweak of a needle or the stray tonic to keep you in perfect health.

From the earliest times, people have stumbled across the healing powers of certain foods and herbs. But how did they discover that sticking a needle in a certain part of the body could have an effect on other parts, even curing disease? Some people say that acupuncture developed out of marma therapy (see ayurveda, pages 22–3). Others think that, after battles, the Chinese noticed some curious side effects of arrow wounds. If the victim survived his wound, sometimes he would discover that a formerly chronic disease had mysteriously improved, or even vanished. From these observations, they surmise, acupuncture was developed.

The underlying philosophy behind traditional Chinese medicine is that good health revolves around the correct flow of *qi*, or *chi*, the subtle energy of the body. Qi flows around the body in channels called *meridians*, and along the meridians lie hundreds of points which link the various organs and functions of the body. While Western doctors often scorn this idea, new instruments such as the PIP scanner (see electro-crystal therapy on pages 235–6) have actually confirmed what the Chinese have known for years: the position of the meridians and the acupuncture points.

If we look after ourselves, eat the right kinds of foods and undertake the right kinds of exercise, we can increase the amount of qi in our bodies. If we fall into bad ways, our levels of qi drop or are blocked and the consequence is lack of vital energy, emotional distress or even disease. The entire Chinese life view is immensely complex and, some might say, almost obsessive. Qi can be depleted or lost through too much, too little or the wrong kind of food, drink, exercise, work and even sex. Even your emotions can fall out of balance and affect your health.

yin & yang

According to traditional Chinese medicine, the world can be divided into two forces, *yin* and *yang*. Yin is considered to be dark, cold, negative, passive and feminine, while yang is light, warm, positive, active and male. Disturb the balance of yin and yang, and the result is disharmony, possibly ill health. In addition, there are the five elements to consider. Every one of us contains the elements of fire, earth, air (known as metal), water and wood. When a traditional Chinese medicine practitioner diagnoses, he or she does not just check for the flow of qi, but also looks to see how much of each element is within the body and what kind of energy is being transmitted. It is then possible to stimulate or quieten unbalanced organs or body systems through food, exercise, massage, herbs or the needles of acupuncture.

OPPOSITE ACUPUNCTURE PLAYS A VERY IMPORTANT ROLE IN TRADITIONAL CHINESE MEDICINE. ITS AIM IS TO BALANCE THE BODY'S VITAL ENERGY, OR QI, AND RESTORE HEALTH. SPECIFIC ACUPOINTS ALONG THE MERIDIAN CHANNELS LINKING OUR BODIES' VARIOUS ORGANS AND FUNCTIONS ARE STIMULATED TO COMBAT IMBALANCES.

what can traditional chinese medicine help?

- Almost every condition will respond well to traditional Chinese medicine.
- Chinese herbs have become famous for treating eczema and other skin conditions.
- Acupuncture is well known as an aid to dieting and giving up smoking.
- Acupuncture also has good effects on emotional and psychological problems.
- A huge variety of conditions respond well to acupuncture – from acute problems such as headaches, coughs and colds to long-standing chronic conditions such as angina, irritable bowel syndrome, premenstrual syndrome, rheumatism and eczema.
- It can help relieve pain and has even been used with great success in childbirth.
- Some practitioners report good results with infertility.
- Mechanical problems are usually treated with tuina, Chinese therapeutic massage.

what can I expect from a session?

WHERE WILL I HAVE THE TREATMENT?

You will be sitting in a chair for the initial diagnosis and lifestyle counselling. Acupuncture and tuina are carried out while you are lying on a couch.

WILL I BE CLOTHED?

You will be asked to remove some clothing for acupuncture. Otherwise, you will be fully clothed.

WHAT HAPPENS?

You will be asked a few questions about your health and past medical history; however, most traditional Chinese medicine practitioners can tell exactly what is going on in your body by taking your pulses and looking at your face, eyes and tongue.

If you are having acupuncture, you will be asked to lie down on a couch. Many acupuncturists use moxa, a herbal mixture which is placed on the acupoint and set alight. When it becomes warm, you tell the practitioner and it is whisked away before it burns the skin. The needle is then inserted and either left there or twisted in and then pulled out directly. This process will continue on a variety of points; some are in very strange places (such as the palate and the pubis!).

If you have a herbal consultation, you will be given a precise mixture of herbs to take – either in pill form or, more likely, loose to be brewed as a tea.

WILL IT HURT?

Acupuncture can be slightly painful, depending on the practitioner and the technique used. If needles are inserted superficially, it doesn't hurt at all. Sometimes, however, they may be inserted deeply and twisted, which can be a somewhat uncomfortable sensation. If tuina massage (see below) is part of your treatment, it can at times be very deep and strong.

WILL ANYTHING STRANGE HAPPEN?

You may feel a tingling or surge of released energy when a needle is inserted. Some people find that old emotions are released through acupuncture or tuina (see below). Also, Chinese herbs can have very swift reactions – you may find a cold, for example, clears almost instantly once you begin herbal treatment, or that you experience a sudden rush of energy.

WILL I BE GIVEN ANYTHING TO TAKE?

Yes, herbal preparations are often included in traditional Chinese medicine. These can be in pill or dried form. If taken in tea form (which is common), some of these taste quite unpleasant. You may also be asked to alter your diet.

IS THERE ANY HOMEWORK?

Yes. Most probably, you will be asked to practise good breathing techniques and to make lifestyle changes. Some practitioners may suggest that you take up chi kung or tai chi.

tuina

Tuina gives a wake-up call to the whole body. It's an exciting and energizing system of massage that leaves your body feeling as if it has been given a thorough spring clean. Its effects on the mind are equally uplifting. Yet tuina is virtually unknown and unused here in the West.

In China, however, the story is totally different. There, it is as well established and respected as acupuncture and Chinese herbal medicine. Tuina massage is routinely used in Chinese hospitals – primarily to treat pain, but also in the treatment of many common ailments. The words *tui* and *na* literally mean 'push' and 'grasp'. This profound, invigorating and energizing form of massage and manipulation focuses deep pressure along the energy lines (known as meridians) and acupuncture points of the body. Tuina's aim is to release blocked energy and restore a balanced flow throughout the entire body, promoting a wondrous sense of health and vitality.

home tuina session

This tuina massage is generally suitable for everyone, but do not massage on inflamed or broken skin, or over skin conditions such as eczema, psoriasis or shingles. You should also not use this massage on anyone with osteoporosis (brittle bones).

1 Your partner should be seated in a comfortable, upright chair with good back support, hands resting in the lap, feet firmly placed on the floor. Standing behind your partner, stroke lightly along the tops of the shoulders. Then squeeze gently along each shoulder with the whole hand, gradually increasing the pressure and starting to knead with the heel of the hand. As you feel your partner begin to relax, knead with the thumb, feeling for any tender or knotted tissue. Grasp the top of the shoulder and squeeze the large muscle there deeply, giving it a slight shake. To achieve the best results, spend at least 10 minutes on this step.

These techniques unblock the energy channels from the head to the shoulders, significantly raising your energy levels.

2 Using your thumb and first two fingers, squeeze the muscles on either side of the neck vertebrae while the other hand lightly supports the forehead. Progress from light to strong pressure, with a definite kneading action. Work from the base of the neck up to the region just beneath the skull, lifting the hand between each position. Change hands frequently. Spend at least 5 minutes on this step. This technique stimulates the bladder and gall bladder meridians, sweeping away the tension that leads to headaches and relieving stiff and aching neck muscles.

3 Standing to the right-hand side of your partner's chair, put your right foot on the chair so your thigh is about level with his or her armpit. With your left hand, grasp his or her right wrist and raise the arm so it rests gently across your knee. Turn the wrist away from you. Grasping the muscle on the top of the shoulder with your right hand, squeeze firmly and

knead deeply between your fingers and the heel of your hand. Continue like this down the arm. Repeat several times, then squeeze with the fingers and thumb lightly all the way down the arm, giving a slight lift between each position. Change hands frequently. Squeezing and kneading clears the energy channels in the shoulders, loosening the muscles.

4 Support your partner's right arm between your hands, just below the armpit. The arm should be completely relaxed. Using the palms in opposition technique (one palm moves in the opposite direction to the other), rub rapidly to and fro, massaging the arm muscles down to the wrist. This technique powerfully stimulates the flow of energy in all the meridians of the arm, which particularly helps the small intestines regain balance.

5 Hold your partner's right hand firmly with both hands, your thumbs together at the top of the wrist. Raise the arm to just below the horizontal and pull gently to loosen the shoulder joint. Then shake 20–30 times with small up-and-down movements. This technique greatly relieves shoulder stiffness, as well as pain in the arm and shoulder area, and the side of the neck. When the correct energy balance is established in your neck, shoulders and arms, you can feel like a new person.

6 Repeat steps 3, 4 and 5 on the left shoulder and arm. You should aim to spend about 10 minutes altogether on steps 3, 4 and 5 on each arm.

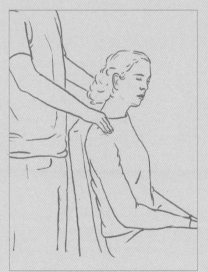

what can tuina help?

- Tuina is superlative for treating neck, shoulder and back pain, sciatica, frozen shoulders, tennis elbow and migraines.
- It can produce profound shifts in emotional wellbeing and is wonderful for beating stress.
- Many conditions can respond well to tuina – including digestive problems, menstrual irregularities and respiratory ailments.

what can I expect from a session?

WHERE WILL I HAVE THE TREATMENT?

You will be sitting in a chair and/or lying on the floor or a couch.

WILL I BE CLOTHED?

Yes, you are usually treated with all your clothes on.

WHAT HAPPENS?

Before the treatment, the therapist will ask a few questions about your health; whether you have had any injuries or serious illnesses, or if you are pregnant. Tuina is not suitable for people with fragile bones or osteoporosis, and practitioners also need to be very careful in treating those with cancer or heart problems. Certain points are avoided in pregnancy because they could induce labour. You are then asked to sit upright in a chair. The name *tuina* may mean to push and grasp, but your body will also be shaken, squeezed, pulled, rotated, rocked and rolled! At times, it feels like the deep-tissue work of Rolfing and Hellerwork, at others like osteopathic manipulation. The treatment starts with your neck and shoulders, before moving down your arms.

You will then move onto a couch and your back, buttocks and thighs will be pounded and kneaded. Finally, you are asked to sit on the floor with your legs stretched out in front. There is a pressure on your spine and, before you realize what is happening, your vertebrae 'pop' in swift succession like a strip of bubblewrap.

WILL IT HURT?

The tuina touch is very deep and can be painful. If you like to doze off during a massage or have a very low pain threshold, this really isn't for you.

WILL ANYTHING STRANGE HAPPEN?

As with most forms of bodywork, you may experience old memories resurfacing.

WILL I BE GIVEN ANYTHING TO TAKE?

No, medication is not part of the treatment

IS THERE ANY HOMEWORK?

You may be given moves to practise on yourself at home, or asked to make adjustments to your diet or lifestyle.

good healthkeeping – the chinese way

There are simple changes we can all make to our daily lives which can help us to live healthier, and even longer, lives.

A good diet is crucial. The first rule is to eat sparingly. The Chinese say you should eat until you are 70–80 per cent full. All food should be chewed thoroughly to allow the enzymes in the saliva to start digestion. Liquids should also be sipped, rather than gulped.

Avoid extremes of temperature – the Chinese tend not to eat or drink things that are either very hot or very cold. Ideally, food should be steamed, poached or stir-fried.

The traditional Chinese diet follows the World Health Organization guidelines almost exactly (see page 57), being high in complex carbohydrates, vegetables and fruits, while low in saturated fat. Fish is rated highly and meat is eaten only in small quantities. Chinese physicians have always recommended eating 'earth' chickens, or free-range chickens, as we know them.

The Chinese diet avoids dairy produce, as it is believed to cause allergies and infections. Eggs are eaten only rarely. The Chinese also avoid most of the nightshade family of vegetables, which includes potatoes, tomatoes and peppers (interestingly, modern nutritionists find that these foods can cause problems for quite a few people). Caffeine and tobacco should also be shunned.

Grains are rated very highly, with rice considered to be the most nourishing of all grains. Pulses such as lentils, aduki beans, kidney beans, chickpeas, mung beans and tofu (made from soya beans) are also important mainstays of the Chinese diet.

Vegetables are usually cooked, as they are considered much easier for the body to assimilate in that form. Also, cooked vegetables are believed to build up the body, while cold vegetables have a more eliminating action.

Red meat is very rarely eaten and then only when the body is depleted – it is considered very rich and to cause aggression and irritability in large doses. However, it can be therapeutic – e.g. a woman might eat a nourishing lamb stew after her period to regain blood and energy.

the chinese kitchen medicine cabinet

Sun Ssu-mo, an ancient Chinese physician in the Tang Dynasty, correctly diagnosed and cured beriberi, the nutritional deficiency disease caused by a lack of thiamine (vitamin B_1) – 1,000 years before European doctors. He wrote: 'A truly good physician first finds out the cause of the illness and, having found that, he first tries to cure it with food. Only when food fails does he prescribe medication.'

Barley meal helps the digestion and drains what the Chinese call 'damp heat' – moving away foods that are stagnant in the system. Boil with rice for two hours.

Brussels sprouts are rich in alkalizing elements when lightly steamed, and particularly good for the pancreas.

Cherries are detoxifying, work as a laxative and stimulate the nervous system. The darker the cherries, the more therapeutic their value.

Chicken raises qi (energy) and is generally uplifting.

Cinnamon bark and euconia bark both possess aphrodisiac qualities.

Cucumber is rich in potassium, sodium and phosphorus. It is good for the nails and hair, as well as promoting excretion of waste through the kidneys.

Ginseng is an energy tonic to lift spirits and raise energy. It is very useful for those who are run down after an illness. Ginseng is also good for mental and physical stamina. (Note: contraindicated for high blood pressure, severe headaches or fever.)

Grapes are often used to cure constipation and gastritis, and as general detoxifiers. They also alkalize the digestive tract and bloodstream. Dark grapes are best.

Horseradish and lemon juice provides quick relief from mucus congestion – useful for coughs, colds, flu, asthma and pneumonia.

Lycii berries tonify the blood. Put them in buns or sprinkle them on porridge.

Mushrooms Shiitake mushrooms are often used as energy raisers. Rei-gen mushrooms are used as immune stimulants said to raise the white blood cell count. Often used by those with HIV/AIDS, they can also be used by anyone for their calming effects. They are said to alleviate stress and help you work with more vision.

Raw beetroot juice is a natural kidney cleanser, dissolving and eliminating any gravel.

Raw carrot and spinach juice detoxifies the digestive tract and helps normal bowel function. It is also used for tonsillitis and pneumonia, can help with rheumatism and colitis, and is believed to strengthen the heart and ease menstrual problems.

Raw, crushed garlic (above left) contains allicin, a powerful natural antibiotic and fungicide that helps prevents colds and flu, and is said to raise libido.

Raw tomato (left) is believed to reduce inflammation of the liver.

Red meat is helpful for blood. It is eaten very rarely by the Chinese, but some practitioners recommend women eat red meat after their periods to make new blood. A typical recipe is to cook lamb with Chinese angelica and lycii berries.

Schizandra helps focus the mind and is useful for those who are studying.

THE ANCIENT WISDOM OF OTHER CULTURES

AYURVEDA AND TRADITIONAL CHINESE MEDICINE ARE THE BEST-KNOWN ANCIENT SYSTEMS OF HOLISTIC HEALTHCARE, BUT THERE ARE MANY OTHERS. SOME HAVE BEEN LOST TO US OVER THE CENTURIES BECAUSE THEIR WISDOM WAS NOT WRITTEN DOWN AND THE ORAL TRADITION HAS DWINDLED IN RECENT TIMES. OTHERS ARE STILL USED AND ARE GRADUALLY BECOMING BETTER KNOWN IN THE WEST. OVER THE NEXT FEW PAGES, WE'LL LOOK AT THREE FASCINATING SYSTEMS.

mongolian healing

Could you blame your illness on your past lives? Maybe you are under the weather because your stars are unfavourable this year? Or perhaps you are being blighted by an evil spirit? Mongolian medicine goes way beyond the merely mechanical – it is based on the belief that health is a fusion of physical, psychological and spiritual. Prayers are as likely to be offered as pills, and exorcisms performed alongside acupuncture. It may sound bizarre, but the latest psychoneurimmunology (the science of mind–body medicine) research would probably agree with many of Mongolian healing's precepts. It also predates the concepts of quantum physics by several millennia, insisting that time is relative (the past and future affect the present) and that we are not separate from our surroundings.

Mongolian medicine was ancient when Genghis Khan rampaged across Central Asia with his hordes. At its heart is what is known as *em-dom*, an ancient folk medicine which has been retained in its purity and offers some unusual (to put it mildly) remedies. Horse milk is used to treat lung complaints. An infection in the umbilical cord of a newborn is cured by burning a piece of the mother's hair, grinding it into ash and putting it on the sore place – it is said to heal overnight. There are incredibly arcane formulae for everything from soothing mouth ulcers to promoting youthfulness.

Mongolian medicine is said to be as ancient as the great healing systems of China, Tibet, the Middle East (tibb) and India (ayurveda), if not more so. In fact, it shares many techniques with them – the use of herbs, moxibustion (the burning of herbs on the skin), acupuncture, massage and manipulation techniques. Even its spiritual practices are not dissimilar – although this side of traditional Eastern medicine is generally played down in the West.

what can mongolian healing help?

- Mongolian physicians will treat almost anything. Even psychological problems and spiritual 'crises' seem to respond.
- Digestive and hormonal problems appear to respond well.
- It is said to improve longevity and make you feel more youthful.
- Mongolian massage is highly effective for back pain, stress-related problems and digestive troubles, and it is claimed that it can even help cellulite.
- It is said to heal psychic wounds and is ideal for people who want greater self-awareness.

what can I expect from a session?

WHERE WILL I HAVE THE TREATMENT?

You will be sitting in a chair for the consultation. If you need massage or acupuncture, you will lie on a couch.

WILL I BE CLOTHED?

You will be fully clothed for the consultation, but down to only underwear for chua ka, the massage.

WHAT HAPPENS?

Diagnosis is swift and efficient. As with ayurveda and traditional Chinese medicine, the practitioner will read your pulses, check your tongue and scrutinize your face. You will then be given a prescription to take. It's a very quick, down-to-earth session. Mongolian massage, chua ka, has been described as 'reflexology for the body' and it feels as if every acupressure point is being hit in turn. It's a really deep, powerful and satisfying massage.

WILL IT HURT?

Acupuncture can be uncomfortable and the massage can be very strong. At times it is almost painful, but the pain is forgotten as your body releases its tension – it's that weird kind of 'good hurt'.

WILL ANYTHING STRANGE HAPPEN?

You will be checked for evil spirits! The physician may decide you need a ceremony or ritual to help your problem.

WILL I BE GIVEN ANYTHING TO TAKE?

Yes, you may be given powders to dissolve in water, or pills.

IS THERE ANY HOMEWORK?

You may be asked to make some adjustments to your lifestyle.

tibb or unani medicine

Tibb is a hidden treasure in the world of natural health. A holistic system of medicine, tibb has been practised across vast areas of the world (Persia and Turkey, in particular) for thousands of years. Even today, it is still the main source of medicine in large areas of India, Pakistan, Bangladesh, Afghanistan, Malaysia and the Middle East. Practitioners say it incorporates knowledge from ancient Egyptian and Greek medicine, from the Chinese and Indian traditions, and from the ancient healing wisdom of Persia and the Middle East. Its extensive pharmacopoeia of herbs is now being investigated by Western pharmaceutical companies in the belief that tibb could hold the secrets to cures for many modern illnesses.

At first sight, tibb (which is also known as unani medicine, Sufi medicine or Graeco-Arabic medicine) appears little different from traditional Chinese or ayurvedic medicine. Like these, tibb recognizes vital energy (known in Arabic as qawa); it shares the concept that medicine needs to be holistic, to look at the whole person; it regards the correct balance of elements within the body as essential to health; and it uses a battery of herbal remedies to combat modern ills. However, although the basic philosophy of tibb shares much with its ancient cousins, it has unique strengths and qualities that make it worthy of a wider recognition around the world.

First, tibb is a very gentle medicine. Where Chinese doctors would treat first with diet, tibb physicians will look at lifestyle. They start at the most subtle levels, trying to adjust a person's breathing. It's a small change, but it can have a huge effect. Next, they attend to the emotions. In India, Pakistan and Bangladesh, where tibb is taught in universities, a major part of the hakim or practitioner's training involves counselling and psychotherapy. Tibb teaches that what a person thinks and imagines can affect his or her health profoundly.

Next, they investigate sleep and sleeping patterns, eating patterns and bowel movement. They will study your working life and how you relax, and try to find ways of making your life work for you in the most healthy yet realistic ways. Then, and only then, would they use herbs if necessary. If you had a structural problem, they might employ osteopathic manipulations or massage techniques (or refer you

middle eastern spices for health

Incorporating healing spices into cooking can be a delicious, as well as simple, way to promote health.

Cardamom is used to flavour tea, coffee and rice in Turkey. In the practice of tibb, it is used in cooking or in a late-evening drink to soothe and promote good sleep. Cardamom is extremely useful in the treatment of hyperactivity.

Coriander is a very useful aromatic which helps to improve the digestion and also has a healthful effect on the heart. Use it to flavour all kinds of cooking, particularly meat dishes.

Ginger is particularly used in the winter and in cold climates to heat the body. It improves the digestion and staves off colds and flu. Ginger also improves energy levels. (NOTE: ginger should *not* be taken if you are suffering from an ulcerative condition).

Honey is the panacea of tibb. Tibb's practitioners advise almost everyone to use honey – both in cooking and taken as a drink. Simply add a teaspoon of good-quality honey to a cup of warm water and drink whenever you need a lift.

Olive oil is used prolifically throughout tibb – internally in cooking and externally for massage and skin oils – as it is said to help almost all conditions and to tone and beautify the body.

Saffron is regarded very highly in tibb and is considered an important healer which strengthens the heart and mind. It is used when people are moody or depressed. Use saffron when cooking rice or add it to warm milk and honey as a subtle way of influencing the emotions.

to other practitioners). Finally, if they felt your problem had a deeper, spiritual basis, they would use what is known as *logotherapy*, finding ways that fit your belief system or religion to soothe your very soul. So, tibb is holistic in the true sense of the word – the physician is looking at every patient on four levels: the physical, the emotional, the intellectual and the spiritual, and treating accordingly.

what can tibb help?

- Tibb has good results with all manner of problems, both acute and chronic. Physicians say there are few conditions tibb ultimately cannot help – although they won't deal with accident or emergency cases.
- It is excellent if your problem has a psychological or spiritual aspect.
- It has good results for a variety of skin disorders and for respiratory conditions.
- In tibb, there is a large variety of herbal tonics that regulate and boost energy. There is even a hoard of supposedly highly potent aphrodisiacs.
- It often helps conditions which have proved resistant to other therapies.

what can I expect from a session?

WHERE WILL I HAVE THE TREATMENT?

You will be sitting in a comfortable chair for the consultation.

WILL I BE CLOTHED

Yes, you will be fully clothed.

WHAT HAPPENS?

The hakim starts with simple questions on your health and lifestyle. He will be keen to know about your birth. (For example, was it difficult? Tibb recognizes many problems as arising from traumatic births.) He will ask about your work, about your eating and exercising habits, your sleep and ways of relaxing. He will also want to know whether you have had any accidents or serious illnesses. It is like talking to a doctor and psychotherapist rolled into one – a wonderful combination. Then your wrist is taken to read your pulses. The hakim will also be assessing your body shape, complexion and whole manner for clues to your basic constitution or *mijaz*. In addition, he will look at your tongue and minutely observe your irises.

You will then be given your prescription, which might include some pampering sessions, gardening for earthing your energy, or perhaps some time out and relaxation, alongside medication.

WILL IT HURT?

No, this is not a painful therapy.

WILL ANYTHING STRANGE HAPPEN?

Some people may find the emphasis on spiritual and psychic matters unusual and perhaps a little disturbing.

WILL I BE GIVEN ANYTHING TO TAKE?

Yes, you may be given some tiny pills to take.

IS THERE ANY HOMEWORK?

Yes, you will be expected to make adjustments in your lifestyle.

tibb home help

- Get up early – ideally, before sunrise and certainly before 7 am. Drink a little warm water and honey on rising to prevent constipation.
- Always eat a good breakfast. Skimping on breakfast or avoiding it altogether will lower your energy levels. Lunch should be a reasonable size, while the evening meal should be light and eaten at least two hours before bedtime. This regime should also regulate your weight – tibb teaches that most Western obesity is caused by eating too much too late at night and not enough at breakfast.
- Tibb emphasizes regular exercise to keep you healthy in body and mind. Walking is excellent (see opposite).
- Make sure you get enough relaxation. Too many people in the West today are overstimulated. If you always feel tired, on a day off, take half an hour's siesta in the afternoon. Have a warm bath with essential oils (lavender is excellent). Massage your feet or head with light oils.
- Incorporate spirituality into your life. Whether it involves prayer, meditation or simple contemplation of the beauty in the world, just ten minutes a day will help bring you peace.
- Don't go to bed too late. Our natural clock would take us to bed no more than a couple of hours after sunset. Try to be in bed by at least 11 pm.
- Cultivate good sleep. If you have trouble sleeping, try meditating before sleep or experiment with gentle massage – on your feet or head. A warm, milky drink is comforting. Start by sleeping on your right side – this promotes restful sleep.

tibetan medicine

Tibetan medicine is ancient and venerable. It also appears to work – startlingly well. Reports have suggested that Tibetan physicians have cured 'incurable' diseases and many desperate people have flown thousands of miles to ask their opinions and to take their unique herbal preparations known as 'precious pills'. The Tibetan tradition of healing has always remained rather arcane and unapproachable simply because few Westerners had the basic tools (a working knowledge of modern and ancient Tibetan) to learn the system, or the patience to complete the training (it takes at least 10 years).

It can be hard to find a bona fide Tibetan physician in the West. However, increasing numbers of Westerners are taking up the knowledge and many are offering a combination of Tibetan massage and nutritional and lifestyle counselling.

Tibetans classify all of life into five energies which combine to create three 'humors' – air, bile and phlegm. Air controls breathing, speech and muscular activity, the nervous system, thought processes and your emotional attitude. Bile governs heat in the body, the liver and the digestive tract. Phlegm controls the amount of mucus in the body and also regulates the immune system. When all the humors are in balance within your body, you will enjoy perfect health. When one or more becomes aggravated or sluggish, problems will occur.

It sounds simple, but Tibetan healing is so precise and so complex that it can be mind-boggling: it takes a very experienced physician to bring about the kind of 'miracle' cures that occur. However, with just a little knowledge we could all make ourselves healthier.

Diet is very important and practitioners believe that often food is the only medicine required to obtain the necessary balance for good health and wellbeing.

what can tibetan healing help?

- Tibetan medicine can benefit most conditions, particularly if you see a fully qualified physician.
- The massage is deeply stress-relieving and can help a wide variety of stress-related disorders.
- You should become more balanced, in both mind and body.
- Tibetan medicine can have a beneficial effect on the mind and emotions – you should feel more centred and in control.
- Depression, anxiety and irritability can be alleviated.
- Digestive problems and hormonal problems seem to respond well to Tibetan medicine.

what can I expect from a session?

WHERE WILL I HAVE THE TREATMENT?
You will be lying on a couch for the massage and sitting in a chair for lifestyle counselling.

WILL I BE CLOTHED?
You will need to strip to underwear for the massage, but you'll be covered with towels. Otherwise, you will remain fully clothed.

WHAT HAPPENS?
Expect careful questioning and pulse-taking (as with traditional Chinese medicine, Tibetan healing checks a variety of pulses to gauge health). In addition, the Tibetans use urine diagnosis for precise information on the person. The massage feels wonderful. It uses spiced or herbalized oils and works on the acupressure points to free blockages.

You will be advised on diet and told which foods to avoid. Lifestyle tips may be given, too.

WILL IT HURT?

No, treatment is not painful. The massage is incredibly relaxing.

WILL ANYTHING STRANGE HAPPEN?

Not really. You may drift off to sleep during massage.

WILL I BE GIVEN ANYTHING TO TAKE?

If you see a fully qualified Tibetan physician, you will be given herbs, often in the form of tiny pills.

IS THERE ANY HOMEWORK?

Yes, you will be expected to make changes to your lifestyle and diet.

what's your tibetan type?

Most people are a combination of types, but the following should give you a rough idea of which humor is dominating you at present.

AIR: Air causes stress. You may sweat very little and could suffer from insomnia, constipation, back pains, dry skin and stomach disorders. Your mind may flit from subject to subject. Symptoms include restlessness, dizziness, shivering, sighing, pain in the hips and shoulder blades, and humming in the ears.
DIAGNOSIS: A clear sign of unbalanced air is watery, almost transparent urine.
DIET TO BALANCE: Avoid cold foods such as salads and ice cream, or make sure you have a hot drink beforehand (such as ginger tea). Base your diet on chicken, meat broths, cheese, onions, carrots, garlic and spices, spinach and leafy greens.

BILE: Bile people often sweat quite a lot. They are precise, analytical people with good mental powers, but can be a little antisocial. They often wake up feeling bright and cheerful but by midday are feeling irritable. Their weak spot is their liver and they can easily overheat. When bile is out of balance, you could feel thirsty, have a bitter taste in your mouth, suffer pains in the upper body, feel feverish and have diarrhoea or vomiting.
DIAGNOSIS: Unbalanced bile is present if your urine is yellow or brownish in colour.
DIET TO BALANCE: Choose cool, light foods such as salads and yogurt, and drink plenty of cool water. Avoid hot, spicy foods, nuts, alcohol and red meat.

PHLEGM: Phlegmatic people are generally heavy; they have even, stable and (sometimes) stubborn personalities and avoid rows. They are prone to oversleeping and like an afternoon siesta. Their problems tend to be bronchial or in the kidneys. If phlegm is out of balance, you could feel lethargic and heavy. You may suffer frequent indigestion or belching, distention of the stomach and a feeling of coldness in the feet. You might put on weight or find it difficult to lose weight.
DIAGNOSIS: Disordered phlegm shows itself in very pale, foaming urine.
DIET TO BALANCE: Keep the digestion warm with spices such as ginger, cardamom and nutmeg. Fennel and peppermint will help the digestion, too. Avoid dairy, as it is mucus-producing, and don't eat too much fruit if you are trying to lose weight.

tibetan tips for health problems

For anxiety and tension – rub either side of your breastbone.

For chesty/phlegmatic conditions – fill a bowl with hot water and add a few drops of ginger oil. Sit with your feet in it until the water is no longer hot, then massage your feet.

For combating stress and putting digestion back into balance – massage the soles of your feet in a circular motion.

For constipation – rub the base of the 'web' of skin at the point where your thumb and forefinger meet. Regularly drink hot water that has been boiled.

For general wellbeing – stand up straight with your arms outstretched, then start spinning slowly round in a clockwise direction (anticlockwise if you are in the southern hemisphere). Keep your eyes fixed on a spot straight ahead of you to minimize dizziness (as you turn round, fix your eyes back on that spot as quickly as possible). You will probably not be able to manage more than six turns to begin with. Practise every day and slowly build up speed, gradually working up to 12 repetitions (no more, or you will lose the energizing effect).

For hayfever – try taking a spoonful of honey every day for a month before the hayfever season starts.

For insomnia – put 2 or 3 drops of ginger essential oil in a base oil (almond is nice and light). Rub it into the soles of the feet before bedtime. Children will fall asleep if you massage the sides of their feet.

For mid-afternoon tiredness – try hot, sweet foods, such as honey in hot water.

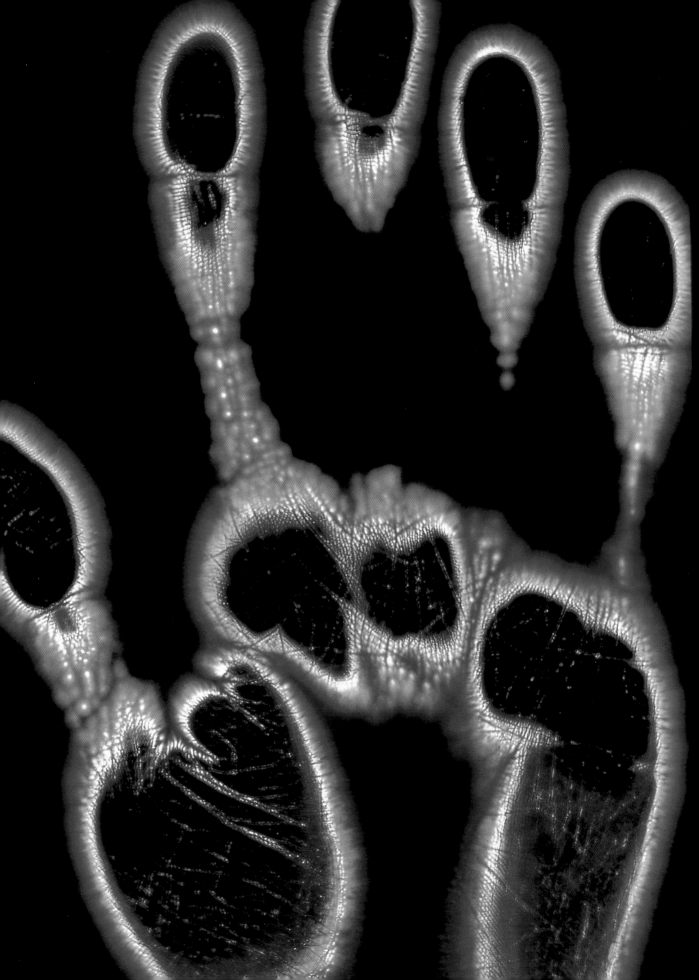

ENERGY MEDICINE

As we have already seen, the ancients understood that we are not just flesh and bones; we are infused with a subtle form of energy that cannot be seen by the naked eye or under the microscope of science. For many years, complementary and alternative therapists have worked with this subtle energy and seen with their own eyes that, by working on the esoteric level, they could affect huge changes in the physical body. Scientists remained sceptical: no one had ever seen a meridian, an aura, a chakra, they argued. In recent years, however, more open-minded investigation into this field has shown remarkable results: you can see the aura and the subtle energy pathways. It has been proven that healers can effect physical change.

We stand on the brink of an explosion in energy medicine. In the future, it will not seem strange to treat cancer with colour, rheumatism with sound. No one will scoff at the concept of flower essences shifting emotions, homoeopathy (where not a molecule of the original substance remains) curing eczema, or acupuncture reversing infertility.

The key to all these ideas lies in the concept of vital energy. Most people tend to think in terms of matter and energy as separate entities. Our bodies are matter: we feed them food which gives us the energy to power them – just as we feed a car fuel to make it move. But, according to the new field of quantum physics, the molecules that compose the physical human body are actually just a form of vibrating energy. In fact, Albert Einstein concluded that matter and energy were actually perfectly interchangeable.

Equally, everything around us is energy: it just vibrates at different frequencies. Just as X-rays, radio and television waves, ultrasonic waves and microwaves have different frequencies, so, too, do the various systems of the human body and the world around us. The cells of the body actually emit pulses of light which scientists surmise may be part of a sophisticated communication system to organize the actions of cells within each body system.

Once you take these ideas on board, the entire concept of energy medicine (and a lot of other mind–body–spirit ideas) instantly makes sense. Directing a specific sound at a particular organ could bring it back in balance by a form of 'entrainment', encouraging the diseased part to vibrate at the right frequency again. A gem, flower or homeopathic remedy's vibrational signature could have the same effect.

Equally, once we recognize that we are powered by energy, it's a swift jump to recognize that energy isn't just physical: we talk about emotional energy; natural energy; spiritual energy; sexual energy. Once we free ourselves from thinking on purely mechanical, tangible lines and see the world around us as energy vibrating at different frequencies, concepts such as feng shui, emotional healing, Tantra and contact beyond death all become quite possible.

The whole field is remarkably complex and astonishing. Fortunately, you do not need to be a quantum physicist to use energy medicine! It can help, however, to understand a few key concepts.

We humans possess several specialized systems that supply energy and information to the organs, tissues and cells of the body at a variety of levels. The various forms of energy medicine view these in different ways, but there are some basic concepts on which most agree.

forms of vital energy

There are many forms of bioenergy in the human body: metabolic energy, bioelectrical energy and biophotonic energy, to name but a few that scientists are now researching to understand how cells communicate. For our purposes, however, we'll focus on that which is known as subtle, or vital, bioenergy (also known as subtle magnetic life energies). Why? Because these are the systems that we can most readily and easily influence for ourselves.

Qi (in the Chinese system) and prana (in the Indian) are the forms of energy with which you may be most familiar. Both the Chinese and Indians have been aware of the

OPPOSITE The aura of a human hand is seen at left in this Kirlian photograph. Auras are subtle bodies of energy, or electromagnetic fields, which surround us all. In the 1930s, Semyon Kirlian provided visual proof of their existence.

existence of subtle energy in the body and the environment for thousands of years – their whole systems of medicine are built upon it, as are their theories of architecture (feng shui in China, vastu shastra in India).

Although both forms of energy are described slightly differently, in reality, they are both ways of describing the energy that is absorbed from the environment around us, from the food we eat and the exercise we take. It can also be inherited from our parents. Qi flows through channels known as *meridians*, while prana flows through channels called the *nadis*, and also through the *chakras*.

Energy medicine also teaches that there are fields of energy that lie beyond our physical form. The best known is the 'aura' (which forms around the body), but there are also etheric energy (which keeps the physical body in correct shape), astral energy (which deals with emotional energy), mental energy (which governs intellect, creativity and thought) and higher spiritual energy or soul energy (which is said to hold our memories from lifetime to lifetime).

Let's take a closer look at some of these concepts.

balance your chakras for health and harmony

Eastern religions teach that the human body contains many spinning spheres of bioenergetic energy, known as *chakras*. The major ones run from the base of the spine to the crown of the head. While scientists insist chakras don't exist because they cannot be seen under the microscope, clairvoyants claim they can easily 'see' them. And the PIP scanner (see Electro-Crystal Therapy, page 235) which takes information from sound and light frequencies in the body now shows what the mystics have known of all along: oscillating spheres of energy in a vertical line down the body.

The chakras are precise monitors of our physical and mental wellbeing. Each chakra is said to spin at a different frequency and, when each one spins at its perfect frequency, the systems of the body radiate perfect health; emotions are centred and balanced and we enjoy optimum health and a deep sense of peace. It's a little like tuning into a radio station: if you're on the wrong frequency, the sound is distorted and unpleasant; once you hit the right frequency, it becomes clear as a bell. However, with all the stresses and strains of modern life, it is easy for the chakras to fall out of frequency. When this happens, we fall prey to illnesses, feel under par or lose our emotional equilibrium.

Each chakra governs different emotions and life issues. By visualizing and meditating on the chakras, you can learn a lot about yourself, increasing your self-knowledge. You can also use your chakras to 'tune in' to various issues or life lessons. For example, if you wanted to connect to the feeling of unconditional love, you would focus on your heart chakra, visualizing it as a beautiful, clear green wheel of energy, vibrating in your heart area.

The table opposite shows the main chakras, their colours and the areas they govern.

healing the chakras

In an ideal world, all our chakras would be balanced, each spinning equally. However, most of us have one or more centres out of equilibrium. Sometimes the body itself will give us clues: a sore throat can be an indication that the throat chakra needs attention, headaches may be a hint that we need to work on our brow chakra and constipation may nudge us into looking at our base.

Alternatively, consider which of the areas in the table opposite cause you problems. Are you often fearful, lacking in confidence and self-esteem? Work with your solar plexus. Do you find you have sexual relationships, but can't connect on an emotional level? You may well need to focus on both the genital and heart chakras. If you're feeling too spacy and unconnected with the 'real world', you may need to ground yourself with your base and stop living in your crown! Let's now take a look at how you can balance the chakras with everyday activities.

THE BASE CHAKRA: You need to reconnect with your body. Start by doing as much physical exercise as possible – choose a sport or activity you enjoy (maybe dance, aerobics, running or swimming). Try massage – find a professional aromatherapist or bodyworker, or ask a friend or partner to give you a massage. Yoga would be excellent, as it heals and balances all the chakras. Gardening and pottery are good grounding exercises if you have a deficiency of base

CHAKRA	LOCATION	COLOUR	GOVERNS
BASE	Base of spine	Red	The physical body, social position, survival
GENITAL	Genitals	Orange	Sensuality and sexuality, emotions
SOLAR PLEXUS	Solar plexus	Yellow	Self-esteem, energy, confidence, will, inner power
HEART	Heart/chest	Green	Love, intimacy, balance, relationships
THROAT	Throat	Blue	Communication and creativity
BROW	Forehead	Indigo	Imagination, intuition, dreams and insights
CROWN	Top of the head	Violet	Understanding, connection with the divine

chakra. On a psychological level, look at your early relationship with your mother: talk to her about it if you can. If it's painful, talk to a trained therapist or counsellor.

THE SACRAL CHAKRA: Learn to trust and enjoy your senses – feel the textures around you, listen to new music and sounds, look at nature and at art, and taste different foods and drinks. Dance can help to liberate this chakra, as can bodywork. Gently try to get in touch with your emotions (with professional help if necessary) to release any old feelings of hurt, anger and guilt.

THE SOLAR PLEXUS CHAKRA: Anyone with problems in this chakra would benefit from doing sit-ups (abdominal crunches) to strengthen that area. Martial arts such as judo or tai chi would be excellent. Psychotherapy can help you build up the necessary strength to release or contain any pent-up anger and strengthen your sense of autonomy.

THE HEART CHAKRA: Breathing exercises will help all those with problems in the heart chakra – join a yoga or chi kung class that teaches breathing. Start a journal, writing down all your feelings and thoughts honestly. Look at your relationships and try to free yourself from suppressed grief and loss (with professional help if necessary). Start to accept yourself – just as you are.

THE THROAT CHAKRA: If you are lacking in energy in your throat chakra, you need to use your voice: singing, chanting, humming, shouting – anything to release the voice. Sound therapy or voicework would be wonderful. If you have too much energy here, practise the art of silence and concentrate on what other people are saying. All problems in this chakra benefit from bodywork or massage to release tension in the neck and shoulders, or you could try the Alexander technique or Pilates. Write your thoughts and unspoken feelings in a journal; write letters (they don't have to be sent).

THE BROW CHAKRA: Try painting and drawing – use whatever materials and colours you like and paint whatever comes to mind. Look at your painting and see what emotions emerge. Write down and work with your dreams. Try meditation or autogenic training. Guided visualizations can be useful, as can hypnotherapy (but only with a qualified expert).

THE CROWN CHAKRA: Meditation could be very useful for you. Be open to new ideas and new information – don't dismiss things until you've tried them. Examine your attitudes to spirituality and religion. If you have an excess of crown chakra energy, you need to connect with your body and the earth – try physical exercise, massage or gardening. If you have a deficiency, open yourself up to the idea of spirituality, drop your cynicism and cultivate an open mind.

how to see auras

You don't have to be psychic or have any particular spiritual 'powers' to be able to see auras. Anyone can learn how to see this energy field: it's a matter of learning how to use our peripheral vision and training our eyes to see something for which we normally don't bother to look.

1 Ask your 'guinea pig' to stand about 60 cm (2 ft) in front of a bare white wall. Avoid colours or patterns.

2 If possible, use natural daylight, but don't have your subject stand in direct sunlight.

3 Now stand back at least 3 m (10 ft) from your subject.

4 Ask the person to relax, breathe deeply and rock gently from side to side, hands unclasped at the sides.

5 Look past the person's head and shoulders and focus on the wall behind him or her. Avoid looking directly at the person, concentrating instead on the wall behind him or her.

6 As you look past the outline of the body, you should see a band of blurred white light around your subject, as if they were in a cocoon. This is the etheric aura.

7 Continue to look past the outline of the body and you should see the subject as if he or she were illuminated from behind, possibly with a bright yellow or silver colour. You may start to notice colours.

8 Some people will have less visible auras than others, so don't worry if you can't see any colours at first.

auras – reading the body

Mystics have talked for centuries of auras, of these bodies of subtle energy, the electromagnetic fields, which surround us all. Thousands of years ago, as we have seen, the Hindus knew of the subtle energy centres called the chakras. In more recent times, Nicola Tesla (in 1891) and Semyon Kirlian (in the 1930s with his Kirlian photography) have proved beyond a shadow of a doubt the existence of these energy radiations that cannot be seen by the naked eye.

The aura is what we recognize as a halo around the heads of very spiritual beings such as Christ, the Buddha, Mohammed, Vishnu and all the prophets and angels. You don't have to be a highly evolved spiritual leader, however, to possess an aura. Each and every one of us has this vibrating energy; it's just that few of us know how to see it. Once you have learnt how to see the aura (and it's really quite a simple process – see the exercise to the left), you gain a unique insight into yourself and the people around you. Reading auras could warn you away from unscrupulous or unpleasant people. It could also let you know when someone is angry, upset, jealous or lying. By catching the clues in the aura, you could stop arguments before they even start. You would know when to give your partner kind, loving support when he or she was feeling low.

According to aura experts, each colour in the aura represents a different aspect of our personality. Red shows strength and courage, and orange signals creativity, while yellow shows an extrovert, confident, logical personality. Green is for balance, love and healing; blue is peaceful and communicative; indigo is psychic and healing; and violet is spiritual and dreamy.

Often it is the very colours that we lack on which we need to focus. Missing colours signify areas of our personality that need to be developed to achieve a healthy and harmonious balance. The physical body is the last to be affected so, if you can catch imbalances and correct them while they are still simply in the subtle body, the aura, you will save yourself a lot of health problems. Change your conditioning and tackle your difficulties and you invite good health.

Auras can also give clues to our relationships. The almost 'chemical' reaction we often experience when we meet people could be due to how our aura reacts to someone else's. If someone feels uncomfortable, their aura will 'shrink' away from the other person's. If one person is pushy and aggressive, their aura can envelop the other's. On the other hand, people who feel comfortable together will show auras that meet happily or even merge into one.

In fact, we have two layers of aura: the *etheric* aura, which hugs the body closely, and the *astral* aura, which is much larger in its extent. When you begin to see auras, it will most likely be the etheric aura you see – purely as a white or transparent shimmering surround to the person. However, with practice, you can start to see the astral aura, too, and also various colours in the aura. You will then be able to start to 'read' a person by their aura.

what the various colours mean

Once you have learnt how to see auras, you can develop your skill by starting to notice colours. Generally speaking, these are the most accepted meanings of the various colours you may see in an aura.

Purple/violet – this colour indicates a person with a strong sense of mysticism and deep interest in spirituality.

Indigo – this means an artistic person who could well have inspired thoughts and possess deep wisdom.

Blue – someone with strong mental powers, intelligence and logical thinking will have a blue aura. Clear blue shows a capacity for intuition. Watch out for dark shades of blue, which could indicate a suspicious nature. A steely blue-grey colour in the aura could denote someone who is very cautious and controlled.

Turquoise – a turquoise aura indicates a dynamic person with hoards of energy. This person will be a good organizer, and he or she will also be someone who likes to influence others.

Green – green is a restful, healing colour which shows a strong sense of balance and a deep inner calm. Watch out, however, for dark green shades in the aura, or the occasional dark green flash across the aura, which can warn of deceit or jealousy.

Yellow – a cheerful personality full of joy, freedom and vitality, compassion and optimism will possess a yellow aura. Yellow also suggests love and a strong sense of caring. However, make sure the yellow is clear and bright. A dark, lifeless yellow points to covetousness and suspicion. A sulphurous, dirty yellow can indicate pain or a hidden source of anger.

Orange – this colour reveals someone full of vitality, warmth and generosity. This is also someone who has power and can be full of inspiration. Too much orange in the aura can indicate pride.

Gold – a little gold in the aura is a good sign. Gold usually indicates someone who is well balanced, kind and generous. A totally gold aura is usually found around great spiritual leaders.

Red – red signifies physical life, vitality, ambition and sexual power. People with lots of red in their auras are often very sensual and have a high sex drive. Watch out, however, for dark or cloudy red, which could point to violent tendencies or hidden anger or rage. Scarlet can indicate lust without love.

Pink – this colour indicates modesty, gentleness and shyness.

Brown – definitely not a good sign in the aura, dirty, dull brown signifies an unsettling, distracting, materialistic tendency. This could be someone who is generally negative in their nature or just happens to have a negative attitude at that time (check the aura over a few days). Brown can also show selfishness and a tendency towards avarice.

Grey – grey can signify dark or brooding thoughts. It also indicates depression, low energy and fear.

Black – beware of this aura: a black aura means someone with evil intent, malice and a very sinister character. A dark, dull, murky, indistinct colour may mean depression or show someone who carries the weight of the world on his or her shoulders. It may also indicate drug dependency or physical illness.

White – a lot of white in the aura may connote someone who has taken or frequently takes drugs. White can also signify illness.

Opaque colours – if the colours in the aura are opaque or misty, this tends to mean unresolved situations or struggle.

Clear, transparent colours – clear, bright colours are a good sign. Generally speaking, they signal clarity and a more complete or settled nature – what you see is what you get. This type of aura indicates someone who is healthy and has a happy disposition.

Dirty, dark colours – in general, dirty, dark colours show unhealthiness, lack of balance and negative emotions such as chronic anger, fear and jealousy.

Flashes of colour in the aura – this can indicate an emotion that is not under control. As you become more experienced in reading auras, you may notice that odd flashes occur as you watch, showing a flash of, say, anger or irritation.

psychoneurimmunology

Psychoneurimmunology concerns the mind's ability to effect change in the body. Only now is this being admitted (and often grudgingly) by Western doctors, but it has been widely practised for millennia by Eastern cultures. The Chinese alone have accumulated a vast reservoir of evidence linking the powers of body and mind, neurology and immunology, and have developed specific techniques for activating that link.

The principal technique in psychoneurimmunology is visualization. Patients are taught to focus their mind to visualize healing energy flowing into ailing organs, to dissolve tumours, repair tissue and so forth. Psychoneurimmunology will always work best if the image used has some meaning for you. One young boy with cancer imagined jet fighters zooming into his body to bomb the tumours. His strategy worked: the tumours shrank and disappeared without any recourse to chemotherapy, radiation or surgery.

Other people with cancer have taken a more literal (but still highly effective) tack. They visualized the cell membranes of the cancer cells within their bodies splitting (the problem with cancer cells is that their membranes stay intact so the immune system does not realize the body is under attack). This tactic has greatly improved the recovery and mortality rates of people with cancer.

Others have helped themselves through chemotherapy by visualizing increased blood cell production while they are having the treatment.

Studies have shown that if people with broken bones visualize the bone mending and regrowing, it genuinely speeds the healing process.

Basically, we are what we think we are. While it is not fair to say that we totally create our own reality (although there is a school of thought that says that every illness we suffer is due to our negative thoughts!), we can certainly use the power of thought and visualization to effect changes in the body and to facilitate our own healing processes.

OPPOSITE VISUALIZATION IS A POTENT METHOD FOR EFFECTING CHANGE IN THE BODY THROUGH THE POWER OF THOUGHT. IT CAN WORK WITH GREAT SUCCESS TO TREAT EMOTIONAL PROBLEMS AND ALLEVIATE STRESS, AS WELL AS TO TREAT PHYSICAL AILMENTS.

do-it-yourself visualization

You can use visualization to help virtually any condition, for relieving stress or for emotional recovery. Try this:

1 Find somewhere quiet where you will not be disturbed. Make yourself comfortable, either on the floor (covered with a blanket if it is cool) or in a comfortable chair.

2 Close your eyes gently and breathe calmly and deeply. Allow as much air as possible to fill your lungs. Become aware of it flowing right down to the very bottom of your lungs.

3 Now take 12 conscious breaths. Each time you breathe in, imagine you are also inhaling total relaxation and calm. As you breathe out, all the stress and anxiety leaves your body.

4 Relax for a minute, feeling how much more relaxed and calm your body and mind feel.

5 Think of a wonderful place in which you feel safe, secure and very happy. It might be an actual place or an image of an ideal retreat, e.g. a cosy room with an armchair and fire, a beautiful desert island with the sun warming your body, or perhaps a dappled glade in a cool forest.

6 Explore all around your place: what does it look, smell and sound like? How does it feel (the warm sun on your skin, the rough texture of bark, the rub of a warm blanket)?

7 Know that this place is safe and sacred. It is a place of inner peace and inner healing. Anything can happen here. Feel all the stress and strain, all the negativity and morbid thoughts simply evaporating as you sit or lie here quietly. Feel your body become lighter, softer, warmer, more peaceful.

8 Now bring healing into your body and your life. Become aware of the area around your heart. Gradually it is being suffused with light, with healing energy. Feel the light spreading out through your whole body (you may feel warmth or coolness, or a kind of tingling). The light pinpoints any areas that need healing and you feel your body respond and change.

9 Stay in your special place, as long as you like. You may want to meditate quietly or just sit and enjoy the relaxation. Know that this place is always available for you.

10 Slowly bring yourself back to waking reality. Become aware of the room and your body. Move your fingers and toes. Give yourself a good stretch. Slowly open your eyes. Rest for a few minutes before you race back to normal life.

HOMEOPATHY

How can a tiny, tasteless white pill (like those shown opposite) that retains not even one molecule of the original substance from which it was derived have a profound effect on the body and mind? It's senseless if you take a mechanical view of the body. If we look at homeopathy as energy medicine, however, it no longer appears impossible.

Homeopathy is one of the fastest growing, and most trusted, systems of natural healthcare. In skilled hands, it can seem like a miracle. Results can often be very swift indeed, particularly for acute conditions. Chronic cases do take longer, but improvements can be sweeping.

Homeopathy was founded by Samuel Hahnemann in the late eighteenth century. He trained as a doctor, but was also a skilled chemist. Instinctively, he felt that the medicine he had been taught was not the answer; often it seemed to do more harm than good. Hahnemann felt that the approach was all wrong and that 'we should imitate nature, which sometimes cures a chronic disease by another and employ in the disease we wish to cure that medicine which is able to produce another very similar disease, and the former will be cured; *similia similibus*'.

The idea wasn't actually new. In the sixteenth century, Paracelsus taught that within each disease lies the key to its cure. Hahnemann and the ancient physicians also realized that to effect a long and lasting cure, you couldn't just cure the disease: you needed to cure the whole person. Then, of necessity, the disease would cure itself.

Hahnemann's breakthrough came with his observations on the effects of cinchona bark which, when it was given to healthy individuals, produced symptoms that were very similar to those of the dangerous malaria fever. However, when it was given to actual sufferers, it appeared to cure the fever. Out of this Hahnemann developed the main principles of homeopathy, testing numerous substances on himself to find out what symptoms they caused. He found, quite bafflingly, that the more dilute the form of the remedy, the more effective it became and, consequently, he began to dilute remedies more and more. He also discovered that there was no point in precisely matching a remedy to a particular disease or condition. Five patients with flu might need five different remedies simply because they would all have slightly different symptoms.

In addition, Hahnemann realized that he needed to look beyond the merely physical. He concluded that mental and emotional, even spiritual, states were just as important to consider as physical ones.

Homeopathy works, we believe, as a form of subtle energy healing. The water, in which the remedies are initially diluted, may extract and store a form of energy which can affect the human body and psyche. As the homeopathic remedy is being prepared and progressively diluted, the physical elements of the substance are removed, leaving their energetic qualities behind. Hahnemann believed the remedies worked very much like a classic immunization, by creating an artificial illness in the patient that stimulates the body's defences, which rise up to cure the original ailment. However, it seems that the remedy, rather than producing a physical reaction at a structural cell level, is producing a vibrational reaction, a vibrational illness to stimulate the body to heal at a vibrational level.

what can homeopathy help?

- Homeopathy can help virtually all conditions – in experienced hands, it can be used to treat everyone from newborn babies to the very elderly.
- Acute conditions such as bee stings, colds and injuries respond well and quickly.
- It has been proved very useful in chronic complaints including arthritis, rheumatism, PMS and menopausal problems, high and low blood pressure, digestive problems and infertility.
- Problems with a psychological aspect respond very well: depression, anxiety, insomnia and stress-related conditions. Some homeopaths have worked with psychiatrists treating patients with severe mental-health problems.
- Children and babies respond wonderfully. It can help to treat a huge range of problems, including ear infections, colic, eczema and asthma.
- Animals also respond well and many vets now use homeopathy as an adjunct to conventional medication.

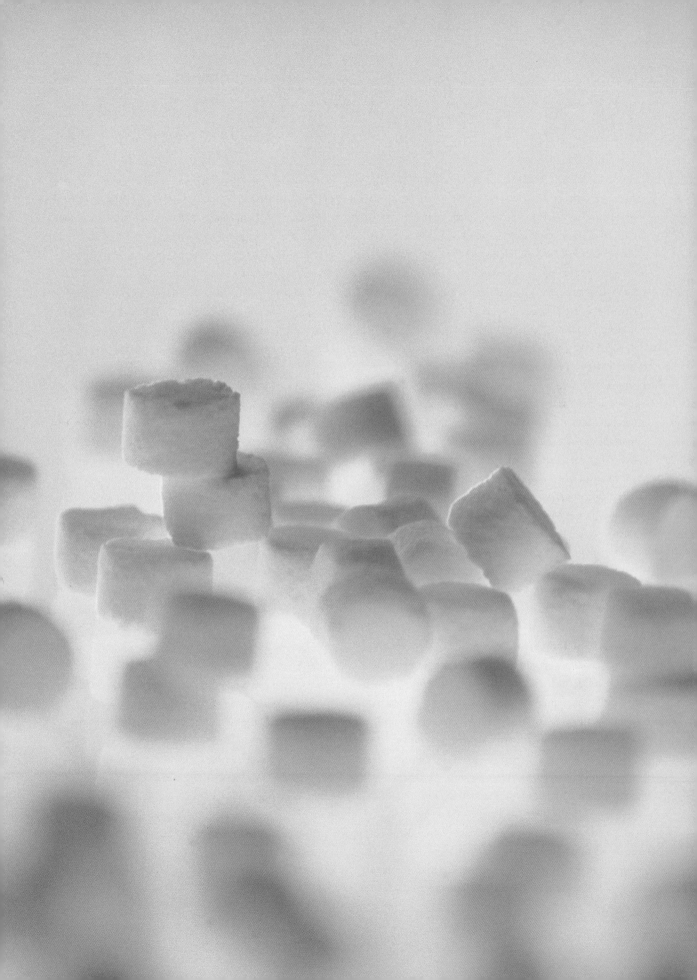

what can I expect from a session?

WHERE WILL I HAVE THE TREATMENT?

You will be sitting in a chair in the homeopath's consulting room.

WILL I BE CLOTHED?

Yes, you will be fully clothed.

WHAT HAPPENS?

Basically you just talk! At your first (and longer) appointment, you will be asked for a full medical history, including dates of illnesses, accidents, operations etc. You will also be asked to describe your present problem in precise detail.

The homeopath will ask you a series of questions, some of which can seem quite odd. Expect to talk about your feelings, your childhood, your dreams, maybe even your thoughts about God. These allow the homeopath to build up a complete picture of you and help to find your ideal remedy.

Some homeopaths will give you a remedy at the end of the session; others will send the remedy to you later.

WILL IT HURT?

No, although painful emotions may emerge.

WILL ANYTHING STRANGE HAPPEN?

Sometimes homeopathy has curious effects. You may find you dream a lot more. You may also find that you feel worse in some way after taking the remedy – this is called an aggravation and shows the healing process is under way. It should not last long, but do always tell your homeopath if you are feeling uncomfortable.

WILL I BE GIVEN ANYTHING TO TAKE?

Yes, homeopathic remedies usually come in the form of tiny white pills or powders, which are virtually tasteless.

IS THERE ANY HOMEWORK?

No, although it is helpful if you make a note of how you feel between appointments, particularly any changes and any dreams.

homeopathic first aid

Although, for best results, you should always see a professional homeopath, every home should have a basic homeopathic first-aid kit. These remedies can dramatically help everyday problems.

For most first-aid situations, obtain your remedies in the sixth potency (often labelled 6x). They are readily available from health food stores and chemist shops or pharmacies. Keep them away from perfumes and essential oils.

Arnica is the great shock remedy. Give it immediately after any kind of accident or shock, whether physical or emotional. It is also very useful after visits to the dentist, after operations and following childbirth because it is incredibly healing.

Arsenicum album is the first remedy to consider when there is any thought of food poisoning – when someone has eaten food that is off or tainted. The classic symptoms are restlessness and irritability, a feeling of desperation, feeling thirsty but wanting only small sips, and intense burning pains.

Belladonna is wonderful for fevers when the face is brightly flushed, for bursting headaches when the face is red, for sunstroke and for sore throats when the tonsils are enlarged and red. It is very useful for bringing down fevers in babies and children.

Calendula (shown opposite) is generally used topically as a lotion or ointment. It is wonderful for any kind of wound or sore, or for soothing rough or chapped skin. Calendula promotes healing and lessens scarring.

Cantharis can help to soothe and heal cystitis. It is useful for any kind of burning pain, especially in the bladder or urethra when connected with urination.

Chamomilla is a classic remedy for teething babies – provided they are fractious and always asking for things, and then tossing them away. This remedy can also help if you've drunk too much coffee and is particularly useful for combating insomnia after an emotional upset.

Gelsemium is the great flu remedy – suitable for the typical variety of flu where you have shivers up and down the spine, an aching back and limbs, and a tight headache. You would not be thirsty.

Ignatia is the great grief counsellor. Give ignatia after any form of emotional shock, fright or grief. It is wonderful for helping with bereavement – not just for humans, but also for pets (remember that children often grieve terribly for lost pets).

Ledum is useful for old bruises and for puncture wounds such as insect stings, splinters or nails.

Nux vomica helps with the ill-effects of overeating or eating the wrong kinds of food; overindulging in alcohol or drugs; overstudying and overwork. Nux vomica is considered the great destresser.

Petroleum is useful for travel sickness of all kinds. Also useful for travel sickness is **tabacum**. Experiment to see which suits you best.

Rhus tox eases sprains of joints or tendons, and can be used after any form of overexertion or strain. It is very useful, with arnica, after surgical operations.

HEALING

We can all heal. As Jesus said in the Bible, 'These things that I do, so can you do and more.' Unfortunately, few of us take it seriously. Yet many of us might be healing every day, without even knowing it. Some would say that every time a doctor or nurse touches a patient with care and concern they are performing a kind of healing. Parent do the same when they cuddle their child, or when they lay a soothing hand on the forehead or give a loving squeeze of the hand. Even total strangers can give the healing touch: some people simply shake your hand or put a hand on your shoulder and you can almost feel their energy leaping out at you.

Healing can be simple: the mere touch of hands. Or it can be clothed in ceremony with recitations of prayers or the chanting of mantras. Which form you choose is up to you.

Healing certainly didn't begin in the Bible. Like so many other natural therapies, healing was a part of most ancient cultures. There is documentation which shows that the Chinese were practising it 5,000 years before the birth of Christ. The ancient Egyptians used it; so did the Greeks and Romans. In many cultures, the laying on of hands has been practised in a straight line from antiquity: both the Native American and the Australian Aboriginal cultures still practise healing in the ancient way.

In the West, however, healing has been rather frowned upon for some centuries, although it is now gaining popularity and credibility once again. In 1956, the British Medical Association (BMA) published a report entitled *Divine Healing and Co-operation between Doctors and Clergy*. The report stated quite clearly that 'through spiritual healing, recoveries take place that cannot be explained by medical science'. At the forefront of the new wave of healing is the National Federation of Spiritual Healers, whose members have been working for the past 30 years to establish bona-fide healing. They are non-denominational and bound by a strict code of ethics. Many hospitals now happily accept them into their wards when a patient asks for their services.

But what happens when someone heals? The process seems so simple. The healer either just touches the patient or hovers their hands above him or her. Some simply sit and think about the patient getting well – even though the patient is many miles away. How can it work? Many healers say that they are bringing their patients into a higher level of being, where they are in touch with the healing power of God or some higher force. Others think in more prosaic terms and say they are using a biomagnetic or bioelectrical energy and bringing the body into balance. However they describe it, what seems to be happening is that the energy system of the body is being balanced.

Many healers will insist that they do not actually heal, but that they merely open up the body so it can perform its own healing. The healer is merely there to act as a catalyst. This is one reason why it is important for the patient to have at least some form of faith in the process. Healers recognize the enormous untapped power of the mind and believe that, if the mind desires healing, the body will follow suit. Hence many healers will use creative visualization or encourage their patients to take responsibility for their own health, instigating changes in diet, exercise, mental attitude, stress relief and so on.

There is no doubt, however, that some people do seem to be 'tapped in' to some enormous fund of energy. They're a bit like live wires, literally buzzing with vital force. Kirlian photographs of healers' hands show bright, darting shoots of energy. And the PIP scanner used in electro-crystal therapy (see page 235) has filmed a healer working on a patient – as she put up her hands, clear shooting energy flew from her hands to the patient's body.

what can healing help?

- Many people turn to healing as a last-ditch attempt, when other therapies have failed.
- It is generally most successful when it prompts changes in the patient's lifestyle.
- People generally find they start to question their lifestyles and discover better ways to live.
- There have been cases of healing instigating almost miraculous cures – but it is unpredictable.
- Many people find healing a particularly soothing and relaxing form of stress relief.

- Because it is so gentle, this therapy is suitable for the very young, the very old and the very weak.
- Healing seems to help dying people – lessening pain and giving a sense of acceptance and peace.
- Animals also seem to respond well.

what can I expect from a session?

WHERE WILL I HAVE THE TREATMENT?

Usually you will be either sitting in a chair or lying on a couch in the healer's room.

WILL I BE CLOTHED?

Yes, you will be fully clothed.

WHAT HAPPENS?

Some healers will talk for a while before healing, using it as a chance to scan your aura (see page 42) and chakras (see page 41). You will then be asked to take off your shoes and jewellery, and then you will either lie on a couch or remain sitting in a comfortable chair.

Healers have different methods. Some will lay their hands gently on your body; others will have their hands hovering just over your body, working on the aura.

WILL IT HURT?

No, healing is totally painless. Usually you won't feel anything.

WILL ANYTHING STRANGE HAPPEN?

Some people feel energy moving in their body by tingling or shivering. Sometimes they can feel warmth or coolness coming from the healer's hands. Some people see colours or scenes from their lives.

WILL I BE GIVEN ANYTHING TO TAKE?

Not usually, although some healers do use flower remedies.

IS THERE ANY HOMEWORK?

It depends on your healer. Some healers will teach you visualization exercises or simple meditations.

do-it-yourself healing

Anyone can learn healing touch – the process is incredibly simple, but will take time and practice to perfect. We will be looking at various types of healing and ways in which you can practise healing yourself and others throughout the book. But let's start now with some simple exercises to awaken your healing powers.

FEELING THE LINK BETWEEN MIND AND BODY

Before you start to heal, try the zero-balancing exercise on page 202, which should convince you that there is a definite link between your mind and your body.

FEELING YOUR OWN ENERGY

1 Rub your hands together quite vigorously for a few moments. Now hold them a few inches apart, as if you were holding a ball. You may feel a tingling or a warmth from your hands. 'Bounce' your hands and feel the energy change as your hands move closer and further away.

2 Now move your hands even further apart, as if you were holding, say, a football or volleyball.

3 Now imagine that in the centre of one palm is a circular patch that can transmit energy. Rub this area with the thumb of your other hand, imagining you are opening up this area. Then repeat on the other hand. If you have any religious or spiritual beliefs, you could ask for help in your healing quest.

SENDING HEALING ENERGY

1 Ask your subject to sit in a comfortable chair, then to relax, close his or her eyes and breathe naturally.

2 Stand with your feet shoulder-width apart. Let your shoulders relax and imagine there is a string gently tugging your head up to the ceiling. Breathe deeply and calmly, connecting with your heart chakra (imagine it pulsing with energy).

3 Now feel your crown chakra (at the top of your head) opening to let in healing energy. Visualize this energy flowing smoothly into your heart and then along your arms and into your fingers.

4 Now direct this energy where you feel it is needed. If you can sense that there is a particular place which needs attention, hold your hands either directly on that part or just above it.

5 If you are unsure where to heal, concentrate on the major chakra sites, starting with the base and moving up to the crown. Check the chart on page 41 for the various chakras. Visualize the healing energy streaming into each centre in turn. As you work, you might feel your hands become stiff or uncomfortable. Quietly shake them to release any negative energy you might have picked up while working. Every so often, pause and breathe to centre yourself.

body

Get the basics right and you will have the blueprint for good health, happiness and wellbeing. In order to enjoy rude good health, you really need only a handful of simple ingredients: good food, good exercise, good breathing and a good environment. In this part of the book, we will look at the simple ways in which you can introduce all of these elements to your everyday life.

We'll start by looking at our basic fuel — food. There is so much conflicting information given about nutrition and diet that we will seek to uncover the truth and discover how to give your body the nutrients it needs. The good diet prescription is not complicated; it will dovetail with any lifestyle and will make a huge difference to your overall feeling of wellbeing.

Exercise is another part of the body equation. Many people baulk at the thought of exercise, having been put off early in life by overenthusiastic parents or sadistic gym teachers! Don't worry: I'll show you how to find the perfect form of exercise for you and how to keep motivated. We'll also look at some wonderful systems of exercise such as yoga, Pilates and chi kung – all gentle, yet amazingly effective.

Even more important – but frequently forgotten – is breathing. We all know how to breathe, but few of us invest time and energy into learning how to breathe really well. Yet good breathing can help our health and certainly increase our energy – it makes us feel truly alive and well. Breathing is a vital science and in this section we look at some simple techniques that can make a huge difference to your life.

Millions of people suffer from sleep disturbances, a very real concern. Good sleep is essential for good health, so we'll look at ways to nudge your system back into good sleep habits. We'll also investigate posture, a word which often fills hearts with dread! No balancing of books on heads, I promise. Instead, we will be checking out the Alexander technique, Feldenkrais and an amazing system called the Mézières method.

There is a lot of information in this section of the book, but there is absolutely no need to be daunted. Bear in mind that even one or two small changes will have a knock-on beneficial effect on your body's wellbeing. Take it slowly and do what you can. You can build up over a period of weeks, months or even years.

NUTRITION: GOOD FOOD

We are fed so much conflicting advice on diet that it's hard to sort the lean facts from the big fat fiction. It seems as though every day we read that we should be eating more protein or less protein; that we should give up all fat or that we should cut down on certain kinds. It can be so confusing that many people simply give up and eat what they like. Yet even a little (let alone too much) of what you fancy can be harmful to your health. Today, our food is so processed, so tampered with that you would be shocked to discover how little goodness it actually contains – and how much nastiness.

Almost all non-organic food is grown with pesticides of some kind. Many of these are health-threatening: some are carcinogenic (cause cancer); some are mutagenic (cause cells to mutate); others could be teratogenic (cause birth defects). The worldwide death rate from pesticide poisoning alone tops 200,000 a year, yet we still spray our crops.

Also causing concern is genetic modification (GM). Altering the genetic structure of a food to improve a particular quality is, warn some, an imprecise science with unpredictable outcomes. Bovine spongiform encephalopathy (BSE), or 'mad cow' disease, continues to pose a real concern, with fears that the disease which can be passed on to humans as variant Creutzfeldt-Jakob disease (vCJD) is on the increase.

glycaemic index – the hidden factor

Research throughout the 1990s has shown that not all carbohydrates are created equal. For the most health benefits, we should be stoking up on foods with a low glycaemic index (i.e. foods that break down slowly, releasing glucose gradually into the body). Apparently, concentrating on these foods in our diet can improve heart conditions, give us more long-lasting energy and help us lose weight. On page 57, the wonder foods that you should include in your diet are listed.

RIGHT It's not a myth: a good, solid, healthy breakfast really sets you up for the day. Muesli, fruit and yogurt are ideal. Try to wean yourself off coffee and try herbal teas instead.

basic safety guidelines for a modern diet

- First and foremost, try to buy as much organic food as possible. It *is* more expensive, but prices are coming down.
- If you can't buy organic, always peel or skin non-organic vegetables and fruit to remove superficial additives (be aware that some pesticides will be absorbed into the food). Always buy organic meat – it's much better to have just a little organic meat than a large piece of non-organic.
- Pick food in season wherever possible. Food grown and harvested at its natural pace will have the most nutrients and vitality. Food grown out of season is usually forced with excess fertilizers and heavily treated with pesticides and fungicides. 'Baby' or miniature vegetables will have been heavily treated, too.
- Choose locally produced food which is less reliant on processing and additives to keep it looking fresh.
- Avoid foods with additives, colourings and preservatives wherever possible. This means all highly processed, convenience foods, including most canned, dried and packet foods, plus ready-made meals and 'fast foods'.
- Avoid smoked meats and fish, and steer clear of sausages and processed meats, which contain high levels of additives and potential carcinogens.
- Be wary of 'diet' foods, which often contain artificial sweeteners and other additives.
- Cut out (or cut right down on) sweets or candies. Most are packed full of artificial colours, preservatives and other additives, which many people suspect of being prime factors in hyperactivity and allergic reactions in children.
- Cut down on red meat (except game), full-fat dairy produce and saturated fat. These can all contribute to heart failure.
- Try not to add salt to your food. Instead, use herbs and spices, or add celery, which has a naturally salty taste.

WONDER FOODS

- whole cereal grains such as barley, whole wheat, cracked wheat (bulgur), oats and rolled oats (good for breakfast), and wholegrain breads
- dried pulses and legumes such as lentils, beans and dried peas. Use them as good sources of protein, in place of meat, in chillis, stews and casseroles
- fruit and vegetables – although be aware that potatoes have a high glycaemic index

supplements – do we need them?

If you're eating a healthy diet, do you really need supplements? The shelves are brimming with vitamins, minerals, amino acids and herbal formulae, but are they truly necessary?

Sadly, many nutritionists now believe that we don't get the micronutrients we need from our daily diet. Few people enjoy the luxury of eating completely fresh, organic, additive-free food all the time. Plus, our modern, stressful lifestyle tends to strip vitamins and minerals from our bodies. Stress, pollution, smoking and alcohol can all scupper our best intentions. Hence, many experts now recommend taking a good-quality multivitamin and mineral compound as a safeguard against possible deficiencies. I think this is a good idea. Choose one from a reputable company (price will usually give a good indication – low-cost multis tend to be low quality): if in doubt, ask at your local health food store or consult your natural health practitioner.

If you are pregnant, you should not take a standard multi, but choose instead a specific antenatal one (ideally, consult a nutritional therapist). There are also now a broad range of multis for a range of people: children (a supplement can be very useful if you have a picky eater), teenagers, women (many find that it can help premenstrual syndrome (PMS) and other menstrual symptoms), sportspeople, menopausal women, and older people.

However, I would seriously warn against self-prescribing anything much more than a multicomplex. The biochemistry of micronutrients is indeed complex and you really need to consult a well-trained, experienced nutritional therapist if you feel that additional supplements would help.

OPPOSITE FRESH FRUIT IS A KEY PART OF EATING HEALTHILY — AND ENJOYABLY. AIM TO EAT AT LEAST FIVE PORTIONS OF FRESH FRUIT AND VEGETABLES A DAY.

the good-health diet

So, after you have cut all the baddies from your diet, what is left to eat? Fortunately, there is plenty of tasty food that should form the basis of your daily diet.

The World Health Organization (WHO) has come up with very simple guidelines based on universally agreed scientific principles. Interestingly, they reflect what most ancient medical philosophies have taught for centuries.

- Around half your daily intake of calories should come from complex carbohydrates (the solid, starchy foods such as bread, pasta, potatoes, cereals and rice). Ideally, choose the wholemeal or 'brown' versions of these, as they retain more nutrients, provide better fibre (which keeps your intestines healthy) and have a low glycaemic index (see page 54). Grains such as barley, millet, buckwheat and quinoa are also a good choice.
- Eat loads of fresh (ideally organic) fruit and vegetables – at least five portions a day (a portion is a piece of fruit, i.e. an apple or orange, or a serving of vegetables). Fruit and vegetables are packed with essential vitamins and minerals, including the disease-fighting antioxidants.
- Cut down on sugars – including syrups, fructose and sucrose (the so-called simple carbohydrates). Sugar simply isn't needed in a healthy diet. If you can't give up sugar (or sweet things) altogether, try to cut down or have a cake or chocolate as a special treat, rather than a daily snack.
- Cut down on saturated fat. Some fat is essential for health – and it's pretty hard to avoid fat entirely – but saturated fat puts us at risk from heart disease and some cancers. The main culprits are fried foods, some cuts of red meat (except game, which is surprisingly healthy) and full-fat dairy produce. Fish is great (oily fish such as herrings, mackerel and sardines do contain fat, but it's the healthy kind), so try to incorporate fish into your diet at least twice a week. Chicken and turkey are low-fat meats; seafood is also a good choice. Investigate vegetarian proteins such as tofu and Quorn, pulses, seeds and nuts.
- Experiment with herbs and spices. They have many health benefits, so get into the habit of adding some spice to your cooking. You will also find that you'll need less salt, sugar and fat because they give added interest to your food.

nutritional therapy

The basic nutritional guidelines that have just been given are literally that – basic.

The cornerstone of all natural health thinking is that we are all individuals with individual needs. The food I thrive on might give you terrible indigestion; the diet that gives you masses of energy might make me put on weight. Equally, the diet that cures one person's arthritis might have no effect on someone else with the same condition. There are simply too many factors to take into consideration.

Nutritionists look at your entire lifestyle and make-up – not just what you eat, but how you work, how you sleep, what exercise you take, how you feel. The goal is to build a complete picture and then find a dietary and supplement programme to bring you back into health. It's also a process of education – finding out why you are imbalanced and how to correct it.

Nutritional therapy may seem like a new fad, but in fact the concept of curing illness with food is exceedingly ancient. Chinese and ayurvedic physicians would always look to diet first. Researchers in the twentieth century began to prove what the ancient sages knew through experience. Christian Eijkman, a Dutch doctor, found that prisoners in the East Indies who ate polished rice got the disease beriberi, while those who ate unrefined rice didn't. Polish biochemist Casimir Funk, working in London, discovered the element in rice husks that prevented the disease. He believed it belonged to a group of chemicals known as amines, so he coined the word 'vitamine', literally meaning an amine (essential) for life.

Nutritional therapy is not a quick fix and it can be tough going. To gain the best results, as with any therapy, you have to be committed and to make sacrifices for your health. You may well be told that you have to give up quite a number of foods for at least a month (to detect intolerances); you might equally be told some home truths about your lifestyle and urged to cut down on harmful practices.

The rewards, however, can be enormous. Many people find that their diet is at the root of some serious ailments.

OPPOSITE OFTEN, WHEN WE THINK WE ARE HUNGRY, OUR BODIES ARE IN FACT CRYING OUT FROM THIRST. KEEP A BOTTLE OF MINERAL WATER NEAR YOU AND DRINK THROUGHOUT THE DAY. AIM FOR ABOUT 2 LITRES (3½ PINTS) A DAY.

what can nutritional therapy help?

- Arthritis and rheumatism respond well to nutritional therapy.
- Allergies and food intolerances can be factors in digestive problems, asthma, eczema and premenstrual syndrome (PMS) – nutritional therapy can help.
- Conditions with an emotional or psychological element such as depression, anxiety, insomnia, irritability and stress can often improve after an adjustment in diet or beginning correct supplementation, as can eating disorders.
- Children can respond well to dietary changes: hyperactivity can often be cured.
- Energy levels almost always increase, mood improves and people usually feel more relaxed.
- Almost all chronic conditions can be helped or alleviated in some way by nutritional therapy.

what can I expect from a session?

WHERE WILL I HAVE THE TREATMENT?

You will be sitting in a chair in the therapist's room.

WILL I BE CLOTHED?

Yes, you will be fully clothed.

WHAT HAPPENS?

First you will give answers to, or fill in, a detailed questionnaire, asking about all aspects of your health: history, current symptoms, energy levels, sleep, work and so on. Some nutritional therapists use kinesiology, dowsing or machines such as the Vega or BEST machine to detect allergies and intolerances, and check for deficiencies. Others will refer you for diagnostic tests.

From all this information, the therapist will work out what foods you should eat and what you should avoid, and also which supplements you need.

WILL IT HURT?

No, there's no pain involved – other than the pain of having to cut out foods you like and crave!

WILL ANYTHING STRANGE HAPPEN?

No, not at all. Nutritional therapy is a really practical, down-to-earth therapy.

WILL I BE GIVEN ANYTHING TO TAKE?

It is most probable that you will be prescribed supplements in the form of tablets or occasionally in liquid form.

IS THERE ANY HOMEWORK?

Yes, basically it's all down to you: having been told what to eat for good health, you are the one who has to stick to the guidelines.

NATUROPATHY

NATUROPATHY IS TO THE WEST WHAT AYURVEDA AND TRADITIONAL CHINESE MEDICINE ARE TO THE EAST – A GENTLE, NATURE-BASED, HOLISTIC HEALTH SYSTEM THAT AIMS TO PUT THE WHOLE BODY IN BALANCE. MANY OF THE NATUROPATHIC 'CURES' CAN BE INCORPORATED INTO EVERYDAY LIFE WITH GREAT EASE. IT'S PART OF THE REASON WHY NATUROPATHS SEE THEMSELVES AS AS MUCH TEACHERS AS PHYSICIANS.

The philosophy of naturopathy is very ancient. Hippocrates spoke of *ponos*, the body's incessant labour to restore itself to normal balance, while Aristotle spoke of the life force having a purpose beyond simply existing. Both insights chime with the naturopath's definition of naturopathy as 'a system of treatment which recognizes the vital curative force within the body'. In its current form, naturopathy has existed for more than 100 years. Its pioneers believed that ill health came about from a mix of hereditary factors, early environment (both before and after birth) and, most importantly, the lifestyle we lead. Most toxic of all is *mesotrophy*, the slow decline of the body's cells, in which poor diet is a factor.

The aim of naturopathy, then, is to allow the body to return to its natural equilibrium and its philosophy dictates that our bodies really do contain the wisdom and power to heal themselves – provided we help them and don't interfere too much. Readjusting our entire lifestyles can be unpleasant, if not downright painful, and naturopathy is certainly no easy option. Naturopaths use osteopathy to correct structural problems. Diet forms a large part of treatment, righting the biochemical balance of the body. Naturopaths also recognize the importance of mental and emotional health. Equally important is the patient's energy or vitality. The most natural cures available are favoured: fresh air and sunlight; fasting and a fresh, pure diet; relaxation and psychological counselling; and, very importantly, the healing power of water.

Some naturopaths are purists and work only with these basic tools. Others have incorporated other disciplines. Most naturopaths are masters of many arts, using herbalism, homeopathy and acupuncture in addition.

OPPOSITE HYDROTHERAPY IS CENTRAL TO NATUROPATHY; HERB AND MINERAL BATHS, STEAMS, SHOWERS AND BODY PACKS ARE COMMONLY USED.

what can naturopathy help?

- Virtually all chronic diseases respond well to naturopathy.
- It has particular success with rheumatic and arthritic conditions.
- Hypertension and allergic and fatigue conditions often improve.
- It can be very helpful in promoting weight loss.
- Skin conditions can disappear or diminish.
- It puts great emphasis on stress relief, so many stress-related conditions respond positively to naturopathy.
- Many people find their psychological wellbeing improves.

what can I expect from a session?

WHERE WILL I HAVE THE TREATMENT?

It depends. You will sit in a chair for the initial consultation. You may lie on a couch for osteopathy or some forms of hydrotherapy; other forms are carried out in a bath, shower or pool.

WILL I BE CLOTHED?

You will be fully clothed for the initial consultation. You would strip to underwear for osteopathy and be naked for some hydrotherapy.

WHAT HAPPENS?

The initial consultation will seem quite medical in its approach and, if you have a serious medical condition, expect to be sent for X-rays, ECGs or blood tests. You may be tested for allergies with a Vega machine. Diet and exercise regimes will then be prescribed. If hydrotherapy is required, you may find yourself being hosed alternately with hot and cold water; lying in therapeutic mud; sitting in a steam 'pod'; or having hot-wax treatments on hands, feet or knees. Constitutional hydrotherapy involves lying on a couch while hot and cold towels are placed alternately over your body.

WILL IT HURT?

Some of the treatments are quite stringent and uncomfortable – although not painful.

WILL ANYTHING STRANGE HAPPEN?

Many hydrotherapy treatments can seem peculiar to begin with.

WILL I BE GIVEN ANYTHING TO TAKE?

Diet will always be a factor. If your naturopath also uses other disciplines, you might be given herbs or homeopathic remedies.

IS THERE ANY HOMEWORK?

Yes, lots. Naturopathy requires a lot of hard work – shifting diet, doing exercise, relinquishing bad habits.

do-it-yourself naturopathy

Water therapy is intrinsic to naturopathy. It's cheap, it's easy to administer and it's literally on tap. There's no excuse for not borrowing a few tips from naturopaths and extending your use of water beyond the usual glass of water to drink and daily bath or shower to get clean. Naturopaths use water in the treatment of injuries, to relieve pain, to reduce fever, as a stimulant *and* a relaxant, and even as an anaesthetic. The following ideas should get you started on your own hydrotherapy.

SALT MASSAGE BATH

If you are feeling low or lacking in energy, this is an essential. It helps the circulation, is useful in easing rheumatic pain and will also get rid of all your dead skin, leaving your body feeling smooth and silky. It's also very simple to do.

It is possible to stop a cold in its tracks this way, but don't do so if your skin is broken – it will sting unbearably.
CAUTION: do not try this if you have high blood pressure or a heart condition.

- Make a slushy paste with salt and warm water. If you can use sea salt, so much the better.
- Apply it all over your body, using circular movements.
- Now get into a bath filled with quite warm to hot water and soak for about 20 minutes.

APPLE CIDER VINEGAR BATH

This is a wonderful tonic if you're feeling tired and is also a prime detoxifier. It is soothing in summer if you are suffering from sunburn or have itchy skin.
CAUTION: do not try this if you have high blood pressure or a heart condition.

- Pour a little apple cider vinegar onto your hands and splash it all over your body.
- Now add a cupful of the vinegar to a warm-to-hot (but not scalding) bath and soak for a while.

MOOR BATH

A mud preparation from Austria containing literally hundreds of minerals and phytonutrients, this is a popular choice among naturopaths and usually readily available from health stores. It promotes deep relaxation and sound sleep. It has also been used medicinally for rheumatic conditions with very good results.

- Pour the suggested amount (see bottle) into a warm but not hot bath. Allow yourself to soak for about 20 minutes.
- Pat yourself gently dry and wrap yourself in a towel. Lie down and relax for at least an hour.

BODY PACK

You will need to enlist the help of a friend for this powerful treatment. Body packs work like a kind of sauna or steam – eliminating toxic waste through sweating.

- Immerse a cotton sheet totally in cold water, then wring it out, leaving it damp. The sheet shouldn't drip, yet needs to be cold to the touch.
- Spread the sheet over a bed or couch (you may wish to put down a plastic sheet underneath) and lie down on it.
- Place three hot-water bottles inside the sheet – one by your feet, one at your waist and one near your chest.
- Have someone wrap the ends of the sheet firmly around you and the hot-water bottles so you are covered from your neck down to your feet. You are now encased in your individual private steam 'room'.
- Relax like this for at least 3 hours. You will start to sweat profusely within 10 to 15 minutes, but the treatment is very relaxing and you will most likely fall asleep. By the end, the sheet will be almost dry and may be discoloured from the eliminated toxins. You will need to wash it before reusing it.

EPSOM SALTS BATH

Have this bath just before going to bed. Epsom salts induce prodigious perspiration and so are superlative for sweating out toxins. This bath is also very useful for rheumatic conditions and can help fend off infections, colds and flu as well.
CAUTION: avoid if you have heart trouble, if you are diabetic or if you are feeling tired or weak.

- Dissolve about 450 g (1 lb) of Epsom salts in a warm bath. (You can work up to this amount slowly over a week or two.)
- Relax for about 20 minutes. Drink a hot herbal tea (thyme or peppermint would be ideal) to increase perspiration and replace any lost fluids.
- Take care as you get out of the bath – you may feel light-headed.
- Do not rub yourself dry. Wrap up in several large towels and go to bed. Wrap your feet up warmly.
- In the morning, or when you wake, sponge yourself down with warm water. Rub your body vigorously dry.

juicing

Naturopaths swear by freshly made fruit and vegetable juices. But just why are juices so wonderful? Fruits and vegetables are rich in micronutrients which have profound healing properties. Many of them actively encourage elimination. The majority of vegetables are highly alkaline in their nature and possess the ability to bind acids and eliminate them through the kidneys and urine.

So juicing is ideal for anyone suffering from 'acid' conditions such as rheumatism and arthritis – provided, of course, you avoid citrus fruits, which exacerbate these conditions.

Some naturopaths say that a day a week on a diet of vegetable juices will be beneficial to almost anyone (see under fasting on page 67 for exceptions and always check with your doctor first). If you do decide on a juice-only day, you should have from 500–700 ml ($^1/_2$–$^3/_4$ pint) up to a litre (2 pints) of fresh juice. For maximum, make several batches of juice over the day. Sip the juice slowly throughout the day – don't slurp it all down. Also, drink plenty of fresh water – either at room temperature or warm.

juices for specific conditions

Certain combinations of juices are renowned for their healing and healthful properties.

ARTHRITIS carrot, celery and cabbage juice.

ASTHMA AND CATARRHAL CONDITIONS carrot and radish juice.

CONSTIPATION cabbage, spinach, celery and lemon juice.

HIGH BLOOD PRESSURE celery, beetroot and carrot juice.

LOW BLOOD PRESSURE carrot, beetroot and dandelion juice.

SKIN CONDITIONS carrot, beetroot and celery juice.

SORE THROATS, COLDS AND FLU lemon, lime and pineapple juice.

TO HELP YOU SLEEP celery juice.

TO OPEN UP SINUSES AND AIR PASSAGES horseradish and lemon juice (125 g/4 oz) of horseradish and 60 g/2o z of lemon juice, combined with a teaspoon of garlic juice and a tablespoon of honey – take a teaspoonful four times daily).

TO SOOTHE THE NERVES lemon and lime juice.

BELOW FRESHLY MADE JUICE TASTES WHOLLY DIFFERENT FROM STORE-BOUGHT VARIETIES – AND IT RETAINS ALL ITS NUTRIENTS. FOR BEST RESULTS, USE RIPE, ORGANIC FRUIT AND DRINK THE JUICE AS SOON AS POSSIBLE.

the juices

Choose fresh, organic vegetables and fruit – ideally those in season. You will need a juicer for these recipes; follow the manufacturer's instructions for use.

Carrot juice is pleasant to drink and one of the best juices to start with if you're new to juicing. It really packs a good healthy punch, too.

- Carrot juice affects the mucus membranes of the body and stimulates blood circulation in the stomach and intestines.
- It is good for constipation, diarrhoea and digestive problems.
- When poor digestion is sorted out, other problems often disappear – headaches, eczema and bad skin can all vanish when the digestion is functioning properly.
- Carrot juice is refreshing and soothing, and helps the body battle against infectious diseases.
- Packed full of antioxidant vitamins, it fights the free radicals that cause disease and ageing.
- Its rich supplies of carotene (provitamin A) are necessary for eyesight and stimulate the production of rhodopsin (visual purple), lack of which causes night blindness.
- Carrot juice is also supposed to help regulate your weight and to give you a beautiful complexion.

Beetroot juice, with its dark purple colour, may look rather unappetizing, but don't let its appearance put you off as it is very beneficial to the health.

- Beetroot contains betaine, which stimulates the function of the liver cells, protecting the liver and bile ducts, and encouraging detoxification.
- Just 100 ml (4 fl oz) of beetroot juice contains 5 mg of iron, as well as trace elements that encourage iron's absorption in the blood.
- Everyone can benefit from beetroot juice, but it is particularly recommended in the first 2 years of life, during puberty, during pregnancy, when breastfeeding and during menopause. Children from 6 months to 2 years need only a teaspoon of juice before meals.

NOTE: beetroot juice is high in sugars. Seek expert advice about its use if you suffer from diabetes or blood glucose problems.

Celery juice tastes a bit salty when drunk on its own, but you can easily mix it with other vegetables to add flavour and give additional health benefits.

- Celery is alkaline and encourages elimination, and hence is recommended for any diseases or problems connected with an accumulation of wastes and toxins, such as arthritic and rheumatic ailments.
- Celery juice also regulates the water balance in the body and is superb for elderly people.

Apple juice is a wonderful source of vitamins, minerals and trace elements. A few apples juiced a day certainly do help keep the doctor away.

- Apples are astringent and can help alleviate diarrhoea.
- They promote elimination of excess fluid and toxins, so are good for arthritis, skin problems and fluid retention.
- Take apple juice when you're feeling under par – it speeds recovery from colds and coughs, and eases catarrh and sinusitis.
- Apples are cooling and so useful in cases of inflammation.
- They can help regulate blood sugar and cholesterol levels, and blood pressure.

Watercress juice is peppery and tangy, and a potent tonic. The plant draws a multitude of vital elements from the soil. You can combine it with other juices if you find the taste too strong.

- Watercress is a superb antiseptic and detoxifier. It is rich in vitamins A, C and E, and the minerals iron, potassium, zinc and calcium.
- Take watercress when you have chest infections, coughs and bronchitis – it is a good expectorant.
- Watercress juice cleanses the blood and so can be helpful in treating arthritis, gout and rheumatism.
- Watercress may help premenstrual syndrome (PMS).
- It is a tonic for the digestion, circulation, kidneys and bladder.

Apricot juice is sweet and delicious, and combines well with less palatable ingredients.

- Apricots are natural laxatives and are therefore wonderful for constipation. Children usually love the taste, so it can be very useful when encouraging them to drink juice.
- Apricots are high in betacarotene, which is protective against lung, skin and pancreatic cancers. If you smoke, you should certainly up your intake of apricots.
- They are very nourishing and easily digested, so are ideal for anyone feeling tired and weak; they are a great convalescence food and ideal for pregnant women, the elderly and children.

CAUTION: some people are allergic to apricots. If you are buying dried apricots, always choose the unsulphured variety as the sulphur used in preserving can also cause allergies.

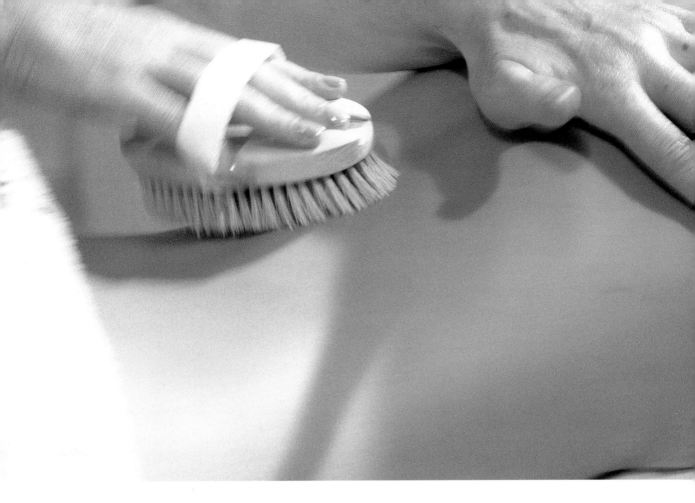

detoxifying

Do we need to detoxify? Sadly, we do. Our world is so polluted that our bodies can benefit greatly from even a short period of rest and recuperation. It need not be Draconian. A few simple changes can have profound effects. Try the following.

1 Alcohol is a big toxic enemy. Cut down your intake as much as possible. Try drinking wine diluted with water if you need to drink socially.

2 If you smoke, do try to give up – you will be doing your body a huge favour. Acupuncture and hypnotherapy can help.

3 Cut down on tea and coffee. To avoid headaches and other side effects of caffeine withdrawal, take it slowly, reducing your intake by a cup a day. Try caffeine-free herbal teas and drinks instead, or hot ginseng essence with honey for a real energy boost.

4 Drink water – lots of it – throughout the day. It cleanses the system, helps flush out toxins and has the added bonus of making you feel less hungry if you're trying to lose weight.

5 Clean up your diet. Highly processed foods and 'junk' foods are full of toxic additives. Follow the guidelines on page 57 and eat as pure and as organic a diet as you can.

6 Treat yourself to a good-quality juicer and enjoy nourishing, energy-packed fresh fruit and vegetable juices for mid-morning and mid-afternoon treats (see opposite). It's worth buying a top-of-the-range model with easy cleaning facilities.

7 Start a regime of skin brushing before your shower or bath to stimulate the flow of lymph and promote good circulation. Use either a damp flannel with a bicarbonate-and-salt mixture or a special skin brush. Start by moving from the feet up the legs towards the back of the knees, then up the thighs to the groin. From the fingers, brush arms towards the armpits, then gently from the neck towards the heart. Then do the back and torso, again always towards the heart. Avoid areas that are broken, tender or irritated. Start with gentle movements, building up to gentle but firm pressure.

ABOVE BODY BRUSHING IS AN ESSENTIAL PART OF DETOXIFYING. GET INTO THE HABIT OF GIVING YOURSELF A BODY BRUSH EVERY DAY BEFORE YOUR SHOWER OR BATH – IT TAKES ONLY 5 MINUTES, BUT MAKES A NOTICEABLE DIFFERENCE.

8 Give yourself a detox-diet weekend.

- BREAKFAST one type of fruit (as much as you like), hot water or herbal tea.
- MID-MORNING SNACK fresh fruit or vegetable juice.
- LUNCH salad of raw vegetables, bean sprouts and almonds (season with orange or lemon juice, garlic and ginger).
- AFTERNOON SNACK fruit.
- EVENING MEAL vegetable soup, salad, steamed vegetables. Drink plenty of water throughout the day.

9 Exercise. All aerobic exercise (jogging, cycling, swimming, stair climbing, brisk walking and so on) helps to maintain the lymphatic flow. Don't conserve energy – run up the stairs, use housework as exercise (scrub to the beat), go to the gym or take a brisk walk at lunchtime, rather than hailing the sandwich trolley from your desk. Probably the best exercise of all for your lymphatic system is rebounding (bouncing on a small trampoline), which need not be expensive. Just 20 minutes a day will really help your detoxifying (and also give you a good aerobic workout).

10 Treat yourself to a massage. Manual lymphatic drainage (see pages 226–7) by a professional is the ideal, but any massage using effluage (firm stroking movements, always in the direction of the heart) is good for detoxifying (and is destressing as well). If you can't afford regular professional massages, form a duo with your partner or a friend and learn how to massage (MLD practitioners will teach you the basic technique or you can learn ordinary massage from videos or on short workshops). Then you can trade massages.

11 Breathe deeply and calmly. Try to set aside 10 minutes each day to concentrate on breathing slowly, rhythmically and deeply, sending air into every cell of your body in order to oxygenate the blood.

- Sit comfortably and start by breathing in while slowly counting in your head to four. Hold for a count of four, then release to the count of four.
- When that feels comfortable, count up to six, hold for six and release for six. Eventually, you should feel able to breathe in to eight, hold for eight and release for eight.

For more breathing exercises, see pages 80–1.

OPPOSITE OUR BODIES CRAVE WATER; OFTEN WHEN WE FEEL WE'RE HUNGRY, IT IS OUR BODIES CRYING OUT WITH THIRST. TRADITIONAL FASTS ALLOWED ONLY WATER, BUT MOST EXPERTS NOW SUGGEST ALSO DRINKING JUICE.

fasting

All over the world, religions have espoused the spiritual benefits of purifying and castigating the body by withholding food. In medieval times, fasting was a way of life. Today, few people see of fasting as primarily a religious experience and it certainly isn't regarded as punishment: fasters are usually seeking a healthier body, brighter mind and clearer emotions.

The traditional fast is pretty tough: you just drink water and that is all. Although this is still practised in naturopathy, many people now practise modified fasts, drinking just juice or eating one type of fruit, usually apples or grapes.

There is evidence supporting the value of periodic, sensible fasting. Research has been carried out since 1880 and, since then, medical journals have carried occasional reports on the use of fasting for the treatment of obesity, eczema, irritable bowel syndrome, bronchial asthma, depression and even schizophrenia. Today, however, most people use it as preventative medicine.

The digestive system uses up to 30 per cent of the total energy produced by the body; by putting the system into a state of rest, we help the body to concentrate on detoxification and healing. On a health level, naturopaths say that fasting can improve your immune function and allow your body a decent chance to deal with its problems; on a beauty level, fasting can make your skin look fresher and more toned, your eyes brighter and your hair more lush.

Fasting is not, however, a good way to lose weight. Six hours after the last meal, the body starts to use glycogen (the carbohydrate stored in the liver and muscles) as its energy source. After 24 hours, your body takes its energy not just from stored fat, but also from the breakdown of muscle. After several days, your metabolism will slow to conserve energy and, if you fast for too long, the ability to digest food may be impaired or lost entirely because the stomach gradually stops secreting digestive juices. Sex hormones are no longer produced and your body loses its ability to fight infection.

Fasting is not for everyone. If in doubt, don't do it. It is distinctly not advised if you are pregnant or breastfeeding, if you have any medical condition and particularly if you have any eating disorder. Always ask your doctor or a qualified practitioner and don't fast unsupervised for more than 24 hours.

HERBALISM

We merrily add herbs to our cooking without a second thought. We certainly don't stop to think about their healing virtues! Yet herbs have been used for centuries as a potent form of medicine. Discovering the healing power of herbs can be a fascinating journey – and can have deep, long-lasting effects.

It is safe to say that herbalism is probably the very oldest of all forms of medicine. It doesn't take much imagination to think that the early hunter–gatherer societies would have discovered, through trial and error, that not only were certain plants good to eat, but that some also had curative powers.

Take any ancient culture and you are bound to find it has a tradition of herbalism. In fact, the herbal tradition stayed firmly centre stage until the advent of modern chemical medicines. Now research is discovering that herbs can be as effective as synthetic preparations – and often more so.

Herbal medicines work on a simple biochemical level. They trigger neurochemical reactions in the body and so directly affect its organs and systems.

Basically, they fulfil three classic functions: they cleanse, they heal and they nourish.

First, before a body can bring itself to health, it needs to rid itself of the toxins and dead and decaying matter that litter the body. Herbs can be used as diuretics, laxatives and blood purifiers to help the processes of elimination and detoxification. The next step is to escort the body back to optimum health: herbs are used to stimulate the body's own self-healing powers and to attack the underlying causes of illness. Thirdly, herbs are used to tone the various organs and to nourish all the systems of the body, helping it keep on an even, healthy keel.

The aim is that, by taking the herbs over a period of time in moderate doses, the biochemical responses of the body will become automatic and it will start fending for itself again, even when you stop taking the herbs.

famous herbal healers

Several herbs have become specially famous in recent years. The following are some you may have heard of:

Aloe vera is a wonderful home first-aid remedy for burns, wounds and sunburn. Buy the gel for topical application. It is also marvellous for insect bites and fungal infections.

Echinacea (purple coneflower) is now well known as a cure-all for colds, flu and other infections. Buy in capsule form and take three 200 mg tablets up to three times a day as soon as you feel yourself coming down with an infection. Do not take echinacea on a longstanding, ongoing basis – use it only as a short course.

Ginkgo is excellent for improving circulation. It is a useful herb for people with diabetes, eye problems, heart conditions and memory loss. However, you should always see a medical herbalist for prescription.

Kava kava is a Polynesian herb proving very useful in anxiety states and for insomnia. It should be avoided during pregnancy.

Milk thistle is a great cleansing herb and very useful if you have been living the high life and need to give your liver some TLC! It is helpful in detoxifying for the same reason.

St John's wort (hypericum) is one of the most popular herbs. It is mainly taken for depression and has proven as effective as conventional antidepressants for many people. However, St John's wort should always be taken under the guidance of a professional herbalist, as it can have side effects and may interfere with the efficacy of other drugs.

Wild yam is a herb that has hit the headlines because of its beneficial effects on menopausal women. Wild yam is believed to be progesteronic (supportive of the body's progesterone cycle), but does not, as commonly supposed, actually contain progesterone in it. See a herbalist if you think that this would be helpful for you.

Saw palmetto is a superb herb for prostate conditions. It's an excellent male tonic herb and careful supplementation can prevent or halt the progression of benign prostatic hyperplasia (BPH). See a herbalist for prescription.

what can herbalism help?

- Herbalism is used for a variety of acute and chronic conditions.
- Herbs can support detoxifying – cleansing and purifying the body.
- Herbal tonics can give a boost and improve energy levels.
- Herbs can be used to ease aches and pains; headaches and migraines; and all manner of eye, ear, nose and throat problems. Skin problems respond well, too.
- Allergic conditions can often be alleviated.
- Urinary disorders, gynaecological problems and digestive problems respond appreciably.
- Herbs can help respiratory and circulation problems.
- Herbs can boost the immune system and so help resist infections.
- Herbs can be very useful in pregnancy and childbirth, and can also be used to treat children.

what can I expect from a session?

WHERE WILL I HAVE THE TREATMENT?

You will be sitting in a chair in the herbalist's room.

WILL I BE CLOTHED?

You will usually remain fully clothed, although some clothes may need to be removed for examination purposes.

WHAT HAPPENS?

Expect a physical check-up and also to answer questions about your symptoms and medical history (emotional life, work, sleep, family history, and so on). It's a very detailed consultation. Your blood pressure may be taken, and heart and chest listened to with a stethoscope. You may have your ears, nose, throat and eyes examined; your abdomen may be palpated (gently prodded and felt) to gauge bowel tone. If necessary, blood tests are given.

WILL IT HURT?

No, although herbal tinctures are very bitter and often unpleasant.

WILL ANYTHING STRANGE HAPPEN?

No, herbalism is a very straightforward therapy – the most akin of all therapies to a visit to an orthodox medical doctor.

WILL I BE GIVEN ANYTHING TO TAKE?

Yes, herbs will be prescribed – usually in tincture form (you dilute them in water and swallow). You may be given dried herbs with which to make an infusion (steeped in boiling water like tea) or a decoction (boiled down into a concentrate). Sometimes pills, lotions and creams are prescribed.

IS THERE ANY HOMEWORK?

You will often be given guidelines for healthier living and diet, and exercise may be suggested.

healing herbs – safe do-it-yourself remedies

Generally speaking, you should always consult a well-qualified herbalist. Herbs are powerful medicines and should not be treated lightly. Some can interfere with other medications; others should not be taken during pregnancy or if you have high or low blood pressure.

However, the following herbs can be used safely by most people (where there are contraindications, these are stated). Most can be grown in your garden.

To use, place 30 g (1 oz) of the dried herb or 75 g (2^1/$_2$ oz) of the fresh herb in a teapot or jug (pitcher). Pour over 500 ml (1 pint) of boiled water (it should have been freshly boiled, but left to stand for a few moments so that it is no longer bubbling). Leave for 10 minutes and then strain. Take the herb in three equal doses throughout the day.

Camomile is your best friend if you're stressed or suffer from insomnia. Drink a cup of camomile tea at night to ease you to sleep. Camomile will also soothe indigestion, stimulate a poor appetite and soothe an irritable bowel. (NOTE: avoid during pregnancy.)

Fennel is the perfect after-dinner digestive. Drink fennel for all kinds of digestive problems, from flatulence to indigestion. (NOTE: avoid during pregnancy.)

Ginger is a safe remedy for morning sickness and is also wonderful for indigestion, nausea and travel sickness.

Hops are another great insomnia aid and are often combined with valerian, vervain, camomile or meadowsweet in herbal teas designed to help you get a good night's sleep. (NOTE: avoid if you suffer from depression.)

Lemon balm can help revive you if you're feeling worn out and depressed. It will also help if you feel you are starting to come down with a cold or flu.

Mint (shown opposite) is another great stomach soother that is wonderful for nausea, travel sickness, indigestion and flatulence. It can ease headaches and is a good pick-me-up. (NOTE: mint can reduce milk flow, so avoid if breastfeeding.)

Nettle is the great cleanser; it stimulates the circulation and makes a superb tonic. It can be very helpful in cleansing the system if you are suffering from conditions such as arthritis, rheumatism and eczema.

EXERCISE

EXERCISE IS AN ESSENTIAL PART OF THE GOOD HEALTH EQUATION. REGULAR EXERCISE KEEPS YOUR HEART AND LUNGS WORKING AT OPTIMUM LEVELS AND HELPS WARD OFF HEART DISEASE. STRESS LEVELS DROP WHEN YOU EXERCISE, SO YOU WILL COME AWAY FROM A WORKOUT OR SPORTS GAME FEELING A GENERAL LIFT IN MOOD. REGULAR EXERCISE CAN PERK UP YOUR SEX LIFE AND GIVE YOU A GOOD NIGHT'S SLEEP; IT CAN ALSO HELP CONTROL BLOOD PRESSURE AND BOOST YOUR IMMUNE SYSTEM.

Of course, if you are concerned about your weight, beginning to exercise is the very best move you can make. Excess flab disappears when you start to work out; your body becomes more flexible and more toned. The more muscle you have, the more fat you burn: you simply can't help but get slimmer and trimmer.

motivate yourself

There's really no excuse for not exercising – yet we manage to invent plenty! It can be tough to get started, so many of us simply don't bother. If you commit to a regular exercise programme, however, you will begin to notice changes quite swiftly. At first, you might be out of breath after just two minutes of jogging or cycling. But rest assured, after a few sessions, you will be up to a good 6 minutes and, within 6 weeks, should be able to breeze through 30!

The following exercise tips will help you boost your motivation levels.

what do you want from exercise?

Check that you're matching your exercise with your goals.
- If you want to change your shape and improve your appearance, go for activities that deliver noticeable results: weight training; circuit training, yoga and Pilates will all change your body shape.
- If you want to lose weight, you need moderately high-intensity sports such as running, stepping, aerobics, fast cycling, brisk walking and power yoga.
- If you want to get healthy without strain, go for low-impact aerobics, swimming, cycling and walking.

- If you want to beat stress, try yoga, tai chi, boxing or skating, plus sports that allow you to go on automatic pilot such as running, walking and swimming.

find an expert

If you can, enlist the help of an expert to get you on the right track. A good gym, for instance, should give you a fitness assessment, a tailor-made programme and bags of encouragement along the way. If you're on your own, you'll probably succeed through trial and error. If you don't like one kind of exercise or routine, or you don't get results after giving it your best shot (it will take 6 weeks of regular sessions to notice a significant difference), change. If that doesn't work, change again. Obviously, you need to give any programme a fighting chance, but don't ever force yourself to do something you hate. If exercise is going to work for you, it has to be enjoyable or, at the very least, challenging!

start small

If you haven't exercised before or not for a long time (and especially if you're returning to exercise after pregnancy), take it easy. If you can get yourself past the first week, you've passed the period in which half of all drop-outs occur. If you work out regularly for six months, you're likely to have created a long-lasting habit. Grin and bear it for that first week (yes, it will be tough) and then it will start to get easier.

The really brilliant thing about exercising regularly is that you soon notice the results. There is nothing more motivating than looking in the mirror and seeing yourself definitely firmer; there is nothing better than seeing a thigh stop wobbling and start rippling.

discover your fitness personality

You love sushi, your best friend hates it. So, where is it written in stone that we should all be doing step and loving it? Just because all your friends adore swimming, why should you? There are a million and one ways of exercising, so you simply need to find those that a) you enjoy and b) fit in with your lifestyle – then the odds are that you'll keep them up.

The following are just a few ideas of how you can tailor your exercise regime to suit your personality and lifestyle.

- YOU'RE A WORKAHOLIC You can't afford the luxury of exercising. But remember that exercise relieves stress and will help you become more energized, more focused, more creative. Try running or cycling to and from work. Visit the gym or fit in a yoga class at lunch-time – it will make you more productive in the afternoon. If you're a competitive type, play squash or badminton with colleagues.

- YOU'RE A STRESSED-OUT MUM You don't have time to think, let alone exercise. Remember first of all that exercise will relieve the stress and make you (and, by extension, your child) calmer. And, if you feel dead on your feet, it will actually give you more energy. Researchers have compared the effects of a sugary snack with a 10-minute brisk walk on volunteers' moods. The snack certainly gave an instant boost of feelgood factor, but the effects swiftly wore off, leaving the volunteers feeling even worse than before. The exercisers, meanwhile, were still feeling great up to two hours afterwards. Many gyms and local fitness centres now have childminding facilities, so check them out, or get together with some friends, hire a trainer and organize your own aerobics class or circuit training. Don't have time? Involve the whole family in exercise: play with your kids (that can be serious exercise in its own right) or bundle everyone off to the park, the boating pond, the ice rink, the swimming pool ... It doesn't have to be the gym or a formal class – just get moving.

- YOU SEE EXERCISE AS ONE LONG, DREARY CHORE You need variety and to pick out activities that don't really seem like exercise. Forget the gym and formal classes – think laterally: rollerblading, dancing, trampolining, horse riding, surfing. What did you enjoy doing when you were a child? See if it still gives you a buzz.

- YOU GET BORED EXERCISING ON YOUR OWN Who says you have to pound the lonely Stairmaster? One of the best ways to motivate yourself is to train with a friend. It's much more fun and, if you like jogging or running, it's much safer, too. If your resolve starts to slip and you're tempted to opt out, you'll not only let yourself down, you'll also letting your friend down (guilt can be a powerful motivator). Apparently, at least 90 per cent of exercisers prefer to work out with other people, rather than solo –

ABOVE EXERCISE IS POWERFUL MIND–BODY MEDICINE. MAKING TIME FOR REGULAR EXERCISE CAN TRANSFORM THE WAY YOU LOOK AND FEEL.

so you're not alone. No friends willing to play the game? Join a circuit class or put your name down for a league.

- YOU LIKE A BIT OF EXCITEMENT We often forget that team sports count as exercise, too. Remember netball? Hockey, volleyball, softball, football, basketball? Why not? You'll meet new people, have fun and get fit almost by accident.

- YOU FEEL SELF-CONSCIOUS ABOUT YOUR BODY AND YOUR ABILITIES Choose something strictly non-competitive. Yoga is ideal because you focus solely on what you are doing. Sometimes you even have to keep your eyes shut! Forget a skimpy leotard – most people wear leggings or sweatpants and a baggy T-shirt. And yoga is a wonderful toner – it gives you beautiful, long, lean muscles.

the mind–body connection

In Part 1 (see pages 12–13), you will have worked out your ayurvedic mind–body type, or dosha. Interestingly, this knowledge can be very useful when it comes to finding a system of exercise that suits you and will motivate you into keeping it up. Some of us just aren't ever going to be good at gymnastics – we simply don't have the physical make-up for it. Equally, others won't have the strength and stamina for long-distance running or shot put. We are all different and, just because you don't like one form of exercise, it doesn't mean you are not the exercise 'type'. You simply haven't yet found the form of exercise that best suits you.

John Douillard, a former athlete and coach, has applied ayurvedic principles to sport and exercise – with remarkable results. Children who formerly hated sport now love it. Athletes who were damaging themselves in search of perfection are now just as good, if not better, without the strain. The key is knowing your type and then choosing a form of exercise that suits your predominant dosha and natural inclinations.

VATA: You are a natural sprinter or runner. You may be good at gymnastics. Pretty well any kind of field sport (with the exception of shot put!) will suit you. Pick sports or exercises that capitalize on your speed and agility, but don't call for a lot of endurance (your weak point). If you play team sports, put yourself in a position where the emphasis is on speed.
PITTA: You have good coordination and can be very (*very*) competitive. Pittas thrive under a bit of stress, so don't bore yourself rigid by taking up synchronized swimming or long-distance running: join a team or get involved with a league. If that isn't possible, try to exercise with someone – the competitive pitta type will even get a kick out of meditating better than someone else!
KAPHA: Kaphas are built for endurance and strength, so pick out sports needing these qualities. Any shot-putter is bound to be a kapha. You will also do well in team sports because you will thrive under the motivation of others. Anything involving distance works well, too: long-distance swimming, cross-country running, race walking ...

stretching

Everyone should make time to stretch. Stretching is simplicity itself, yet it is absolutely wonderful for both body and mind. If you carry out a careful stretch routine before and after exercise or sports, you will help to protect your muscles and joints from injury. If you spend your days stuck at a desk or behind the wheel of a car, stretching can release stress and help relax any tense muscles.

Stretching will also improve your posture and you will be far less likely to suffer from neck, shoulder and back pain, headaches and bad digestion.

Virtually anyone can follow a simple stretch routine. However, if you do suffer from a bad back, you should seek professional advice before stretching.

Try to make the simple stretch routine opposite a daily habit. Practise it in the morning to give your body a wake-up call and also to help you unravel after a long day at work. You can also use it whenever you find yourself feeling tired and stressed – whatever the time of day.

OPPOSITE STRETCHING IS LIKE A WAKE-UP CALL FOR THE ENTIRE BODY.
IT IS NOT ONLY ESSENTIAL BEFORE AND AFTER ANY FORM OF VIGOROUS
EXERCISE, BUT SHOULD ALSO BE ENJOYED IN ITS OWN RIGHT.

simple stretch routine

Take off your shoes. If possible, wear loose, comfortable clothes. Take the stretches slowly and carefully: don't overstretch. The idea is to feel the stretch, but not to cause yourself any discomfort or pain. Don't 'bounce' the stretch to make it more intense: once in the pose, hold it without movement. If you cannot achieve the full stretch, go as far as you can. You will find that, with practice, you swiftly increase your flexibility.

Before you begin, warm up your muscles by marching on the spot, swinging your arms as you walk. You may prefer to dance to the radio. It doesn't matter what you do as long as you warm up before stretching – for at least 5 minutes. Using a mini-trampoline, or rebounder, is a great way to warm up – and it will wake up your lymphatic system, too.

1 CALF STRETCH Facing a wall, stand a little distance away and, crossing your arms, lean them against the wall. Now lean your forehead against your hands. Bend your left knee and extend your right leg out behind you. Keep both feet parallel, pointing straight ahead. Slowly move your hips forwards, keeping your feet flat, until you feel a slight stretch in the calf muscles of the extended leg. Hold gently for a slow count of ten. Now change legs and repeat.

2 QUADRICEPS AND KNEE STRETCH Keeping your right hand on the wall for support, reach behind your back with your left hand and grasp your right foot by the toes. Keep your supporting knee softly bent; tuck your pelvis forwards and stand up straight. Hold gently for a count of 20 and release. Now do the same with the other hand and foot.

3 GROIN STRETCH Sit on the floor with the soles of your feet together. Put your hands on your feet and pull your heels in towards your body. This is a strong stretch, so don't worry if you can't get very far at first. Now gently pull your body forwards, towards your feet, keeping your back erect until you feel a stretch. Hold for a count of 20. As you hold the stretch, concentrate on relaxing your arms, shoulders and feet.

4 HAMSTRING STRETCH Still sitting, straighten your left leg out in front of you. Keep your right leg bent as in the groin stretch, but now bring the sole of the foot to face the inside of the outstretched leg (as far as you can). Keep the extended leg slightly bent. Now bend forwards slightly, from the hips, with your hands relaxed on the floor next to the extended leg, until you feel an easy stretch. Touch the top of the thigh of your left leg and check it is feeling soft and relaxed. Keep the foot of your extended leg upright, not turned out. Hold for a count of 30. Now release the stretch and repeat with your right leg extended.

5 UPPER HAMSTRINGS AND HIP STRETCH With your left leg extended in front of you, bend your right leg and bring it up towards your abdomen, cradling it in your arms like a baby. Gently pull the leg towards you until you feel an easy stretch. Hold for a count of 20, release and then repeat with the other leg.

6 ARCH STRETCH Sit on your toes (kneeling, but so you are resting your buttocks on your heels with your toes on the floor). Keep your hands on the floor in front of you for balance. Gently stretch the arches of the feet. Hold for a count of ten.

7 ARM STRETCH Bring yourself gently to your feet. Raise your left arm above your head. Grasp it at the elbow with your right hand. Now, let your left hand drop down behind your shoulder blade (or as far as it can go). Gently pull the left arm back and in towards the head. Keep your arm, neck and shoulders relaxed. Hold for a count of 20, then release and repeat on the other side.

8 ALL-OVER STRETCH Stand upright with your feet shoulder-width apart, feet facing forwards. Extend your arms in front of you at chest height with palms touching. Now separate them bring them slowly back and down, then on behind your back. Clasp your hands behind your back with your arms extended straight down (hands level with your buttocks). Now inhale deeply, pulling your shoulders back. Exhale and bend forwards, raising your arms (still clasped at the hands) over your head. Return very slowly to an upright position with your arms held loosely behind your back with hands clasped. Slowly twist to the right and then to the left. Repeat the whole stretch three times.

9 BACK STRETCH Sit down and bring your knees up to your chest (with your ankles crossed). Clasp your knees with both arms. Drop your head down to your knees and roll backwards on your spine. Roll forwards and backwards several times.

10 SPINE STRETCH Lie down on the floor. Lift your pelvis slightly and then release. Bend your knees and slowly let them twist over to the right. Turn your head to the left and press your shoulders into the floor. Hold for a few minutes, then bring your knees back to centre and repeat on the other side.

yoga

Yoga is a wonderful form of exercise for absolutely everyone. It has myriad benefits. It puts health-giving pressure on all the body's organs and muscles systematically. It tones the liver, lungs, kidneys, spleen, intestines and heart. The precise postures of yoga (known as *asanas*) cause the blood to circulate more freely, nourishing your organs and softening muscle and ligament tissue. Deep stretching brings the skeletal, fascial and muscular systems back into alignment; it also lubricates the joints, making you far more flexible.

Yoga is used to ease bad backs, to help heal asthma and for breathing difficulties. It can be a splendid exercise both during and after pregnancy. Some yoga teachers run special classes for new mothers to which they can take (and include) their babies! However, do ensure that your yoga teacher is properly qualified (usually the term yoga therapist conveys this) to handle medical conditions.

Yoga helps to detoxify the body – and also the mind. When you practise yoga, your nervous system shifts into 'relax' mode, switching from the sympathetic to the parasympathetic nervous system, so you feel calm, cool and in control.

cautions

- If you are a beginner, always go to a qualified teacher, rather than trying to teach yourself from a book or video.
- Find a well-qualified teacher. If you have any health problems (particularly a heart condition, back trouble or if you have had any kind of surgery), you should find a yoga therapist (who has had a strict medical training), rather than a yoga teacher.
- Don't push yourself beyond your limits. Yoga is not competitive – everyone works at his or her own pace and within the body's limits. Start small – you will soon find you can stretch further or work harder.
- Make sure your yoga teacher is aware of any health or fitness problems you have before the class. A good teacher will be able to tell you which postures to avoid and will often give you specific postures to help your condition.
- If you are pregnant, you will need to avoid certain postures. Again, you should see a yoga therapist or find a class specifically designed for pregnant women.

the sun salute – a complete workout for body, mind and spirit

The Sun Salute or Salutation to the Sun is a well-known yoga routine. It is perhaps the most effective series of exercises you can do for your body. In ancient India, the Sun Salute was a part of daily spiritual practice and was performed in the very early morning facing the sun, the deity for health and longevity. If you are feeling very keen, follow this practice and greet the dawn with this series of exercises. Otherwise, perform them on rising, facing east.

There are 12 spinal positions and each stretches different ligaments and moves the spine in different ways. At first, this series of exercises will seem jerky and uncoordinated, but persevere. As you begin to learn the positions off by heart, you will find you can move fluidly and smoothly from one to another. Start off with just one whole set and gradually build up to the optimum 12. You may find it helpful to record the instructions on a tape recorder until you become familiar enough with them to do without.

1 Standing upright, bring your feet together so that your big toes are touching. Your arms are by your sides. Relax your shoulders and tuck your chin in slightly – look straight ahead, not down at your feet. Bring your hands together in front of your chest with palms together, as if you were praying. Exhale deeply.

2 Inhale slowly and deeply while you bring your arms straight up over your head, placing your palms together as you finish inhaling. Look gently backwards towards your thumbs. Lift the knees by tightening your thighs. Reach up as far as possible, lengthening your whole body. If you feel comfortable, you can take the posture back slightly further into a bend.

3 Exhale as you bend forwards, so that your hands are in line with your feet. Your head should be touching your knees. To begin with, you might find you have to bend your knees in order to reach the floor. Eventually, with practice, you should be able to straighten your knees into the full posture.

4 Inhale deeply and move your left leg away from your body in a large backward sweep, so that you end up in a kind of extended lunge position. Make sure that you keep your hands and right foot firmly on the ground. Your right knee should be positioned between your hands. Now bend your head upwards, stretching out your back.

5 Exhaling deeply, bring yourself into an arched position. Your arms are in front of your head, palms facing directly in front, arms shoulder-width apart. Your back should be in a straight line, with your head in line with your arms. Keep your feet and heels flat on the floor.

6 Exhale and lower your body onto the floor. This is a curious posture known as *sastanga namaskar*, or the eight-curved prostration, because only eight parts of your body should be in contact with the floor: your feet, your knees, your hands, your chest and your forehead. Try to keep your abdomen raised and, if you can possibly manage it, keep your nose off the floor so only your forehead makes contact. Don't worry if it's an impossibility at this point – just keep the idea in mind.

7 Inhale deeply and bend up into the position known as the cobra – hands on the floor in front of you, arms straight, bending backwards as far as feels comfortable. Look upwards.

8 Exhale deeply and lift your back into position 5 (known as the dog). Remember to keep your feet and heels (if you can) flat on the floor. Once again, with regular practice, you will find that this becomes easier.

9 Inhale deeply and return to posture 4, this time with the opposite leg forwards, so that your left foot is in line with your hands, while your right leg is stretched back.

10 Exhale deeply and return to posture 3.

11 Raise the arms overhead and bend backwards as you inhale (as for posture 2).

12 Return to a comfortable standing position, feet together, with your arms by your sides. Look straight ahead and exhale. To close, bring your hands back together in a position of prayer.

further yoga postures for health and vitality

As you become more proficient in yoga, you can extend your practice. Once you have performed your sun salutations, you may like to include these postures, all of which will help to increase energy and eliminate toxins. Perform them slowly and carefully in a controlled manner. Never race. If you feel any pain, stop doing that exercise. You should just feel a gentle stretch.

PRAYER POSTURE

This gentle posture puts all your internal organs into balance. It encourages deep breathing and helps to align your spine into its optimum position. It is also deeply calming for the mind.

1 Stand with your feet together and parallel. Aim to stand tall without straining – imagine you have a string connecting your head to the ceiling.

2 Check your head – it should be easily balanced on your neck, with eyes gazing softly ahead. Your chin should be neither tucked in nor jutting out.

3 Tilt your pelvis slightly forwards and keep your knees straight, but soft – don't lock them.

4 Now bring your hands palms together in front of your chest, as if you were praying.

5 Relax your jaw, your facial muscles and your shoulders. Breathe softly and regularly. You may want to focus lightly on an object in front of you, or you can gently close your eyes.

6 Hold this pose for a few minutes or for as long as you feel comfortable. Then bring your hands back down to your sides and resume your normal stance.

THE TREE

This is a classic yoga posture which is superb for improving your balance, concentration and coordination.

1 Stand up tall and straight. Your feet should be close together and parallel. Fix your eyes gently on something (you will need to keep your eyes open for this posture), and breathe naturally and regularly.

2 Lift one leg and place the sole of your foot against the inner side of your other thigh. You can use your hands to place it there. Keep focusing on the point ahead of you.

3 Now bring your hands up into a prayer position in front of your chest.

4 Hold the posture for as long as feels comfortable. Focus on your breathing. Think about the strength and poise of a tree – its roots firm in the ground, its branches reaching towards heaven.

5 Rest for a few moments before repeating the posture with the other leg.

CHILD POSTURE

This looks very simple, but has very deep effects. It massages your internal organs, promoting good circulation and aiding elimination. It also helps to keep your spine supple and flexible.

1 Kneel down, keeping your legs pressed together. Lower your buttocks so that you are sitting on your heels.

2 Now bend forwards slowly until your forehead is resting on the floor. You may not be able to get this far, but don't worry, just go as far as is comfortable. If it helps, you can rest your head on a cushion.

3 Bring your arms behind you so your hands rest on the floor next to your feet. Relax.

4 Stay in this posture for as long as you feel comfortable. Try to keep your breathing regular and relaxed.

THE MOUNTAIN

This seated variation of the mountain posture tones your abdominal muscles and improves your breathing. It can help sluggish circulation and can also tone the muscles in the back.

1 Sit cross-legged on the floor. Hold yourself upright and breathe naturally and easily.

2 Inhale and stretch your arms up over your head to form a steeple shape over your head. Keep the insides of your arms close to your ears. Bring your palms together if you can and press them together as if you were praying.

3 Hold this posture for as long as you can comfortably do so. Remember to breathe easily and regularly as you hold the pose.

4 Exhale and slowly lower your arms to your lap. Rest for a few moments and then repeat.

OPPOSITE REGULAR YOGA PRACTICE MAKES YOU FEEL ALERT *AND* RELAXED. YOU SHOULD FIND YOU ARE BETTER ABLE TO CONCENTRATE AND THAT YOUR SLEEP IMPROVES. IT IS A FORM OF EXERCISE ALMOST EVERYONE CAN ENJOY.

chi kung – simple but effective

Chi kung (also known as qi gong) is another marvellous form of mind–body exercise. It combines breathing techniques with precise movements and mental concentration. If you practise chi kung regularly, you will reap myriad benefits; your energy levels will increase, while your stress levels fall. Practitioners say you might also prevent or cure any number of chronic or acute diseases. Chi kung is said to improve concentration and even increase creativity and inspiration.

Best of all, absolutely anyone can do chi kung. If you are too weak to stand, there are sitting exercises. If you can't even sit, there are lying-down exercises! Chi kung has helped people in wheelchairs and those recovering from illness and injury – even the very elderly can benefit.

Don't think, however, that because chi kung exercises look simple, they are consequently easy. Chi kung is a precise discipline, demanding meticulous concentration and patience. It is also surprisingly tough on the muscles.

Ideally, you should strive to practise chi kung every day, even if only for 5 or 10 minutes. You can try the following exercises to start with. Wear loose, comfortable clothing and keep your feet bare.

the starting posture

This is the basic starting posture of chi kung. It puts you in the correct position and helps you to become aware of your entire body.

1 Stand with your feet shoulder-width apart. Make sure you find your natural balance – your weight should be neither too far forwards nor too far back, or it will lead to tension and tiredness.

2 Feel the rim of your foot, your heel, your little toe and big toe relaxed on the ground.

3 Keep your knees relaxed. Check to ensure that your knees are exactly over your feet.

4 Relax your lower back. Relax your stomach and buttocks.

5 Let your chest become hollow. Relax and slightly round your shoulders.

6 Imagine you have a pigtail on top of your head that

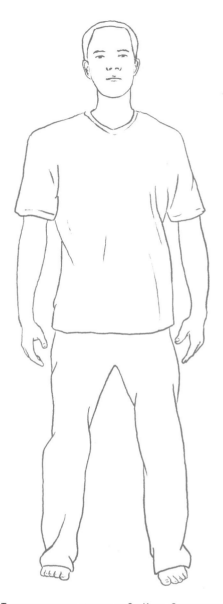

ABOVE The basic starting posture of Chi Kung. Chi kung may look easy, but it is deceiving. Although its postures and exercises are simple in essence, in practice they can be very demanding. The benefits, however, are well worth the effort.

is tied to a rafter on the roof. Let your head float lightly and freely. Relax your tongue, mouth and jaw.

7 Stay in this position for a few moments, with your hands hanging loosely by your sides.

8 Now spend some time visualizing the five elements of Chinese philosophy. Start with earth (imagine the feeling of weight and rootedness); then water (looseness and fluidity); air (lightness and transparency); fire (sparkle – remember this should be fun!); and space (envisage the space within each joint, muscle, breath and your mind).

9 Throughout your chi kung practice, keep bringing your mind gently back to your posture – this will help to keep your mind restful.

holding the dantien

This exercise stimulates the dantien, which in chi kung is considered to be the storehouse of chi or qi, the body's vital energy. It is also good for circulation and lymph drainage, and helps to promote deep, effective breathing. The dantien is located about an inch or so below the navel.

1 Stand in the starting position (see left).

2 Men should place their left hand on the dantien, and then the right hand over the left. Women should place their right hand on the dantien, with the left hand over it. Relax your whole body and lightly concentrate your thoughts on the dantien.

3 With the legs straight but not locked, breathe into the dantien. You will feel your abdomen inflate under your hands as you do this.

4 Slowly bend your knees and breathe out. Your abdomen will deflate into the body on the out breath. Repeat this exercise for at least two minutes – as you get more used to it, you can continue it for longer.

supporting the sky

This exercise is excellent for the lungs and breathing – it is superb when performed first thing in the morning because it empties the lungs after sleeping. It's also very helpful if you have backache. Incidentally, it could be very beneficial if you suffer from repetitive strain injury (RSI).

1 Stand in the starting position (see left).

2 Hold your hands in front of your dantien so the palms face up and the fingers point to each other.

3 Raise your hands up past the front of your chest, with the palms now facing the body. Breathe in. As your hands come up, keep your back straight and, when the hands reach the face, roll your hands over (so that the palms face upwards). Stretch your arms up and look upwards.

4 Open your arms out to the sides and lower them while bending the knees. Keep the back straight until the hands

are in the starting position, but now with your knees bent. Breathe out at the same time. Repeat at least five or six times for the maximum benefit.

turning the head and twisting the tail

This exercise helps to get the kidneys working well, so that they can efficiently eliminate toxins. It strengthens the spine and helps keep it flexible and strong. It takes a fair bit of coordination, but do persist, as it is highly effective.

1 Stand in the chi kung starting position (see left), but with the arms held out and raised at the sides of the body to shoulder height.

2 Place your weight on the right leg, keeping both legs relaxed. Lean to the left while raising your right arm slightly. Allow the left arm to curve downwards, so the tips of your fingers touch your left thigh about where a trouser seam would be. Turn your head to look into the palm of the right hand. As you perform this move, exhale.

3 Come back to the starting position with your arms held out and raised at the sides, breathing in as you do so.

4 Now shift your weight onto the left leg and lean to the right, raising your left arm slightly and curving the right arm downwards, so the fingertips touch the right thigh. Turn your head to look into the palm of the right hand. Breathe out as you perform this move.

5 Repeat at least five times for each side, keeping your movements slow and flowing.

dragon stamping

This exercise is great for your circulation and balance, both mental and physical. It helps to calm the mind and, if performed in the morning, helps you to become focused and energized for the day ahead. Make sure that you are breathing out as you rise and in as you return – it's easy to get it the wrong way round, which is far less effective.

1 Stand in the starting position (see left).

2 While breathing out, rise slowly onto your tiptoes, as high as you can. Stretch your body upwards through the back, keeping the abdomen relaxed. At the same time, point your fingers down and inwards, stretching your arms downwards as you do so.

3 Return your heels slowly to the ground on the in breath and relax. Repeat at least five times.

breathing

We take breathing for granted. We all know how to do it and, because we are doing it all the time, we tend to forget about it. However, if you truly want to improve your health, there is no escaping the need for good breathing. Even if you do nothing else for your health, simply taking the time and trouble to learn how to breathe in the optimum way can deliver truly amazing benefits for you, body, mind and spirit.

Why? Because, quite simply, breathing is the way we pull in oxygen and circulate it around the body to 'feed' each and every cell. Equally, breathing is the way we push out carbon dioxide and waste products, 'cleaning out' each and every cell. You simply can't overdose on deep good breathing – the more oxygen you can send around your body, the better.

The more effectively you can clear waste from your body, the better. Practitioners of Eastern practices such as yoga and chi kung say that breathing fully can do everything from improving your moods to increasing your resistance to colds and illness, fostering better sleep and even minimize the effects of ageing. It feeds the brain, calms the nerves and has a measurable effect on a number of medical conditions, lowering heart rate and metabolic rate, normalizing blood pressure and decreasing the risks of cardiovascular disease.

So what's wrong with our breathing? Basically, we nearly all breathe too shallowly, almost cautiously, only using a tiny portion of our lungs. It has been estimated that, when we breathe in, we take in only around a tumblerful of air when we could, in fact, take in at least three times that amount. Why do we need to take in more air? Because the lungs are made up of some 700 million air sacs, of which the greater

ayurvedic breathing

John Douillard, a trainer who uses ayurvedic principles in his work, teaches all his students to breathe through the nose at all times. This may seem strange if you are used to gasping in huge gulps of air, but Douillard insists that this is the only way to enable the body to enjoy the benefits of exercise without overstretching or stressing it. His 'Darth Vader' breath is a form of pranayama (see right) called *ujjayi* or the 'victorious' breath. This form of breathing is also taught if you take up ashtanga or power yoga. In fact, it is nigh-on impossible to practice ashtanga without it.

- Breathe in through the nose.
- Breathe out through the nose, slightly constricting the throat so you make a guttural sound – like Darth Vader in *Star Wars*. You will feel a sensation in your throat, rather than your nose.
- Notice that your stomach muscles slightly contract as you breathe out.

You will find at first that, breathing in this way, you can work for far less time. Don't panic. Just slow down your workout to suit your breath and your body. You will quickly find that, breathing in this way, you will be able to return to your former fitness levels – and even surpass them.

proportion lie in the lower lungs. When we breathe shallowly, we don't ever wholly expel all the waste gases and detritus in the lower lungs. We also run the risk of losing vital elasticity in the lower part of our lungs. On a more esoteric level, good breathing techniques transport vital energy (qi, chi or prana) right around the body. As you become more proficient, you can boost the power of your breathing by visualizing health-giving energy flooding into your lungs and thence to your entire body as you inhale and stale, spent energy pouring out as you exhale. In China, it is said that breathing like this will enliven your metabolism and invigorate all the cells of your body, producing good health and long life.

Fortunately, there are very simple exercises that can help bring our breathing back to its optimum fullness and freedom. The yogic tradition in India developed a whole science of good breathing. They called it *pranayama*, the art of breath control and expansion. In China, the effects of the breathing that forms an integral part of the chi kung (or qi gong) exercises have been rigorously tested. Hospitals have cured patients of tuberculosis using solely chi kung. Experiments have also shown that chi kung exercises can increase lung capacity from an average of 428.5 cc to 561.8 cc. While the patients were performing the exercises, their lung capacity expanded right up to 1,167.8 cc. Their breathing rate calmed and dropped, and their brainwaves dropped into the theta level, allowing the patients to remain alert, yet deeply calm.

The average person breathes around 16 times a minute, while a chi kung practitioner, through practice, breathes slowly and deeply just five or six times a minute. Once you start breathing properly, you should notice changes in your entire life. Some people say that how you breathe is a good indication of how you look at life as a whole. Symbolically, breathing is all about taking in the new and eliminating the old.

The Buddhist traditions regard every new breath as giving new life and every exhalation as a little death. Taking in deep, joyful breaths is seen as a way of affirming life and vitality. Breathing minimally and shallowly is turning your back on life or accepting it only grudgingly. As one proverb states: 'Life is in the breath. Therefore, he who only half breathes, half lives.'

OPPOSITE LEFT FEW OF US LEARN HOW TO BREATHE PROPERLY, YET SIMPLE BREATHING TECHNIQUES CAN HAVE A PROFOUND EFFECT ON BODY AND MIND.

simple techniques for better breathing

CHI KUNG – THE ABDOMINAL BREATH

1 Stand with your feet about shoulder-width apart, your knees slightly bent. Relax your shoulders. Imagine that a string runs from the top of your head to the ceiling, holding you upright but not rigid. Place your hands gently over your stomach, just below your navel.

2 Take in a slow, steady breath through your nose, allowing your abdomen to swell out like a balloon as you breathe. Hold the breath gently.

3 Exhale, allowing the breath to come out slowly through your mouth as the stomach subsides.

This form of breathing directs qi, or vital energy, right around the body. As you become more proficient, imagine health-giving energy flooding into your lungs as you breathe in and stale, spent energy pouring out as you exhale. Apparently, regular practice improves not only your health, but also your beauty!

PRANAYAMA – THE BREATH OF LIFE

1 Lie down on the floor and make yourself comfortable. Bring your feet close to your buttocks and let the feet fall apart, bringing the soles of the feet together, hands resting gently on the floor. (This may feel uncomfortable. If so, you can put cushions under your knees.) This posture stretches the lower abdomen, which enhances the breathing process.

2 Breathe down into the diaphragm, feeling the abdomen expand and contract. Breathe naturally at your own pace, pausing for a second or two between each breath.

3 Now extend the breath so it comes up from the abdomen into the chest. Continue this cycle, pausing slightly between each breath.

4 Finally, bring your knees together and gently stretch out the legs. Allow yourself to relax comfortably on the ground for a few minutes. (You may feel more comfortable with a cushion under your lower back or your neck.)

CAUTION: anyone with chest problems should take these exercises very slowly and carefully, preferably under the guidance of a trained yoga therapist. Anyone with a heart condition, blood pressure problems or glaucoma should not hold the breath. Again, consult a trained yoga therapist.

POSTURE

WHEN THINKING ABOUT WAYS TO IMPROVE OUR WELLBEING, OUR POSTURE DOESN'T USUALLY COME TO MIND. YET WE COULD ALL FEEL A LOT BETTER IN BODY, MIND AND SPIRIT IF WE PAID A LITTLE MORE ATTENTION TO OUR POISE.

As young children, if we were lucky, we possessed unselfconscious poise and perfect posture. We were ideally balanced and fluid. But, as time and modern living take their toll, we tend to adapt ourselves to a harsh environment and a stressful life. We begin to lose our easy freedom of movement when we start adapting to our environment – sitting in badly designed chairs, spending hours at the wheels of our cars, facing difficult emotional trials and traumas. We unconsciously acquire patterns of movement that work against our bodies' design and, in so doing, build up tension.

Long-term tension and bad posture can set us up for back pain and more. The ribs are attached to the upper (thoracic) spine and, when we stoop or round our shoulders, the lungs are not able to expand properly. With long-term misuse, respiratory problems can occur. Habitual slumping in an (albeit comfortable) armchair puts pressure on all your internal organs. Your heart, digestion, lungs and so on are all squeezed and therefore cannot work as effectively as they should. Inevitably, slouching can cause problems if continued on a long-term basis.

Basic good posture involves having your body in the best possible alignment: with back and abdominal muscles equally strong and the spine in the optimum position. Good posture will help your body operate more effectively, but can even affect your mood as well. All the nerve pathways that leave the brain eventually go through muscles, so there is a definite connection between what we think and what we experience. People with an upright posture tend to be confident and extrovert, while those who slump and slouch may veer towards depression and uncertainty. Turning that around has interesting effects. If you are feeling down and depressed, try sitting up straight with your eyes looking ahead – you'll find it automatically lifts your mood.

OPPOSITE EVERYTHING WE DO IN DAILY LIFE – FROM SITTING IN A CHAIR TO CARRYING A PILE OF BOOKS, CAN AFFECT OUR POSTURE.

good posture – the basic rules

STANDING

- Stand straight: think about standing on both feet. This may sound strange, but most people actually slouch to one side, putting their weight on one leg, which puts them out of balance. Study the basic posture of chi kung (page 78), which will put you in a good standing position.
- Practise the pelvic tilt: tuck your bottom in and pull your stomach in so that you are using your muscles almost like a girdle to hold yourself in. This provides good support for the lower back.
- Bring your chin in: most of us poke our chins out far too far. The head should be balanced, with the chin tucked in.

WALKING

- Take even strides: some people pull themselves along, overusing their hamstrings (the back of the thighs); others lean forwards and overstride. The healthiest way to walk is to take even strides.
- Keep your balance: we are designed to balance on one leg after the other. Don't throw your weight around.
- Walk low: high heels can throw the pelvis forwards which, in turn, will throw the whole body out of alignment. This will eventually cause shortening in some muscles, which could lead to back pain. Low, well-cushioned shoes are best for everyday wear. It's fine to wear high heels for special occasions – just don't wear them all day, every day.

SITTING – FOR WORK

- Chair comfort: you should be seated with your knees lower than your pelvis. The seat should be high enough for you to relax your shoulders, leaving your arms at a 90-degree angle to your desk. If the chair has arms, they should be low enough to fit under your desk.
- Screen daze: if you use a screen at work, your computer should be on a stand, rather than on the desk, so that you can look directly at it, rather than down towards it. Equally, make sure it is placed directly in front of you, rather than off to one side.

SITTING – TO RELAX

- Don't slump: slumping in front of the television may feel comfortable, but it's the worst possible position for your back. You should have a reasonably firm support behind you – a firm cushion will help.
- Watch your eyes: if you're watching television, you should be directly facing it with your head balanced. Don't twist. If you're reading a book or magazine, lift it up towards you, rather than bending over your lap.

SLEEPING

- Get the right support: a good mattress is essential. Too soft and the curves of your back sink in and reinforce bad posture – but, equally, too hard can be uncomfortable.
- Choose your pillow carefully: it needs to be malleable enough to mould to the curves of your neck. There are specialist pillows available on the market that ensure this, or you could roll up a hand towel and place it inside your pillowcase to provide a good support for your neck.
- Lie well: it's fine to sleep on either your side or your back, but avoid sleeping on your front with your head to one side. It twists the upper neck and can create imbalance.

WHAT TO AVOID

Certain movements and practices will play havoc with your posture – and your health. These are the main ones to avoid.

1 The heavy shoulder bag: a shoulder bag actually pulls up the shoulder, causing your body to overbalance and twist to compensate. A rucksack is ideal or, at the very least, keep shifting sides when carrying heavy bags.

2 The telephone shrug: clutching the telephone between ear and shoulder may result in 'telephone neck syndrome', which can cause searing pain between the shoulder blades. If you spend most of your day telephoning, use a headset.

3 The reversing rick: when reversing a car, don't pull your head back sharply and jerk your neck around. Instead, try dropping the tip of your nose towards your shoulder and then turning it while imagining your shoulder lengthening.

4 Post-exercise trauma: good posture after vigorous sport is very important. Don't slump in the changing room. Stand up and walk about instead.

5 The hip bend: bever pick up anything by twisting and bending – always squat before lifting.

alexander technique

A straightforward, down-to-earth technique could make you taller and slimmer. It can see off silence stress and banish the blues. It can even give significant relief from back and neck pain and the ache of arthritis. Yet this technique is no new wonder therapy, no esoteric healing – it's been taught for years. It's called the Alexander technique.

It was developed by Frederick Mathias Alexander, an Australian born in 1869. Alexander was a successful actor – until he started to lose his voice during orations. A host of doctors and voice coaches could find nothing wrong with him, so Alexander reasoned that he was doing something during his performance to cause the problem. With the use of a series of mirrors, he analysed his movements and discovered he was pulling his head back and down onto his spine with an enormous amount of tension. The tension was impairing his breathing and causing constriction of the larynx.

Alexander began to experiment and finally came up with a solution for the tension. He gave his body three main orders: 'Allow the neck to be free'; 'Allow the neck to go forwards and upwards'; and 'Allow the back to lengthen and widen.' These mental instructions both relaxed the tension and freed his voice. In addition, he discovered that the asthma he had suffered from since birth also vanished.

Alexander was so intrigued by these findings that he developed an entire system that would enable almost anyone to regain the comfort and ease of movement they enjoyed as babies and small children.

Our bodies will cope with postural abuses for some time, but then, generally from our thirties on, they start to complain. We begin to develop neck and back pains; we start getting headaches or migraines; we feel permanently tense and stressed, and have trouble sleeping. Some of us develop breathing problems because our lungs are cramped; others suffer digestive problems because we are squashing our colons. The Alexander technique offers us a solution, teaching us how to unravel taut, tense bodies.

The Alexander technique may not be exciting or trendy, but it does work. And, once you have learnt the technique, it is yours for life – along with all the benefits of a body that is deeply relaxed and comfortable in itself.

what can the alexander technique help?

- Alexander technique teachers don't claim to help or cure anything, but do say that it is almost always therapeutic.
- Many people (especially those with neck and back pain, and arthritis) are referred by their doctors.
- Many psychologists find that the Alexander technique can often help to clear depression. There seems to be a strong link between posture and psychological problems. Simply 'straightening up' and looking the world in the eye appears to have an instant effect on mood.
- Arthritis seems to respond well.
- Some people with asthma find they breathe more easily after learning the Alexander technique.
- It improves coordination and flexibility.
- Its pupils regularly report that they feel easier in themselves, that they have more energy and less stress.
- Many people 'grow' (in fact, they are actually straightening up) by as much as 3 or 4 cm (an inch and a half) after learning the Alexander technique, and they also appear to lose weight. We have a tendency to sink into our hips, so therefore, by encouraging a lengthening of the torso, a redistribution of fat tissue takes place and the body becomes taller and thinner.

what can I expect from a session?

WHERE WILL I HAVE THE TREATMENT?

You will be in the teacher's room.

WILL I BE CLOTHED?

Yes, you remain fully clothed throughout.

WHAT HAPPENS?

The technique is usually taught in individual lessons or small classes. Your teacher will meticulously observe how you use your body when you are standing, sitting and walking. He or she will then teach you how to change your patterns of movement subtly to restore your body to its natural balance. Don't expect miracles overnight – a basic course will consist of around 30 lessons and many people go on to take still more.

WILL IT HURT?

No, it's not painful at all.

WILL ANYTHING STRANGE HAPPEN?

No, not really. The exercises are all pretty straightforward.

WILL I BE GIVEN ANYTHING TO TAKE?

No, medication is not part of the treatment.

IS THERE ANY HOMEWORK?

Yes, lots. You will be expected to put everything you learn in the lessons into practice.

do-it-yourself alexander technique – relieving tension

This simple Alexander exercise can help relieve muscular tension. It involves lying on the floor with your head supported by a small pile of books. The number of books you will need will depend on your height and the curvature of your spine. Stand normally with your heels, buttocks and shoulder blades lightly touching a wall. Get a friend to measure the distance between your head and the wall, and add about $2^1/_2$ cm (1 in) to the measurement – this is the height of books you will need. Choose paperbacks (they're much more comfortable!).

- Lie on your back on the floor by going on all fours, then gently rolling onto the books. Bring your feet as near to your buttocks as is comfortable, so your knees point to the ceiling. Your hands should gently rest on either side of your navel.
- Lie like this for about 20 minutes. During this time, try to become aware of any tension in your body. Is your back arched so it is not fully in contact with the ground? Are your shoulders hunched? Are your shoulder blades not fully in contact with the ground? Do the books feel hard because you are pulling your head back, causing tension in your neck? Can you feel one side of your body more in contact with the floor than the other? Can you feel tension in your legs – do they want to fall in or out to the sides? Can you feel more pressure on the outside or the inside of your feet?
- Don't move or try to correct any problems – that will only make them worse. Instead, apply conscious thought to help release tension. If your back is arched, think of it lengthening and widening. If your shoulders are hunched, imagine them dropping away from your ears. If your leg wants to fall out, think of your knees pointing up to the ceiling.
- Before getting up from the floor, pause for a moment – think about a less stressful way of rising to your feet. Roll over onto your stomach and go on all fours. Assume a kneeling position and then put one foot in front of the other to come back up to a standing position.

feldenkrais method

The Feldenkrais method has been described as a way to 'find the cat in you' – teaching effortless movement through improved mind and body coordination. It's the secret behind the poise and control of countless actors and dancers, and the magic ingredient that can give sportspeople the edge in improving their performance or fine-tuning their game.

The Feldenkrais method was developed by Moshe Feldenkrais, who was born in Russia in 1904 and gained a PhD in engineering and physics. When he damaged his knee playing football, he was told that the only treatment was (possibly ineffectual) surgery. Feldenkrais decided to tackle the problem himself, applying his knowledge of structure and motion, combined with his martial-arts training.

He concluded that stiffness and pain are often caused not by physical defects, disease and degeneration, but rather by limitations in movement. Re-educating his body to move more freely and easily, he cured his knee and began a quest to help other people find the same release. By gently moving their bodies in unfamiliar ways, Feldenkrais found his 'students' could become more aware of how their bodies moved and, by repeating the actions, could actually alter the neuromuscular patterns that organize and control movement. The result was freedom from pain, increased flexibility and a wonderful feeling of truly inhabiting the body.

Feldenkrais is often compared to the Alexander technique, and the two systems certainly share the same emphasis of educating the body into freedom of posture and movement. However, whereas Alexander seeks the ideal, for perfect posture, Feldenkrais will be happy with a simple improvement on what you already have.

what can the feldenkrais method help?

- Physiotherapists often refer clients to Feldenkrais teachers for help in easing pain, chronic back problems and neuromuscular diseases.
- It can help people recover from accidents and strokes.
- It's a wonderful destresser – particularly for people who spend a lot of time in front of a computer.
- It can help minimize the severity of repetitive strain injury (RSI).
- 'Clumsy' children can benefit.
- Elderly people find it helps them move with added freedom.
- It gives flexibility, strength and suppleness, which, in turn, makes people feel more confident.

what can I expect from a session?

WHERE WILL I HAVE THE TREATMENT?

You will be in the teacher's room on a couch, or in a hall if you are being taught in a class.

WILL I BE CLOTHED?

Yes, you stay fully clothed throughout.

WHAT HAPPENS?

The Feldenkrais method is taught in two distinct ways. One-to-one sessions are known as Functional Integration and comprise manipulation, generally carried out on a low couch. It's all very gentle, minimal and pleasant. You will be asked often to 'check in' with your body, noticing sensations and getting in touch with how you feel. You will also be taught how to perform the minute movements for yourself. A lot of visualization is involved, to help your body make the right moves. There is no pulling or straining; everything is done slowly, carefully and mindfully. You can also learn the method in Awareness through Movement classes and workshops, in which small groups carry out gentle exercises guided by a teacher. Many of the movements taught in class are drawn directly from babyhood and childhood, so you're quite likely to find yourself rolling or twisting on the floor just like a toddler. Great fun!

WILL IT HURT?

No. You may notice some clicks and pops, but it's very pleasant and soothing.

WILL ANYTHING STRANGE HAPPEN?

Often you will be asked to compare the two sides of your body, halfway through the session. You may be surprised to find that the side that has been worked on will feel quite different from the one that hasn't.

WILL I BE GIVEN ANYTHING TO TAKE?

No, medication is not part of the treatment.

IS THERE ANY HOMEWORK?

Yes, you will be expected to practise at home what you learn in sessions or classes.

mézières method

The Mézières method teaches that perfection is possible. Within us all lies the potential to become 'a Greek god or goddess': no saddlebag thighs, no bulging bottoms, no rounded shoulders, no flabby waists. It isn't merely a fantasy: this unique form of bodywork really can resculpt the body. By returning your body to its ideal form, you will automatically bring yourself to a better state of health.

The method is well respected in its native France, where it has been quietly revolutionizing bodywork for the past 40 years. Its originator was Françoise Mézières, a teacher of physiotherapy and anatomy. Like all physiotherapists, she had been taught that the muscles in the back are generally too weak and need to be strengthened. But one day, while examining a patient, it suddenly struck her that in fact the very opposite was true: the muscles in the back were actually too strong. Their strength caused them to become shortened and to lose their elasticity, creating tension and eventually pain. This imbalance of muscle strength was occurring all over the body, but it was particularly pronounced in the back because the muscles in the back overlapped to form a chain running the entire length of the body.

There was, she realized, absolutely no point in relieving stiffness or shortening in just one muscle or muscle group, as it would simply cause compensatory shortening in another area: the whole chain needed to be stretched and readjusted at the same time. This concept flatly contradicted everything Mézières believed in, everything she taught her students, so she set out to disprove her theory. Two years later, after constant observation and evaluation, she admitted defeat and began to reshape entirely her way of working.

The Mézières method is no easy ride. It involves intense, painstaking work by practitioner *and* patient. Expect to have sessions once or twice a week and for it to take several months, possibly a year, to reshape a body. Practitioners say you can often get rid of pain in one session, but it will never be long-lasting unless you work hard to correct the cause of that pain. This correction involves literally unravelling the distortions of the body – it's a little like slowly and patiently taking the kinks and knots out of a badly twisted rope and stretching it so that it once again it lies smooth and flat.

what can the mézières method help?

- People report a radical reshaping of their bodies after using the Mézières method.
- Aches and pains often disappear with this therapy; so, too, can arthritis and sciatica.
- The Mézières method can correct long-term distortions of the body, from kyphosis (dowager's hump) and scoliosis (spinal curvature) to flat feet, knock knees and bow legs.
- It has a positive effect on mood as well, improving confidence, easing depression and soothing anxiety.
- Practitioners promise that the Mézières method can correct almost any problem, bar those that are congenital or caused by fractures or mutilations.

what can I expect from a session?

WHERE WILL I HAVE THE TREATMENT?

You will be lying on the floor in the therapist's room.

WILL I BE CLOTHED?

You will be asked to strip down to underwear.

WHAT HAPPENS?

First, the practitioner gauges your posture, asking you to stand with feet together, ankles, knees and toes touching, then to bend forwards slowly as if to touch your toes. You will be observed from all angles, as the practitioner decides how to proceed.

You will then lie on the floor while the practitioner puts your body into precise positions. It sounds simple, but it's tough work. You feel rather like an overpacked case: press on one side and something pops out the other side. The practitioner may use his or her body weight to maximize to the stretch, sometimes kneading tense, stiff muscles to help them yield.

WILL IT HURT?

It can be quite uncomfortable at times. You may have pins and needles after the session and it's quite common for your legs to feel numb in the early stages.

WILL ANYTHING STRANGE HAPPEN?

You may well feel totally different after a session, as if you have been given a new body.

WILL I BE GIVEN ANYTHING TO TAKE?

No, medication is not part of the treatment, although some practitioners may advise you on diet.

IS THERE ANY HOMEWORK?

Yes, for best results in reshaping your body, you will practise the Mézières method at home.

pilates

Pilates has sprung to fame in the past few years. Adored by dancers and sportspeople, it is a gentle exercise system which aims to put you back in touch with your body. The result is perfect poise, fabulous flexibility and freedom from aches and pains.

Pilates was developed more than 60 years ago by Joseph Pilates, a German who was interned in Britain during World War I. He developed a system to maintain the health and fitness levels of himself and his fellow internees while they were in confinement. Later, Pilates moved to New York and his studio became a magnet for ballet dancers, sportspeople, actors and actresses, among many other wise mortals who wanted to learn the workout that gives strength without bulky muscles; the method that promises harmony between your mind and your muscle.

The Pilates method works through resistance – using equipment with tensioned springs, gravity or your own body weight. Pilates is wonderful for correcting any postural imbalances and bad habits, by increasing the mobility, strength and elasticity of your muscles. Considered to be one of the safest forms of exercise ever devised, it is regularly recommended by osteopaths and physiotherapists.

Pilates uses flowing, controlled movements with specific breathing patterns to improve both coordination and muscle stamina. Every movement is carefully monitored to ensure you are using the correct muscles in precisely the correct way.

what can pilates help?

- The Pilates system is invaluable as rehabilitative exercise after injury. It can also help prevent old injuries recurring.
- Pilates is extolled by dancers and sportspeople. Actors, singers and musicians use the method to improve their breath control, grace and coordination.
- It improves posture, relieves back problems and is superb for toning and streamlining the body.
- It is a totally safe form of exercise for use during pregnancy.
- Pilates can help prevent the onset of osteoporosis.
- Stress and stress-related problems respond well.
- It can help repetitive strain injury (RSI).
- The Pilates method is ideal for older people who want to maintain mobility.

what can I expect from a session?

WHERE WILL I HAVE THE SESSION?

You will be in a Pilates studio filled with special equipment – machines, mats, large balls – or a simple room without equipment.

WILL I BE CLOTHED?

Yes, you will wear comfortable clothes for the session. Generally, you will go barefoot.

WHAT HAPPENS?

The teacher will start by finding out about you – your lifestyle, any problems, what you want to achieve. He or she will also check your posture, looking for any imbalances and tension. You will then be taken through a warm-up leading into a series of stretches and exercises. Every movement in Pilates is focused (you will be taught to be mindful of your body throughout)

and fluid. You will constantly focus on centring and pulling your stomach muscles in. Every exercise uses the breath in a specific way, as you breathe in through the nose and out through the mouth. These exercises are very precise – because they have been designed to work specific groups of muscles – so expect constant supervision throughout. Often you will perform an exercise in several different ways, with each variation more advanced. However, you will always be advised to work at your own pace and level: nothing is ever pushed in Pilates. Like yoga, it is non-competitive. If you practise regularly, you will soon notice your core strength increasing, allowing you to perform the more advanced variations with ease.

WILL IT HURT?

No, it's not painful. However, you may find some of the exercises quite difficult to begin with.

WILL ANYTHING STRANGE HAPPEN?

No, Pilates is a pretty down-to-earth system.

WILL I BE GIVEN ANYTHING TO TAKE?

No, medication is not part of the system.

IS THERE ANY HOMEWORK?

Yes, for best results, you should not only practise Pilates at home as well, but also as often as possible.

LEFT AND ABOVE EVERY EXERCISE IN PILATES IS PRECISELY DESIGNED TO TARGET SPECIFIC MUSCLES. THE MOVES PICTURED HERE ARE QUITE ADVANCED AND YOU WOULD BUILD UP TO THEM GRADUALLY. EACH MOVE IS FOLLOWED BY ONE WHICH STRETCHES THE OPPOSITE GROUP OF MUSCLES, SO YOUR BODY IS ALWAYS KEPT BALANCED AND IN ALIGNMENT.

home pilates

SLIDING DOWN THE WALL

This releases tension and is great for the spine.

1 Stand with your feet shoulder-width apart and parallel, with your back about 45 cm (18 in) from a wall.

2 Bend your knees and lean back into the wall (as if you were sitting on a stool).

3 Breathe in and feel yourself lengthening up through the spine as the breath fills your lungs.

4 Start to breathe out and gently pull your stomach in, as if you were bringing your belly button back towards the spine.

5 Still breathing out, relax your head and neck so you can let your chin drop forwards. Imagine your forehead has a weight pulling it forwards.

6 Now slowly start to roll forwards. Keep your hands and arms, and your neck and head, relaxed. Make sure your bottom stays glued to the wall. Let yourself roll forwards one vertebra at a time, as if you were being peeled off the wall.

7 Go as far as you feel comfortable (eventually you will be able to reach the floor). Now hang in your furthest position and breathe in.

8 Breathe out and pull your belly button to the spine again. Rotate your pelvis so the pubic bone moves towards your chin (remember these are tiny movements).

9 Slowly, vertebra by vertebra, curl your spine back into the wall as you come up. Repeat this exercise six times.

FOOT CIRCLING

This simple exercise helps keep your ankle joints flexible.

1 Sit on the floor with your legs stretched out in front of you, a little more than shoulder-width apart with your knees facing up to the ceiling. (NOTE: if this is uncomfortable, put a pillow under your bottom to tilt you forwards slightly). Place your hands on the floor beside you to balance yourself.

2 Now feel yourself lifting out of your hips, keeping your spine straight.

3 Rotate your feet around in outward circles (your right foot will be going clockwise and your left foot anticlockwise).

4 Keep your knees still and work from your ankles to get a really good range of movement.

5 Repeat with your feet rotating in the opposite (inwards) direction. Repeat the whole exercise ten times.

ENVIRONMENT

ARE YOU LIVING IN A HEALTHY HOME? IT IS IRONIC THAT, WHILE MANY OF US MAKE SO MUCH EFFORT TO KEEP OUR BODIES HEALTHY WITH GOOD FOOD, REGULAR EXERCISE AND SERIOUS STRESSBUSTING, WE TEND TO FORGET ABOUT OUR HOMES. YET THE ENVIRONMENT WHICH SURROUNDS US IS VITALLY IMPORTANT, AS ESSENTIAL AS A HEALTHY DIET. THERE ARE SIMPLY LOADS OF TOXINS IN EVERY HOUSE — HIDDEN DANGERS WHICH CAN COMPROMISE OUR HEALTH. FORTUNATELY, THERE ARE SOME VERY PLEASANT WAYS BY WHICH YOU CAN TURN YOUR HOME INTO A HEALING SANCTUARY.

the polluted home

There are literally hundreds of potential indoor air pollutants. Any new curtains, carpets or furniture coverings may be emitting formaldehyde gas, a highly toxic substance which can cause irritation to the eyes and throat, and exacerbate allergies. Home insulation, roofing timbers and pressed-wood and fibreboard furniture and fittings can also emit harmful chemicals, while that fresh coat of paint could release solvents such as toluene, xylene and benzene (all potentially toxic) and might contain mercury (which may cause brain damage) as a fungicide. That's just the tip of the iceberg.

It all sounds terrifying, but don't panic — there is much you can do to make your home healthy.

- First, don't bring in more toxins. Whenever you redecorate or refurnish your home, avoid using synthetic materials: choose 100 per cent wool carpets or natural floor coverings such as sisal and coir; pick eco-paints that are water-, milk-, mineral- or plant-based.
- Recycled wooden floorboards look fabulous (check out salvage merchants). Use old wood to build feelgood, safe furniture. MDF may be the new wonder material, but it can emit harmful chemicals, as can pressed wood and fibreboard.
- If you have an open fire, have your flue checked and swept regularly. Make sure that all your heaters and boilers are regularly serviced.
- Choose all-natural fabrics for your curtains and soft furnishings — synthetic fabrics can emit noxious chemicals such as vinyl chloride, styrene and formaldehyde.

- Let the air into your home (it helps to flush out toxic build-up). Open your windows for at least 15 minutes twice a day.
- If your clothes are dry-cleaned, leave them outside with the plastic covers off for 30 minutes before bringing them inside.
- Fill your house with plants (see the box below).
- Modern household cleaners and pesticides may be effective, but they're also highly toxic. Choose alternative cleansers, especially eco-friendly ranges that do not contain harmful chemicals (look in your health store).
- Minimize the use of electrical appliances, keeping them switched off when not in use. All of them give off electro-magnetic radiation, which may cause insomnia, high blood pressure, anxiety and general ill health.
- Replace any fluorescent bulbs (which can cause headaches, depression, nausea and eye strain). If possible, use daylight bulbs, which are particularly helpful if you suffer from seasonal affective disorder (SAD).
- Call in professional help to remove any old lead paint and asbestos in your home. Don't attempt to do this yourself.
- Install a water-purification system for your domestic water supply and have ionizers in your home.

OPPOSITE MANY HOMES, NO MATTER BEAUTIFUL THEY LOOK, ARE FILLED WITH TOXIC MATERIALS WHICH CAN CONTRIBUTE TO POOR HEALTH.

cleansing plants

Your house plants can be staunch allies in healing your home. Remarkable research by NASA found that certain species actually remove chemical pollutants from the air. Some people believe that plants can also help prevent the ill effects of electromagnetic radiation, so keep some around your computer and television. Choose from the following:

- peace lilies
- sansevieria (mother-in-law's tongue)
- spider plants (*Chlorophytum elatum vittatum*)
- golden pothos (*Scindapsus aureus*)
- *Syngonium podophyllum*
- philodendrons

decluttering your home

1 Set aside a specific time for decluttering your home. Make it fun: put on some favourite music; burn some aromatherapy oils (something fresh and stimulating such as lemon, grapefruit or pine). If you know that you'll be overcome with nostalgia, take some clematis Bach flower remedy. Promise yourself a treat at the end of your decluttering (even if it's just a glass of freshly squeezed juice or a cup of herbal tea – and a magazine).

2 If you have loads of other people's stuff, put it all in a box and ask them to come and collect it. Say you're having a clear-out and that anything remaining after, say, a month, will be donated to charity.

3 If you have a family heirloom that you really don't want, offer it to other members of the family. If no one wants it, agree to sell it and have a family outing with the proceeds. Don't be guilt-tripped into keeping it!

4 Nearly new clothes and expensive mistakes can go to dress agencies, or be given to friends. Take any unwanted clean, serviceable clothes to charity outlets.

5 Furniture and unwanted (working) electrical goods can be advertised in your local newspaper (often for free or a small fee). Otherwise, charities for the elderly and disabled people will often come and collect them.

6 Donate magazines to hospitals or your doctor's/dentist's/vet's surgery. Clip out any newspaper cuttings you need and put them in a book, then recycle your newspapers and other clean paper products.

7 Keep an 'essential papers' file for your important documents. Keep sentimental letters and keepsakes in a beautiful box. Put important contact details in an address book, personal organizer or on a computer disk. Then let go of all the other papers: recycle or have a bonfire!

8 Old medicines can be dangerous; old cosmetics can go rancid. Safely dispose of old medicines (usually to your pharmacist) and dump cosmetics older than a year.

9 It's not hygienic to use chipped or cracked crockery. Use it to make mosaics if you're artistic; otherwise, put it in the garbage (trash).

10 Weed out your book and record collection and sell any unwanted items to second-hand stores or give them to charity outlets or jumble sales.

clear the clutter

If your home is piled high with clutter and mess, you will never feel comfortable and relaxed in it. On a physical level, clutter attracts dust and cobwebs. In energetic terms, it prevents qi from circulating freely – the energy stagnates. Psychologists also believe that, when we are surrounded by confusion, our minds become equally confused and anxious.

Decluttering is the first step that any feng shui (see pages 94–5) consultant will advise you to take and it will make an enormous difference to your feeling of wellbeing. The Chinese believe that, when we get rid of the old, it allows room for something new to take its place – an idea worth holding on to if you find it hard to let go!

How you clear the clutter is up to you. Some people like to have an enormous clear-out, going through the whole house like a whirlwind and filling an entire skip! Others will need to take it more slowly, maybe focusing on a different room (or even just a drawer) each week.

the smell-good home

Scent is another way to make your home harmonious with a minimum of effort. Change the smell of your home and you can shift its atmosphere and mood from soothing sanctuary to vibrant party place whenever you wish. However, don't be tempted by artificial fragrances and air fresheners: synthetic smells are a common trigger for asthma and hayfever. Instead, seek out pure aromatherapy products. Use them in a fragrance burner, add them to a bath or fill bowls with warm water and add a few drops to scent a room gently (place on a radiator to release the odour over a longer time).

The following are the best oils for starting – but don't use aromatherapy products if you are pregnant, unless you consult a trained aromatherapist first.

- Geranium lifts your mood – use it if you're feeling down or to welcome guests into your home.
- Lavender is wonderful for deep relaxation.
- Lemon is uplifting. Put a few drops in the washing-up liquid.
- Peppermint is energizing, but can increase your appetite (so avoid if you're trying to lose weight!).
- Rosemary can help concentration – burn some on your desk as you work.
- Ylang ylang is sensuous and sexy! Use it whenever you want to bring romance and passion into your life.

geopathic stress

Could harmful energy fields radiating from deep beneath the earth be ruining your life and be hazardous to your health? Many complementary health practitioners are convinced that abnormal energy fields generated by underground streams, large mineral deposits or faults in the substrata of the earth could be seriously compromising the health of millions. They call the condition geopathic stress (GS) and hold that it can be a major contributing factor in everything from migraines to cancer, from nightmares to divorce.

The evidence suggests that geopathic stress certainly does exist. In Germany, geopathic stress has been researched since the 1920s and is taken very seriously. Experiments have shown that bacteria grow abnormally when grown over currents of underground water, while mice inoculated with disease will fall ill far more rapidly when kept over a vein of subterranean water. Builders in Germany and Austria now test sites before building, and many will routinely give guarantees that new buildings do not have lines of 'bad' energy passing through them.

All this sounds terrifying, but practitioners reassure that, even if your house does suffer from geopathic stress, your health need not necessarily be affected. Apparently, geopathic stress comes up through the earth in thin bands or small spirals, so it will only affect you if you are sleeping directly on top of it or sitting in it all day. It is very easy to move your desk or your bed to avoid it.

detecting geopathic stress

If you think geopathic stress might be affecting your home, you can try some do-it-yourself detection for yourself.

- Experts say that geopathic stress is most probably affecting people who complain of constantly feeling tired and below par. Everything is an effort. They are easily depressed and irritable. They suffer endlessly from colds, while illnesses, aches and pains will not respond to any treatment. Children become disruptive and badly behaved.
- Because geopathic stress comes up from beneath the earth in thin lines, it can easily affect just one person in the house – a line can pass through just one side of a double bed or one armchair. So, it is quite possible for only one member of the family to be affected.
- If you suspect you suffer from geopathic stress, try putting cork tiles under your bed or favourite chair for a few weeks to see whether you start to feel better. Cork tiles seem to neutralize the rays for a limited period. If you do start feeling better, try moving your bed or chair.
- Watch where your pets sleep. Cats, strangely, adore geopathic stress and will often choose to sleep on a bad spot, while dogs will avoid it at all costs. If your cat always makes a beeline for your favourite armchair, try moving it to the dog's favourite spot.
- Babies are apparently very sensitive to geopathic stress. If your baby constantly rolls over to one corner of the cot, he or she may be attempting to escape geopathic stress. Move the cot to another part of the room and see whether your baby stays put.
- If you feel you are affected by geopathic stress, try switching on a hairdryer and running it all over you, with the side of the dryer touching your body. 'It sounds crazy,' admits geopathic stress expert Jane Thurnell-Read, 'but, if you do it once a week, it does seem to help.'

Of course, if you think that geopathic stress may be a serious problem for you, it is well worth finding a reputable dowser (see the resource section at the back of the book).

ABOVE LEFT A BOWL OF ROSE PETALS IS A DELIGHTFUL AND SUBTLE WAY OF BRINGING UPLIFTING, CHEERING SCENT INTO YOUR HOME. DON'T BE TEMPTED TO USE ARTIFICIAL ROOM FRESHENERS — THEY ARE FULL OF CHEMICALS.

colours for the home

Colour has the power to lift our spirits, to soothe our souls, to enliven us or calm us. By bringing colour into your home, you can subtly but very effectively change the atmosphere of the house. See colour therapy (pages 233–4) for more ideas.

- Ideally, your bedroom should always tend towards the cooler hues – soft blues, greens and mauves, which will slow down the brain and soothe the nervous system. But do incorporate some vibrant red or pink (in the form of cushions or throws) if you want to liven up your sex life!
- Pick warm shades for kitchens and living rooms. Colour therapists say that pink or peach encourages people to draw closer together, share feelings and discuss them. Pink also helps people to relax, let go, unwind and feel at ease; it dispels stress and tension. Orange, yellow and apricot are equally suitable. Orange, in particular, is a very sociable colour – ideal for living rooms where people congregate.
- Soft indigo or violet are wonderful if you have a meditation or retreat room. They can also be soothing for guest rooms.
- If you live in a studio apartment or have to double up your living and sleeping space, go for soft greens – they are soothing enough for sleep, yet comfortable for daytime, too.

feng shui

Feng shui evolved around 5,000 years ago in China. The ancient Chinese believed that invisible life energy (known as qi, or chi) flowed through everything in life. It's the same philosophy that underlies acupuncture – if the energy in your body is moving freely and easily, you will stay fit and healthy. Should it become stagnant or blocked, however, you will most likely fall ill. In acupuncture, needles are used to free any blockages and to regulate the smooth flowing of qi. The principle is much the same in houses and offices, but various 'cures' are used instead of needles.

The Chinese believed that the buildings we live and work in require quite as much attention as our bodies; as a result, they developed this complex science for 'healing' our environment. Centuries of observation suggested to them that different areas of the house or room attracted specific energies. Furthermore, the Chinese believed that certain configurations (the layout of rooms or even the position of furniture or features) could either help or hinder the free, smooth flowing of energy. If the energy was blocked or allowed to flow too swiftly, it would cause corresponding blockages and problems in life. Fortunately, however, they realized that very small but specific changes ('cures' such as hanging wind chimes or crystals in particular places or using certain colours) could correct such disharmony and put a life back on track. Augmenting particular areas with auspicious colours and objects could even create better energy and hence better opportunities in life.

At its core, the philosophy of feng shui teaches that, by making small shifts to your home, you can affect everything in your life – from your finances to your health, and even your marriage and sex life.

Although feng shui sounds mystical, it is taken very seriously, not just in its native China but all over the world.

mapping your home

One of the fundamental principles of feng shui is in the *ba-gua*. This is an imaginary octagonal template that divides any space (your entire house, an apartment or office or simply a room) into eight areas (or corners). These represent wealth, fame, marriage, children, helpful people, career,

knowledge and the family. In order to work out the ba-gua of any room or house, the position of the main door is important. If it lies in the middle of your wall, it is in the position known as career. If it is to the left of centre, it is in the position known as knowledge, and if it is to the right, it is in the position known as Helpful People. Imagine yourself standing with your back to the door with the ba-gua laid over your space. Then work your way clockwise around the room.

You can apply the ba-gua to any building or room. Having worked out what lies where in your house, you can often see whence your problems may be emanating. Not all houses are built perfectly square and symmetrical – often you will find you are missing an area of the ba-gua. An L-shaped house might well be missing the marriage area. Equally, the marriage area in your bedroom might be the place where you keep a cluttered desk or the dirty laundry. Neither of these would help your relationships because the qi would become stagnant and heavy. If money is a problem, make sure your wealth area is clean and clear (and maybe add a feature such as a water fountain or fish tank to boost finances).

feng shui in your home

Fortunately, there are umpteen very simple 'cures' used in feng shui that can help resolve problems in your home's qi. They are generally cheap and simple to implement.

- Ensure everything in the house works well: check electrics and plumbing; replace broken light bulbs and cracked window panes; make sure doors and windows don't stick. The fabric and mechanics of your home correspond to your body; keep them running smoothly and you should stay fit.
- Keep shapes soft and rounded where possible. Avoid sharp corners. Softly rounded sofas and chairs; big, squashy bean bags; and organic shapes are feng shui heaven.
- Boost the qi of your home by adding healthy green plants, fresh flowers and maybe a goldfish tank or water fountain.
- Hang wind chimes by your front door so they tinkle as you enter (they boost the energy of your home), but make sure they do not actually touch the door.
- Use mirrors to reflect pleasant views into the home. If you look out over an unpleasant view or a large building overshadows your home, hang a silver ball (from New Age stores) from a red ribbon in your window – this will deflect the harmful qi.
- Keep the toilet seat down! Otherwise, you will be simply flushing wealth energy away.

vastu shastra

Vastu shastra is the Indian equivalent of feng shui, a complex science of spiritual architecture. In essence, the two systems are very similar. Both teach that, for good health, harmony and happiness we should live in symmetrical buildings and that there are beneficial directions in which to site the various rooms of the house and the furniture within it.

While feng shui has the ba-gua, a map of the various directions and the corresponding areas of life, vastu shastra has a mandala or sacred diagram called the *vastu purusha mandala*. The story goes that a formless being threatened to cause disruption between heaven and earth. The gods seized the creature and laid it face down on the earth, where it took the form of a human being (the purusha). Vastu practitioners say that the mandala (sacred image) forms the basis for understanding how energy moves through any given space.

Cosmic energy is said to enter a building through the purusha's head in the northeast, move along its arms in the southeast and northwest, and finally gather at its feet in the southwest. So, to attract vital energy inside the home, it is crucial to keep the east, northeast and north clear, open and unobstructed. Once the energy has entered the house, it is important to ground it. So, the ground in the south and west is traditionally kept slightly higher and it has fewer openings, less open space and more solid walls.

Houses built according to vastu shastra principles generally face east to maximize the amount of early sunlight entering. In ancient India, the rising sun with its gentle heat and light was seen as a source of vitality, while the setting sun had far too much heat and glare. Ideally, every house and building should echo the sacred geometry of the cosmos, harnessing spiritual power and vital energy. This is spiritual architecture in its purest form – a kind of yoga for houses. So what do you do if your house doesn't face east or if your kitchen is in the wrong area? First and foremost, you should try to shift the rooms, so a vastu consultant may suggest you relocate your kitchen. Hardly a cheap option! However, there are more practicable ways to get round the problem. You may be advised that the cooker (stove) – the symbolic heart of the kitchen – be put in the southeast corner of the west room.

Although vastu shastra is complex, its practitioners promise it is well worth the effort. Applying vastu shastra to your home, they say, can bring you good health, great relationships, a happy family life and serious wealth.

BELOW ALTHOUGH A CLEAR, UNCLUTTERED BEDROOM IS A BOON, IT IS NOT ADVISABLE TO HAVE YOUR BED AGAINST A WALL OF FLOOR-TO-CEILING WINDOWS. THIS WOULD MAKE YOU FEEL UNSETTLED AND POSSIBLY UNSAFE WHEN IN BED.

tips for vastu shastra success

GENERAL CONCEPTS

1 Houses should ideally be square or rectangular in shape – and sited within a square or rectangular plot of land. Avoid triangular or irregular plots.

2 The back of the house should be slightly higher than the front to contain the energy coming in the front door.

3 The front of your house should have more openings (doors and windows) than the back.

4 Ideally, your home should face east, to attract the energy of the sunrise. If it faces in another direction, ensure that east is kept open and is not blocked by trees or other buildings.

5 Never have three doors in a line – a very bad design in vastu shastra practice.

6 Avoid having your toilet in the northeast, a position that is considered far from ideal.

7 The central part of the house is very sensitive. Do not have a staircase or a toilet here. Traditionally, this area would have been an open courtyard (impractical for most of us today), but do try to keep this area as clear, clean and stable as possible.

FRONT ENTRANCE AND HALL

1 Your front door should ideally face east. It should be the biggest door in the house.

2 Paint an 'ohm' symbol on your front door – at eye level – to improve your home's energy and vitality.

3 Always keep the area near the front door unobstructed and open, to allow the maximum amount of energy to flow into the house.

4 Place lower, lighter furniture near and around the front door. Any taller, heavier furniture should be placed in the area diagonally opposite (furthest away from the door) to hold the energy down.

BEDROOMS

1 The main bedroom should be in the southwest corner of the house or apartment. You should then sleep in the southwest corner of the room with your head facing south. If this is impossible, have your head facing west. It is not good to sleep with your head facing north.

2 Don't let your bed touch the walls on any side, as this will inhibit energy flow.

3 Children should sleep in the west corner of the house. Cots and beds should be in the southwest of the room so their heads face west. A green bulb will help enhance intelligence.

KITCHEN

1 If possible, place your kitchen in the southeast of the house – this is linked with the fire element in Vedic texts. Face the east when cooking. The sink should be towards the east of northeast.

2 To stimulate your appetite and that of your family, paint the walls soft pink or orange.

3 Place a mirror on the eastern wall to help strengthen your finances – good food mirrors financial strength.

DINING ROOM

1 The dining room should be a relaxed spot in which you can enjoy calm eating. Paint the walls soft pink, orange or cream.

2 Place a mirror on the east or north wall of your dining room, or perhaps even both.

3 Your dining table should be rectangular – avoid egg-shaped or irregular-shaped tables. Keep the dining table away from the walls of the room.

4 If possible, the dining room should be situated in the west of the house.

5 Paintings of the rising sun and the beauty of nature (without animals in them) will create a good feeling.

LIVING ROOM

1 Ideally, living rooms should be sited in the north, east or northeast part of the house.

2 Place furniture in the south and west, allowing plenty of space in the north and east of the room.

3 Put an indoor plant in a heavy pot in the south or west of the living room.

4 Recommended colours to use in your living room are white, soft blue and soft green.

5 Bless your living room to help attract beneficial energies to your home. Use incense, smudging (see page 168), clapping, drums, bells, prayer – whatever feels right for you.

NOTE: feng shui and vastu shastra share many characteristics, but there are discrepancies between the two. The best advice is to follow the system to which you are intuitively drawn.

SLEEP

Good sleep is vital for our health and happiness. The world seems a brighter place after a good night's slumber. When our sleep is disturbed, on the other hand, nothing seems right. Sleep experts believe that lack of sleep can be blamed for up to 40,000 road crashes a year, for bad decision making in business and even for such disasters as Chernobyl. On a more domestic level, any parent of a poorly sleeping child will tell you that persistent lack of sleep is one of the most exquisite forms of torture ever invented!

But how much sleep do we truly need? Ask the experts and you end up confused. Some say we all suffer from sleep deficit – sleeping, on average, between an hour and 90 minutes less than we should. Others maintain that we need only between 5 or 6 hours, and that most of us are actually oversleeping. So whom should we believe? The answer has to be our own bodies, which undoubtedly know how much sleep we need and when. Most of us will sleep for around 8 hours a night, but some people happily manage on 5 or 6, while others feel lousy without 9. Curiously, our very personalities can determine how much sleep we need. American experts have discovered that short sleepers tend to be efficient, energetic, ambitious people who are relatively sure of themselves, socially adept and decisive. They are satisfied with their lives, while their social and political views are conformist. Long sleepers, by contrast, are nonconformist with mild neurotic problems and tend to be less sure of themselves. They appear to be more artistic or creative.

It's not really how much sleep we get that is important for our health and wellbeing, it is the kind of sleep we get – quality over quantity. Sleep is divided into three types: light, deep and REM (or dreaming) sleep. Cut down on sleep and our bodies will compensate by automatically cutting down first light sleep and then, if necessary, REM sleep, too.

The importance of REM or dreaming sleep is another thorny topic of debate among scientists. Some insist that our dreams are merely the detritus of the day, spewed out like so much garbage. Others are convinced that, by using our dreams creatively, we can resolve many of our waking problems. Many researchers are fascinated by the idea of 'lucid dreaming', of learning how consciously to direct your dreams. Dr Rosalind Cartwright of St Luke's Medical Centre in Chicago found that people who cope best with divorce tend to have helpful dream patterns. She recommends reshaping dreams to have a happy ending. 'Once the dreaming changes, the morning mood changes,' she says. 'If people stop having unpleasant, guilt-ridden, anxious dreams, they wake in the morning more refreshed and better able to face the world.'

If you still feel grouchy and tired when you wake, despite having wonderful healing dreams, there could be another answer. Many scientists believe the Spaniards, far from being lazy, have had the right idea all along with their afternoon siesta. The body's circadian rhythms show that we are ready for sleep around 3 or 4 pm and that many overtiredness problems could be solved by a half-hour nap in the afternoon. Researchers have discovered that careful use of naps can help long-distance truck drivers, overworked junior hospital doctors and residents, and those on night shifts; an afternoon catnap significantly sharpens mental alertness and improves mood.

what happens when we sleep?

Remarkably little is known about the actual physiological effects of sleep, but the facts, as they emerge, are intriguing. In the first 3 hours of sleep. large amounts of growth hormone are released into the body. Although the reasons for this in humans are not quite clear, growth hormone in animals is known to give immune systems a boost. As deep sleep ensues, more immune activities get under way. Levels of other hormones rise rapidly, too, such as prolactin, which is believed to regulate glucose and fatty acids in the blood, reduce water loss in the kidneys and generally balance our bodies. Melatonin, understood to influence regeneration and regulate water, is also released. So, while we slumber, our bodies appear to be fine-tuning, balancing and protecting.

Deprive yourself of the correct amount of sleep and you could find yourself becoming more irritable and antisocial. Your memory will not be as good and your coordination may be impaired. Your sex life may even suffer – research has discovered that our sex hormones are suppressed when we deprive ourselves of sleep.

beating insomnia

Insomnia, the inability to sleep or sleeping poorly, often starts in infancy. Sometimes there are simple causes, such as bad habits or the effects of moving house. Sometimes, however, there is the deeper fear of separation. Parents who suffered childhood separation themselves often associate sleep with loss. Losing consciousness becomes frightening for them and they pass their anxieties on to their child.

As we grow up, our sleeplessness generally falls into three categories: transient insomnia, brought on by a change in routine such as jet lag or switching shifts; short-term insomnia, caused by illness or emotional problems; and chronic insomnia, which has myriad causes ranging from depression or anxiety to abuse of drugs or alcohol.

A doctor's standard response to 'I can't sleep' has often been simply to give a prescription for sleeping pills, but medical research is now showing that, far from being valuable lifelines, these drugs can cause more problems than they solve. Benzodiazepine drugs (such as temazepam, nitrazepam and triazolam) are most commonly prescribed, but research has shown them to be highly addictive. Withdrawal after long-term use can cause severe side effects such as cramps, vertigo, palpitations, panic attacks and seizures – not to mention rebound insomnia. Fortunately, doctors now view sleeping pills with more caution and are starting to use them only as a short-term rescue package for crisis management.

try homeopathy

The following remedies are readily available from pharmacists or health stores. Take them in the 30x potency. Choose the remedy that most closely fits your symptoms. Of course, if you can, consult a professional homeopath.

- ACONITE for acute insomnia, caused by shock, fright, bad news or grief. You may be woken by nightmares and have fear, anxiety and restlessness. You feel better for fresh air, in a cool room, and feel worse at night, in a warm, stuffy room, with heavy or stifling bedclothes.
- ARENSICUM ALBUM for waking between 1 am and 3 am because of anxiety or an overactive mind. You are sleepy during the day, but anxious at night. You are restless in bed, with anxious dreams and nightmares. You feel better for warmth, warm drinks and sleeping propped up in bed, and worse when alone, cold or drinking alcohol.
- CHAMOMILLA for irritable babies who refuse to be calmed and sleeplessness caused by teething, anger or colic. They moan while asleep and their eyes are half open. They feel better when carried or travelling in car, worse after 9 pm, after burping, in cold, windy weather and when too hot.
- IGNATIA for sleeplessness caused by shock, emotional stress or grief. You have mood swings, no thirst and your limbs jerk when falling asleep. You feel better for being distracted, worse for coffee and alcohol, cold and fresh air. You crave sweet things, but they make you feel worse.
- LACHESIS for menopausal sleep problems. You may feel suffocated or hold your breath as you go to sleep. You awaken suddenly and it may feel as if the bed is swaying. Night sweats and anxiety are common, and you may awaken feeling unwell. You feel better for fresh air, but worse for tight clothes and warm, stuffy rooms.
- NUX VOMICA for waking around 3 or 4 am feeling bright and cheerful, and not sleeping again until just before usual getting-up time. Your sleeplessness is due to irritability, overwork or working late. You are drowsy in the evening and after food, suffer nightmares, and feel better for warmth, in the evening and when left alone. You feel worse for alcohol, overeating (especially spicy foods), noise and lack of sleep.
- PULSATILLA for early waking with an overactive mind and/or recurrent thoughts. You have anxious or vivid dreams and night sweats, and throw off bedclothes feeling too hot, but then pull them back because you feel cold. You feel better for cool drinks and affection, but worse in a stuffy room.
- SEPIA for difficulty falling asleep. You wake up early feeling unrefreshed. You are exhausted and depressed by mental stress and overwork, and feel irritable and sleepy during the day. You suffer headaches, nausea and dizziness due to tiredness and night sweats. You feel better for naps, exercise and fresh air, but worse in thunderstorms or heavy weather.
- SULPHUR for awakening at the slightest noise and finding it difficult to get back to sleep. You feel hot and thrust limbs out from under the covers. You have vivid nightmares, disturbed and unrefreshing sleep, wake in the early hours and then sleep late. You are kept awake by a continuous flow of ideas. You feel better for lying on the right side, but worse for stuffy rooms and a hot bed.

other alternative approaches

- Try yoga, meditation and breathing techniques – these can all help if stress is a factor.
- Relaxation or visualization tapes can often help you relax and sleep (try the exercise in the box at right).
- Acupuncture can alleviate insomnia and has been known to cure unpleasant dreams and nightmares.
- Hypnotherapy can help you to break bad habits.
- From the nineteenth century until the twentieth, in mental asylums, anyone who was particularly agitated would be put in a neutral bath. Have your bath at just above body temperature and, if you add Epsom salts, you can create your own home flotation tank. It has a very calming, relaxing effect, but you do need to spend a good half-hour there.
- White chestnut, a Bach flower remedy, can be very helpful if you can't switch off mentally. This remedy is specifically for thoughts that go round and round, and can have quite miraculous results. Put a couple of drops in water and sip.
- Herbs can help. Basil tones and calms the nervous system – it acts as a natural tranquilliser. Try pesto soup for supper. Valerian has been used to wean people off Valium and

winding down

This is a progressive relaxation technique.

- Lie or sit with your eyes closed in a dark room. Beginning at your toes, tense your muscles, hold for a count of three, and then relax them.
- Tense and release all the major muscle groups in the body, working from your toes and fingertips up to your neck and facial muscles.
- Breathe deeply as you do this exercise. Take a deep breath in through the nose, hold for a count of five, and then exhale slowly through the mouth while repeating the word 'calm' in your mind.

other tranquillizers. Take 1–2 g of the dried root as a tea 45 minutes before bedtime. Passiflora is also a soporific; try 1–2 g of the dried herb as a tea, as for valerian.

- If you are feeling anxious, try kava kava, which gently relaxes you. Follow the dosage on the packet, but you may find you need to adjust it (some people find the herb makes them drowsy during the day). Don't take this herb for longer than 6 weeks continuously and avoid during pregnancy.
- Aromatherapy is very soothing. Use either a few drops of oil in the bath or on a tissue next to your pillow: use lavender, camomile and neroli to relieve anxiety and to calm, soothe and balance the mind and emotions. Use bergamot for insomnia linked to depression. Benzoin is useful when worries are causing sleeplessness. Clary sage is for deep relaxation (but not to be used with alcohol). Marjoram, sandalwood, juniper and ylang ylang are all warming and comforting.
- A massage (ideally before bedtime or late afternoon) will often work wonders if you are suffering insomnia. Choose from the oils listed above as needed.

solving insomnia – without sleeping pills

FIRST PRINCIPLES

- Look for any underlying psychological causes behind your insomnia and, if necessary, seek appropriate help (such as counselling, stress management etc.).
- Keep your room cool and airy.
- Avoid caffeine, alcohol and heavy meals late in the evening.
- Make sure your bed is comfortable and right for you.
- Ensure you get enough aerobic exercise, but don't exercise too close to bedtime.
- Have a warm bath and a milky drink before you go to bed.
- Avoid refined carbohydrates, sugar, alcohol, tea and coffee, carbonated drinks and excess bran.
- Avoid going to bed hungry – low levels of blood sugar in the brain can cause insomnia.
- Be careful of low-calorie diets – they affect sleep hormone levels and interfere with sleep.

how to make your bedroom a sanctuary

Your bedroom should be a sanctuary from the world – a safe, secure place in which you leave the cares of the day behind. However, it seems that retreating to bed could actually be contributing to our stress and malaise. Any number of health problems can be caused by unseen dangers in bedrooms, ranging from allergies to headaches, from memory loss to depression. Here's how to turn your bedroom into a safe, soothing sanctuary.

- First of all, clear out all the clutter (see page 92). Your bedroom should be calming to the mind, which is not possible if you have piles of work and mess around you.
- Try to avoid working in your bedroom. If this is impossible, place your desk or workspace behind a screen so that you cannot be reminded of work while you are in bed.
- If possible, keep bookshelves out of the bedroom – they distract the mind. Keep ornaments restrained as well; lots of knicknacks are distracting (and also attract dust).

safety-proof your bed

It's frightening to think we may be snuggling down in the equivalent of a chemical factory. If your bed is made from chipboard or particleboard (pressed-wood shavings held together with resin), however, it may well be emitting dangerous formaldehyde gases into the air. Formaldehyde has been estimated to cause sensitivity in around a fifth of the population: symptoms include insomnia, tiredness, coughing, skin rashes, headaches and throat and eye irritation. It is also a suspected carcinogen (causing cancer). It's not just the beds either: many sheets are coated with a formaldehyde finish to help prevent wrinkling.

In addition, your mattress and pillows could be stuffed with polyurethane foam, which not only makes a pleasant home for allergy-causing dust mites, but has also been linked with respiratory troubles and skin and eye irritations. So what do you do?

- Choose iron or untreated solid-wood bedframes. Antique (or more than 10 years old) bedframes are an alternative, as most formaldehyde gas will have gone after 10 years.
- Choose sheets made from unbleached, percale or 'green' cotton for summer. Cotton flannel sheets are ideal for winter. If you can afford it, buy natural linen sheets.
- Think about switching to a pure cotton mattress – without flame-resistant finishes. Futon mattresses are also safe. Choose cotton-filled pillows.
- If you're sensitive to dust mites, buy special mattress and pillow covers to alleviate this problem.

TOP RIGHT YOUR BEDROOM SHOULD FEEL WARM, INVITING AND SAFE. SMALL DETAILS, SUCH AS A WATER BOTTLE COVERED IN SOFT FABRIC, CAN HELP.

make your bedroom a pleasure zone

Remember that your bedroom should be a place of rest and relaxation. Keep that thought in mind as you decide what to include and what to exclude. As far as possible, keep your bedroom dedicated to sleeping – and, of course, romance.

- Make your bedroom as comfortable as possible. Heap the bed with sumptuous cushions and pillows (stuff them with herbs such as lavender and geranium for a good night's sleep).
- Choose soft, gentle lighting. Avoid harsh overhead lights and pick soft bedside lamps or uplighters instead. Candles work wonderfully in bedrooms; choose ones made with pure aromatherapy oils (rather than synthetic fragrances) for soporific scents. But do put them out before you sleep.
- Fresh flowers make your bedroom special. Choose scented flowers such as old-fashioned roses, lilies and freesias. Plant window boxes with night-scented stocks, lavender and camomile for sweet dreams throughout the summer.
- Buy an aromatherapy burner and scent your bedroom with your favourite scents – try ylang ylang, sandalwood, geranium or lavender for starters. Put a few drops of lavender oil on a tissue and tuck it by your pillow.

mind and emotions

Our minds and emotions play as large a role as our bodies in maintaining health and wellbeing. As we've already seen, our minds affect our bodies and vice versa: truly, there is no way to disengage the two. Yet few of us think to give ourselves mental and emotional workouts.

Nowadays, there is really no excuse for not 'mindworking'. Simple techniques can help you stressproof your life and reduce your levels of tension and anxiety, helping you cope with everyday life.

Meditation has been proven, in numerous studies, to be an incredible stressbuster. If you have never tried it before, now could be the time to give this incredible system a chance. If you have tried it but found it too difficult, mindfulness techniques offer many of the benefits without the hard work, while autogenic training is a tried and trusted formula with a proven track record.

In the past, psychotherapy gained a reputation for being long-winded and intrusive. Many people felt they couldn't justify the time, effort and money required for long-term analysis. Yet new forms of 'talking therapies' offer all manner of variations on the counselling theme. Whatever your disposition, time and finances, there is bound to be something for you – and it is good to talk.

Later in this vital section, we will look at work – how to escape the feeling that work is drudgery and make it really 'work' for you. We will also look at simple, effective ways to improve your everyday relationships – with friends, family, colleagues. It isn't all hard work: discovering how to give your sex life a boost has to count as good fun! Meanwhile, boosting your creativity with dance, art and music can be a real eye-opener. Many of us simply don't allow ourselves the time to explore our natural creativity, but it can bring untold benefits.

Finally, our dreams offer a wonderful way of working in the most natural way with our psyches. Dreaming gives us a direct route to the unconscious – it's the way our deep-rooted emotions, fears and anxieties can communicate with our waking, conscious mind. We'll look at ways to work with these messengers of the night.

This section will help you to pinpoint the areas in your life that need attention and offer some interesting solutions and routes to explore. I would never expect you to take everything on board, but hope that you will gain a good idea of what might work for you.

STRESS

STRESS IS A FACT OF LIFE. WHETHER IT BE SUPERHUMAN DEADLINES AT WORK, THE HASSLE OF THE MORNING COMMUTE OR BABIES WHO JUST WON'T STOP CRYING, THE CAUSES OF STRESS ARE SOMETHING FEW PEOPLE ESCAPE. YET, ACCORDING TO DOCTORS, STRESS CAN BE A SILENT, DEADLY KILLER.

Under stress, the body produces the hormones cortisol and adrenaline, which cause changes in heart rate, blood pressure and metabolism to prepare the body for fight or flight. In normal life, we can hardly run away from the office or punch the boss, so the body does not get rid of the excess hormones, resulting in unproductive, or harmful, stress.

Untreated, long-term, continual stress can manifest itself in depression, anxiety, palpitations, ulcers, headaches or irregularities in the menstrual cycle. Allergic reactions can even be triggered by stress. Fortunately, doctors are starting to become more sympathetic towards the problem. Whereas the old tendency was either to dismiss the question entirely or to fob the patient off with tranquillizers, many doctors are now suggesting self-help techniques such as deep breathing and relaxation, hypnotherapy and meditation to teach people how to deal with the condition.

Yet many people feel they have no right to admit to stress, and dismiss the whole idea. They argue that we never used to have all this stress: in the 'old days', we just got on with life and didn't waste time complaining about intangible problems such as stress. Well, it may well seem like that, but do remember that we no longer live in the world of yesteryear. We live in a world that is changing faster than ever before. There are people alive who grew up without air travel, without television, without computers and the Internet, without superstores and convenience foods. Life was totally different. Not that there weren't stressful factors – certainly poverty was far more prevalent and life could be excessively hard – but the sheer speed of life wasn't there. Nowadays, we are all jugglers – balancing home and career in ways our ancestors simply couldn't have envisaged. The causes of modern stress are myriad. But how do you deal with it?

The key to combating stress is realizing what pushes your buttons, what causes you stress. Do you feel stress just on the odd occasion or is your problem more deep-seated?

coping strategies

shock tactics for short-term stress

These tactics can be useful for occasions when you need immediate relief from tension and stress.

1 Don't fly to the coffee machine or reach for a Coke – caffeine merely exacerbates your stress responses. Drink a long, cool glass of water or fresh orange juice instead. If possible, take a walk or jog around outside in the fresh air for a few minutes. At the very least, have a good stretch – this gets the oxygen circulating around your body, gives you fresh energy and stops rising panic.

2 Vent your spleen. If it's feasible, shouting, screaming or groaning is a marvellous way of releasing stress. If you can't do it literally, pretend you're doing it – we hold a lot of tension in our jaws and the action of screaming or groaning is a great way to release that tension. Invest in a punchbag for the home or workplace, wherever, and give it a good thump or six. Exercise classes such as Boxercise and Tai-Bo can be brilliant ways of alleviating stress. So, too, can all the martial arts.

3 Practise constructive vandalism: beat the hell out of bubblewrap. It sounds acutely weird, but studies have shown that popping bubblewrap (apparently, the big bubbles work best) dispels pent-up nervous energy and muscle tension.

strategies for medium-term stress

If you regularly find yourself at boiling point, it's time to adopt some longer term self-preservation techniques.

1 Adopt a good-mood diet. Doctors have always recommended regular meals to combat stress, but now they know that the foods we eat can truly affect our mental state. Depression, anxiety, an inability to concentrate, panic attacks, mood swings, forgetfulness and lethargy – all symptoms of stress – can be triggered by sensitivity to certain foods. The anti-stress diet is high in fruit, vegetables, legumes, nuts and grains – very similar to the sensible eating plan introduced in Part 2 (pages 54–7). In particular, grapes, millet, wheat germ, brewer's yeast, oats, molasses and buckwheat are touted as anti-stress superfoods. Foods to avoid include all refined carbohydrates, sugar, tea and coffee, sweetened commercial drinks and excess bran. Ideally, the way you are already eating will reflect this. If not, go back to the earlier information on a healthy diet and consider changing your eating habits.

2 Exercise – strenuously. A good, tough aerobic workout can release stress like virtually nothing else. When the body cannot rid itself of the excess hormones generated by stress, the result is a harmful state in which the mind and body are permanently aroused. If you're stuck in this twilight zone, you need to kick yourself into a state of pure physical, rather than pure mental, arousal. You can then swing back into the state we know as rest. If you're not exercising yet, look back at pages 70–81 and try to find a system that suits you.

3 Float. Regularly floating in the equivalent of an isolation tank is one of the best stressbusters going. Not only does it relieve stress, but it also enhances creativity, decision making and problem solving (see pages 106–7).

4 Have sex! Seriously. Researchers think that orgasm may be a release mechanism for the body, in a similar manner to other body reactions such as laughing and crying. It appears that sex defuses the chemicals produced by stress in much the same way as intense exercise. During lovemaking, the muscles of the body become highly tensed; after orgasm, the body completely relaxes: it's like a very extreme version of the relaxation exercise known as progressive relaxation (see page 100), where you move through the body tensing and then relaxing each set of muscles. During sex, your body does this automatically and to a much greater degree. More information on good sex is given on pages 138–40.

long-term solutions for deep, dark stress

1 Delegate. You're not superman or superwoman – you cannot do absolutely everything and, believe it or not, the world will not fall apart if you say no occasionally. Stress-management counsellors all recommend taking stock of your life and deciding what's important and what can go by the wayside. Write a list of what causes you stress and consider if there is anything that you can drop or delegate.

2 Meditate or practise mindfulness (see pages 108–10). Try these techniques if you feel stress taking over your life.

3 Practise mental circuit training. If meditation seems too far-out and mystical, follow the example of cosmonauts and astronauts, airline pilots and Olympic athletes: learn autogenic training. Autogenic training is recognized as one of the finest stressbusters in the Western world. It gives you instant stress relief wherever and whenever you need it, lowers blood pressure and cholesterol, relieves insomnia and eases migraine. Yet it is easy to learn and, afterwards, you need only spend a few minutes a day on the exercises – or use them when you feel yourself becoming severely stressed. See pages 112–13.

4 Factor in 'time out' during each and every day. It need only be 5 minutes in the morning and afternoon, but stick to this religiously. Use it to lie down and relax, or place your palms over your eyes and lean forwards on your desk. Even short pauses can break the stress pattern.

If, after trying these strategies, you still find stress is ruling your life, seek expert help. Try your doctor first – he or she may be able to refer you to a psychologist specializing in stress management. Otherwise, the psychological associations or your natural health centre should be able to put you in touch with someone who can help.

be kind to yourself

Pampering yourself is a brilliant way to beat stress. Think about the following.

1 Set aside a small amount of time every day to do something just for you. It could be an hour's massage; half an hour soaking in the bath with soft music, candles and exotic oils; or simply quarter of an hour curled up in a chair with a novel or a magazine.

2 Make a list of the ten things that give you the most pleasure and embed them in your life on a regular basis.

3 Take frequent open-air breaks. Borrow a dog for a walk in the park; meet friends for a picnic or hike, rather than lunch or the cinema.

4 Surround yourself with people who support you. Often we see people because we feel obliged to or so we don't hurt their feelings. Think honestly about your friends – about who makes you feel relaxed and good about yourself. Choose whom you really want to see.

5 Place yourself in a calm, nourishing environment. Whether you live in a big house or one small room, make it your personal haven. A lit candle lifts a room's energy and is calming and soothing. Treat yourself to fresh flowers.

6 Acknowledge the stress in your life but don't let it rule you. Be gentle on yourself and approve of yourself – it's incredible how much stress we create for ourselves by disliking ourselves and giving ourselves a hard time.

7 Smile. Smiling automatically releases endorphins, chemical feelgood messages to the brain, so you almost instantly feel less stressed.

floating

Lying in pitch darkness and utter silence in 45 cm (18 in) of highly salted water sounds a strange way to beat stress. Yet floating is one of the very best (and certainly one of the most pleasant) ways of stressbusting.

The principle behind floating is simple. It was developed in the 1950s by Dr John C. Lilly, a medical doctor who was also trained as a psychoanalyst and a specialist in neurophysiology. Lilly was intrigued by what happened to the brain and body when all external stimuli were removed, and conducted experiments in the soundproof chambers that the navy used to train its divers. From this, he developed his own tank and continued his research. The results were far-reaching – many said far-fetched. People who floated claimed they thought and worked better, could learn more easily and concentrate better. Some said their creativity improved; others even said they felt younger and healthier. Some claimed their sex lives rocketed. Almost without exception, participants insisted they felt much more calm and relaxed.

Several centres in the USA have spent the past 20 years analysing what actually happens when we float. Their results have shown that floating can indeed do all those things – and more. The almost complete sensory deprivation caused by floating seems to agree with both our bodies and our minds.

what can floating help?

- Blood pressure and heart rate fall, while oxygen consumption improves.
- People suffering chronic pain find that they can obtain relief, often not just for the time they float, but for up to 3 days afterwards. Research suggests this can be attributed to the way floating stimulates the body to produce endorphins, natural painkillers.
- Musicians, actors and writers frequently float because floating allows the right hemisphere of the brain to operate freely, leading to much more creativity and imagination, and improving the ability to solve problems.
- Students revising for exams float while listening to tapes of their revision material – the 'superlearning' effect of floating helps them take in far more than a normal hour's study.
- Many psychotherapists find that therapy is much more effective with the client in a tank, rather than on the couch: not only do clients relax quickly, but also they find it much easier to recall past experiences and are much more responsive to positive suggestions and visualizations.
- One of floating's most successful applications is in the treatment of addictive behaviour: overeating, smoking, drug taking and alcoholism all respond remarkably well.
- Phobias often clear up quickly and anxiety states frequently disappear altogether.

what can I expect from a session?
WHERE WILL I HAVE THE TREATMENT?
You will be lying in around 45 cm (18 in) of highly salted warm water in a darkened cubicle. These cubicles range in size, although most are small.

WILL I BE CLOTHED?

You will be either naked or wearing a swimming costume.

WHAT HAPPENS?

The procedure will be explained to you and then usually you will be left by yourself. You get undressed, shower and step into the tank. You then lie with your head propped on an inflatable pillow. Some centres will play music (or you can bring your own tapes) or you can float in silence. There will be a prearranged signal when your time is coming to an end. After this, you simply get out, shower again and get dressed. Usually, you will relax for at least a short time to allow yourself to 'come to'.

WILL IT HURT?

No, it does not hurt at all. It's actually very pleasant.

WILL ANYTHING STRANGE HAPPEN?

You may spontaneously recall childhood incidents or suddenly find solutions to tricky problems. Some people report almost 'out-of-body' experiences. You may fall asleep and dream vividly.

BELOW ALTHOUGH FLOATING MAY SOUND CLAUSTROPHOBIC, IT IS SURPRISINGLY COMFORTABLE. THE CHAMBER IS NEITHER HOT NOR COLD, AND, AFTER A FEW MINUTES, YOU LET GO OF TENSION AND DEEPLY RELAX.

do-it-yourself flotation

Flotation tanks are expensive – and do take up room. If you don't have your own or can't get to a flotation centre, you can still enjoy the healing and relaxing effects of Epsom salts.

1 Dissolve about 450 g (1 lb) of Epsom salts in a warm bath, then allow yourself to soak.

2 Relax for about 20 minutes. Drink a hot herbal tea (thyme or peppermint would be ideal) while soaking to increase perspiration and replace lost fluids.

3 Be extra careful as you get out of the bath – you may feel light-headed.

4 Do not rub yourself dry. Wrap up in several large towels and go to bed, making sure you wrap your feet warmly.

5 In the morning, or when you wake, sponge yourself down with warm water. Rub your body vigorously dry.

CAUTION: avoid Epsom salts baths if you have heart trouble, if you are diabetic or if you are feeling tired or weak.

MEDITATION

Meditation, the art of stilling the mind, has been practised for literally thousands of years. It is a remarkably straightforward technique which can fit into our daily lives with the greatest of ease. In recent years, meditation has been scientifically recognized as being highly effective in treating a range of problems, both physiological and psychological.

From the Indian tradition of yoga to orthodox Christianity, from the mountains of Tibet to the plains of the USA, various forms of meditation have been used for millennia. It began as a religious practice, similar to contemplative prayer, but, over the centuries, it became obvious that meditation's benefits stretch way beyond the spiritual.

Meditation is simply a means of creating calm in the mind. Stop for a moment and become aware of your thoughts. They will probably be jumping all over the place; odd worries, concerns and images will spring into your mind. Meditation, however, helps us train the mind to filter out the unwanted chatter of everyday life, taking us to a still, peaceful place where both mind and body can fully relax. Many meditators find that just 20 minutes of meditation is as refreshing as several hours' sleep. This happens because the deep relaxation that meditation brings about puts our brains into a particularly restful frequency, akin to deep sleep.

The ancient yogis said that meditation was a powerful tonic which produced an acceleration of energy in the body, rejuvenating cells and holding back the ravages of time. For thousands of years, disciples had to take their word for it, but now science is proving that meditation really is potent medicine. Hundreds of scientific studies into meditation have produced impressive evidence. Researchers have found that meditation reduces hypertension, serum cholesterol and blood cortisol, which is related to stress in the body. It has been found effective in reducing the effects of angina, allergies, chronic headaches, diabetes and bronchial asthma, and can help lessen dependence on alcohol and cigarettes. Meditators, researchers found, see their doctors less and spend 70 per cent fewer days in hospital. Anxiety, depression and irritability all decrease, while memory improves and reaction times become faster. Meditation, it appears, gives us more stamina, a happier disposition and even helps us enjoy better relationships.

how to meditate

Meditation is simplicity itself to practise. An experienced meditator can meditate anytime, anywhere. When you first start to meditate, however, it can be very helpful to choose a place that is quiet and warm, one where you will not be disturbed. Ideally, you should be seated – in whatever position you find comfortable. That might be on the floor, cross-legged, perhaps sitting on a cushion. It could equally be sitting upright in a supportive chair with your hands

LEFT Meditation is throwing off its image of lotus-positioned yogis: while you can practise it in the classic cross-legged or lotus pose, it is just fine to sit in a straight-backed chair.

basic meditation exercise

1 Sit with an alert yet relaxed body posture, making sure you feel comfortable (either in a straight-backed chair with your feet flat on the floor or on a thick, firm cushion, 7.5–15 cm (3–6 in) off the floor).

2 Keep your back straight, aligned with your head and neck, and relax your body.

3 Start to breathe steadily and deeply. Notice your breathing and observe the breath as it flows in and out, feeling your abdomen falling and rising. Give it your full attention.

4 If you find your attention starts to wander, simply note the fact and gently bring your thoughts back to your breathing, to the rising and falling of your abdomen.

5 Always try to sit for around 20 minutes. Don't jump up immediately afterwards. Bring yourself back to normal consciousness slowly. Become aware of the room around you, gently stretch and 'come back' fully before standing up.

There are many different ways of meditating. If the exercise above does not suit you, you could try these alternatives:

Candle meditation – Sit in front of a lit candle. Focus your eyes on the flame and watch it. Keep your attention on the flame.

Counting meditation – Slowly count from one to ten in your head, keeping your attention on each number. If you feel your attention wandering (undoubtedly it will!), simply go back to one and start again.

Sound meditation – Choose a sacred sound, a favourite word or phrase. It could be something like 'ohm' or 'shalom', a vowel sound like 'aaaah' or a phrase such as 'I am at peace' or 'The Lord is my Shepherd'. Choose one that has meaning for you. Quietly repeat it – experiment to find the best way.

CAUTION: most people should have absolutely no problems meditating. but it is worth mentioning that, in isolated cases, people have experienced negative effects. The act of stilling the mind can sometimes bring repressed memories to the surface. These can prove disturbing or frightening; if this occurs, it would be wise to consult a trained counsellor or psychotherapist. There have been very rare instances of people suffering quite severe psychological disturbances. These seem confined, however, to people who have a history of psychological illness.

resting gently on your knees. It's not a good idea to meditate lying down, as you may well fall asleep.

You don't actually need any props at all for meditation, although some people find it helps to watch the flickering flame of a candle. However, for most meditation, it is usual to keep your eyes gently shut to cut out external stimuli.

The easiest way to start meditating is to join a class. There are all kinds of meditation, to suit every disposition. Many yoga classes incorporate meditation using sound or breathing to focus the mind. There are classes available in chanting – from Eastern mantras to overtone chanting (as in Gregorian chant). Some classes advocate meditating on a word or symbol reflecting your personal spiritual beliefs. But you can learn to meditate on your own if you prefer. All it takes is a quiet room, 20 minutes and a touch of self-discipline.

mindfulness

We spend our lives trying to be happy, but often end up chasing our own tails. We project happiness into the future, promising ourselves that we would be happy if only we could win the lottery, get a better job, a nicer house, less stress, more money … Yet the key to true happiness lies not in the outside world, but deep within. Mindfulness is meditation brought up to date, pared of its mystical and religious connotations and honed to slot into the most frenetic Western lifestyle. The simple idea is to give people control of their lives by teaching them how to listen to their minds and bodies, rather than be tossed around by the world outside.

Mindfulness is the brainwave of Jon Kabat-Zinn, the scientist with a PhD in molecular biology who runs the Stress Reduction Clinic at the University of Massachusetts Hospital. The clinic was started in 1979 in the light of a realization that, although the hospital could treat patients with chronic physical ailments, their problems would recur after a while. Kabat-Zinn felt sure that the answer lay in teaching patients how to kickstart their own healing powers. He spent years finding the best and most straightforward method. His choice lay in Buddhist and yogic practices, which he then adapted for Western consumption. The results have been impressive: he has found his form of meditation can help to clear psoriasis much faster, can relieve chronic pain and can also lessen

EVERY SO OFTEN, BECOME TOTALLY AWARE OF WHAT YOU ARE DOING AND HOW YOU ARE DOING IT. WHETHER YOU ARE STRETCHING (LEFT) OR SHOWERING (OPPOSITE), FOR INSTANCE, NOTICE HOW YOUR BODY FEELS AND PAY ATTENTION TO YOUR THOUGHTS AND BREATHING.

summon up deep emotions such as grief, sadness, anger and fear that have been unconsciously suppressed over the years. Equally, however, it can summon up feelings such as joy, peacefulness and happiness. Many people find that it helps them to discover what they really want from life.

making mindfulness work for you

- Make mindfulness the very first thing you do each day. Wake up a little earlier than usual and, before you even move, notice your breathing; breathe consciously for a few minutes. Feel your body lying in bed and then straighten it out and stretch. Try to think of the day ahead as an adventure, filled with possibilities. Remember, you can never really foresee what the day will hold.

- Try stopping, sitting down and becoming aware of your breathing once in a while throughout the day. It can be for 5 minutes or even 5 seconds. Just breathe and let go – allow yourself to be exactly as you are.

- Set aside a time every day to just be: 5 minutes would be fine, or 20 or 30. Sit and become aware of your breathing; every time your mind wanders, simply return to the breath.

- Use your mindfulness time to contemplate what you really want from life. Ask yourself questions: 'Who am I?', 'Where am I going?', 'If I could choose a path now, in which direction would I head?' or 'What do I truly love?' You don't have to come up with answers, just persist with the asking.

- Try getting down on the floor once a day and stretching your body mindfully, if only for a few minutes. Stay in touch with your breathing and listen to what your body has to tell you.

- Use ordinary occasions to become mindful. When you are in the shower, really feel the water on the skin, rather than losing yourself in thought. When you eat, really taste your food. Notice how you feel when the telephone rings.

- Practise kindness to yourself. As you sit and breathe, invite a sense of self-acceptance and cherishing to arise in your heart. If it starts to go away, gently bring it back. Imagine you are being held in the arms of a loving parent, completely accepted and completely loved.

feelings of anxiety and depression. He has instructed patients whose illnesses range from heart disease to ulcerative colitis, from diabetes to cancer. 'We teach these people to develop an intimacy and familiarity with their own bodies and minds,' he explains. 'This leads to a greater confidence to learn from their symptoms and to begin to self-regulate them.'

You don't need to be sick to benefit from mindfulness meditation. Its simple techniques can help everyone live life with greater certainty and self-confidence. At its most basic level, mindfulness simply involves stopping and becoming aware of the moment. The easiest way to do this is to focus on your breathing, gently letting go any stray thoughts or worries that emerge. Kabat-Zinn asks his patients to strive for 45 minutes of mindfulness a day, but stresses that even a few minutes makes a great difference. 'It can be 5 minutes or even 5 seconds,' he says, 'but for those moments, don't try to change anything at all, just breathe and let go. Give yourself permission to allow this moment to be exactly as it is and allow yourself to be exactly as you are.'

Mindfulness may be simple, but it is not necessarily easy, he warns. Not only does it require effort and discipline, but also the very act of stopping and listening can often

autogenic training

Autogenic training (AT) has been dubbed 'meditation for Westerners'. It consists of a series of simple mental exercises designed to switch off the 'fight or flight' stress mechanism of the body and allow you to deal with the traumas of the day coolly, calmly and in total control. It's the ideal choice for anyone who wants a scientifically researched, simple and straightforward, streamlined method of stress relief.

Autogenic training originated in Germany in the 1920s and was formulated by a Berlin doctor, Dr Johannes Schultz. Another German, Dr Wolfgang Luthe, took the concept of autogenic training and developed it into its current form. More than 3,000 scientific publications have run reports on the beneficial effects of autogenic training, making it one of the best-documented and most consistently researched methods of stress relief in the world.

So what does this mind workout comprise? Quite simply, it's a case of learning how to focus your attention inwards through a series of mental exercises. There are three basic components: first, the art of passive concentration (quietly allowing your mind to focus on your body); secondly, the repetition of certain phrases or words that allow you to target certain parts of the body and induce feelings such as heaviness or warmth; and, thirdly, the positioning of your body into certain standard postures to cut out the effects of the outside world. The three positions involve lying flat on the floor in a totally relaxed position (somewhat akin to a yoga asana); sitting in a chair with your hands resting on the arms of the chair or on your thighs; or perching on the edge of a hard chair in a kind of slump, with the back and head loosely drooping forwards.

It's a highly flexible system: once you've learnt it, you can practise it sitting in your office, on the train, in a parked car or lying in bed. Next, you are taught how to focus on sensations in the body, imagining warmth in the arms and legs. Breathing is calm and easy; you learn how just to watch your breathing, rather than trying to control it. Simply thinking about the exercises makes you feel calm.

The system is taught in weekly one-hour sessions over a period of 8 weeks. People generally find they become far calmer, easier and more relaxed. They sleep better, too.

Sportspeople have found that their performance improves with autogenic training. Creativity seems to shoot up and many businesspeople discover that not only do their stress levels drop, but also their communication skills and ability to make clear, effective decisions improve dramatically. The reason, apparently, is that autogenic training brings the two sides of the brain into better balance, allowing you the benefit of the intuitive, imaginative right side of the brain, which is normally switched firmly off during waking life. In addition, when you practise autogenic training, you tend to need, on average, an hour's less sleep at night.

You should always be taught this technique by a fully qualified teacher. Not only should everyone have a medical consultation before starting the course, but also it has to be emphasized that this is not a superficial cosmetic relaxation technique: it works at a very deep level. Aside from the sheer physical effects that autogenic training can have, it can also work profoundly on the mind. Sometimes, hitherto deep-hidden anxieties, feelings of anger or frustration can surface when you start the training. Occasionally, people report headaches or chest pains. It is clearly very important to have qualified advice on hand.

what can autogenic training help?

- People report feeling calmer and more able to cope through the use of autogenic training; they are in control of their lives, rather than feeling that life is controlling them.
- Autogenic training has been proven to relieve tension and insomnia significantly and to lessen anxiety.
- It lowers both blood pressure and blood cholesterol (a key measure in preventing heart attacks). In fact, its effects can be so dramatic that people with medical conditions have to be carefully monitored while they train. Some diabetics have found they needed to halve the amount of insulin they take when they practise autogenic training, and other forms of medication can also be decreased in dosage in many cases.
- It is helpful in psychosomatic disorders and has been used to help people with cancer.
- There has been early work with infertility – it was found that a significant number of women have high levels of the stress hormone prolactin, which acts as a natural contraceptive and stops conception. When they practised autogenic training, these women found the hormone levels dropped and a good

proportion conceived. The benefits continue after conception: pregnant women who practise autogenic training report that it reduces the stress of childbirth.

- Many airlines use the technique to combat insomnia and jet lag in their staff, and it is used quite widely in other industries to reduce stress and improve performance at all levels. Autogenic training has even been taught to astronauts and cosmonauts, as part of their space-training programmes.

- Some therapists are experimenting with using it to counter the effects of Parkinson's disease.

what can I expect from a session?

WHERE WILL I HAVE THE TREATMENT?

You will be sitting on an upright chair, relaxed in an easy chair or lying on a couch or the floor (the three ways of practising autogenic training).

WILL I BE CLOTHED?

Yes, you remain fully clothed throughout.

WHAT HAPPENS?

The teacher will explain clearly how autogenic training works. Each week, you will focus on a different part of the body and learn how to get in touch with it and how to gain an element of control over its degree of relaxation. For example, to begin with, you will work at inducing a feeling of heaviness and relaxation in your arms, later learning to spread this feeling to all your limbs. You will then learn to regulate your heartbeat and breathing, bring softness to the solar plexus, relax tension in your shoulders and feel coolness on your brow.

As the weeks progress, you will learn how to combine the various commands into a system of inducing complete relaxation throughout your whole body and mind.

WILL IT HURT?

No, there is nothing painful about autogenic training.

WILL ANYTHING STRANGE HAPPEN?

Some people feel slightly uncomfortable about getting in touch with their heartbeat or breathing. You may find the process stirs up old emotions.

WILL I BE GIVEN ANYTHING TO TAKE?

No, medication is not a part of the treatment.

IS THERE ANY HOMEWORK?

Yes, between lessons, you will be expected to practise autogenic training exercises several times during the day. The more you practise, the more effective the treatment.

do-it-yourself autogenic training

To get the most from autogenic training, you need to be taught the technique on individually. However, these relaxation tips are based on its philosophy.

1 Sit down and close your eyes for a moment. Practise quiet observation of yourself. Check for body tension: are you clenching any muscles? Don't try to change anything; just be aware of it. If you have an ache or pain, such as a headache, quietly observe it. Decide that it is a form of stress release that may be beneficial. Rather than seeing it as a problem, take an interest in its movements or intensity. Watch your breathing. Let it lead you wherever it wants, whether in the form of sighs, shallow panting or quiet abdominal breathing. Don't change it; just go along with it.

2 When you feel tense or upset, retreat to somewhere private, such as your bedroom or bathroom, and 'shake' it out of your system. Loosely shake each limb in turn and feel the wobble. When you catch yourself saying 'I could scream', do it. Bury your face in a pillow and let rip. No one will hear you and you'll feel much better. If you need to cry and can't, make some moaning sounds with dry sobs and you may start yourself off. Think how a child cries automatically – at times we need to relearn natural responses.

3 Have some fun. When did you last have a really good laugh? Ring up a friend and arrange a crazy night out. Go to a show: let some playtime back in your life. Above all, allow yourself to believe you're a worthwhile person, warts and all. Decide that your feelings are part of you. Express them safely and honestly (in private), then turn your thoughts to a more positive outlook.

4 Quietly become aware of your heartbeat. Don't try to alter anything: just be aware. Think of what an amazing job your heart does. You can continue this awareness by focusing on your breathing. Notice how you breathe. How far do you take the air into your lungs? Do you breathe deeply or shallowly? Make sure you take this exercise very slowly and carefully – if you feel uncomfortable at any point, stop.

TALKING THERAPIES

Not long ago, no one would ever admit to seeing a psychotherapist or psychiatrist – it was tantamount to admitting you were insane. Now the situation is different. Psychotherapy has become acceptable – in some places, even fashionable. But do you really need it? In the past, you would see a mind therapist only if you had severe depression or mania, or a phobia that prevented you from getting on with your life. Nowadays, people see therapists for a host of reasons – some serious, some seemingly quite trivial.

The whole issue of psychotherapy is complex. As we have already discovered, our minds and bodies are not separate entities. Many seemingly psychological problems disappear when you adjust your diet and start to exercise. Lots of people have found they have been 'cured' of their depression with a simple prescription of regular exercise. Equally, many others have found 'mental' problems such as anxiety or irritability miraculously disappear when they shift to a healthy wholefood diet. Shyness, lack of confidence and poor self-esteem can gradually dissipate when people start a programme of bodywork. There simply isn't any way to divide the body from the mind and emotions, as we have already discussed.

When problems seem intractable, however, you may decide that some form of psychotherapy could help you clarify your life and sort out the problems. If this is the case, trust your instincts and find yourself a therapist. Do bear in mind that psychotherapists aren't gods – they can't wave a magic wand and sort out your problems for you. They are not there to give you the answers on a plate, but to help you find the answers for yourself.

There are as many different forms of psychotherapy as there are days in the year and the mere idea of choosing a therapist can be as off-putting as ordering from a very long menu in a completely foreign language. Should you go for psychodrama or psychosynthesis? What is the difference between primal integration and primal therapy, or even primal integration and postural integration? Psychobabble? It's a veritable Tower of Babel.

All therapies do, however, have one basic aim: to make you feel better about yourself, to help you get the most out of life. It is just that they approach it in very different ways.

the four major approaches

Let's try to clarify what's on offer. As far as psychotherapy proper goes, there are basically four main approaches: psychoanalytic, behavioural, cognitive and humanistic.

- Psychoanalysis follows the patterns laid down by Sigmund Freud. He believed that our behaviour is influenced as much by the unconscious as the conscious mind and that certain instinctual urges, such as aggression or sex, are often driven into the unconscious.

- Behavioural psychotherapy teaches that the environment 'conditions' people to behave in certain ways and that we all adapt our responses to fit in with our surroundings. In other words, if you reward someone for doing well, they will continue to do well; if you reward them when they fail, they will continue to fail.

- Cognitive psychotherapy contends that we make sense of our world via specific views and assumptions that have been learnt, or conditioned, by our earlier experiences. By changing our beliefs and attitudes, it teaches, we can change our behaviour.

- Humanistic psychology is the umbrella name for a collection of approaches tied together by shared beliefs. Emphasis is put on how we as individuals experience the world and the sense we make of it, with particular regard to self-esteem, self-awareness and feelings. Generally included are the existential approaches, the work of Abraham Maslow, Thomas Szasz and Ronald Laing. It is also bound up with the human potential movement and encounter.

Most therapists will practise one of these four approaches or a combination. However, there are literally hundreds of offshoots and subschools, all with their own theories. Also, don't forget that bodywork therapies (such as Rolfing, SHEN® et al.) can have a psychotherapeutic effect, as can many of the more creative therapies that are investigated later on in this section. To make things more complicated, no two therapists will work in exactly the same way, even when ostensibly practising the same therapy.

how should you choose your therapy?

It may sound unscientific, but really the only way is to read about the different approaches to see which, if any, appeal. Next, send off for their literature to get more precise, detailed information. Many centres organize introductory events such as lectures or workshops. If you prefer the idea of one-to-one therapy, good therapists should be only too happy to give an introductory session to see if you get on with one another. Umbrella organizations such as those listed at the back of the book can also offer advice.

How much you can afford is another pertinent question. Traditional one-to-one analysis and psychotherapy demand a long-term cash commitment. Group work is cheaper and often runs in courses. Some approaches (such as Rolfing and Hellerwork) consist of a set number of sessions, so the expenditure has an end in sight. At the other end of the scale, co-counselling costs virtually nothing once you are trained.

Often there's a temptation to decide on the kind of therapy that matches your personality. Precise, strait-laced people tend to be drawn to the rigour and order of analysis; creative, expressive people may well feel happier with a more expansive therapy such as dance or primal therapy. Yet people who intellectualize too much may well derive numerous benefits from a 'non-intellectual' approach such as dance, while the expressive types lay find a more logical approach interesting and challenging.

Ask yourself in what kind of situation you would feel most comfortable. Many people find the idea of talking about their feelings in a group terrifying; for others, there is 'safety in numbers'. Some like the idea of hitting emotions head-on in confrontational therapies such as encounter or primal. Introverted people who are scared of expressing themselves may find a gentle approach such as art just what they need.

The major decision you face is group versus individual therapy. One-to-one therapy is a natural choice if you find the idea of groups frightening or have difficulty forming close relationships: ideally, you will develop a bond with your therapist and you will be able to discuss personal matters in confidence. Group therapy also has advantages. It provides feedback from varying types of people, not just the therapist. It also enables the therapist to observe you in a more natural situation, interacting with the other members of the group. Equally importantly, it gives you a chance to see that you're

not alone in your problems: realizing that other people have equally difficult lives can make you feel far less isolated.

Most people still opt for a 'talking' therapy – analysis, psychotherapy etc. – but this is by no means the only option. You can also choose therapies that don't demand you probe your psyche directly. If you haven't tried bodywork, consider this as a possibility. While bodyworkers stress that they are not psychotherapists (and will often refer you to a counsellor if very strong feelings emerge), their work can be an ideal introduction. Similarly, in creative therapies such as dance, you do not have to talk at great length about yourself.

There is a theory that, as long as you really want it to work, virtually any therapy will do the trick. It really is a case of finding an approach that interests you and that you feel would be of the most benefit to you. Some would say that you will be subconsciously drawn to the right one!

a brief a–z of therapies

This is a necessarily short introductory outline of the major types of therapy you are likely to come across.

ADLERIAN PSYCHOLOGY (INDIVIDUAL PSYCHOLOGY):
Adlerian counsellors see each person as driven by his or her self-chosen goals – often based on how we perceived life as children. Adler saw life as having three main tasks: work, relationships and society/the community. The therapy is carried out either one-to-one or in groups or workshops.

ART THERAPY: See pages 112–13.

ASTROLOGICAL COUNSELLING: Carl Jung began the interest in astrology as part of psychological healing; now there is a growing trend towards combining astrology and counselling. Basically, this holds that the planets' positions can influence the client's personality and life. Through counselling and interpretation of the client's birth chart, insights are given and advice offered. Sometimes the counsellor will draw up charts for partners or other significant people in the client's life to see where conflicts and problems occur.

BIODYNAMIC PSYCHOTHERAPY: See pages 125–6.

BIOENERGETICS OR BIOENERGETIC THERAPY: This is a body-orientated form of therapy based on the belief that the body, mind and emotions are linked – by observing tensions in the body, you can diagnose problems within the psyche. Releasing these bodily tensions means emotional issues will surface to be resolved. Therapy involves exercises to release tense muscles; great attention is given to breathing, movement and voicing. Bioenergetics can be learnt in groups or one-to-one.

CLIENT-CENTRED THERAPY: Developed by Carl Rogers, this is sometimes known as Rogerian counselling. Practised either one-to-one or in groups, it has at its core a belief that the client's view of the world is always valid: the therapist will not try to interpret the clients' behaviour or change the way they see themselves. This is a gentle therapy in which the therapist listens with empathy to the client and then seeks to reflect the thoughts and feelings expressed.

CO-COUNSELLING: This is a form of do-it-yourself counselling in which two non-professionals counsel one another. One takes on the role of client; the other becomes the therapist. After an agreed length of time, they switch places. Training courses in co-counselling last about 40 hours. You can then join a network which puts you in touch with prospective partners.

COUNSELLING: This term is widely used for a huge variety of approaches. Counselling can simply involve quiet listening, advice-giving or comforting, or it may mean psychotherapy.

COUPLE THERAPY: Offered to all couples, regardless of marital status or sexual orientation, couple therapy attempts to resolve conflict within a relationship. Both partners are required to attend so that both sides of the problem can be observed. Many people find it a very useful way to talk about their feelings and hurts without the process degenerating into argument. If there are children, they are often involved, too.

DANCE THERAPY: See pages 148–50.

DRAMA THERAPY: Often used for the physically and mentally challenged and for children with severe behavioural problems, drama therapy is another of the creative therapies that offers a safe environment for exploring potentially difficult emotions.

DREAM THERAPY: See pages 145–7.

EYE MOVEMENT DESENSITIZATION AND REPROCESSING (EMDR): This relatively new therapy from the USA appears to be having swift and profound effects in treating phobias and post-traumatic stress. The therapist flicks a finger back and forth in front of the patient's eyes; the patient follows the movement and brings to mind what is causing the problem.

EXISTENTIAL PSYCHOTHERAPY: Quite unlike most other psychotherapies, this is as much about digesting existential philosophy as it is about coming to terms with oneself. Existentialism looks at the 'big' questions of life: death, alienation, suffering, responsibility. Not an easy approach, it appeals to those interested in the philosophy and writings of Friedrich Nietzsche, Jean-Paul Sartre, Martin Heidegger et al.

FAMILY THERAPY: Often used when a child in a family has problems, the therapy focuses not on the individual, but the family as a whole. The entire family is included in therapy and one or two therapists assist. It is mostly carried out within child guidance units, psychiatric departments and social services.

FLOWER REMEDY THERAPY: Highly diluted essences of flowers are believed to influence your mood and emotional state. Therapists will ask questions to determine the client's predominant state and then prescribe different essences. Flower remedies are usually used with other forms of therapy – frequently counselling or hypnosis. See pages 236–9.

GESTALT: Dissatisfied with Freudian psychoanalysis, Fritz and Laura Perls evolved Gestalt therapy in the 1960s. The focus shifted from the verbal to the non-verbal, with more attention being paid to how people behave than what they say. Gestalt therapy is usually conducted in groups.

GROUP-ORIENTATED PSYCHOTHERAPY: This umbrella term covers therapy in which working within a group framework is considered useful and therapeutic. Rather than being simply therapy carried out in a group, the group becomes a key part of the therapy. Often the therapist stays in the background. The group may simply free-associate or members may focus on what is happening in their lives at that moment.

HYPNOTHERAPY: This involves the therapist leading the client into a state of deep relaxation. From here, the therapist may simply offer positive statements to the subconscious mind or involve the client in a more dynamic experience, exploring feelings, re-enacting situations or going back into dreams to discover their messages. The client is always aware of what is going on and never loses control.

JUNGIAN PSYCHOTHERAPY (ANALYSIS): Carl Jung widened Freud's idea of the unconscious, believing that, apart from the individual unconscious, we all share a 'collective unconscious', a vast pool of shared knowledge and feelings. Jung believed we need to integrate our conscious and unconscious minds, and worked with dreams, fantasies and symbols. Central themes include the exploration of archetypes (the shadow, the wise person etc.); the relationship between our masculine and feminine sides (the animus and anima); and the power of myth. Jungian analysis is conducted one-to-one, with the analyst and client sitting upright facing each other. There is less focus on the past, more on the present and future.

KLEINIAN PSYCHOTHERAPY (ANALYSIS): Following the work of Freud, Melanie Klein focused on the importance of the early years of life. Her central theory was that, as babies, we feel conflicting emotions of love and hate, primarily towards our mothers. These conflicts remain unresolved and create tension in later life. Kleinian analysts encourage clients to express good *and* bad feelings, transferring them from the mother to the analyst, so that they can be explored and understood.

MEN'S THERAPY: A response to women's therapy, men's groups have suffered a certain amount of ridicule (with images of naked men beating their chests and banging drums in the woods). However, the rationale is as valid as that for all-women groups: sometimes it can be much easier to discuss painful issues within same-sex groups. Men's therapy is always conducted in groups, although each group may have a different emphasis. Some focus specifically on the issue of masculinity, while others discuss more general concerns.

MUSIC THERAPY: Music can easily change or affect mood and so has wide applications in therapy. It is often used to release feelings and to help those with physical or mental disabilities.

NEURO-LINGUISTIC PROGRAMMING (NLP): See pages 121–3.

OPEN ENCOUNTER (ENCOUNTER): This group therapy encourages people to forget about what is and isn't 'done' in 'polite society' and to explore their true feelings. It has no rigid format: the group will deal with whatever emotions or impulses arise. Sometimes this involves truthful speaking; at others, physical activity such as kicking or beating a cushion.

PERSONAL CONSTRUCT THERAPY: This therapy has some novel attributes. It usually starts with self-characterization – the client writing a biography of himself or herself as if it had been written by a good friend. From this, the analyst evaluates the client's self-image then creates a fictional character who views the world in a totally different way from the client. The client is then asked to 'be' this character for a week.

PRIMAL INTEGRATION: This is a quite separate entity from primal therapy. Practitioners do not see it as a therapy as such, but rather as a growth process, a journey of self-development which incorporates elements of a spiritual path. Like most forms of therapy, the aim is integration, becoming whole. Practitioners use a variety of methods, including bodywork and investigating feelings, dreams and fantasies.

PRIMAL THERAPY: Arthur Janov held that unhappiness and neurosis are caused by deep-seated childhood pain. Primal therapists believe that this can be exorcised by reliving it. The focus is on the client's hurt and any incidents of abuse or neglect. Clients are encouraged to release their pain in any way they like – curling up and crying, or screaming and punching cushions. The therapist acts as support. It is quite intense: for 3 weeks, the client is seen every day for up to 3 hours. A more relaxed programme is then followed for a year.

PSYCHOANALYSIS: Founded by Sigmund Freud, this is the archetypal image of therapy à la Woody Allen: the highly charged relationship with the 'shrink', the couch, the transference of emotions connected with figures from your life on to the analyst, the concept of resistance (withholding key feelings). Very formal and highly structured, it requires a huge investment of time, effort and money. The analysand or patient sees the analyst four or five times a week for several years. The patient lies on a couch, with the analyst sitting behind or out of direct eye contact, and is asked simply to talk or free-associate, saying whatever comes to mind.

PSYCHOANALYTIC PSYCHOTHERAPY: This is a watered-down, more practical version of full-scale analysis which still follows Freud's principles. Sessions tend to be once or twice a week and the patient and analyst generally sit facing each other.

PSYCHODRAMA: If you feel as if you live life like an actor on a stage, psychodrama may well appeal. Its creator, Jacob Moreno, felt that 'all the world's a stage'; psychodrama is group psychotherapy combined with theatre. The 'director' (therapist) encourages the 'protagonist' to re-enact scenes from his or her life, while other members of the group take on the supporting roles. Ideally, fresh insights will occur and a form of catharsis follows.

PSYCHOSYNTHESIS: Roberto Assagioli trained in Freudian analysis, but focused on the 'higher' unconscious – the source of inspiration, joy and peak experiences. He sought to blend the concepts of Western psychology and Eastern mysticism. Psychosynthesis aims to draw together all the different roles we play, all the warring, contradictory parts of the psyche. A variety of techniques is used, from painting and drawing to guided imagery and engaging in inner dialogues with different parts of your self.

SOLUTION THERAPY (SOLUTION-FOCUSED OR BRIEF THERAPY): See page 120.

TRANSACTIONAL ANALYSIS: A Canadian psychotherapist, Eric Berne developed transactional analysis and, in 1964, wrote the bestselling book *Games People Play*. His theory is that we live our lives according to scripts that originate in childhood, but which affect our whole lives. Examples would be 'Be Perfect', in which we always feel we should do better, or 'Hurry Up', where we always feel we are running out of time. By learning to identify and understand our hardwired scripts, we can understand and change our behaviour. Initial sessions involve learning the theory and the language of transactional analysis. It is usually conducted in groups.

TRANSPERSONAL PSYCHOTHERAPY: This is a branch of psychotherapy that emphasizes the spiritual and the search for meaning in life. The key concept is the idea of self or the soul, which seeks to unite itself both to its own different aspects of personality and to Jung's idea of the collective unconscious. Sessions are either conducted on a one-to-one basis or, quite often, in groups or workshops. Guided imagery, meditation, dream work, drawing and painting are often used and therapists frequently focus on unblocking the chakras, the Eastern energy centres of the body.

WOMEN'S THERAPY (FEMINIST THERAPY): This is based on the recognition that women have three common issues: autonomy or power, self-nurturing and anger. In women's therapy, women are encouraged to direct anger, to confront the restrictions placed on them and to learn to look after themselves, as well as others. It often incorporates elements of Gestalt, transactional analysis and client-centred therapy.

self-counselling – the basic plan

This is a very condensed version of an outline for self-counselling. You will need to find a time and place where you won't be disturbed. Allow yourself a clear, uninterrupted hour for each session. Take a break of a week between each session.

SESSION ONE Focus on what you want to achieve.

- First, write down the changes you want to make – whatever comes into your mind. If it feels more comfortable, speak them into a tape recorder before copying them onto paper.
- Now go over your account and notice the kind of language you have used. Change negative phrases to positive ones – i.e. rather than say 'I want to stop smoking', phrase it as 'I will become a non-smoker.' 'I won't be so unassertive' could be 'I will stand up for my rights.' Make sure your changes are clear and measurable – make your goals very precise.
- Check your goal doesn't depend on other people changing. You can never guarantee a change in other people – the only person over whom you have that kind of control is yourself.
- Do you know anyone who has achieved what you want? He or she could give valuable advice or provide a good example.
- Think about how you will actually be different when you have achieved your desired change. Define in detail what you and others will be able to see and hear you doing differently. Be very specific. Check that the changes you are contemplating are safe for you. Think through the results of any changes you want to make. If you became more assertive with your employer, for example, you might lose your job. Are you ready and willing to risk making the changes you want? Is the change really for you? Make sure you are seeking to change for your own benefit.
- Return to your original statement. You may want to rewrite it in the light of your answers to the previous questions.

SESSION TWO Look at what is happening in your life now.

- What is actually happening to me now? (Be specific – keep to what is happening, rather than what you think may be happening.) What is not happening? What are other people doing or not doing? Now ask what you are thinking. It is important to distinguish between thought, feeling and action. What are you feeling? What are you doing? What would you prefer to be happening? What would you be doing if you were succeeding? What are you willing to do to start? How is that

different from what you are actually doing? What is the worst thing that could happen? How might you sabotage yourself?
- Listen to the language that you have used. Is it vague? Make it precise. Are your problems based on fact or on how you perceive the situation? Be honest with yourself.

SESSION THREE Write your life script. This may well help you gain insight into your behaviour and feelings in the present.

- What is your earliest memory? Is there a family story about your birth? How were you named? Describe your parents. Describe yourself. What was your parents' advice to you? What did they want you to be? What made them angry with you? How did they express their anger? What do you like most, and least, about yourself? What do you wish your parents had done differently? If, by magic, you could change anything about yourself, for what would you wish? What do you want most out of life? Do you think of yourself as a winner or a loser? What will it say on your tombstone?
- Can you see any patterns emerging? Are there any attitudes or beliefs from the past that are affecting you in the present? The script can give important clues – you may be able to see clear connections between your present ways of thinking, feeling and behaving, and the early decisions you made.

SESSION FOUR Resolving differences. At this stage, there is a variety of different techniques and approaches you can use to help you leave the past behind and move forwards to make the changes you desire. Sometimes just recognizing where thoughts and beliefs come from can provide a breakthrough, but often you will need to do more work. One suggestion is to use the 'empty chair' of Gestalt therapy. This is very useful if the earlier sessions have shown that you have 'unfinished business' with anyone in your life (either alive or dead).

- Set up your room so you are sitting opposite an empty chair or floor cushion. Imagine the person to whom you want to speak is sitting in the chair. Voice what you want him or her to hear.
- When you have finished having your say, move to the empty chair yourself and pretend you are the other person. Let him or her speak through you – the response may be very predictable or you may be surprised by what you say or feel.
- Let the conversation continue – switching chairs as necessary – until you are satisfied that you have said all you wish. Now sit quietly and reflect on any insights you have gained.

SWIFT SOLUTIONS

WHILE MANY OF THE 'TALKING THERAPIES' CAN DEMAND A LONG COMMITMENT, A NEW BREED OF PSYCHOTHERAPIES AIMS TO GIVE A QUICK YET EFFECTIVE FIX. THESE STRATEGIES CAN BE SURPRISINGLY POWERFUL AND ARE CERTAINLY WORTH A TRY IF YOU FEEL THAT STANDARD PSYCHOTHERAPY IS NOT FOR YOU.

solution therapy

Traditional therapies usually take months (and sometimes years) to see results, but brief therapy, or solution-focused therapy (to give it its full name), will often dispatch people after one or two sessions. It may seem incredible, yet the changes that can occur following that short spell can appear truly miraculous, with effects that can last forever.

The new wonder therapy was developed in the USA by researcher Steve De Shazer. He discovered that, despite the common concept of psychotherapy needing to be a long-term process, in actual fact people attended an average of only seven sessions. If they could get what they needed so quickly, he reasoned, surely a new model could be developed that expected and facilitated rapid results. The result was initially called brief therapy, but many now prefer the title solution-focused therapy, or simply solution therapy.

While standard therapists and analysts will spend hours looking at your 'problem', solution therapists are not really interested in how your life isn't working. Instead of focusing on the problem, solution therapists look at the time when the problem does not exist. Say you have a panic attack that lasts for an hour. Normal therapy would probably focus on that one hour, whereas solution therapists are interested in the 23 hours of the day when the panic attack didn't happen. In other words, you have strategies that stop you from having panic attacks all day long and the solution therapist would want to find out what they were and how you could continue the strategies to cover that one stray hour.

Central to solution therapy is the idea that, even before we come to therapy, we have methods in place for coping with our problems. The therapist is not there to instruct, but to encourage us to believe in our innate problem-solving facility.

what can solution therapy help?

- It has proved successful for anxiety problems, those who suffer depression and even for people with severe addictions.
- Survivors of abuse frequently benefit and the model is also of immense help in family and couple therapy.
- Solution therapy could help you stop smoking or lose weight.
- This therapy is about crisis resolution, rather than personal growth. It's good for people who want a quick resolution, but not those who want to explore feelings or look into the past.

what can I expect from a session?

WHERE WILL I HAVE THE SESSION?

You will be sitting in a room with (usually) two or more therapists.

WILL I BE CLOTHED?

Yes, you will be fully clothed.

WHAT HAPPENS?

First, therapists will ask clients why they have come and how they would like them to help. Then, as early as possible, they ask what they call the 'miracle question': 'If you woke up one day and your life was exactly how you wanted it to be, how would you know?' Naturally, most people's first response is something like 'I would feel better', 'I would have won the lottery' or 'My husband would still be alive' – seemingly impossible daydreams, foolish wish fulfilment. However, out of these dreams, the therapists may uncover perfectly realistic goals. By careful questioning, the team will find out precisely what winning the lottery, for example, may mean. The questioning continues to build up a solid map of behavioural changes – some large, some very small. It's the small and insignificant that solution therapists suggest form the first steps of change. When you achieve them, you will have the motivation and encouragement to take the next step, and the next, and so on.

WILL IT HURT?

No, this is not a painful therapy – either physically or emotionally.

WILL ANYTHING STRANGE HAPPEN?

No, solution therapy is very down-to-earth and practical.

WILL I BE GIVEN ANYTHING TO TAKE?

No, medication is not part of the treatment.

IS THERE ANY HOMEWORK?

Yes, you will be asked to make initially very small shifts in your life.

nlp – the master communicator

What makes one person succeed where another fails? How is it that some people can debate metaphysics in a foreign language, while the rest of us still stumble over 'Two beers, please'? Are we simply genetically wired to be either superachievers or also-rans, or can we change the program? The advocates of neuro-linguistic programming (NLP) insist that there's a swift, scientific, precise technique that will stop you languishing in the mire of mediocrity – we can, they insist, all become superpeople. If one person in the world can do it, according to NLP, so can you – you just need to learn precisely how they do it and then copy them. This is a technique called 'modelling', which can, if properly applied, give us a precise map to achieve the same excellence as the person we model.

NLP started in the 1970s in California, when Richard Bandler (a mathematician and Gestalt therapist) and John Grinder (a professor of linguistics) began to question exactly what made some people brilliant in their work, while others remained mediocre. They selected three acknowledged experts in the field of therapy and 'modelled' them, finding out exactly how they worked, how they thought, how they perceived, how they moved and spoke, what minute processes took place and precisely the sequence in which they happened. Their findings led to NLP: not really a therapy, more a precise tool for understanding human communication and improving it – a way of working out what causes excellence and how we can each achieve it. Bandler and Grinder swiftly went on to model athletes, dancers, teachers, businesspeople, even politicians. The results were so impressive that they put their findings together and called this system for analysing excellence NLP. It's like taking an advanced driving course – but for living.

The first lesson is that, in order to communicate effectively with someone, you have to know which 'mode' they are in. We have three modes of functioning – visual, auditory and kinaesthetic (feeling) – and you can usually tell which mode a person is using at any given time by their body posture, the speed of their speech, their breathing and even the words they use (see page 122). NLP teaches that much of our misunderstanding arises when people communicate in different modes – when a person in visual mode tries to communicate with someone in an auditory state, for example. Good communicators 'match' the person they are talking to, so if they are talking to a 'visual' person, they, too, will go into visual mode, speaking rapidly, breathing quite high in the chest and using 'visual' words and phrases such as 'I look at it this way', 'I see what you mean' or 'What's the overall picture?' Suddenly you are speaking the same language.

Following on from this is rapport building, in which, by subtly mirroring the person we are talking to (adopting a similar posture/speaking at the same speed/ breathing in synchronization), we can almost instantly put someone at ease.

Basically, it is all about learning how brains work and how different people's brains work in different ways. Simple techniques can prove highly effective in any

mapping miracles – solution therapy

Solution therapy can be ideal when you want simply to resolve a problem or crisis, rather than delve deeply into your psyche for weeks on end. If you are in need of crisis resolution, try asking the following questions.

1 If you woke up and all your problems and worries had disappeared, how would you know a miracle had happened?

2 How would you behave differently? (Be as precise as possible.)

3 How would your family and friends behave differently?

4 How do you think your family and friends would know a miracle had happened? How would they see the differences in you and your behaviour?

5 Are there parts of the miracle that are already happening in your life?

6 How have you made these things happen? Is it possible for you to make more of them happen?

7 What elements of your life at present would you like to continue?

8 On a scale of nought to ten, where nought is the worst your life has been and ten is the day after the miracle, where are you now?

9 If you are on, say, four, how would you get to five? What would you be doing differently?

10 How would your family know you had moved up one point?

situation, from soothing the boss or getting through to the kids, to communicating honestly with your partner.

Understanding how brains work is also fundamental to the ability to model. In order to copy someone exactly, it's not enough merely to mimic their physical moves, you have to get inside their head, to find out the processes behind an action. If, say, you wanted to model an expert skier, you might first watch his or her technique very carefully. You might move your body in the same motions as you watch, until they feel like a part of you. Next, you would make an internal picture of an expert skiing, then conjure up a disassociated image of yourself skiing – like watching a film of yourself modelling the other person as precisely as possible. Next, you would step inside that picture and experience how it would feel to perform the same action precisely the way the expert athlete did. You would repeat this as often as it would take for you to feel completely comfortable doing it. This strategy, say NLP practitioners, could give you the specific neurological strategy that could help you perform at optimum levels. Then you would try it in the real world.

are you visual, auditory or kinaesthetic?

NLP teaches that we each favour a specific 'pathway' or mode of perceiving the world – visual, auditory or kinaesthetic. But how can you tell?

- Have someone ask you a question that requires you to recollect something in the past, e.g. what did you do last weekend? If, when you answer, you look up to the other person's right, you are predominantly visual. If your eyes slide from the left to the right of their face, you are mainly auditory. If you look down and to the left then right before answering, you are working in a kinaesthetic pathway.
- How do you best learn a new subject? Do you memorize a page of information (visual), repeat facts out loud (auditory) or write down what you are learning (kinaesthetic)?
- What kinds of words do you use to express yourself? Do you talk in terms of seeing ('I see what you mean', 'The picture is clear', 'Look at me when I'm talking to you'): all primarily visual. Or do you talk in terms of hearing ('I hear what you're saying', 'I'd like to sound them out', 'Listen to me when I'm talking to you'): auditory. Or do you express yourself in terms of feeling ('I feel it in my bones', 'It really touched me', 'Can't you feel the difference?'): kinaesthetic.

swish technique – turning past failure into present success

The swish technique from NLP offers a swift way to change negative patterns of behaviour. It is often used to help people overcome fears and phobias – such as of public speaking or flying – or handle difficult situations better – so they can prevent habitual arguments, cope with a difficult boss, become more assertive.

1 Identify the behaviour you want to change. Close your eyes and decide on a cue picture. This is what you might see, hear and feel just before you start the behaviour that you want to change. So, for example, it might be you feeling and looking small and unimportant.

2 Now create a picture of how you would like to look and feel and sound instead – if you were to be in your ideal, confident, energized state. Make the picture really clear and really powerful. You should feel a little shiver of energy when the picture's just right.

3 Now imagine your unpleasant cue picture is on a huge movie screen. It's big, clear and in full colour. It should be pretty unpleasant to see.

4 Now place the picture of the new confident you on the screen, down in the bottom left-hand corner. Make this picture small and in black and white.

5 Now you can start 'swishing'. Imagine the small positive picture zooming up to fill the whole screen, completely obliterating the negative picture. As the picture expands, it becomes bright, multicoloured and clear. In contrast, the negative picture shrinks away into a corner, gradually becoming small and dark.

6 Open your eyes, stamp your feet and shake your arms out. Clear your mind of the picture.

7 Now repeat the procedure (steps 4 and 5) as quickly as possible, stopping and blanking the screen in your mind's eye between each swish.

You can boost your confidence by swishing just before you have to go into any difficult situation. The difference it makes should be enormous.

- If you're assessing children, there are other ways of gauging which mode they use. When they are angry, do they look you in the eye with defiance (visual), scream and shout (auditory), or stamp their feet or throw themselves to the ground (kinaesthetic)? What would they notice first on a walk in the park? Other children, the birds and animals around (visual); the sound of music playing, dogs barking or people shouting (auditory), or the wind, the rain, the cold or the heat (kinaesthetic)?

This all sounds very interesting in theory, but what help is it practically? Well, if you decided to learn a new language, it would be helpful to choose a method that allowed you to work in your most comfortable pathway. A series of audio tapes would not be enough for a kinaesthetic person, while an auditory person would not do so well with a simple textbook. A visual person will always manage better with clear text and diagrams, an auditory person through spoken words and a kinaesthetic with practical examples. In an ideal learning situation, all three pathways will be used.

NLP can also help you to understand people and to communicate better. People find that they get on much better with their boss or a difficult member of their family if they can talk the same language, picking up on which pathway the person works in and shifting their language to match that person. It's subtle but highly effective and, if you are interested in good communication, well worth investigating in greater depth.

timeline therapy

Timeline is a precise, swift technique which developed out of NLP. By changing your relationship with time, you can transform your whole life. Time line therapy teaches that the only difference between people who just dream and the people who live their dreams is that the people who live their dreams do something different with their thinking. At a deep, subconscious level, they truly believe things will happen.

make time work for you

You may find it easier to practise these exercises with a partner guiding you. Sit down comfortably in a chair and relax. Some people may find it easier to close their eyes.

FINDING YOUR TIME LINE: Have someone give you the following prompts. As you think about the time in question, you will find you access the information in a particular place in your mind's eye (i.e. up to the left, down to the right, over to the side). If you find it hard to work out where you are holding time, have your partner observe your body language. You may indicate where the thought is held by a movement of the hand, the eyes or your head.

- Think of something you might be doing in 3 months.
- Think of something you might be doing in 3 years.
- Think of where you might be 10 years down the line.
- Think of something that happened last week.
- Think of something that happened 6 months ago.
- Think of something that happened 5 years ago.

Pay attention to where your thoughts are. See if you can draw a line between them. It might go from side to side, forwards and backwards, or be quite convoluted. This is your time line. Become used to it – imagine where events lie on it.

make your dreams come true

Think about something you really want to happen. Now make your dream as specific as you can.

- Ask yourself: 'What is the last thing that has to happen for me to know that I have achieved my dream?' What would you need to see, to hear, to feel, to know you've achieved it?
- Really imagine that scene. See it in clear detail. Make it just right, as perfect as it can be, as real as it can be.
- Step slightly out of the picture, but keep it clearly in your mind's eye. The emotional intensity will feel slightly less, but that's fine. Freeze-frame the picture, like a snapshot.
- Rise up way above your time line, imagining it stretching out below. Hold the picture with you and imagine you're floating out above the future. Now let the picture go; let it float down onto the time line, onto the right time for your dream to become reality. Watch it settle on the line and watch all the events between then and now realigning themselves to support your outcome.
- When you are ready, float back to the present.

You have now set your subconscious to 'create' the future for you. But remember you might still have to put in some effect. Time line will create the opportunities – you have to take them.

BODYWORK FOR EMOTIONAL BALANCE

MIGHT THE MASSAGE TABLE TAKE OVER FROM THE PSYCHOANALYST'S COUCH? TRADITIONALLY, IF YOU WANTED TO WORK ON YOUR EMOTIONS, YOU TURNED TO THE TALKING THERAPIES. MANY PEOPLE ARE NOW FINDING, HOWEVER, THAT, BY WORKING WITH THE BODY, THEY ARE OBTAINING SWIFTER, MORE EFFECTIVE RELEASE FROM EMOTIONAL DISTRESS AND UNRESOLVED TRAUMA.

The joy of bodywork as therapy is that you don't need to confess your darkest secrets: you don't even need to know your darkest secrets. Bodyworkers believe that our bodies know the truth and the truth can be stretched, squeezed or simply touched out of us. It was biochemist Dr Ida Rolf who, in the mid-twentieth century, discovered that manipulating the fascia, the connective tissue of the body, could bring about profound changes to both body and emotions (see Rolfing, pages 205–6). By manipulating and stretching the fascia back to their original position, she could reprogram neurological pathways and return her patient to alignment and, eventually, physical comfort. Rolf also found that, when she changed the body on a physiological level, her patients changed on a mental and emotional level as well.

Virtually every bodywork practitioner – from acupuncturists to zero balancers, from osteopaths to reflexologists – affirms that touch (whether deep or light) seems to draw psychological material from the body. Bodyworkers are convinced that their therapies will become a recognized part of healing emotions, as well as straightening bodies. Many 'somatic' therapists work with the breath, asking clients to lie down and deepen their respiration until it stirs up feelings and memories. Others encourage their clients to use movement to express how they feel or perhaps sound, asking clients to make sounds, rather than coherent speech. Yet more work directly with the body, using touch and manipulation to trigger change.

OPPOSITE EXPERIENCE SHOWS US THAT VARIOUS FORMS OF TOUCH, SUCH AS ROLFING OR OSTEOPATHY, SEEM TO BRING TO THE SURFACE OLD MEMORIES, HURTS AND BURIED EMOTIONS HELD IN THE MUSCLES.

biodynamic therapy

As children, we are just ourselves: spontaneous, exuberant, intuitive, really 'alive'. As we get older, however, we gradually learn to hide our feelings from the world for fear of ridicule or disapproval. Biodynamic therapy aims to put you back in touch with your true, uninhibited personality. Many people find that they gain the courage to take up new challenges, to take calculated risks, to dare to change their lives.

This unique therapy employs a variety of techniques. One week you could find yourself sitting in a chair talking about your life, as in regular psychotherapy. The next session you may end up pummelling your fists into a mattress on the floor. Then again, you are equally likely to spend an hour on a massage couch with your therapist giving you a deep bodywork massage. The massage is perhaps the most famous (or infamous) part of biodynamic therapy – it is singular in that the therapist gauges the effect of the bodywork by listening intently to your stomach through an anaethescope. The rumblings of the digestive system, they believe, give a clear indication of whether or not you are releasing emotional blocks.

Biodynamic therapy was developed more than 30 years ago by Norwegian-born Gerda Boyesen. A psychologist and physiotherapist, she realized that she could get even better results in her psychotherapy by working on the body as well as the mind. She found, like many other bodyworkers, that emotions were held in the body and that, through certain kinds of deep massage, they could be released. But she also noticed that the greatest release came when the gut started rumbling. She listened, experimented and finally developed what she called *psycho-peristalsis*, a finely tuned technique which encourages the body literally to 'digest' emotional stress through deep, powerful massage.

soothing the emotions

Acupressure (using the pressure of your fingers or thumbs to stimulate acupuncture points) can have quite impressive results on the emotions. Try the following:

If you're feeling irritable – Place your fingers under your ears, behind the lobes. Tilt your head back slightly and you should find a small hollow just beneath the bony ridge of the skull. Press firmly on the points behind both ears with a deep, steady touch – it should be tender, but not too painful. Hold for about 30 seconds. These points will also help clear your head if you are feeling confused and tired, or help to stave off headaches.

For repressed emotions – If you are holding onto a negative emotion, try using your thumbs to work in from your armpits towards the bottom edge of your collarbone – you will probably find two quite tender spots. Apply enough pressure to feel a certain amount of pain, and hold the points for a few moments. Keep breathing while you press, imagining the tension and emotions disappearing every time you breathe out.

To help you become calm – Find the point that lies in the 'web' between the thumb and first finger of your left hand. It will probably be quite tender. Breathe deeply while you apply firm, even pressure for a few moments. You can do this unnoticed in public when you feel your nerves becoming taut.

what can biodynamic therapy help?

- A large variety of problems respond well to biodynamic therapy.
- The massage can clear headaches and migraine.
- It has a good success rate with shyness, depression and anxiety, and also with panic attacks and addictions.
- Many people try this therapy because they simply feel there has to be more to life and want to explore their potential.

what can I expect from a session?

WHERE WILL I HAVE THE TREATMENT?
You will be sitting in a chair in the therapist's room, or lying on a couch or on a mattress on the floor.

WILL I BE CLOTHED?
Yes, you remain fully clothed for all parts of the therapy.

WHAT HAPPENS?
The therapist generally suggests what form each session takes – talking, massage or vegetotherapy. If you have vegetotherapy, you

ABOVE TRY PRETENDING YOU'RE SCREAMING TO SOOTHE STRESS. STRETCH YOUR MOUTH WIDE, TENSE YOUR FACE AND NECK MUSCLES, AND CLENCH YOUR FISTS. THEN ALLOW YOURSELF TO RELAX TOTALLY.

will lie on your back on a large mattress and allow your body to move in whatever way it wishes, perhaps clenching your fists or stretching or rolling. The therapist will usually ask you to focus on the feelings in your body and possibly exaggerate the movement.

WILL IT HURT?
The massage can feel quite tender or painful in places.

WILL ANYTHING STRANGE HAPPEN?
The therapist will listen to the rumblings of your gut with an anaethescope during massage.

WILL I BE GIVEN ANYTHING TO TAKE?
No, medication is not part of the therapy.

IS THERE ANY HOMEWORK?
No, you will not usually be given any homework.

SHEN®

SHEN® is a scientifically researched form of energy healing which aims to release emotions trapped in the body, giving blessed freedom from pain and tension, and a greater sense of confidence and ease into the bargain. It's one of the most effective ways of releasing repressed and painful emotions.

At first sight it seems like 'spiritual' healing or techniques such as reiki or jin shin jyutsu. The difference is that SHEN is not mystical or God-given; it is precise and scientific, a happy marriage between the often inscrutable world of ancient natural healing and highly sceptical modern science.

SHEN was developed by Richard Pavek, an American scientist whose original disciplines were aeronautics, electronics and chemistry. Energy healing, he realized, really did work in many cases, but he was astonished to find that the healers could not explain how or why their techniques worked. Pavek regretted this a 'deplorable lack of science' and set out to put healing on a solid scientific basis.

Working on the laws of physics that state that magnetic and electrostatic fields move in a circular motion, Pavek observed that all living things have an energy field, which he called the *biofield*. This biofield flows in certain set patterns. He then became fascinated by the field of psychosomatic illness, disorders that have quite physiological symptoms, but which cannot be traced to any mechanical, neurological or biochemical dysfunction in the body. He noticed that, while orthodox medicine and psychological approaches could do little for such patients, bodyworkers (whether masseurs or deep-tissue or bone manipulators) seemed to have the most success. They often found that they were releasing suppressed emotions along with tense muscles or trapped nerves. Pavek realized that only by releasing the energetic blockage with a clear flow of bioforce energy can the old hurt be released and the physical and emotional effects relieved.

what can SHEN® help?

- SHEN® has consistently good results with the kinds of conditions that frequently won't respond to either medical or psychiatric care, and so-called psychosomatic illnesses.
- Any physical condition that has an emotional basis usually responds well, including chronic pain, premenstrual syndrome (PMS), irritable bowel syndrome, bulimia, anorexia and other eating disorders.
- Anxiety attacks and phobias can be helped.
- It is superb for post-traumatic stress syndrome.
- Many cases of migraine respond. One of the most startling claims for SHEN is that it can halt around 60 per cent of migraines in the middle of an attack.
- It has been used successfully in rape crisis centres and can be very helpful in cases of physical, emotional or sexual abuse.

what can I expect from a session?

WHERE WILL I HAVE THE TREATMENT?

You will be lying on a special SHEN cradle (rather like a camp bed), on top of a massage table.

WILL I BE CLOTHED?

Yes, you will be fully clothed.

WHAT HAPPENS?

The practitioner will explain how SHEN works, then ask you for a detailed case history, quizzing you not only on your medical history, but also on whether you have experienced any prolonged or unexpressed grief, any depression or insomnia, any compulsive behaviour, excessive worries or anxiety attacks. SHEN can treat almost anyone apart from the psychotic or suicidal. Practitioners will not treat you, however, until they are happy that you have a good support network at home or are working with a trained counsellor or psychotherapist. The reason for this is that often old emotions can surface days after the treatment and they need to be sure you will be supported if anything distressing arises. You are then invited to take off your shoes and any jewellery, and lie on the cradle, with your eyes gently closed.

The practitioner simply holds your body, with his or her hands in specific spots – it's very gentle, very supportive. At the end of the session (usually an hour) you feel incredibly relaxed.

WILL IT HURT?

No, it won't hurt at all.

WILL ANYTHING STRANGE HAPPEN?

Some people 'see' past scenes or remember past emotions. It's not uncommon to cry or feel angry. Some people shake or twitch, as old energy is shifted. Others simply fall asleep.

WILL I BE GIVEN ANYTHING TO TAKE?

No, medication is not a part of the treatment.

IS THERE ANY HOMEWORK?

No, but many people learn SHEN to help family and friends.

WORK HARMONY

How many of us, hands on heart, are in jobs that we really love? Doubtless the answer is very few. Yet our work is how we spend the majority of our waking lives. Doesn't it therefore seem more than a little strange that we are quite resigned to the fact that work is usually a drag? That work should be hard, difficult and relatively unpleasant? Earning money must, by its very definition, be something serious. But why? Why shouldn't we enjoy our work?

Work takes up such a hefty chunk of our lives that it seems criminal to continue with a job that makes us truly unhappy. Few of us take the time to analyse precisely why we do the work we do and where exactly the problems lie. We often make career decisions in haste, in panic, at the drop of a hat. Although you may insist that you hate your job, it is worth sitting down and asking exactly what it is you hate about it. It may well be only one element of your work that you dislike. Armed with that knowledge, you are in a much better position to decide whether to do the same work in a new company, to alter the kind of work you do in the same organization or to change both your job and your company.

You do have a choice. The trouble is that we often end up in a job through force of circumstance and then believe that we can't change. Why not, though, fit what you enjoy being good at with the ideal career? By analysing precisely what constitutes your 'job personality', you can make your working life more profitable, more involving and much more fun.

It's worth setting aside a day, or a couple of evenings, to work solely on yourself and your career. It is vital to give yourself your undivided attention. Before you start, try to get into a relaxed state. Take some deep breaths, stretch, roll your neck slowly round. Detach yourself from your normal tasks and commitments. Don't look on these exercises as a chore. Pretend it's a game, have fun and feel free to use coloured crayons, paints or huge pieces of paper – whatever appeals. If you want to draw pictures, that's great.

Above all, be honest. Remember, no one needs to see this except you. Put down everything you can think of, however silly or unrelated it may appear. Some people have forged incredible careers by unearthing skills and pleasures in things they did at school or at a youth club.

our family script

We acquire many of our deep-seated beliefs about work at a very young age from previous generations for whom the concept of work was often intrinsically bound up with notions of duty, discipline and hard slog. Consequently, we are almost all following other people's work scripts, obeying decisions we made almost subconsciously before we even entered the workplace. By becoming aware of your scripts, you can let go of a large number of preconceptions about the nature of work, about the kind of job you are in and about your expectations.

- Ask yourself your thoughts about work. For example, do you think: 'I never get what I really want'; 'I have to fight and be tough to make myself heard'; 'I have to have a "proper" professional career, like a doctor or lawyer'?
- Write down whatever comes to mind, however silly it may seem. Spend some time pondering where those thoughts originated. Did you feel dissatisfied at school, perhaps? Or was your father never promoted beyond a certain level? Did your parents tell you how much your education was costing and that you owed it to them to get a 'sensible' job?
- Look at your thoughts logically. Decide whether they are appropriate for you now. If not, be willing to let them go. Merely by being aware of your internal script, you can reassess your work pattern.

finding your job personality

Realizing that most of your conclusions about the kind of work you should be doing are based on other people's decisions means you can now look at what you really want.

- Make an audit of all your skills, your knowledge, your attributes and qualities, your hobbies. Start from as early as you like and put down everything that you can think of. Include the subjects you learnt at school and college;

You will now have a good idea of where your skills and areas of expertise lie. You may well feel you would like to develop a skill or start using an old skill again. You might consider that your present job really doesn't represent your true skills and breadth of knowledge. Jot down any thoughts that come into your head and then move on.

the ideal workplace

Your present job might already be using all your skills and knowledge, but you are still unhappy. The trouble could well be where you are working. Once you know what your skills are, you must question the context in which you want to use them.

- Look back at your audit and make a list of the environments in which you have either worked or learnt. For each stage of your life, ask yourself about the kind of organization you were in: was it large or small, public or private sector? What did it produce (did it make things, disseminate information, help people, etc.)? Was the workforce primarily male, female, or mixed? Did you work alone, in a small team, as part of a large structure? Note any patterns. Were you always happiest working primarily on your own, but reporting to a small group of co-workers? Do you like to be part of a large, organized team involved in caring?

- Ask yourself what you really want from a workplace. Do you like working for established businesses; for new, growing concerns; for non–profit-making organizations? Do you like working for an organization that manufactures things (if so, what kind of things?); one that processes information (how do you like to deal with information?); or one that works with people (exactly what kind of people? What age range, what background? Individuals or groups? Easygoing or difficult people?).

- Would you be happy if you changed your work environment? For instance, instead of teaching large groups of adults, would you like to give one-to-one help to children with special needs? Would you rather be working for a small, personal company than an established, large, safe firm? Maybe you simply need to change the way you work. If you are lonely working on your own, perhaps you could become part of a team or work under the auspices of a larger department which would give support and feedback.

ABOVE WORK IS ESSENTIAL TO OUR SELF-ESTEEM AND WELLBEING. SADLY, MANY OF US LABOUR IN JOBS THAT WE HATE OR FIND BORING.

the jobs and careers that you have had and the qualities and skills they called for; the extracurricular activities and hobbies you enjoyed; and any workshops or training.

- Don't judge what you are writing – for example, don't think, 'Acting in school plays is irrelevant to me as an accountant.' Everything is important, from playing in the softball team to enjoying caring for your younger siblings.

- Decide which are your favourite three skills. Flesh out each skill with stories from your past: how you used this skill, what the situation was, who was there, how it felt. Can you think of any skills you enjoyed using on lots of occasions? Say you like organizing: be very precise about how exactly you enjoy organizing. Do you enjoy organizing people or data or things? Do you enjoy organizing in a methodical, logical way or using your intuition and gut reactions? Were you part of a team, managing the team or working alone?

- Look at your stories and decide which are your favourites.

your work language

Lots of people have discovered that they enjoy the skills they use, but hate the language they have to speak. Yet a solicitor does not have to speak just 'solicitese': she could also speak the language of film or theatre, of medicine, of psychology, or of shipping, depending on the environment in which she pursues her skills. An administrator might love his job, might feel very happy with the size and structure of the organization for which he works, but hate the fact that it deals in military uniforms because, over the past few years, his views on defence have fundamentally changed. You can never be happy in a job if you wince every time you hear certain words or phrases.

- Look at your subject list, your list of areas of knowledge, and highlight any that you couldn't stand working with all day long. Which are your favourites? Which would you be happy talking about and hearing about all day long?

creating your ideal job

You should now have most of the information you require to discover your ideal work situation. Pull it all together and find the anatomy of your ideal job.

- Think about anything you might have missed in the previous exercises. Ask yourself what your dreams are – if this were the last day of your life, what would you regret not ever having done? Incorporate any answers into your job anatomy.
- Indulge in some playful thinking around matching your favourite things to possible jobs. Be inventive, be silly, don't analyse. Think of ways to link even the most incongruous qualities: use it as a test of your lateral thinking.

making links

Now is the time to start thinking about the external factors: what is out there and how to match what employers want with what you have to offer. Don't immediately fly to the nearest employment agency or job advertisements. People who think in unorthodox patterns stand far more chance of success. If you reply to an advertisement in a newspaper,

your odds are pretty slim — you could be competing against hundreds of applicants. If you go for a job from an employment agency, you will still be up against a fair few. But if you target a specific organization and convince its personnel that you are tailor-made for it, you are competing against nobody. Yes, you might argue, but there is no vacancy. Perhaps not, but people who know precisely what they want and match their skills to a specific organization often prove irresistible.

- Spend some time asking yourself the following questions. Which of my skills could be used in a variety of occupations? Which jobs would allow me to use my favourite skills in a field based on my favourite subjects or areas of knowledge?
- Which organizations or companies employ people in these roles? Which of these organizations do I like? Which of these organizations need my skills and knowledge?
- Ask friends or family to give some input. Show them your list of criteria and see if they have any thoughts or hunches.

the core statement

If you prefer a more unusual approach to career appraisal, try the core statement. It's a clever technique which helps people discover the kind of role in life that could make their 'soul sing.' It has put frustrated businesspeople back in the fast lane and helped firms build teams of highly motivated workers. It can give absolutely everybody a clear insight into what really makes them tick — and tick joyously.

The core statement is, very simply, a clear, concise statement of your life's purpose. It outlines the criteria that have to be fulfilled in order to keep you contented and committed to your path in life — to make you adore your days, rather than just get by. Composing it rarely takes more than an hour and, once you have it, you have it for life.

All of us have quite specific roles that we feel happiest playing in life. While one person may relish new challenges, another may love nothing better than the safe and secure. Where one person thrives working alone, another may feel lost without the support and stimulus of a team or family.

Our core statement tends to be clearest in childhood, before we succumb to the pressures of school and work. It's as if there were a line of arrows leading through our lives that shows where we should be going. Unfortunately, many of us veer away from that path – as a result of pressure at school or college, or in the workplace. Also, while most of us think that our daily grind is simply something to endure, people who practise the core-statement philosophy point out that such an attitude could be positively injurious to our health and happiness. When the gap between what we should be doing and what we are doing becomes too great, we start to become stressed and eventually even sick.

To be happy and efficient, we need to be working in the right environment, in the right way or with the right people. Sometimes all you need is a small adjustment to make all the difference. The process itself is simple, yet also great fun. It requires you to look back over your life and pinpoint the times when you were utterly enthralled by life, totally absorbed or totally exhilarated.

It isn't always practical to do precisely what you want. Life is not perfect, but you can get within a certain bandwidth. If you can't be totally fulfilled at work, you need to compensate for that by doing what you love in your leisure time.

finding your core statement

You can start to understand what makes you 'sing your song' by thinking about the following. Work with another person, as he or she may notice which phrases are stressed or repeated.

1 Find a joyful childhood memory. Have your partner ask you the following: 'What were you doing?' 'What made it special?' 'How did you feel?' 'Was anyone with you?' 'What did you enjoy the most?' Write down the key phrases and words.

2 Think of a good time in your life, at any period. Repeat the questions and again write down key phrases or words.

3 Repeat the above process with the following:
- talk about a fulfilling work experience
- explore a hobby or pastime
- capture a moment when you felt complete.

4 Now identify the most important key phrases and words and write them down on paper. Which keep recurring? Where are the patterns? Which represent the most important circumstances or attitudes? If you could have only three or four of these phrases or words, which would they be?

5 Try to compose a sentence that incorporates these phrases and has real meaning for you. When you hit on the right statement, it will instinctively feel right – some people laugh or even cry. Play with words until yours emerges.

the harmonious workplace

We've already seen how important our home environment is to our health and wellbeing, yet many of us don't even consider the places in which we work in the same light. In general, most offices are not healthy places. Some have even been dubbed 'sick' because they actively make the people who work in them feel constantly low, lacking in energy and under the weather. Many of the materials in modern offices are toxic and, if you have a particular sensitivity, could make you feel very uncomfortable or even ill.

The following strategies may help to reduce office sickness. You will find many of the hints apply equally to homes.

- Use heating and air conditioning as little as possible: extra layers of clothing or fans to circulate cool air are healthier ways of regulating the temperature.
- Make sure that all heating and air conditioning systems are regularly serviced and checked.
- Keep the office well ventilated at all times. Having a window open will permit toxic fumes to escape. Even if the weather is unpleasant, at least open the windows for a few minutes before work and after lunch.
- Try to ensure that all electrical equipment (which emits electromagnetic fields) is unplugged when not in use. Position helpful cleansing plants (see page 90) by your computer, photocopier, fax machines and so forth.
- Avoid passive smoking. If people you work with smoke, try to designate a specific room for smoking.
- Work under natural light, if possible. Sit by a window if you can and/or use daylight bulbs in your desk lamp. Where possible, try to avoid fluorescent lighting.
- Ionizers can help improve air quality. Water can help balance the humidity of your office, so install a fish tank (it's good feng shui to have fish as well) or a bubbling water feature (again, great feng shui).
- If your office is going to be redecorated or refurnished, try to persuade your office manager to have it done with non-toxic paints and solvents, and to choose fabrics, flooring and furniture that has not been treated with chemicals.
- Try to persuade office cleaners to use environmentally friendly, non-toxic cleaners, detergents etc.

using feng shui
in the workplace

Just as feng shui can make a difference to your home life, it can be very important at work as well. Many big corporations now insist on having feng shui consultants analyse their workplaces for the best possible flow of qi, vital energy. You, too, can take advantage of this subtle energy to make your workplace more pleasant and your career more successful.

There are simple guidelines for success and happy working conditions in the office.

- Your desk should always be positioned diagonally opposite the door, with you facing the door. You need to be able to see everyone who walks into your office the moment they enter. This makes good sense psychologically (no one can creep up on you and surprise you), but is also said to be the 'power position' that will give you control, concentration and a sense of natural authority.
- Computer workers who have their backs to the door will become stressed. According to feng shui, sitting with your back to the door, whatever your job, can even cause you to be demoted or made redundant. If, for whatever reason, you really can't change your desk position, put up a mirror so that you can see people approaching. Mirrors can also be used in offices to draw in money-endowing water views (if your office looks out over any kind of water, make sure a mirror reflects the view). Water is considered to equate with wealth and success. What happens if your desk is immovable and your boss frowns on the idea of mirrors? Slip a mirror into your desk drawer facing the desired direction, as a symbolic protection.
- If you are the boss, make sure you don't sit too close to the door of your office, particularly if other workers or secretaries share it with you. If you do, you will be treated as an underling and lose respect. Workers in better and more advantageous spots will become insubordinate.
- If you work for a difficult boss and you have to sit directly in front of or behind him or her, be sure to place either a crystal paperweight or a bowl of water on your desk. It will deflect any criticism or intolerance. If you can put goldfish in your bowl, even better.

- Watch out for workers who sit close to the door. They tend to leave early and avoid overtime. A mirror positioned to take the worker's attention away from the door will cure this.
- If you can, incorporate a fish tank into your office, preferably positioned in the wealth corner. A tank with a bubbling aerator is most effective. Ideally, you should have eight red fish and one black one.

feng shui your desk

Your desk is the key to success at work. Whether you want a better relationship with your boss or a nice fat raise, you need to use the art of feng shui to boost your opportunities. Where you place your desk and what you place on it can make the difference between make or break in business – be you a big boss in a corporate office or self-employed in a corner of your living room. Ideally, your desk should be positioned so you are sitting with your back against a solid wall with a good view of both the door and the window. Above all, make sure you keep your desk free of clutter: if your desk is buried under a pile of paperwork, it will make you feel tired and depressed before you start your day.

Here's how to arrange your desk to boost your career.

- Keep a bright, functional desk lamp on one side of your desk – this helps to hold your attention. Place it on the far left-hand side of your desk to improve your finances. If you would rather increase your recognition, put it directly in front of you. If you need to get on better with people, place it in the top right-hand corner.
- Fresh-cut flowers stimulate mental activity and cleanse the atmosphere. The colour and number of flowers are important: four red or purple flowers in a vase will help boost your income; two yellow flowers in the top right-hand corner will help you get on with people. In general, flowers will boost your creativity and recognition.
- Your telephone can sit in either the bottom left-hand or bottom right-hand corner of your desk. The right side is ideal, as it will make people more helpful when you call them. If you are left-handed, keep your address book on your right instead to gain a similar result.
- Keep essential reference books on your left-hand side, the knowledge area.
- Opposite your desk, make sure you have something that stimulates your creativity or reminds you of your goals.

LEFT Using feng shui principles on your desk at work is one way to take control of your working life. Even quite simple changes can bring about surprisingly dramatic results.

Revisit the information on NLP (pages 121–3). Be aware of how your colleagues view the world and, if you find yourself slipping into disagreement, try using their language to make them feel less threatened and more understood.

If you find yourself in a difficult situation, with an argument brewing, try the following tactics

- First of all, say: 'Let's have a 5-minute break and come back to this.' A pause will allow both/all of you to calm down and rethink. Use this time to go somewhere quiet and to work through these suggestions.
- Take a few minutes to sit calmly and breathe deeply. Feel yourself breathing out the anger and irritation, and breathing in new ideas and responses. Do some of the breathing exercises on pages 80–1.
- Write down the reasons for the disagreement. Pour out all your feelings of anger and irritation onto paper (it may be a good idea to write an imaginary letter to the person or people). This can help release the negative emotions safely and also put things in perspective.
- Try seeing the other point of view. If you find this hard (or even downright impossible!), the empty-chair technique from Gestalt therapy is useful (see page 119). Sit on one chair and imagine the other person sitting on the other. Describe exactly how you feel. Now swap chairs and imagine you are the other person. Put yourself in his or her shoes and talk to the other chair as if you were the other person talking to you. What might he or she be thinking, feeling? What might he or she really want to say? Swap chairs again, continuing the conversation (or argument) for as long as it takes to understand both sides of the question (there always are two sides to every question).
- Take two drops of beech flower remedy under your tongue. Beech will help you stop being overcritical and angry. If your colleague(s) will take some, too, so much the better.
- When you return to the other person or people, visualize love and understanding flowing from your heart chakra towards others. You may like to visualize it as a beautiful pink-gold bubble of unconditional love. Although this may be difficult, do try your best!

- If your work is creative, try to have a rounded desk. If your work involves figures or is very precise, a square desk is better, but ideally still with rounded corners.
- Try to use a square briefcase or handbag to make you more inclined to complete projects.
- When cheques come in, put them in the top left-hand corner of your desk, perhaps weighted down by a beautiful paperweight. Place your invoices here, too, before you send them out.
- If you work in a team or want to get on better with your colleagues, put a photograph of your work team in the top right-hand corner of your desk. Place a candle in front of it to boost the good energy.

getting on with people

Sometimes the hardest thing about a job is the people with whom we work. When a crowd of people work together in close proximity, it's understandable that not everyone will get on all the time. Recognizing that we are all very different can help. There are also some interesting techniques that can help head off problems and resolve any conflicts that do emerge.

RELATIONSHIPS

RELATIONSHIPS CAN OFTEN SEEM LIKE THE GREATEST MYSTERY OF LIFE. THERE ARE SOME PEOPLE WITH WHOM WE JUST 'CLICK' — WE FEEL AS IF WE HAVE BEEN BEST FRIENDS ALL OUR LIVES. FOR OTHERS, WE FEEL AN INSTANT ATTRACTION, AN INTERNAL CHEMISTRY. YET OTHERS SEEM TO RUB US THE WRONG WAY — ALMOST BEFORE THEY SPEAK OR ACT. PSYCHOLOGISTS HYPOTHESIZE THAT WE ALL HAVE 'MAPS' THAT HARDWIRE US TO FIND SOME PEOPLE MORE ATTRACTIVE THAN OTHERS, BASED ON EARLY EXPERIENCES AND FAMILY BACKGROUND. ASTROLOGERS ATTRIBUTE IT TO OUR STAR SIGNS AND THOSE OF THE PEOPLE WE MEET.

Whatever the reasons, there is no doubt that relationships can cause the greatest joy — and the greatest heartbreak — of all aspects of life. Most people would say that a good primary relationship is the most essential aspect of life, swiftly followed by close ties to family and friends. In this section, we're going to look at ways to improve our relationships.

keeping relationships on track

A good relationship needs careful nurturing, regular care and attention. It's not enough to cross your fingers and trust to luck that your partnership will flourish over the years — like a car, successful relationships need frequent servicing and regular check-ups. If your relationship is to run at peak performance, it needs regular maintenance. For healthy, happy relationships, some things need checking every day, some every week, while each month and year call for an in-depth overhaul. Try to insert the following into your emotional life.

every day

- SHARE YOUR WORRIES We all lead tough, frantic lives. Many of us wage a constant struggle to balance work, children, household, friends, money, health. It's all too easy to find yourself wallowing in a pit of self-pity and forget that your partner has a tough life, too. Your relationship should be something that helps you both through the morass, not a further millstone round your neck. Try thinking about what would make his or her life better and, with a little luck, he or she will do the same for you. When you've had a tough day and you can't wait to unburden all your fury and frustration, wait — just 2 minutes — before you hurl it at your partner. Give each other a few minutes to enjoy just being in each other's company. Have a hug, hang on tight and appreciate that here's someone nice after all the monsters at work/on the bus/on the roads ... and then, only then, should you launch into the 2-hour tirade against the world.

- START THE DAY WITH A KISS The alarm clock rings and you both stumble out of bed, in the perennial morning frenzy. Try setting the alarm for 5 minutes earlier and start your day with a kiss and a cuddle. Even if you are miles apart, you could always give each other a daily 'alarm call'. It only takes two minutes and starts the day on a happy note.

- THINK ABOUT WHAT YOUR PARTNER WOULD LIKE What would make his or her day? It doesn't have to be red roses or expensive presents, but how about taking his car through the carwash or buying him a bottle of his favourite Belgian beer, or putting on her favourite record? The most valued presents are often the most offbeat or the most simple: how about a birdfeeder for outside her office window; a subscription to the magazine she loves; a long, luxurious neck rub; or a ready-run bath with bubbles, candles and a glass of wine on the side?

- MAKE TIME Sometimes it's hard to remember you even live together, you see so little of each other. How about getting up just a little earlier to share breakfast, or even just coffee? Or a phone call at lunchtime? A good rule of thumb is to set aside 15–20 minutes to talk every day in order to debrief, catch up and say hello.

- DON'T GO TO SLEEP ON AN ARGUMENT Whatever it takes, try to stick to an agreement that you clear up anything that has annoyed you throughout the day before you turn off the light. That way you can start each day fresh.

OPPOSITE IT IS WORTH SPENDING TIME AND ENERGY WORKING ON CLOSE RELATIONSHIPS. STRONG, HAPPY RELATIONSHIPS NOT ONLY MAKE US FEEL GOOD, BUT ARE ALSO VITAL FOR HEALTH AND WELLBEING.

the vital questions

If you want to check your relationship is on track, ask each other and yourself the following questions, devised by psychotherapists to gauge how well relationships are faring. They will help to pinpoint areas of potential difficulty and bring them out in the open for healthy discussion.

Decide whether you agree or disagree with each statement, and the level to which you agree or disagree.

1 I am happy with what my partner expects of me.

2 agree with my partner's goals and plans.

3 I am satisfied with the ways in which we resolve our differences.

4 My partner is not too busy for us to do enough things together.

5 I am comfortable with my partner's different moods.

6 We agree on whether to have children, and how to raise them.

7 At times I need my personal space and my partner gives it to me.

8 I am happy with the way we show affection for each other.

9 I am not worried about being unsatisfied with my partner sexually.

10 We are able, when necessary, to talk out problems when we disagree.

Use your answers as the starting point for discussion with your partner. If you find it hard to understand your partner's point of view, try the empty-chair technique on page 119.

once a week

- HAVE A SPECIAL NIGHT Pick your least favourite day of the week. You could go to the cinema, for a walk in the country or out to eat. Or order in food and stay home with a video. Make time to give each other a massage or just talk.

- CHECK OUT HOW YOU BOTH FEEL Spend time each week finding out exactly how the other is feeling, voicing anxieties and irritations, and letting go of resentment, fear or anger. Pick a time when you aren't rushed. Maybe sit down with a glass of wine or have lunch together.

- GIVE SMALL SURPRISES Leave a note on the pillow when you have to get up before your partner does, or in the suitcase or underwear drawer if either one of you has to go away for a few days. Attach a simple note saying 'I love you' to a posy of flowers on the pillow, or a bar of sandalwood soap in the bathroom.

- SET ASIDE TIME FOR SEX We'll look more at this in the next section of the book, but, for now, use your imagination and experiment by changing your lovemaking scenario from time to time. For instance, you might want to break away from the mistaken idea that making love should only be done at night and in bed.

once a month

- SHARE AN ADVENTURE Widen your horizons and do something completely different. Try something wild like hang gliding, horse riding or jet skiing. Take a weekend course in, say, massage, gourmet cookery or orienteering. You could spend a day at the races, an afternoon messing around in a rowing boat or take a picnic in the park. If you both fancy different things, make a list and take it in turns each month to try 'your' adventure.

- HAVE AN ADVENTURE – ON YOUR OWN Every psychologist and relationship expert agrees we all need time out, time alone to pursue our own thoughts and interests, to see our own friends. Take time out to indulge yourself: a weekend in the country, a day's pampering at a health spa, an afternoon wandering round an art gallery or a long, self-indulgent lunch. Allow yourself some space and time. Absence really does make the heart grow fonder.

- CHEERFULLY COMPROMISE Once in a while, give him or her a special treat day. Choose all the things you know he or she loves: pottering around secondhand bookstores, watching football or trawling country pubs, a day's shopping, a smart lunch, perhaps a mini-facial and a soppy film. Just make sure you remember to have your special day, too.

once a year

- ASSESS YOUR RELATIONSHIP Set aside time at least once a year to evaluate where you are as a couple. Ask yourselves questions. What values do we share? What do we both want right now? What do we both want for the future? Look at the current reality. What's working? What isn't? What do you appreciate or value about each other? How well does the relationship meet your needs? Look at possibilities. If the relationship could be any way you wanted it to be,

how would it be? What would be different from the way things are now? Take your time. Set aside an evening (you could make it more appealing by including a nice dinner with wine and candles). Both of you should write down your answers to the questions above and then discuss them together – you might be surprised by the answers.

- LEARN SOMETHING NEW – TOGETHER Taking up horse riding or squash, chess or backgammon gives you a reason to spend regular time together and gives you new interests. Learn a language. When you're fluent, reward yourselves with a holiday to the country in question.

- FANTASIZE Write out a list of 100 things you each want to do in your life – from the mundane (have a haircut), through the interesting (learn ballroom dancing or raise ducks), to the extreme (travel round the world for a couple of years, change jobs or move to the country). Read out your lists and compare your wishes. You may well find fantasies in common – work towards turning them into reality. A shared goal can really cement a relationship.

- MAKE A LONG-TERM COMMITMENT If you aren't already married or living together, you don't necessarily have

ABOVE SET ASIDE TIME JUST TO SIT AND TALK. SHARE CHILDHOOD MEMORIES AND REMEMBER GOOD TIMES YOU HAVE SPENT TOGETHER. DISCUSS SMALL PROBLEMS BEFORE THEY BECOME LARGE ISSUES.

to go for an engagement ring or a house, but, if you are committed to your relationship, it helps to make a symbolic gesture. Anything could do: buy a washing machine together, rescue a dog from an animal refuge, take out a joint membership to the gym, or set up a joint savings account for the holiday of a lifetime. There is something powerful about seeing your names linked on an official document!

- MAKE RITUALS Set aside time once a year to celebrate your relationship – it's a way of spiritually rejuvenating your relationship. See more about rituals on pages 174–9. It doesn't have to be a strictly spiritual ritual: it might be treating yourselves to a smart hotel for a night or a break to Paris or Barcelona, or even a champagne breakfast in a hot-air balloon. You could incorporate some of the other ideas given here, such as listing your fantasies or checking out how you both feel about the relationship. Or you could just devote the time to sheer fun and enjoyment.

SEXUALITY

Touch is essential for both our physical and our psychological health. Research has even shown that premature babies need touch in order to grow normally. We certainly don't lose that need for closeness, warmth and touch as we get older — touch is also life-sustaining for us as adults. And there is nothing so close, so intimate and so totally accepting as the touch of one lover on another. Sex makes us feel more than just desirable — it allows us to feel wanted, cared for, protected and safe. It makes us feel good about ourselves.

why sex is good for you

A good sex life is incredibly beneficial for our health and wellbeing. Here's why.

- IT REDUCES STRESS Sex releases chemicals in much the same way as intense physical exercise does. In addition, during lovemaking, the muscles of the body become highly tensed; following orgasm, the body completely relaxes. Sex is like a very extreme version of the relaxation exercise known as progressive relaxation, where you move through the body tensing and then relaxing each set of muscles. During sex, however, your body does this automatically and to a much greater degree. A large study by the Institute for Advanced Study of Human Sexuality confirms the theory that people who have fulfilling and happy sex lives generally show far fewer stress symptoms than those who don't: they are less anxious, less violent and hostile, and are far less likely to blame their misfortunes on others.
- IT MAKES US FEEL BETTER ABOUT OURSELVES A healthy, happy sex life can boost our self-esteem like nothing on earth. No other activity is so intimate, so personal — it's like baring your very soul. When your partner responds with love and affection, it bestows a sense of wholeness. Of course, sex will only boost your self-esteem if you're with the right partner.
- IT SOOTHES SLEEPLESSNESS A bout of lovemaking is probably the last thing you would think of when you can't get to sleep. Yet research shows that an orgasm can be the perfect trigger to a good night's sleep because serotonin

(the hormone that induces sleepiness) is released after orgasm. Also, insomnia is most often brought on by anxiety and tension. Sex relieves that tension.

- IT CAN HELP TO HEAL SORROW AND GRIEF Expressing ourselves through sex can have a profound healing effect. When you're feeling depressed or sad, it's all too easy to withdraw into yourself. Lovemaking makes you connect with another person at a very deep, nurturing level. Sex also produces endorphins, feelgood hormones that elevate mood, so a session of sex when you're feeling low could be the best possible antidepressant.
- IT HEALS YOUR HEART Sex really can provide you with a mini-workout (it's been estimated that a woman burns around 4.2 calories a minute during sex, compared to 4 calories per minute playing tennis). Obviously, you're not going to keep going long enough to notch up as many calories as a full tennis match, but you will still give a toning effect to your heart and lungs. However, sex also has far more subtle effects on the health of our hearts. A prime risk factor for heart disease is lack of love. One study looked at the sex lives of women hospitalized for heart attacks. Of these, 65 per cent reported some form of sexual dissatisfaction or frigidity. For a control group, the researchers asked the same questions of women hospitalized for non–heart-related problems and only 24 per cent said they had difficult or non-existent sex lives.
- IT COULD EXTEND YOUR LIFE There appears to be a strong connection between immunity and sex — a healthy sex life can make us more resistant to disease and stress. It seems that the arousal, excitement and physical release of sexual activity enhances the natural ability of the immune system to ward off illness. A typical orgasm boosts the body's T3 and T4 lymphocyte cells (the ones that fight infection) by up to 20 per cent. This comes as no surprise to many alternative practitioners, who have long believed that touch alone can help improve immune function. A study at the University of Miami seems to prove the point: massage alone raises levels of serotonin, the neurotransmitter that triggers the increase of immune-defence cells.

how to use sexual energy to help and heal

In order to have health-giving sex, you need to have a healthy, open, honest relationship. Here's how to pave the way ...

- Make sure you both really enjoy your lovemaking. The art of a truly happy sex life is good communication, say sex therapists and relationship experts. Talk about sex – about what you enjoy and what you don't like as much. Be honest, but careful – don't blame your partner, just say how you feel.

- Become sensual as well as sexual in your everyday life. Give your body and mind sensual treats: this means eating and exercising well; wearing clothing that feels good on your skin; enjoying a languid bath with essential oils, or an invigorating shower. Engage your senses to the full.

- Learn how to give a simple massage and have your partner learn, too. There are plenty of books and videos giving simple instructions, or follow the instructions on page 140.

- If you seem never to have time for lovemaking, make a regular 'appointment' for sex. Although it may sound rather unromantic, sex therapists all agree that these appointments can do wonders for your sex life – adding a frisson of anticipation to the day.

- Give yourselves enough time. The most frequent reason for women being dissatisfied with sex is that they feel they are not given enough time and attention. Lovemaking is a vital part of your relationship: allow it the time it deserves.

- Keep the romance alive in your life: give your partner small surprises. This need not mean flowers. It could be a new book or CD; a photo frame with a picture of you in it; or a favourite food or drink. Leave a loving message – on the bed, on the answerphone, on e-mail. Suggest a surprise

outing or have a picnic in bed. Revitalize your love life with books and videos. Bring a new element into your bedroom with fresh ideas: books such as Anne Hooper's *Kama Sutra* (Dorling Kindersley) make for fun bedtime reading. If you are interested in Tantra (where sex meets mysticism), read the books by Margo Anand (*The Art of Sexual Ecstasy* and *The Art of Sexual Magic*, both Piatkus).

- Turn your bedroom into a private sanctuary. Avoid having work in the bedroom, take out the television, put a lock on the door so you know you can have privacy. Make it really comfortable – add sumptuous velvet cushions (according to feng shui, they should be red or deep pink).

the art of sacred sex

The ancient Indian art of Tantrism teaches union with God through lovemaking. In the original tradition, sex was merely a means to an end: adepts were not seeking better orgasms, but a deeper religious experience. Here in the West, few of us are prepared to complete the years of arduous training that a Tantric has to undergo. However, practising aspects of Tantrism can have a remarkable effect on your love life – and on your relationship with your partner. The ritual given here is based loosely on the complex Tantric ceremony known as *maithuna*. It can give surprisingly intense results very swiftly.

1 Make sure your bedroom is as beautiful and sensual as it can possibly be. Follow the guidelines already given above, paying attention to the look of the room, the scent of it, the

ABOVE BE SURE NOT TO LET YOUR SEX LIFE BECOME MUNDANE AND PREDICTABLE – EXPLORING NEW TECHNIQUES TOGETHER CAN NOT ONLY FOSTER INTIMACY, BUT ALSO DEEPEN YOUR SENSUALITY.

sounds around you and the feel of coverings. Red candles can provide soft, sensual lighting and suggest passion.

2 Prepare a tray of delicious, exotic finger food (just small nibbles, not a heavy meal). Add a decanter of wine and two beautiful glasses (be careful not to overdo the wine, though).

3 Both of you should shower or bathe (either separately or together). Spend time connecting with your body. Dress in light, flowing clothes.

4 Sit down and spend time simply enjoying each other's company, talking, eating and drinking together. You may feel moved to touch and caress each other. You might want to try some yoga together or breathing in time with one another, or simply sit gazing deep into each other's eyes.

5 You may already feel aroused. To prepare yourselves for sacred intercourse, however, the man should meditate on the image of the vulva, the yoni, picturing it as warm, welcoming, moist and soft, opening and closing like a flower. Concentrate on the soft aroma of musk and imagine the sound of a deep heartbeat, a slow rhythm of the earth, the pulse of life.

6 The woman, meanwhile, meditates on the penis, the lingam, visualizing it as erect, mentally examining its different textures. The scent to imagine is patchouli. The sound is that of a faster, more insistent throb.

7 The man should now move gently forwards and enter the woman deeply and solidly. Any position can be adopted, but many people prefer sitting face to face.

8 For a while just move slowly, the woman milking the penis (squeezing and releasing it with her vaginal muscles) and the man thrusting gently.

9 Next, allow yourselves to become totally still. Stare deeply into each other's eyes. Imagine yourselves linked at the various chakras: at the head, the throat, the heart, the solar plexus and particularly the genitals.

10 Imagine your entire genital area surrounded by a pulsing orb of deep red light.

11 Now synchronize your breathing, slowly and deeply breathing towards your partner's mouth.

12 Imagine the energy generated from your genitals spreading up your spines and throughout your entire bodies. Remain in this position for as long as is comfortable. Even if you manage just a few minutes, it should still result in an unusual experience for you and your partner.

sensual massage

Giving and receiving massage is a wonderful way to relax and to foster love and trust. It helps you both become aware of each other's bodies in a safe, loving way. It is also deeply sensual and the perfect prelude to lovemaking. Don't worry that the massage won't be perfect or professional enough. The aim is to give your partner pleasure, and almost any touch (providing it feels good to your partner) will do that.

1 Make your bedroom comfortable and pleasant. Make sure it is warm enough, clear the clutter and (because oils may stain) put a towel over the bed or wherever you intend to give the massage. Choose some relaxing music you both like. You may want to light some candles and burn some relaxing essential oils (lavender or camomile) or romantic oils (such as sandalwood or ylang ylang) in a burner.

2 Make up your massage oil. Use 8 drops of one of the oils above in 4 teaspoons of a base oil such as sweet almond.

3 Start on the back with your thumbs on either side of the spine, fingers pointing towards the neck. Allow your hands to glide slowly up the body and around the shoulders. Draw your hands lightly down the side of the back to your starting position. Don't worry if your technique is a bit stilted to begin with – just relax and ask your partner for feedback (he or she might like your touch to be firmer, or gentler).

4 Fleshy areas such as hips and thighs can be kneaded gently. Lift, squeeze and roll the skin between the thumb and fingers of one hand and glide it towards the other hand.

5 Curl your fingers into loose fists, keeping the fingers (not the knuckles) against the skin. Work all over the body. Make small circling movements on the shoulders, palms of the hands, soles of the feet and chest.

6 Form your hands into cup shapes and, with quick, light movements, move over the skin as if beating a drum.

7 If you feel adventurous, emulate Hawaiian masseurs, who use their entire arms or their hair to touch the body.

8 Gauge how your partner feels (if you can't tell, ask!). If they are in the mood for sex, kiss them gently all over. Very softly stroke the thighs and breasts, gradually moving into lovemaking.

OPPOSITE YOU DO NOT NEED TO BE AN EXPERT TO GIVE A SENSUAL MASSAGE. FOLLOW THE BASIC TECHNIQUES GIVEN ABOVE AND THEN SIMPLY LET YOUR SENSES AND INTUITION GUIDE YOU.

FAMILY

WE ALL WANT TO PLAY HAPPY FAMILIES. WE'D ALL LIKE TO BE CALM, GENTLE, WISE GROWN-UPS WHO HAVE PERFECT RELATIONSHIPS WITH OUR LOVING PARTNERS AND OUR HAPPY, CONFIDENT CHILDREN. UNFORTUNATELY, MOST FAMILIES END UP BICKERING AND SQUABBLING, SULKING AND SCREAMING AT SOME POINT. HOW CAN YOU TALK TO A CHILD WHO SIMPLY DOESN'T WANT TO LISTEN? HOW CAN YOU GIVE YOUR PARTNER, YOUR CHILDREN AND YOURSELF THE TIME YOU ALL NEED? HOW CAN YOU PROTECT YOUR FAMILY FROM THE DANGERS WITHIN THE SOCIETY IN WHICH WE LIVE? HAPPY FAMILIES IS CERTAINLY NO GAME; IT'S MORE LIKE MISSION IMPOSSIBLE.

When you stop to think about it, it's not that surprising. These are the people with whom we live intimately; the people who see our bad sides as well as our good; the ones who have to put up with our horrible habits, our lousy moods, our everyday frustrations and irritations. It is simply not reasonable or realistic to expect to have the 'perfect' family all the time. There are plenty of things you can do, however, to make your home a happier place and to bring more joy and fewer frayed tempers to family relationships.

ABOVE LIFE IS STRESSFUL, BUT DO MAKE TIME TO ENJOY ACTIVITIES TOGETHER AS A FAMILY. A DAY AT THE BEACH IS HEAVEN FOR CHILDREN AND CAN BE FUN FOR ADULTS, TOO. RELAX AND ENJOY FOR A FEW HOURS.

ways to promote peace

- LISTEN Often misunderstandings arise because we simply don't listen to each other. Children feel hurt and ignored. Partners feel left out. Make time to listen.
- PRESS THE PAUSE BUTTON Everyone needs a remote control with 'pause' on it, to be used before we lash out at the people around us. It's natural to want to hit back when someone hurts us, but resist the urge. Think how your reaction will affect the other person before you reply.
- BE NICE That's a tough one, isn't it? Bring the principle of 'random acts of kindness' into family life. Think of little things that make people's lives easier or more pleasant. It could be taping a favourite television programme if someone's out; it may be doing the washing up; it may be cooking a favourite meal or picking a posy of wild flowers.
- STOP NAGGING Resist the urge to criticize and complain: give each other compliments, rather than constant nagging. Think of something nice to say to everyone regularly.

When you're wrong, apologize. We all make mistakes, so say sorry and mean it. Hard as it may be, don't nag children all the time: let go of the little things and boost their confidence by letting them 'win' sometimes. Toddlers going through the 'no' stage can be particularly testing. Make a few totally rigid rules (about consideration and safety) and let the unimportant things go.

- BE LOYAL AND RELIABLE Keep any promises you make – always. Be loyal at all times to your family. Defend its members when they're not around. Let go of grudges. Yes, we all make mistakes, we all do rotten things from time to time, but try not to hold on to grudges for hours, weeks, months or even years! Let go of the past and start afresh.
- SPEND TIME TOGETHER Set aside certain times during the week when you act together as a family. Perhaps you can make it Sunday lunch or an evening when you all go out (for a walk, to the movies). Let everyone have an input – take it in turns to choose what the outing will be.

your family space

When we live alone, we can organize your space exactly as we want it. Once we start sharing our homes with a family, however, the issue of personal space really comes to the fore. We all have varying requirements and a home needs to reflect everyone's wishes and desires. Not paying attention to this oft-forgotten aspect of family life can be the source of a lot of grudges and unhappiness. Spend some time on this exercise.

1 First, you need to draw a floor plan of your home. It need not be draughtsman quality, but try to make the proportions roughly accurate. If your home has several floors, do a plan for each one. Make several copies and let everyone in the house have their own to colour.

2 Label each room on your plan and mark in all the major pieces of furniture.

3 Pick a colour for each family member and start to colour in the plan. Think about who uses each space and mark it accordingly (you may have stripes in some places!). For example, someone may have a chair that is supremely 'theirs'.

4 Let the colours show the division of tasks in the house. One person may do all the cooking, so the cooker (stove) is 'theirs', or even the whole kitchen – bar the table where you eat! The table may be commandeered for homework by the children, however, and so be shared.

5 Balance out how much each person uses each room and colour in the room accordingly.

What you end up with may well prove surprising. You may have colonized huge parts of the house for yourself or you may realize that you have been virtually squeezed out. The children may have no place to call their own. Certain rooms may be out of bounds to certain people. Have a good, long think about why this might be – and if it really suits your needs.

Of course, different people in the family may have different perceptions of how the space is used. View the plans as providing a starting point for a debate, and try to be fair.

- Is the division of space fair?
- Who wants or needs more?
- Can you think, together, of ways that would give everyone what he or she needs?

This may seem impossible, but a solution can usually be found. For example, some people need certain spaces only at particular times. It could be perfectly fine for the kitchen to be a homework zone, providing the books are cleared away afterwards so an adult can use the space for making pottery or writing the great novel! Children sharing a bedroom need to have their 'own' walls for posters and such, or they could divide the space with furniture or a decorative screen.

what kind of family do you want?

Few of us stop to think about what we actually want from our families. Often we express our thoughts only in negative terms: we don't want a family like the one we grew up in or we don't want to be like so-and-so ... Change the focus and think what you do want.

Set aside an evening to discuss your 'ideal' family, your goals and aspirations – what you see as your 'purpose' as a family. It could be a nice idea to have a special family meal beforehand and then discuss the following.

- What kind of family do you really want to be? What words come to mind when you think about your ideal family?
- To what kind of home would you like to invite your friends?
- What embarrasses you about your family? Don't be nasty or vindictive, but do be honest.
- What do you love about your family? What makes you feel warm and good? What makes you want to come home? If your feelings about family and home are negative, is there anything that feels good about it?
- If you had to write a 'mission statement' for your family for the coming year, what would it be?

Sit down and talk about this. Above all, listen – every family member should have a say. You might be surprised by what is important to each of you. This could provide the basis for an important family heart-to-heart. Together, come up with a short list of the things that are most important to you all about your family. You may wish to write them up on a large card or poster, which could be put somewhere you can all see it and act as a reminder of what your family is about.

DREAMWORKING

Dreams are the medium through which our unconscious minds try to communicate with us. Most of us, however, ignore these messages from the night. This is a shame, as our conscious minds are so overloaded with all the practical considerations, fears and conventions of everyday life that we often cannot see the wood for the trees. Our unconscious, free of such restrictions, generally knows precisely what we really need. Learn to listen to your unconscious and it could help make your waking life much more fulfilling. Your relationships should improve, your career could change — listening to your unconscious could even help your health.

We spend a third of our lives asleep and, even though you may not remember your dreams, there is no doubt that we all, without exception, dream each and every night. It's curious, therefore that so few people bother to consult the oracle in their own heads. It's not even as if the concept of dreamworking were anything new. The Old Testament is full of references to prophetic dreams, while in ancient Greece people would regularly spend a therapeutic night in a Temple of Sleep, where they believed the god of the temple would send healing dreams. Native Americans have used the power of dreaming for centuries — they would regard ignoring a dream as sheer stupidity.

In the West, however, dreaming has been very much marginalized for centuries, dismissed as either florid imagination or simply the mind's way of disposing of the detritus of the day. It wasn't until Sigmund Freud started investigating dreams that these pyrotechnics of the night started to be taken seriously. Yet even Freud saw dreams simply as repositories for all that lies repressed in human nature. It was left to Carl Jung to map the dream world and it is Jung that most modern dream therapists follow when they travel into the land of night.

Working with your dreams can equip you with a passport to a renewed sense of creativity. It can be a fresh way of tackling tricky problems and relationships. Our dreams can offer us a means of realizing our deepest desires and coming to terms with our deepest fears.

Dreams can often suggest solutions of which the waking mind has not the faintest glimmer. One woman suffered a humiliating harangue from her boss at work. That night, she dreamed of her hated school headmistress and was struck by the comparison between the two authority figures. She realized that she was feeling exactly the same sense of powerlessness, helplessness and childlike desire for revenge that she had felt as a child. The perception made her snap out of this childish response and remain level-headed.

Working even more deeply, dreams offer us a direct route to the past. They give us a second chance, an opportunity to look back at our mistakes, traumas and hurts, and reassess them in the bright light of the present. Many psychotherapists of various disciplines will use dreamwork in this way, unravelling the past and often, in the process, leading their clients to a far greater sense of perspective and of ease. Interestingly, it is not only emotional or mental relief that comes from working with the past. Often, physical symptoms will disappear when you uncover the original reason for becoming tense or stiff. This experience can be powerful and sometimes painful; many people may feel more comfortable working with a trained therapist for this aspect of dreamwork.

However, you can still go a long way on your own, if you are prepared to be totally honest about the past. All too often we tend to see what we want to see, to discover what we want to discover. It could be a good idea to enlist the help of a close friend, who could perhaps point out an interpretation we might avoid ourselves (although, ultimately, it is your dream and only you can say what it really means).

Above all, don't deny your dreams. Even if they appear disturbing, distressing or even disgusting, they might have a purpose. A little time spent working out their messages, trying to understand the meaning behind their symbols, could make your waking life far easier and more pleasant. In other words, make friends with them — however seemingly mad or bad. Like all good friends, they will in return do their best to help and support you.

OPPOSITE Dreamcatchers are believed to catch bad dreams in their web, allowing the person sleeping below to enjoy restful sleep. But even nightmares may have their purposes.

recalling your dreams

Before you can even start to work with your dreams, you have to be able to recall them in the first place. There is no one, infallible way to remember dreams. Some people find that simply saying aloud before sleep that they want to remember their dreams helps. Some ask for a dream on a particular topic. Others meditate. Still others just wait to see what happens. There are, however, a few points which seem to be of universal help:

- On waking, it can help to stay lying still in your sleeping body position to recall your dream.
- Try saying it aloud or telling someone else your dream as soon as you wake.
- Having a 'dream book' or journal by your bed to write in as soon as you open your eyes can be a very useful way of capturing a dream. Sometimes writing down and rereading your dreams can aid in understanding them. If you prefer, draw an image that sums up your dream.
- Sometimes a simple ritual before sleep, such as spending 10 minutes gazing at a candle or into a glass of water, burning aromatic herbs or dancing to a favourite piece of music, can help lead us into dreams.

ABOVE CHOOSE A BEAUTIFUL JOURNAL IN WHICH TO RECORD YOUR DREAMS. KEEP IT BY YOUR BED SO THAT YOU CAN JOT DOWN DREAMS IMMEDIATELY ON WAKING. YOU MAY ALSO WANT TO USE A TAPE RECORDER.

exploring dreams, talking to your dreams

How can you work with your dreams once you have recalled them? Try these simple techniques.

- Say you dream of the sea, a lion or a school. Don't race to find a dream dictionary and simply look up the symbol. It isn't as straightforward as that. You need to think about the personal associations you may have with the sea or with a lion. Write down everything of which it reminds you. Often quite surprising insights can appear and frequently the symbol will draw into your conscious mind long-forgotten incidents from the past.
- Use the empty-chair technique (see page 119). Take two chairs or two cushions. Sit yourself on one and imagine your dream (or a figure from it) is sitting on the other.

Try speaking to your dreams, telling them how much you want to remember them. You may feel silly at first, but persevere, as it can be very illuminating. Switch seats and speak as if you were the dream replying. Say whatever comes into your mind, without censoring it or feeling embarrassed. Give the dream a voice – let it describe itself and tell you what would help it to surface. You may well be very surprised at what comes up.

- A creative way to start exploring dreams is through painting or drawing them (see the section on art therapy on pages 152–3). The result may be a literal picture of what happened in the dream or it may be more of an expression of the mood of the dream through shape and colour. Don't ask other people to 'interpret' your painting, although it can be helpful to discuss it with someone else. Ask them what they notice about it.

- Use the technique of 'dreaming your dream on', otherwise known as 'active imagination'. If a dream finishes on an uncertain or disconcerting note, try continuing it in waking time. To get in the right frame of mind, find a quiet, dark place where you won't be disturbed and let yourself deeply relax. Start to imagine your dream in all its detail, not just visually, but with all your senses – hearing the sounds, accessing the feeling in your body. There may be a vivid character in the dream whom you want to question. If so, simply ask the character if it would like to talk to you and then wait for the answer. Be patient: you have to wait for the reply and not rush to give it yourself. You will get a sense of when it's coming and, in this way, it won't just be something your conscious mind is making up.

who do you meet in your dreams?

Generally, the people whom you meet in dreams will tend to be different aspects of yourself, often those repressed in waking life. There are no hard and fast rules – and it isn't worth looking up your figure in a 'dream dictionary' – but these are some common correspondences.

- THE SHADOW One powerful image that often appears is the 'shadow', a dream character that normally manifests as someone of the same sex as yourself. Jung said that the shadow represents all the things about ourselves which we find unacceptable and so try to repress. Hence, if expressing or feeling anger wasn't acceptable in your family as you grew up, your shadow may appear as an angry or violent man or woman. If you can talk to your shadow and become on good terms, it will allow you to express your anger appropriately without flying off the handle. Ruthlessness is a common shadow for women because lots of little girls aren't allowed to be ruthless. Try putting your shadow in the 'other' chair in the empty-chair technique (see opposite).
- THE QUEEN A very common image in dreams is the queen, which, for a woman, usually represents her sovereignty

and power. For a man, the queen tends to represent his ability to deal with the feminine side of his nature.

- ROCKS STARS AND FILM STARS These generally represent the hero, excitement and creativity. Dreaming about a star means you want to project the part of you that craves attention and the centre stage.
- BABIES These represent new life of all kinds. Dreaming of babies often occurs when people need to develop other sides of themselves – often when their children have grown up and left home.

unpleasant dreams

Don't be disgusted or horrified by your dreams – no matter how vile they may appear to your waking, conscious self. There are messages in every dream, however disturbing.

- GOING TO THE TOILET IN PUBLIC This is a very common dream. Urinating in public usually represents spontaneous self-expression, while defecating generally represents your creativity. Either of these dreams usually means you haven't yet found your true way of expressing yourself.
- BEING NAKED IN THE STREET Another common albeit disconcerting dream, this classically indicates a fear of revealing who you really are. Normally, it will suggest that you need to reveal more of your true personality.
- BEING CHASED Usually, whatever or whomever is chasing you represents an aspect of yourself that wants to make contact with you. Animals can represent your instinctual nature – it may be that you are leading too cerebral a life. Try talking to the creature or using the empty-chair technique (see opposite).
- HAVING SEX Jung found that sexual dreams usually signify creativity. If you are making love with someone of the same sex as yourself, this usually indicates that you are trying to get in touch with your own feminine or masculine energy.
- TAKING EXAMS A common dream in which you realize that you are due to take an exam (or speak in public or run a race, etc.) yet have not done the necessary preparation. This indicates anxiety and fears that may be holding you back. Maybe you're a perfectionist with unrealistic expectations of yourself – try to be less critical.

CREATIVITY

When we were young, we probably sang at the tops of our voices; we twirled and danced, fancying ourselves ballerinas; we painted and drew without giving a thought to whether the result was 'Art' (with a capital 'A') or not. As we grow older, however, we tend to give up artistic pursuits and leave them to children or the professionals. Yes, we may venture onto the dance floor (providing we've had a few drinks for Dutch courage), we may even sing along with the radio (providing no one's listening), but that's about it.

A growing band of therapists are claiming, however, that if we could only get back to that childlike enjoyment of art, dance and song, we could all become much healthier and happier. Over the next few pages, we'll take a look at simple ways to kickstart your creativity.

dance therapy

All forms of dance are wonderful self-therapy. Dancing is one of the primal instincts of humankind: from the dawn of time, we have felt the urge to move our bodies in a rhythmic way. In fact, dance was originally often a sacred urge – dance would bring the community together for celebration, for sacrifice and to mark the passing seasons of the year and the seasons of life. In our modern Western culture, we have lost touch with our dance heritage. We no longer dance to conjure up the deer for good hunting. (Why bother when our food is lying prepackaged on the supermarket counter?) We no longer dance to honour the earth; instead, we trample all over it. Yes, we dance at weddings and the odd Christmas party, but we no longer leap over the Beltane fires or spin around to welcome the rising energy of the new year. Yet, in losing our dance, we have lost part of our souls.

On the most basic level, dancing is good exercise – it gives your cardiovascular system a workout and stretches your muscles. It's also a wonderful form of stress relief. It really doesn't matter which kind of dance you choose. If you've always fancied floating around a ballroom, why not start now? If serene circle dancing seems suitable, join a circle (it's blissfully calming). If, on the other hand, you fancy kicking up a storm with salsa, Irish jigging or Ceroc, go for it. Of course, it need not be organized dance – you may feel able to connect with your inner self or the earth and start to move. Most of us, however, have lost the knack. That's why some forms of dance have been specifically designed to produce a deep therapeutic effect on mind and body. One of my favourites is Biodanza.

biodanza

While most dancing leaves you totally exhausted, Biodanza leaves you bouncing with boundless energy. It can take away stress and improve your sleep; it can even give you the nerve to chuck no-good lovers and begin new relationships. After a year of Biodanza, its growing band of aficionados swear, your life will be totally different.

Biodanza is tricky to categorize: it's much more than a dance form, but it's not technically a therapy and Biodanza's practitioners certainly don't like to tout it as a cure. Its creator, Chilean psychologist and anthropologist Rolando Toro, came up with the idea for Biodanza back in 1960. He wanted to reintroduce a dance that could express deep feelings and allow people to really connect to each other. He felt that, by dancing in a manner true to our essential 'inner' self, we could literally dance ourselves back to health and happiness, learning to love our bodies and to feel happier in society. He worked at first with mentally disturbed patients and discovered that certain kinds of music would make them move in different ways. This would, in turn, bring about startling changes, in both their bodies and their emotions. Research showed that the moves were stimulating different parts of the nervous system.

The theory is quite complicated, but the dance itself is simple and great fun. Now well established in the USA,

South America, Switzerland, Italy and France, Biodanza is used not just for general wellbeing, but also as a specific therapy for people with eating disorders, those with mental disabilities, children with autism or Down's syndrome, and people suffering from asthma, cardiovascular problems, Parkinson's disease, osteoporosis or gastrointestinal disorders. The very young, the very old, pregnant women – everyone can benefit.

There is absolutely no need to be a 'good' dancer. There is no 'correct' way of doing exercises. The point is to find your own dance. As Rolando Toro puts it: 'Our proposal is to dance to our own life. To retrieve the condition of being the owners of our body, our emotions, as a whole, a unit.'

writing

Many of us dream of writing a novel, penning poems or scribbling an autobiography, yet few of us ever knuckle down to it. We find plenty of excuses – we don't have time, we were never 'good' at writing, nobody would want to read what we have to say. The words remain unwritten. That's a pity, because writing can act as a potent form of self-therapy, illuminating the past and helping us understand ourselves in the present. Writing freely can clear emotional blocks, unshackle creativity and help us in almost every area of life.

It's not about writing a bestseller – although, once the creative juices start flowing, you may end up a published author. It's more about freeing yourself from writing's taboos and learning how to access your innermost feelings.

Psychologists have long recommended we keep journals to record our daily thoughts, claiming that writing down our innermost thoughts and feelings, uncensored, can help emotional growth. Freud pioneered free-association (saying or writing whatever 'pops' into your head), while Jung advocated 'active imagination' (letting the imagination run free to explore dreams or fantasies). Let's look at some simple ways to use the written word as therapy – and for fun.

You will need to set aside a decent amount of time for these exercises – at least 10 minutes for the actual writing of each exercise, plus time to settle yourself beforehand and some time afterwards to muse on what happened in the exercise. Pick a time when and place where you won't

be disturbed – you won't be able to write just what you feel if you know someone is going to pop up behind you and read over your shoulder! Choose a pen that feels comfortable and writes easily, and either loose sheets of paper or (if you intend to keep a record of your work) a bound notebook.

Before you start, it may be a good idea to sit quietly for a few minutes and focus on your breathing, allowing yourself to become calm. You may like to light a candle or burn some aromatherapy oil to give yourself a sense of ritual.

get in touch with your feelings

Start by trying out different ways of writing about your feelings, thoughts and attitudes. It doesn't matter if what you write is absolute rubbish, embarrassing, fanciful or whatever. Nobody else need ever see it. Try these exercises – just for fun. Work quickly, so you don't have time to censor yourself.

1 RIGHT HERE, RIGHT NOW Start by looking at your immediate surroundings. What catches your attention? It could be your cat curled up on a sofa, the rain on the window panes, a cobweb in a corner. Describe two or three of the things you notice, being very precise in your descriptions: what do they look like, smell like, feel like, taste (!) like? How do they make you feel? What thoughts come into your head when you describe them? What is your mood, your feelings, your thoughts? Keep writing for about 12 minutes on this.

2 A SPECIAL PLACE We all have 'special' places of the past, most usually from childhood. What outside places do you remember from when you were small? It might be a beach, a playground, a small patch of land that was magical to you. Describe the place in as much detail as you can – again, think about using all your senses. How do you feel about this place now? How did you feel then? What happened in that place? Again, spend about 12 minutes on this exercise.

3 DESERT ISLAND THOUGHTS Imagine you are marooned on a desert island – it's beautiful and safe, with plenty of food and water, and a nice shelter. Think about the following:

- What and whom would you most miss? Why?
- What wouldn't you miss? Why?
- Which three things would be your desert island objects (excluding things such as television, computer, telephone!)?
- What would be your one desert island book?
- How would you live from day to day? Would you be able to cope with being alone? How would you do it?

RIGHT FINDING A PEACEFUL CORNER IN WHICH TO WRITE OUT YOUR THOUGHTS AND FEELINGS CAN BE THERAPEUTIC. YOU NEED TO FEEL VERY PRIVATE AND TO BE SURE THAT YOU WON'T BE DISTURBED.

flow-writing

This technique works at unleashing the huge reservoir of ideas, images and feelings that make up our unconscious minds. Our minds are like giant icebergs; only a tiny part (the conscious mind) appears above the water. Below lies a huge mass of unconscious (but highly important) information. Flow-writing bypasses the controlling conscious mind and allows this hidden material to come to the surface.

You will probably want desperately to direct your writing, but resist the urge. Don't plan, just write whatever comes into your head. Don't worry if you panic or dry up. Simply repeat the last few words you've written until something new suggests itself, then continue. Try not to censor yourself – it doesn't matter if what you write seems trivial or silly. Equally, it's fine if embarrassing or private feelings come up. This is for you — nobody else ever need read it. Don't worry about whether you have the right word or your writing is logical or your grammar perfect – just 'go with the flow'.

If you find this hard, start off with one of these sentences:

'For the first time in my life I …'

'In my heart of hearts, I really wanted to …'

'It's been many years since …'

'My deepest fear was that …'

'Nobody ever knew that …'

After you have written each piece, underline any sentences, phrases and words that catch your attention. You may find that one of these phrases or words is the impetus for a fresh bout of flow-writing. You can use this technique if you know you have an area you want to explore. Simply pick a sentence that plugs you into that time or incident, and off you go.

using sound for healing

You don't have to be a singer or have a good voice to benefit from singing, toning or making sounds. It isn't about perfect pitch or making a beautiful sound: it's all about gaining confidence and being who you want to be.

'So many people were told they couldn't sing at school,' says sound therapist Susan Lever, 'that they were tone deaf or maybe told off when they were singing and it stops them enjoying singing. We have a lot of early messages that it's not okay to be who we are. Sometimes we try to copy other people's voices, we try to get rid of dialects or we have "telephone voices". Playing with sound helps people feel safe. They can relax and feel it's okay to take risks and explore.'

First of all, take a look at the ideas on sound therapy (pages 250–1). Groaning, sighing and humming are simple, effective ways to start using your voice.

Take every opportunity you can to use your voice – sing along to the radio while you're doing the housework, belt out rock tunes or opera arias as you drive in your car. If you can find somewhere really private, you might even try screaming. Many therapists say that, if you can unleash your inner scream (and apparently most of us have one), you can plug into some deep, powerful feelings – and at the same time release a lot of stress and tension.

Sound doesn't have to be loud, however, to be effective. One of the most powerful techniques for healing with sound is toning pure vowel sounds that correspond with the chakras (the energy centres of the body; see pages 40–1). Start with a deep guttural 'uuuh' at the base of the spine; then 'ooo'

(the genital chakra); 'oh' (the solar plexus); 'ah' (the heart); 'eye' (the throat); 'ey' (as in hay, for the third eye) and finally 'eee' (for the crown). The sounds get higher as you move up the body. Tone each one for several minutes.

Making sound can really change your mood. If you feel low and you make happy sounds, it will lift you without a doubt. Your breathing will automatically change and so will your physiological state. You will find you have a lot more energy, a lot more confidence and a lot less stress.

Above all, the aim is to find your natural voice and relearn how to speak and sing without strain or effort. Often that involves relaxing and teaching yourself to let the voice come naturally from the whole body, rather than holding it tight in the throat. Once this happens, you may discover some surprising side effects. Letting your voice come from your whole body will often start to release long-standing blocks and tensions. If you *have* always spoken or sung from your throat, it is probably a protection mechanism. Start singing from your heart or your abdomen and you might find something else coming up, such as old grief, hurt or anger.

art as therapy – painting your way to health

Daubing paint or scribbling with a pencil, say art therapists, has the power to heal. You don't have to be Van Gogh and you don't need any art-school techniques. Painting whatever you want to, straight from the heart, can apparently put you in touch with repressed emotions and long-buried hurts.

Psychologists explain that art has the ability to bypass our conscious, 'thinking' mind and connect directly with our subconscious, where all our deepest fears and hurts are buried. Paint and you could discover hidden sides to your personality; you could gain in confidence and self-esteem; you might even find that physical ailments disappear or are alleviated when you allow yourself a creative outlet.

Art has been used as a tool by psychotherapists since 1810. Since then, many experts have discovered that, when people paint freely, they are able to express feelings and give a form on paper to fears and terrors that they are utterly unable to express in words. Art therapy is most definitely not about painting or drawing 'properly': you don't have to make pretty or lifelike pictures, but rather simply pick up your paintbrush and see what happens. Art therapist Michael Edwards suggests you sit quietly and breathe deeply before painting. Then just see what appears on the paper. Afterwards, he suggests you try 'talking to your pictures'. It sounds crazy, but he promises that you could have some very interesting responses. 'Write a commentary or simply scribble a letter to your painting. Ask it questions: it might answer. I know it sounds nuts, but it does seem to work.'

The process isn't always easy or fun. Art leads people gently into their psyches. Sometimes distressing things come up, but somehow they can be contained by the paper. In other words, you might feel terrified about, say, a nightmare, but by painting it out you can take back a certain amount of control over your fears. Art therapists are loath to claim miracles, but sometimes people even find physical problems disappear.

healing your mind and soul with art

To get a feel for art therapy, try these exercises. As with all these creative exercises, you should find a time when and a place where you won't be disturbed. It doesn't matter which art materials you choose – some people like to paint large (on huge sheets of paper or newspaper) with poster paints; others prefer scribbling on smaller sheets with felt pens, crayons, chalks or charcoal. You could go to an art shop and see which materials draw you. Don't censor your choice – one woman I met found she worked best painting on glass!

- Put aside all expectations of painting a 'proper' picture. That isn't the point. You may not even paint anything recognizable. Some people simply use colour or shapes or symbols. Others don't use paintbrushes – they prefer to splat paint on with their hands or fingers, or even feet!

- You may find it's easier to paint with your non-dominant hand (so, if you're left-handed, try using your right hand). Perhaps you could shut your eyes while you paint. Maybe you could even dance as you paint! All these suggestions tend to free your unconscious and allow it to take over.

do-it-yourself art therapy

Paint your lifeline – Take a large piece of paper and any art materials you like. Imagine that the paper represents your lifetime – the beginning, the now, the future and the end. Sit quietly for a few moments and then fill the paper in whatever way you like. Don't expect anything or try to draw 'properly'; use whatever symbols or images you feel are appropriate. You might choose to depict events in your life or simply choose different colours to represent different parts of your life or feelings. When you have finished, be aware of how you feel – both in your mind and your body. What is your painting saying? Does it yield clues to how you think or how you feel about your life? What are the themes and questions in it? Don't throw it away afterwards – keep it and look at it from time to time to see if any new insights arise.

Paint a fairy story – Fairy tales and myths have powerful effects on our psyches. Think back to your childhood – is there one particular story you remember? It may be a favourite or one that frightened you at the time. If you don't have a particular tale, find a book of tales (the Brothers Grimm are a good choice) and pick a story that appeals. Reread your story. Which image is the most powerful in the book? Again, choose art materials and paper. Depict your chosen image any way you like. You may even be drawn to use other materials, maybe making a model out of clay or scrap or natural objects such as sticks, stone or grasses. Once you've finished, look at your image. Think about how you feel when you see it. What does it remind you of? Write down your feelings or stray thoughts.

Paint a dream – Dreams are also powerful ways to access our feelings. This is looked at in more depth in the dreamworking section (pages 145–7), but it can be a good exercise to attempt painting an image from a dream, or trying to express the mood of a dream with paint or other art materials.

Paint yourself – How do you see yourself? Lay a huge sheet of paper on the floor. Lie down on it and ask someone to draw around your outline. Fill in the silhouette any way you want. You may want to cut out pictures from magazines or newspapers; you may prefer just to use colours. Are there any parts that feel 'cut off' (perhaps you feel drawn to get out the scissors and snip them away)? Are there any parts you don't want to colour in? Are there any parts that seem brighter, more 'real'? How does this exercise make you feel about your body?

soul

4

What is a soul? We can touch our bodies, but no one has ever actually touched a soul. We can sense our minds working, we can feel our emotions, but our soul is somehow far more ineffable. Many mystical traditions hold that the soul is the part of us that is divine and eternal. When our bodies have turned to dust and our minds are no more, we exist as pure soul. But exactly what does that mean in daily life?

I think you can sense your soul and, with practice, you can become more and more aware of it and its needs. Think of a time when you were overcome with wonder, with love or beauty. It could be the sight of a newborn baby gazing up at you. It might be the vision of a sunrise or sunset, when the earth is bathed in breathtaking beauty. It could be the majesty of a mountain range or the tiny miracle of a snowdrop pushing through the rock-solid frozen earth. It might just be a warm feeling as you sit listening to your friends chatting or a sense of peace as you quietly muse on your own. At these, and other, moments, we catch a glimpse of our souls – we feel an inkling of something deep within that is not caught up in the day-to-day detritus of life.

The aim of this section is to find simple, effective ways by which we can nurture this relationship with our souls. If we want to get the most out of our lives, to feel fulfilled, exhilarated and peaceful, we need to address our soul just as much as our bodily and psychological requirements. In some ways, the soul connection is the most important. If your soul is in good form, everything else should fall into place because we find soul everywhere – in the incredible entity we call a body, in the halls of our minds, in nature, in our work, in our personal lives, in our sexuality, in our dreams. We explore our souls both in the joyful moments and in the dark abysses of depression, fear, sorrow and anger.

As we come to recognize our souls, we may even feel the tug towards something larger, more wise and powerful than us: we start to feel our connection to Spirit. In the past, the most common way to explore this was through organized religion. This is still a valid path and one we look at in the first part of this section. However, we don't just find our connection to Spirit and 'God' within a church or mosque, a synagogue or temple, so we will also be looking at alternative ways to find a sense of unity with Spirit.

THE SPIRITUAL TRADITIONS

THERE ARE MANY PATHS TO THE DIVINE. SOME PEOPLE GROW UP WITH ONE PARTICULAR RELIGION AND IT RESONATES SO DEEPLY WITHIN THEIR SOULS THAT THEY FOLLOW IT ALL THEIR LIVES. IN MANY WAYS, THEY ARE THE LUCKY ONES. THEY HAVE A CERTAINTY ABOUT THEIR SPIRITUAL LIVES THAT CAN BE DEEPLY COMFORTING AND REASSURING. FOR OTHER PEOPLE, FINDING THE RIGHT PATH CAN BE A LONG AND OFTEN PAINFUL PROCESS. SOMETIMES IT ENTAILS LONG PERIODS OF SEARCHING AND EXPERIMENTING – OFTEN ACCOMPANIED BY INTENSE DISAPPOINTMENT. IF THIS APPLIES TO YOU, DON'T BE DISCOURAGED. THE JOURNEY MAY BE DIFFICULT, BUT WE ALL TEND TO GET THERE IN THE END.

The 'standard' religions have a weight, tradition and power that can make them deeply welcoming. They are not, however, the only way. Today, many people are rediscovering ancient religious traditions such as shamanism or Wicca and paganism. Still others will feel drawn to forge an individual relationship with Spirit. Go with your heart, listen to your soul. Truly, it doesn't matter whether you find God (Goddess, Supreme Creator, whatever it is that underpins the universe) in a babbling brook or in the vaults of a cathedral. All that is important is that your spirituality soothes your soul, that it has meaning for you and that it brings you peace.

In this section, we will look briefly at some of the great spiritual traditions of the world.

christianity

Christianity is the world's largest religion – about a third of the world's population regard themselves as Christians, although Islam is projected to become the dominant religion during this century.

In general, all Christians follow the teachings of Jesus Christ, a Jewish preacher born c 7–4 BCE. Most Christians regard Jesus as the son of God and one of the Holy Trinity (Father, Son and Holy Spirit) who was incarnated as a man, born of a virgin (Mary). He preached God's word before being condemned to death and crucified. On the third day after his death, Jesus was resurrected and ascended to heaven.

There is a wide divergence between the teachings and beliefs of the various Christian sects. Some believe that we are born fundamentally sinful and that we can only be 'saved' from hell and damnation through a life of repentance and prayer. Others are far less judgmental and consider the concept of hell as symbolic, rather than an actual location for eternal torment and punishment. At its most simple, Christianity really comes down to two tenets: love God and be kind to others.

Prayer is the most common form of worship. In the past, retreats and pilgrimage, alongside fasting and meditative techniques, were part of Christianity and many people are now returning to these practices. There is also renewed interest in the varying forms of Christian mysticism, such as Gnosticism, and in the wisdom of early Christian mystics and sages such as Hildegaard of Bingen and Meister Eckhart.

Christian mysticism emphasizes the relationship between man and God, and also God and the world – teaching that God can be found within us and also in the world around us. Through diligent practice, we can obtain a sense of oneness with God. As Hildegaard of Bingen put it: 'The mystery of God hugs you in its all-encompassing arms.'

islam

NOTE: Muslims always follow the name of the prophet Muhammad with the words 'peace be upon him'; when written, this is abbreviated to 'pbuh'. As a mark of respect, we have followed this practice.

OPPOSITE WHETHER YOU ARE DRAWN TO THE GREAT TRADITIONAL RELIGIONS OR FEEL AN URGE TO FOLLOW YOUR OWN PATH, MAKING TIME FOR YOUR SOUL CAN GIVE GREAT PEACE AND COMFORT.

Islam is the second-largest world religion – and it is expanding very fast. It is also the youngest of the world's great religions. Islam is generally believed to have been founded in 622 CE by the prophet Muhammad (pbuh). Muhammad (pbuh) was raised in the desert but travelled widely, meeting people of a wide variety of religious beliefs. At the age of 40, in 610 BCE, he received divine revelations from the angel Jibreel (or Gabriel) while he was in Mecca. He was given the task of converting his people from their pagan, polytheistic beliefs and what he saw as their moral decadence and materialism.

Muhammad (pbuh) taught that we need to relinquish our selfish individual needs and personal will, surrendering instead to the divine will of God – the word *Islam* means 'surrender'. These revelations, the divine words of God, were written down and became the Qur'an, the divine scripture, or writings, that all Muslims follow. The Hadith, a collection of the sayings of the prophet Muhammad (pbuh), is used as an additional guide for living.

The principle of 'surrender' is readily demonstrated by a Sufi (see below) teaching story in which a man knocks on God's door. 'Who's there?' comes the voice of God from inside. 'It's me,' says the man. 'Well, go away,' says God, 'there's no room in here for two.' The man walked away and wandered around alone in the desert until he realized his mistake. He then returned to the door and knocked again. Once again, God asked, 'Who's there?' This time the man answered, 'You.' 'Then come in,' replied God.

Muslims have a series of duties including regular prayer, charitable donations, fasting and pilgrimage. Perhaps most often misunderstood is the concept of Jihad (struggle). While some fundamentalist Muslims have seen it as a literal call to enforce conversion to their faith, via crusades and bloodshed, the vast majority of Muslims see it as a personal, internal battle, a struggle with one's self.

Islam is a very moral religion: devout Muslims reject alcohol, gambling and the taking of drugs. They recognize Jesus, but regard him as a prophet, rather than a deity. Other prophets such as Abraham and Moses are also respected. Muhammad (pbuh) is seen as the last of the prophets.

There are several strands of Islam. One which is gaining popularity in the West is Sufism. This is a highly mystical path, characterized by its profoundly beautiful spiritual poetry which talks about the longing for union with God and often expresses this in 'romantic' terms, with God as the deeply Beloved with whom the Sufi shares an intoxicating and passionate sacred love.

hinduism

Despite its great antiquity, Hinduism remains a vibrant faith today and is the world's third-largest religion. It is said to have originated in the Indus Valley around 4000 to 2200 BCE.

There are literally thousands of different strands of Hinduism and, to the novice, it may seem very confusing and even contradictory, with different sects worshipping a variety of deities. There is, however, basically one eternal truth: we are all part of God and God is within each of us. 'Atman is Brahman' means the Higher Self (our true spiritual identity, rather than our common ego) is God: our consciousness is simply an expression of the cosmic consciousness.

The Hindu sage Ramakrishna said: 'The ego is like a stick dividing water into two. It creates the impression that you are one and I am another. When the ego vanishes, you will realize that Brahman is your own inner Consciousness.'

Although the entire universe is experienced as one divine entity, this deity is also expressed as a trinity: Brahma (the Creator, who continues to create new realities); Vishnu or Krishna (the Preserver, who preserves these creations) and Shiva (the Destroyer, who can destroy, but be compassionate as well). Humans are seen as being trapped in samsara, a meaningless cycle of birth, life, death and rebirth. Karma (the accumulated sum of our good and bad deeds in life) will determine how we live our next life. The aim is to live as pure a life as possible so we can be reborn at a higher level and eventually achieve enlightenment and escape samsara.

There are various paths towards spiritual enlightenment, known as *yogas*. The hatha yoga we do as exercise was originally a path towards God through mastery of body and mind. Tantric yoga was initially a difficult path towards union with God through precise use of sexual energy. Other forms of yoga include bhakti yoga (which emphasizes prayer, worship and devotion) and gnana yoga (which is more intellectual, focusing on meditation, study of scripture and philosophy). Many Hindu practices are now used widely in the West, such as meditation, physical yoga and pranayama (breathing).

buddhism

Buddhism was founded in Northern India, inspired by an Indian sage called Siddhartha Guatama, or simply Buddha, who was born in 563 BCE. At the age of 29, he left his family and career in order to seek truth. In 535 BCE, Siddhartha reached enlightenment and assumed the title of Buddha (which means 'One who has been awakened').

Buddhism has become enormously popular in the West in recent years – probably because of the extreme simplicity and clarity of its teachings. There is no belief in a 'God' as such, no need for personal saviours.

Buddhism teaches that we suffer because we fear death. Yet, in truth, there is no death because there is no separate 'self' to die. We are not individual souls, but all part of an indivisible whole. Our problems stem from the illusion (samsara) of our separation. The principal aim of Buddhism is to experience nirvana, the blissful state of enlightenment in which we are one with all of creation, all of consciousness.

Of course, the ego can have trouble with this philosophy – particularly the notion that each of us is like a drop of water which will eventually be absorbed back into the infinite ocean. Buddhists, however, insist that enlightenment is actually incredibly comforting, bringing the certain knowledge that our essential beings will never die.

Many Buddhist practices are also finding general favour today. Mindfulness (see pages 109–10) is a classic Buddhist practice. Meditation is used, too, and some Buddhists practise chanting, pilgrimage, ceremony and rituals.

Zen Buddhism is a form of Buddhism mingled with some elements of Taoism (see page 160). Founded in the sixth century CE by an Indian Buddhist, Bodhidharma, its aim is for us to discover who we are: to experience our true 'Buddha nature' in the emptiness of mind. In this state of 'empty mind', we have no sense of ourselves as individuals, but rather as part of the greater consciousness. Classic Zen practice is 'sitting', meditation's most basic form. Zen is also famous for the bizarre and seemingly illogical advice and practices of its masters, who seek to shock the mind into spiritual realization. A classic example is: 'What is your original face?' Such questions defeat the rational mind and may ultimately cause the seeker to stop striving and purely 'see'.

judaism

NOTE: it is forbidden for Jews to spell the name of the deity in full, so they write 'G-d'. As a mark of respect, this practice has been followed here.

Judaism was founded around 2000 BCE when the G-d of the ancient people of Israel established a divine covenant with Abraham, making him the patriarch of many nations. He was followed by the patriarchs Isaac and Jacob. Moses was the next great leader of the ancient Israelites; he led the people out of captivity in Egypt and received the Law from G-d. There are around 18 million Jews in the world, mainly in the USA (around 7 million) and Israel (4.5 million).

There are two main books of scriptures. The Tanakh consists of three groups of books: the Torah (which contains Genesis, Exodus, Leviticus, Numbers and Deuteronomy); the Nevi'im (the Prophetic books of Isaiah, Amos etc.) and the Ketuvim (the Writings, including Kings, Chronicles etc.). The Talmud contains stories, laws, moral debates and medical knowledge, and is composed of material from two sources: the Mishnah (six 'orders' containing series of laws from the Hebrew scriptures) and the Gemara (including comments from hundreds of rabbis from 200–500 CE). The Gemara explains the Mishnah with other historical, sociological, legal and religious material.

Judaism teaches that there is only one G-d, who is Creator of everything and is without body. The entire world is seen as inherently good and its people basically good, creations of G-d. Believers can come closer to G-d by following the divine commandments. There is no saviour needed nor any other intermediaries. G-d communicates to the Jewish people through prophets and monitors people's behaviour, rewarding them for good deeds and punishing evil. One's actions are seen as very important and Jewish life is regulated by a large body of law – basically, the Ten Commandments of Moses are a synopsis of the Law (in all, there are 613 commandments found in Leviticus and other books).

Judaism celebrates a wide variety of festivals and regular worship is also expected. Prayer and study are an intrinsic part of Jewish life. Recently, many Westerners have become fascinated by the esoteric branch of Judaism, the Quabalah.

taoism

The word *Tao* (pronounced 'dow', to rhyme with 'now') roughly translates as 'path', or 'the way'. The Tao is considered to be the force, or energy, which moves through and within all things in the universe. A deep mystical concept, the Tao can signify pure consciousness, an emptiness which is yet full or supreme oneness with creation. It is also seen in more prosaic terms as the way things are, the way life works.

The founder of Taoism was Lao-Tse (604–531 BCE), who was a contemporary of Confucius. He sought a way of avoiding the persistent warfare that plagued society and wrote down his ideas in a book, the Tao Te Ching, which is a combination of psychology and philosophy.

Taoism became a religious faith in 440 CE, when it was adopted as a state religion in China and Lao-Tse became venerated as a deity. Sadly, much of the Taoist heritage was destroyed during China's Cultural Revolution, instituted by China's former Communist leader Mao Tse-tung in 1966. Today, there are around 20 million practising Taoists and interest in the Tao is growing as people discover its concepts, often through acupuncture, tai chi, feng shui and the I Ching.

The goal of the Taoist is to become one with the Tao, the essential life energy of the universe. Understanding and wisdom are achieved not by prayer to a deity, but through observation of the world and its signs, inner contemplation and meditation. The world is seen as divided into two opposites – yin and yang – which should be kept in perfect balance. We humans, however, usually manage to upset this balance and one or other will become dominant, causing disharmony, disease and disturbance. Taoists strive to care for their bodies as well as their souls. It is considered essential to nurture one's qi (vital energy) and to keep yin and yang in balance. Similarly, one should develop virtue: seeking compassion, moderation and humility. Kindness is seen as a great virtue, as is careful planning and forethought.

One of the key concepts of Taoism is wu wei, achieving action through minimal effort, popularized in the West by the psychologist Carl Jung. Wu wei is explained as follows: it is the practice of going against the stream not by struggling against it and thrashing about, but by standing still and letting the stream do all the work.

jainism (jain dharma)

Jainism traces its roots to the 24 Jinas (literally meaning 'those who overcame') in ancient East India. The first Jina was supposedly a giant who lived around eight and a half million years ago. The most recent, and last, Jina was Vardhamana, or Mahavira, who was born in 550 BCE and founded the Jain community. It took 13 years of deprivation for him to achieve enlightenment and, in 420 BCE, he starved himself to death. Jainism contains many elements in common with Hinduism and Buddhism, although it is far more ascetic. The world's four million Jains live almost entirely in India.

Jainism teaches that the universe is without beginning or end; it exists as a series of layers:

- the supreme abode where the Siddha or liberated souls live
- the upper world: heavens where celestial beings live
- the middle world: earth and the rest of the universe
- the nether world: seven hells with various levels of punishment
- the nigoda: where the lowest forms of life reside
- universe space: layers of cloud surrounding the upper world of celestial beings
- space beyond: an infinite zone without soul, matter, time, motion or rest

We are all bound by karma, and moksha (liberation from constant reincarnation) is only achieved by enlightenment (which, in turn, can only be achieved by the harshest forms of ascetic living). There are five essential principles for life:

- AHIMSA This is basically non-violence. It is taken to the most extreme form – you must not commit mental, verbal or physical violence on any living thing, even an insect or vegetable. Jains consume only what will not kill the plant or animal from which it is taken – i.e. milk, fruit and nuts.
- SATYA This is speaking the truth always.
- ASTEYA This means not stealing.
- BRAHMA-CHARYA This is the soul's conduct – remaining faithful to one's spouse.
- APARIGRAHA This means detachment from people, places and material things. Some Jains even go as far as to reject clothing and go naked at all times.

confucianism

Confucianism is not a religion as such, but more a series of codes of moral conduct. It was founded by K'ung Fu Tzu (commonly known as Confucius in English). He was not a prophet or philosopher, but, as he liked to put it, a 'transmitter', relaying the wisdom of the ancients. K'ung Fu Tzu was born in 551 BCE, in what is now the Shantung province of China. His writings are mainly concerned with morality, ethics and the proper use of political power. During his life, Confucius wandered through China accompanied by a small band of students; he spent his last years teaching in his homeland.

There are around six million Confucians in the world today. Many combine the ethical teaching of Confucianism with Taoist and Buddhist beliefs.

The major ethical beliefs of Confucius include:
- LI Ritual, correct ways of behaving
- HSIAO Family values – love between parents and children, siblings, grandparents etc.
- YI Righteousness
- XIN Honesty and trustworthiness
- JEN Benevolence, kindness to others
- CHUNG Loyalty to the state

The Confucian tradition recognizes four major life passages, which are governed by ritual and celebration:
- BIRTH The spirit of the fetus (the T'ai-shen) is believed to protect the expectant mother and deal harshly with anyone who bothers her. There is a Confucian ritual for disposing of the placenta after birth and the new mother is made to rest and carefully fed a special diet for a month following the birth.
- ATTAINING MATURITY A group family meal of chicken celebrates the transition to adulthood.
- MARRIAGE An elaborate six-stage celebration takes place which involves minutely observed rituals for proposal, engagement, dowry, procession, marriage and reception, and, finally, morning after (breakfast).
- DEATH A willow branch is carried to the cemetery in order to symbolize the soul of the person who has died. Mourners contribute to the cost of the funeral and liturgies are performed on set dates for the first three years after death.

shinto

Shinto was founded in Japan in around 500 BCE (or possibly earlier). It was originally a form of shamanism featuring nature and ancestor worship, divination and fertility cults. The word *shinto* comes from the Chinese *Shin Tao* ('Way of the Gods'). It was, and remains, a loosely based religion, with no written scriptures as such (although there are valued texts), no real figureheads and no body of religious law. Many Japanese follow both Buddhism and Shinto – in Shinto, Buddha is seen as another Kami or nature deity, and Buddhists in Japan regard the Kami as manifestations of Buddhas.

There is a large number of Kami, emanating from the original 'divine couple', Izanagi-no-mikoto and Izanami-no-mikoto, who gave birth to the Japanese islands. Their offspring became the various clan deities. Amaterasu, the Sun Goddess, was one of their daughters and is regarded as a chief deity. Many others are related to natural objects and creatures. There are guardian Kami in particular areas and locations; clans also have their particular protective Kami. The Kami are generally seen as benign protectors.

All of humanity is regarded as 'Kami's child' and hence sacred. So, too, is nature – to be close to nature is thus seen as being close to the gods; natural objects are often worshipped as sacred spirits. Ancestor worship is an integral part of Shinto and family life is very important – the main celebrations and rituals are all to do with family, birth and marriage. A strong emphasis is put on morality, cleanliness and kindness.

There is much of interest in Shinto for modern spiritual seekers and many of its practices are being taken up, in particular by those who practise Wicca, shamanism and druidism. Seasonal celebrations are a strong part of Shinto and there is a tradition of venerating sacred places, such as springs, mountains and trees. Ritual dance is common. Shinto believers make shrines and altars both within the home and in nature. They also visit communal shrines for celebrations and rituals. Charms are made and worn for healing and protection. Origami (literally, 'paper of the spirits') is about much more than making pretty shapes out of paper: it is made as a gift to spirits and placed on or around Shinto shrines. The paper is folded, rather than cut, out of respect for the tree spirit that gave its life to make the paper.

sikhism

Many people regard Sikhism as a Hindu cult, but, although it does contain elements of Hinduism (as well as Islam), Sikhism is fundamentally different and unique. *Sikh* means 'learner' and it was founded by Shri Guru Nanak Dev Ji (1469–1538), who was born in the Punjab. He received a vision in which he was instructed to preach the way to enlightenment and God.

There are around 22.5 million Sikhs worldwide. Their goal is to build a close loving relationship with God. This is seen as almost akin to that of a bride longing for her husband. God is regarded as a powerful yet totally compassionate entity. He is present in everything, from the greatest spiritual seeker to the lowliest grub. There is one God who alone should be worshipped, but, as with Islam, He has many names. Sikhs do not deny the other gods of Hindu belief, but consider them lesser gods who should not be worshipped. Like Hindus and Buddhists, they believe in karma and reincarnation. Sikhs totally reject the caste system of the Hindus, however, believing that everyone has equal standing in the eyes of God.

Sikhism is strongly non-elitist and it is customary in its temples to sit on the floor to emphasize that everyone is of equal value. Many Sikhs follow the teachings of living gurus. They pray many times a day and also worship in temples known as *gurdwaras*.

bahá'i faith

Just as Christianity arose from Judaism, so the Bahá'i faith developed from Islam. It is now a worldwide faith with around six million followers. They believe that there is only one God, the source of all creation who is transcendent and basically unknowable. However, he has sent and continues to send great prophets to reveal the word of God. These prophets are considered to have been: Adam, Abraham, Moses, Krishna, Zoroaster, Buddha, Jesus Christ, Mohammad and the Báb.

'The Báb' was the title assumed by Siyyid Ali-Muhammad (1819–1850 CE), who lived in Persia. It means 'the gate' and, on 23 May 1844 (considered the founding of the faith), he explained that the purpose of his mission was to herald the arrival of 'One greater than Himself', who would fulfil the expectations of all the great religions. His followers became known as Babis and many were martyred for their beliefs in the religious unrest that followed. The Báb was executed in 1850, as he was seen as a threat to orthodox Islam.

The Manifestation predicted by the Báb was one of his followers, who became known as Bahá'u'llah and spent the last 40 years of his life in prison or exile. His son Abdu'l-Bahá became leader after his death.

The Bahá'i believe in the unity of all the great world religions – not that they are identical, but that they have all sprung from the same source. They assert that every person has an immortal soul, which, at death, passes to the spirit world – 'a timeless and placeless extension of our own universe'.

Prayer and fasting are a strong part of the faith; work is regarded as a form of worship and holy days are observed. Members of the faith also make at least one pilgrimage to the Shrine of the Báb and the houses in which Bahá'u'llah lived. They believe that unity is the key to peace and that eventually the world will be ruled by one single government, led by Bahá'is. Principles of freedom of speech, equality and tolerance are strongly promoted and they believe in scientific enquiry guided by spiritual principles. However, this tolerance is not extended to homosexuality and women are excluded from serving in the Universal House of Justice, its highest religious court.

vodun or voodoo

This grouping includes related religions such as Candomble, Macumba, Santeria, Lucumi and Yoruba.

A variety of religions with shared concepts and beliefs can be traced back to the West African Yoruba people. When the Yoruba were forced into slavery, they took their religion to Haiti and other Caribbean islands. The word *Vodun* equates to an African word for 'spirit'. Very similar religions (Umbanda, Quimbanda and Candomble) can be found in South America.

There are an estimated 60 million people practising Vodun worldwide. Each group follows a slightly different spiritual path and worships a slightly different pantheon of spirits, which are known as Loa. Traditional belief includes a chief god, Olorun, who is remote and unknowable. He authorized a lesser god, Obatala, to create the world and all life in it. However, these two gods had a battle that led to Obatala's temporary banishment. There are also hundreds of lesser gods and spirits, including Erzulia, goddess of love; Erinle, spirit of the forests; Ogou Balanjo, spirit of healing; Ogun, spirit of war; Baron Samedi, spirit of the graveyard; Agwe, spirit of the sea; Sango, spirit of storms; and Osun, spirit of healing streams. Many Loa are similar to Christian saints, in that they were once people who led exceptional lives. Vodun has many other features in common with Roman Catholicism and, indeed, in the past many slaves worshipped the Loa under the guise of Christianity.

Vodun ceremonies aim to make contact with the spirits and gain their help and favour by the offering of gifts and animal sacrifices. These ceremonies are elaborate, consisting of a feast prior to the main ritual; creation of a *veve* (a pattern of flour or cornmeal on the floor – each Loa has a particular pattern); chanting, rattling and drumming; and dancing by the priest (called a *houngan* or *mambo*) and the students (*hounsis*) until someone becomes possessed by a Loa and falls. The possessed dancer will be treated with great respect and takes on the characteristics of the Loa. An animal is usually sacrificed – its blood feeds the Loa. It is normally then cooked and eaten.

Followers of Vodun believe that each person has a soul composed of two parts: a *gros bon ange* (literally, 'large good angel') and a *ti bon ange* (or 'little good angel'). The ti bon ange leaves the body during sleep and when a person is possessed by a Loa during a ritual. These are dangerous times, when the ti bon ange can be damaged or captured by evil sorcery while free of the body (this corresponds to the belief in the astral body).

Vodun is a much misunderstood religion, mainly through the efforts of Hollywood! It conjures images of zombies, human sacrifice, graveyard rituals, murderous curses, necromancy and black magic. Certainly, it is fair to say that some hougans do engage in sorcery and a few mix both good and bad magic, but generally magic is used to bring healing and good fortune. Zombies, meanwhile, are considered to be people under the influence of powerful drugs, with no will of their own. As for the classic 'voodoo dolls' of horror movies, they are not commonly used; only occasionally in South America are they employed as a means of cursing.

pagan religious traditions

The terms *pagan* and *neo-pagan* refer to a collection of separate religions which share common themes. These include Wicca and witchcraft, paganism and heathenism, shamanism, druidism, Asatru (Norse paganism), goddess worship and re-creations of ancient religious traditions such as the Celtic, Egyptian, Greek, Roman, Sumerian and Norse (among others).

These systems of belief were all persecuted in the past and, in many cases, little remains of the original practice and tradition. Modern followers have had to reconstruct their religions from ancient sources of information. Some have used channelling (obtaining information from the spirit realm) or intuition to fill the gaps.

Even today, these groups face much misunderstanding and persecution. Christianity, in particular, has confused the pagan faiths with Satanism (which has nothing to do with paganism and is, in fact, an offshoot of Christianity).

All pagans worship and revere nature. There is a deep reverence for the life force and the cycles of life and death within nature. Pagans celebrate a wheel of seasonal rituals which, while having deep spiritual meanings, are also an excuse for festivity and socializing.

Paganism puts great emphasis on individual responsibility and integrity. The classic pagan tenet is 'Do what thou wilt, but harm none' – which is often woefully misunderstood. It means that every individual has the duty to discover his or her Self and to develop it as fully as possible, in harmony with the outer world. We can do whatever we feel it requires to fulfil this, providing we do not hurt anyone else. Most pagans venerate both female and male principles of life – the Goddess and the God.

The pagan path is becoming very popular. People are drawn to the flexibility of this spiritual tradition (you can practise it in small groups or on your own). It is also very much in tune with present-day thoughts and concerns (the environment, balance between the sexes, self-development, interest in ritual and ceremony). Most pagans also believe that fun and laughter should be an essential component.

PRAYER

In the past, prayer was as essential a part of everyday life as meals. As a child, I was taught to pray and indeed prayed in a very formulaic way for close on 25 years. But, nowadays, few people, apart from those with standard religious beliefs, actually pray.

This is a shame, as prayer is a very simple, yet immensely comforting, piece of soul work. It is 'talking' to God, Goddess or whatever it might be that is larger and knows more than us. Prayer means setting aside a time to unload our worries, our concerns and our anxieties – and also to share our joys, our triumphs and our gratitude.

Prayer is an intrinsic part of many religions: Christians pray to God, Christ and (in the Roman Catholic tradition) to Mary, Mother of God. Muslims turn towards Mecca and prostrate themselves in prayer. Hindus pray to the numerous deities of the Hindu pantheon. Wiccans pray to the Goddess, pagans to Mother Earth. A prayer can be as simple as 'Thank you, God,' or 'Please protect me and keep me safe', or it can

be an elaborate series of words which form a traditional prayer. By ignoring or dismissing prayer, we just may be missing out on something deeply important. Psychologist and theologian Dr Walter Weston certainly thinks so. He has spent years researching the science of prayer and shares some remarkable findings in his book *How Prayer Heals*. 'The evidence indicates that humans accumulate, attune, focus and transmit an energy that heals,' he writes.

Recently, research has shown that prayer can significantly help AIDS patients. A study by the American Psychosomatic Society in Florida divided 40 equally ill patients into two groups. The group receiving prayer did not know that volunteers from ten religions and healing traditions were praying for them for an hour a day for a week. After 6 months, the group who had been prayed for had spent an average of 10 days in hospital compared to 68 days for the control group. Those receiving prayer also reported a decrease in emotional distress.

what does prayer mean to you?

Are you very resistant to the concept of prayer? Many of us recoil from the idea of prayer because of bad childhood experiences. Prayer might conjure up feelings of kneeling for long, boring periods, hands clasped, until your knees are sore. Or it might be associated with dreary visits to church, synagogue, mosque or temple. Take a few moments to think about what prayer means to you.

- When you think about praying, what images and sensations come to mind?
- What feelings and emotions emerge? Some of us will find resentment towards parents lies under the surface, or dislike of a priest or religious leader. I can clearly remember feeling very angry as a child that people in the church were hypocrites – acting as if they were religious, but gossiping cruelly before and after the service.
- Did you enjoy praying or dislike it? What did you like or dislike? Often it's the form of prayer that is the problem.

mantras – a different form of prayer

Many people now commonly use mantras as a form of prayer and meditation. A mantra is simply a word or phrase used repetitively to enter a state of prayer and awareness of God. It can be just one word, such as 'ohm', or a series of words, such as the Hari Krishna chant.

Muslims repeat the name of Allah or the other Names of God; Quabalists tone the G-d-names; Tibetan Buddhists turn the prayer wheel chanting 'Aum mani padme hum', while Catholics recite the rosary while fingering rosary beads and Hindus repeat a mantra as they pass each bead of the mala through their fingers.

OPPOSITE CLOSING OUR HANDS IN PRAYER IS ONE OF THE CLASSIC SYMBOLS OF RELIGIOUS LIFE, BUT IT IS NOT NECESSARY TO USE TRADITIONAL PRAYERS IN ORDER TO TALK TO GOD OR SPIRIT.

finding the kind of prayer that works for you

There is no 'right' way to pray. You have to find what works for you. The following are just suggestions, nothing more.

- Some people will feel drawn to rediscover some of the beautiful old melodic prayers of traditional religion. You may want to move outside your childhood, or best-known faith, and explore other traditions – perhaps the poetical Sufi tradition, or a Quabalistic prayer, or the prayers of the early Christian mystics, or even non-denominational New Age–type prayers.
- You may wish to make up your own prayers – or find pieces of poetry or prose that have meaning for you. Of course, you do not need to have a proper 'format' – many people simply talk to God, as if He/She/It were another human being. If you find it hard to talk to someone in your head, use the Gestalt empty-chair technique (page 119) and imagine God is sitting on the chair opposite you.
- You may wish to chant a mantra or try toning sounds.
- Some people find the best prayer is silence. Simply sit, kneel, stand or lie, and still your mind.
- Gazing at a religious object, painting or symbol can often become a form of prayer. It need not be a purpose-made artefact – it could be a stone, a piece of wood, a shell or a beautiful view or corner of nature. Some people pray leaning against a tree, or gazing into a fire or pool.

hints on praying

If you're really stuck, think about the following:

- God, or the Higher Power, loves you unconditionally. Nothing that you say will shock. He or She will simply be delighted to hear from you!
- Don't worry about what words you use or don't use. It is your intention that matters, not how clever your vocabulary is.
- Use your prayer time as an opportunity to be totally honest, totally yourself. Share every part of your life – good and bad. Prayer isn't necessarily about just spiritual matters – God will be as interested in your exam worries or your insomnia as your quest for inner knowing and piousness!
- Be prepared for your prayers to be answered – though not always in the way you expect. Prayer can be very powerful.

SACRED SPACE

How do you feel when you walk into a church or temple? There is usually a sense of peace, an indefinable sense of walking into somewhere sacred, holy. It is what the Greeks called *tenemos*, a sanctuary. We all need places where we can feel safe and secure, peaceful and protected – on a daily basis. These need not be anywhere as grand as a synagogue or mosque – we can find peace within our own four walls.

When we walk through our front doors, we should be able to leave the stresses and strains of the outside world behind. A home should provide us with a sanctuary for the soul, a haven for the senses. It should be an oasis of calm and security, a place where we can be totally ourselves.

Think about how you feel when you walk into your home. Does a wonderful sense of peace and happiness descend on you, or do you feel irritated and stressed the moment you step through the door? If your house is a true haven, you will feel full of wellbeing – able to relax completely when needs be; energized and vitalized when that's the order of the day. If you constantly feel depressed, jumpy, nervous or just plain exhausted in your home, it is not serving your soul needs.

Why should our homes be so very important? I believe it's because a home is a symbol of the world; it represents our own mini-world, our own Mother Earth. When we feel safe and comfortable in our homes, we feel more able to deal with the often frightening outside world. Deep in our psyches, we recognize that a house or apartment is far more than a mere structure: our home not just a place where we can keep out of the elements; it's far more than merely somewhere to eat and sleep.

what do you need from your home?

We are all different. Your ideal home may be a country cottage or cabin, simple and full of rustic charm. For someone else, the perfect place is an inner-city loft, vibrating to the constant hum of humanity. It could be a one-room apartment or a huge mansion. Before we set out to make our homes sacred, we must discover exactly what we need from them. There are many ways to find the elements of your perfect home. Try these:

- What kinds of home did you live in as a child? Think back. What did you like about them? Are there any elements of those homes that fill you with nostalgia?

- Let your mind wander over the places you loved when you stayed in them. Maybe a certain holiday cottage? A hotel or retreat? What did they have in common? Often this will not be the physical structure of the place, but a feeling. Try to pinpoint that feeling and figure out ways by which you might reproduce it in your home.

- Get out some paints and paper, and try painting an image of your soul home. It need not be an actual representation – it could be a series of colours or shapes. Don't think too much about it, just paint and see what happens. You might like to try painting with your non-dominant hand or with your eyes shut. Then sit back and see what your intuition says about the images you have created.

- Take out a pile of magazines and make a treasure map. Look for images that spell 'home' to you. You may be surprised at what your unconscious craves. Cut out the pictures and make a montage on a large sheet of paper. Place it somewhere you will notice it throughout the day – you can add or take off images as you see fit. It doesn't matter if the homes are out of your price range or beyond possibility – you are looking for the elements. You may not even choose pictures of homes or interiors – they could be pictures of people looking calm, families enjoying themselves or just colours or impressions. It's a kind of esoteric wish list.

making a soul home

Once you know what you need from your space, you can start to make it a healing home, a soul home. A soul home is certainly not a place of clutter and chaos, but equally it is not a show home. Investing your home with soul is not about spending a fortune on new furniture and interior designers:

it's about making your home a refuge for the senses, a retreat for the spirit. Some houses make you feel uncomfortable the moment you walk in. They look beautiful, but you hardly dare sit down in case you crease the cushions. You worry that your children might make a mess or your dog put pawprints all over the carpet. This kind of house is a statement – like the latest designer clothes or the smartest sports car. Hollow. The ideal soul home is nothing like that: it should be an oasis of delight and refreshment. How your home looks is important, but it also needs to feel good. Where possible, choose softly rounded shapes – in feng shui terms, soft contours help good energy to flow. In human terms, we tend to feel more comfortable nestled in a generous sofa with plump cushions than perched on a stiff, square chair. Think about sense-friendly textures, too. Given the choice between a luxuriously sensuous sheepskin rug and a scratchy, itchy synthetic rug, on which would you prefer to stretch out? Choose natural fabrics and furnishings as much as possible – they connect us with the natural world and make us feel more at home.

do-it-yourself home protection

It's one thing adding texture and comfort to your home, but how do you bring in the right atmosphere and mood? Many of the techniques in this book (particularly the space-cleansing techniques on page 169) will help, but you can start by trying this very simple ritual, a version of which exists in virtually every ancient culture:

1 Stand in the centre of your home and spend a few moments simply centring yourself. Close your eyes and gently follow your breathing. Feel the tension dropping away from your body and mind.

2 Now visualize a small glowing point of light deep in your heart. It shines with a clear, pure, bright white light.

3 Expand the point of light so that it becomes a bubble of light, one that surrounds your entire body. You know that, within this bubble, you are safe and protected, serene and secure.

4 Now take the bubble out even further, so that it encompasses your entire house or apartment, cocooning it in healing, transformative light. Imagine the protective bubble removing any negativity from your home, leaving it a pure, beautiful place of safety and serenity.

5 Gradually come back to normal awareness, armed with the knowledge that you have started to transform your home.

the elements

One of the nicest, and easiest, ways to bring a sense of magic and joy into your space is to ensure you have all the elements represented. This gives a home balance. Most people tend to favour one or two elements, and you can often tell which they are by the look and feel of their homes. For example, fiery people will generally be drawn to strong, vibrant, powerful colours, while watery people will tend to gravitate towards artistic homes full of paint effects and often piled high with clutter! Air homes are typically clean, airy (of course!) and spacious, and tend towards minimalism. Earthy homes will have lots of wood and stone, and natural colours such as greens, browns, taupes and russet – autumnal (fall) hues.

If you can, try to introduce all four elements. Here are some suggestions.

EARTH Earth grounds us, gives us safety, stability and a centre. It often represents the physical, our bodies and the earth itself.

- The most obvious way of bringing earth into your home is with natural stone and rock.
- Salt, too, represents earth and can be very useful in rituals and cleansings. Natural sea salt is best.
- Crystals are powerful storehouses of earth energy. Visit a crystal store and let your intuition pick the stone 'meant'

for you. You could dedicate a crystal as your 'house' stone, or even have one for each room. For example, a rose quartz is a lovely protective stone for a child's bedroom.

WATER Water soothes and calms, and it is purifying and healing. It often represents our emotions.

- Install an interior waterfall – it's soothing and also very good feng shui (see page 94–5).
- Bowls of water – perhaps with added flowers or petals – bring the element of water into the home and also provide valuable humidity.
- Introduce water into rituals by spraying rooms with a plant mister – you can add flower remedies (see pages 236–9) or aromatherapy oils (page 218) if you wish, to intensify the beneficial effect.

AIR Air is invigorating, fresh and incisive. It often represents the intellect, the sharp power of the mind.

- Incense, smudging (page 170) and burning aromatherapy oils (page 218) all attract the spirits of the air and can be used in ritual (see pages 174–9).
- Open your windows once or twice a day and let the fresh breeze blow through your home.

BELOW OUR WORLD IS SURROUNDED BY AND MADE UP OF THE FOUR ELEMENTS — WATER, EARTH, FIRE AND AIR. BY BRINGING THESE INTO YOUR HOME, EVEN IN SMALL WAYS, YOU CAN ENLIVEN THE ATMOSPHERE AND CREATE A MUCH-NEEDED SENSE OF HARMONY AND BALANCE.

FIRE: Fire is pure energy – it ushers in new possibilities and is also protective. Fire often represents the will and the energy of the heart.

- Candles can be used both in rituals and to energize your home. But make sure they're safe (placing them in a bowl of sand or water is a good idea – and keep them well away from children and animals).
- An open fire is a comforting place beside which to meditate and dream.

space cleansing

Space cleansing is one of the simplest yet most effective ways of shifting your home's atmosphere. It's an intrinsic part of most ancient cultures, yet here in the West it's a forgotten art. Vestiges of it remain in the wafting of incense around a church; the bells ringing out are a form of sound cleansing, purifying the parish.

Imagine how your house would be if you hadn't physically cleansed it for ten years? Not a pleasant thought. Yet few houses have ever been spiritually cleansed and so they become full of stagnant energy, old atmospheres and stuck emotions.

That may sound strange, but think about this. How often have you walked into a room and thought you could 'cut the air with a knife'? You are picking up the heavy emotional energy left by an argument or row. How often have you walked into a place and thought: 'I don't like the feeling of this place'? or, conversely, walked in and thought: 'Oh, this is nice. I feel at home'? You are picking up on the 'atmosphere', the layers of emotional energy that have attached to the walls of the place.

Cleansing your home on an energy level is one of the most important things you can do to make it really your home, rather than the repository of the feelings, emotions and 'stuff' of its previous inhabitants.

clearing clutter

Before you can start the esoteric work, you need to clear the clutter that invariably accumulates in every home. You don't have to get rid of everything, turning your home into a minimalist showpiece, but you do need to clear out the mess so that you can focus on what is important in your life. See the section on clutter on page 92.

Remember that mess and clutter affect us on three different levels. Physically, clutter attracts dust and dirt, so a messy house will be a nightmare for anyone who suffers from allergies. You can never properly clean a messy house – and cleanliness is next to soulfulness! Psychologically, clutter makes us feel irritable and tense. Piles of disorganized letters and bills; rooms stuffed with objects; newspapers, magazines and toys lying everywhere all make us feel anxious – our subconscious knows there is work to be done and worries. Finally, on an energy level, clutter is a nightmare, as qi, or subtle energy, cannot flow smoothly and easily. It becomes stuck and turns stagnant, affecting our health and wellbeing. If you still find this process hard, think about what the Chinese sages said: when you clear away your clutter, you are making room for something new and exciting to come into your life.

how to space cleanse

1 Take a bath or shower. You might like to add a couple of drops of rosemary oil, which helps to purify your aura. Dress in clean, comfortable clothes, but keep your feet bare and remove all jewellery and your watch.

2 Go to the centre of your home and spend a few moments with your eyes shut, quietly breathing and centring yourself. You may be able to contact the spirit of your house and ask for its help. If you have any religious beliefs, you may like to ask for help in whatever way feels right to you.

3 Start to 'clap out' your home. Move slowly and steadily around your home, clapping in every corner. Clap your hands, starting at the bottom of the wall and swiftly clapping on up towards the ceiling, as high as you can. You may need to repeat this several times in each spot – until the sound of your clapping becomes clear. As you clap, visualize your clapping dispersing any stagnant energy.

4 When you have finished clapping, wash your hands.

5 Go around your home balancing the energy with a bell or a rattle. Imagine the sound clearing any last vestiges of old energy.

6 Return to the centre of your space and once more close your eyes and breathe. How does your home feel now? Can you detect the difference?

7 Stamp your feet to ground yourself and have a good shake and stretch. It's also a good idea to have something to eat and drink after this ritual.

NOTE: do not perform space cleansing if you are unwell, pregnant or menstruating, or if you feel nervous or apprehensive.

do-it-yourself smudging

Smudge sticks are available in most New Age shops (commonly made from sagebrush, cedar and/or sweetgrass).

1 Light the end of your smudge stick and let it burn for a few minutes until the tip starts to smoulder.

2 Take off your shoes and remove any jewellery. Stand in a relaxed posture.

3 Feel the earth solid beneath your feet and ask Mother Earth to keep your feet solidly and safely on the ground.

4 Feel your head lifting up towards the sky and ask Father Sky to remind you of your link to Spirit. Remember you stand between the earth and the sky, balanced.

5 Now waft the smoke towards your heart. Hold the smudge stick away from you and use a feather to waft the smoke towards you, then take the smudge smoke over your head, down your arms and down the front of your body. Imagine the smoke lifting away all your negative thoughts, emotions and energies.

6 Breathe in the smudge, visualizing the smoke purifying your body from the inside. (Note: be careful if you suffer from asthma or respiratory difficulties.)

7 Bring the smoke down the back of your body to the ground. Visualize the last vestiges of negativity being taken back into the earth and away into the air.

8 Next, ask the spirits of the herbs to replace any negativity with pure, positive energy. Imagine you are surrounded by gentle, loving energy. Breathe in positivity, courage and love.

9 Thank the smudge stick, then put it out by dowsing it in earth or sand.

smudging

Smudging is the common name given to the Sacred Smoke Bowl Blessing, a powerful cleansing technique from the Native American tradition. Smudging calls on the spirits of sacred plants to drive away negative energies and put you back into a state of balance. It is the psychic equivalent of washing your hands before eating and is used as an essential preliminary to almost all Native American ceremonies. Smudging can be used to cleanse yourself before any form of ritual work or space cleansing. Before you undertake any form of ritual work, you should smudge the items you will be using (such as crystals, bowls of water, salt, candles etc.). Smudging can also be used as a form of space cleansing in itself.

shrines and altars

People have built altars and shrines for thousands of years. Archaeologists have found evidence of primitive altars, sacred objects and figurines all over the world: building altars is a very deep-seated human urge.

Altars have taken many shapes and forms. The first were probably the natural sacred spaces: places that seemed to our ancestors heavily imbued with the sacred; perhaps the dwelling place of a god, goddess or nature spirit. Mountain tops, caves, springs and groves were freely venerated. Offerings would be left and, over time, the place would become a natural shrine. As humans learnt more sophisticated building techniques, they used their architecture to create temples, churches and mosques as homes for Spirit.

Throughout history, the simpler tradition of home altars and shrines has endured. Many religions have continued the practice unbroken to the present day: step into any orthodox Hindu or Roman Catholic home and you will usually find a shrine. Images of Buddha and Kuan Lin will adorn the homes of a Buddhist or Taoist. For Native Americans, the medicine wheel is a gateway to Spirit, while most modern Wiccans have one or more altars with images of the Goddess and nature.

Personal altars can serve many purposes. Above all, they offer us the chance to make the Divine personal – an altar should always reflect our personality, our beliefs, our needs. Everything you place on your altar should have meaning. That way, whenever you see your altar, you become mindful of the sacred in your life.

Equally, you can make altars for specific purposes – to bring more of a certain energy into your life. Altars serve to concentrate our intentions. So, if you want to bring more success, or love, or peace into your life, you could construct an altar specifically geared to that purpose.

OPPOSITE AN ALTAR IS A PLACE TO STOP AND BE CALM AND AWARE – IF ONLY FOR A MOMENT. IT IS A SMALL PLACE OF REFUGE, AN AID TO STILLING THE MIND AND FOCUSING.

candles

There are many varying associations for the different colours, but I find these work well:

Blue – for meditation or bedroom altars where you want to relax and be soothed.

Purple – for psychic development or spiritual awareness. Purple is good for a private meditation altar.

Green – for a healing altar, to bring balance, peace and harmony. Green can also be used in rituals to attract wealth or abundance.

Yellow – for friendship and joyful altars; use also when you want to increase your communication, good luck and wisdom. This is a good colour for a home-office altar or for a teenager facing exams.

Red – for passion and energy. Red is good for attracting romance and sex.

Pink – for when you are seeking love or wanting to conceive a child.

building a home altar

Every home should ideally have a central 'home' altar that holds the spirit of the house and offers refuge and a home for the sacred. You may automatically know where it should be – maybe there is already a sort of subconscious altar there. If not, close your eyes and centre yourself, breathing calmly. Ask for guidance on where to place your altar – from your higher self, from your guardians, from the spirit of your home. You will most likely find that you suddenly get a strong feeling or a vague sense of where your house altar should be.

However, you don't have to stop at just one altar – you can build them all over your home. Many ancient cultures have some kind of shrine or sanctuary on or around the threshold of the house, offering protection and signalling the shift from the outside world into the sacred home. A kitchen is a natural place for a homely altar offering thanks for all your blessings. A living room could be home to a family or friends altar, celebrating love and warmth. More private altars can be sited in your bedroom, study and meditation space. Even small spaces – such as window ledges, the top of a cupboard or a series of hanging baskets in your bathroom – can make effective homes for altars.

There are no set rules as to what you should put on your altar. Simply follow your intuition and be guided by what feels right. However, if you feel uncertain, there are various tried and tested formulae that will start you on the right track. Let's look at how to build a basic home altar.

The fundamental ingredients include candles, a bowl of water, an incense holder or aromatherapy burner, matches and a bowl of salt. Optional extras for your altar could include a healthy plant or vase of fresh flowers, favourite photographs, crystals, representations of divinities, natural objects (such as stones, wood or shells) and other meaningful objects.

The first items on the list represent the four elements, which are traditionally represented on any altar for balance and connection. Place them as you see fit. You may like to add flowers or petals to the water in your bowl. Choose an incense or aromatherapy oil that you like or which suits your purpose for your altar. The colour of the candle you choose may also reflect your purpose (see the box at left).

Now add any items to personalize your altar. If you are building a home altar, it is customary to include pictures of members of your family or items made by them. Things that represent your common or various interests can be included, too. If you have a favourite deity, it is good to include an image or symbol: a figure of Buddha or the Goddess, a cross or Star of David etc.

Feel free to play around with the arrangement until it feels right. Light your candle and let your mind wander over the altar. Does it provide a focus for meditation? Does it set your mind on interesting pathways? If so, it is doing its job.

Once you have grasped the basic principles of altar building, you will find it simple to create altars for any room or any purpose. Just bear in mind that you are providing a visual focus for your intent, so include items that have particular meaning and resonance for you.

seasonal altars

Later in this section, we will be looking at how to get back in tune with the natural world, with the shifting rhythms of the seasons. One lovely way to start this process is to build seasonal altars – to mark the shift from one season to the next and to help you prepare for the lessons of that time.

WINTER SOLSTICE (YULE) 21 December: This date marks the Celtic Christmas and is a great family festival. It is a time to focus on the people we need, rather than the people we like! It is also a time to recognize that conflict has a place in life and that we must learn how to deal with it. A time to focus and to reflect, this is when we should gather our intent for the year to come. Most of us subconsciously make a Yule altar in the form of a Christmas tree or a mantelpiece arrangement, but it is also good to think consciously about it. Traditional colours are red and green. Consider including:

- evergreens such as holly, mistletoe and ivy
- bells and brightly coloured baubles
- photographs of people who can't be with you at Yuletide
- sweets and candy, mince pies, spices such as ginger or cinnamon, oranges (perhaps made into pomanders by sticking cloves in them in pretty patterns)
- a glass of wine, sherry or punch
- candles in brightly coloured bowls
- your resolutions for the year to come

SPRING EQUINOX 21 March: Marking the first day of spring, this festival ties in neatly with Easter for Christians and celebrates the return of life. It's a time for spring cleaning (both physically and emotionally); a time to get rid of whatever has stuck to you over the winter – both things and people you have outgrown. It's an expansive time – to reach out for what you need to move forwards in life. Construct a joyous, colourful altar, maybe covered with a clear green cloth. Think about including the following:

- spring flowers, buds and branches of pussy willow
- eggs – either natural or painted or dyed
- hares, which are the traditional animals associated with the spring equinox, but you can also include the Easter bunny and chicks, or any young animals
- hot-cross buns

- images of the Goddess, who returns after her winter descent underground, or Christ on the cross, who died and was reborn
- green and yellow candles
- seeds (you could plant them afterwards – something nice to do if you have children, or even if you don't!)

SUMMER SOLSTICE (MIDSUMMER'S EVE) 21 June: This is the peak of the expansive energy of the year and the summation of what you are and have become during this upward surge of the year's energy. It's a time to gather together in large groups. This is an outward, sociable festival, a time to learn about your place in society and the world. It is a time to examine what you want from life and to look at who you really are. It's often celebrated as a big party! Let your altar reflect this:

- predominantly red – a red cloth and red candles
- lots of summer fruits and berries
- heaps of summer flowers – the more colourful and profuse, the better
- if possible, magical midsummer herbs such as St John's wort, mugwort, vervain and thyme
- pictures of friends and joyous party images

AUTUMN (FALL) EQUINOX 21 September: This is a new phase as winter starts to draw closer. The Earth Goddess has departed into the earth and the leaves are turning. It's a time for purification, for quiet, inward work when we stop to adjust ourselves to a less outdoor part of the year. It's a time for long-term planning, for letting go of parts of ourselves that no longer serve our essential being. It's a time to reconcile the opposites within us – looking at male and female, dark and light, young and old. Your altar should reflect this:

- rich, russet autumn (fall) colours – deep reds, rusty yellows, dark greens, burnt oranges for your cloth and candles
- wreaths of oak leaves and nuts
- pumpkins, squash, apples and other fruits of the harvest
- pine cones, nut kernels and dried herbs
- coloured yarns, beads or shells – you could make necklaces, weaving in symbols of what you want from life
- muslin herb bags (afterwards, place them in drawers to deter moths or use as bath bags)
- opposing pairs of things – two stones, one black and one white; something rough and something smooth; something old and something new

RITUAL

RITUALS OCCUPY A STRANGE PLACE IN MODERN SOCIETY. WE EITHER LOVE ALL THE PARAPHERNALIA THEY ENTAIL OR HATE THE DISRUPTION THEY BRING. SOME PEOPLE LOOK FORWARD TO GATHERINGS SUCH AS CHRISTMAS AS A TIME OF FAMILY, FRIENDS AND FUN; OTHERS FEEL HORROR AS THE FIRST CHRISTMAS CARDS APPEAR IN THE STORES, DREADING A SEASON OF STRESS AND STRAIN. ALMOST ALL OF US, HOWEVER, WHATEVER OUR THOUGHTS, GO THROUGH THE MOTIONS. ASIDE FROM STOICALLY BATTLING WITH CHRISTMAS, WE DUTIFULLY BAKE BIRTHDAY CAKES AND WE DON OUR BEST CLOTHES TO GO TO WEDDINGS, BAR MITZVAHS AND FUNERALS. SOME OF US EVEN STILL MAKE IT TO THE TRADITIONAL CELEBRATION OF HARVEST FESTIVAL.

Many people would say, in fact, that we have far too much ritual in our lives. Isn't life busy enough without having more plans to make, more occasions to celebrate? Compared to our forebears, however, we are seriously lacking in rituals. Ritual might seem outmoded, even unnecessary, but many experts insist that, in order to lead balanced, healthy lives, we need much more ritual, not less. Many psychotherapists believe that rituals – and plenty of them – should make up a central part of our lives.

We're not talking about dispatching a bunch of flowers for Mother's Day, a card for Father's Day or snatching a last-minute box of chocolates for Valentine's Day. For rituals to be healing and life-enhancing, they have to be more than duty – they have to have meaning. We don't need more commercial trappings; we don't need bigger and better Christmases: we simply need more personalized ones. Do you find yourself following exactly the same pattern every year at Christmas? Do you look forward to it or does its approach fill you with a sense of burden and horror at its commercialization? Are your rituals too rigid? Have they stayed the same over the years despite obvious changes in family members' ages or beliefs? If a ritual no longer works for you, you need to change it. Rituals should grow and evolve all the time.

An example might be reinventing a ritual to celebrate an anniversary. You might go out together or cook a special meal at home. You could give gifts that symbolize the past year you have spent together – something really thoughtful that has meaning. You might then talk about what you both want for the next year of your life – you could use it as a

time to make your lists (as discussed in the relationship section on pages 135–7).

On a much smaller note, you might decide to start every morning with a kiss and end every evening with a word that you want to symbolize the next day – even tiny things such as this are rituals and, what's more, powerful ones.

ancient ceremonies

Rituals were a central part of life for our ancestors. In pagan times, each year that passed was marked with regular seasonal festivals in which all community members participated. Experts believe that these were not, as has been commonly assumed, an attempt to control nature, but rather a means of coming to terms with the shifting rhythms of the seasons. By following the ups and downs of the year, people got to grips with the cycles of their own lives, learning that there are times of great energy and joy alongside times of quiet introspection; times of birth and rebirth, but inevitably also times of sadness, loss and death. Perhaps it is a subconscious yearning for these lost or denigrated celebrations that has, in part, caused the rising interest in paganism and other native, earth-based religions, with their plethora of satisfying rituals and celebrations.

Shan, a therapist and pagan priestess who taught me so much about ritual, insists on the importance of seasonal rituals: 'The seasons of the year are less crucial to our modern lives, with imported food, heated houses and indoor work,' she says. 'But our bodies and emotions still go through their important changes, which we are foolish to ignore. They can greatly enrich our lives if we honour their primal wisdom.' She notes that, according to the pagan calendar, there are eight festivals a year, about one every 6 weeks. 'That gives us about 5 to 6 weeks of workaday life, then a break for a holiday or celebration – an entirely pleasant and very healthy rhythm,' she adds.

Between these seasonal festivals, our forebears celebrated important life events – birth, adolescence, menstruation,

RIGHT EVEN IF YOU DON'T HAVE HOURS TO SPEND CARRYING OUT ELABORATE CEREMONIES, TRY TO MAKE TIME IN EVERYDAY LIFE FOR SMALL BUT VALUABLE RITUALS THAT OFFER A SHORT BREAK FROM THE DAILY GRIND.

marriage, menopause and death. A few rituals remain, but are often stifled or derisory. Think of the wedding where the heart of the ceremony has been lost amid the paraphernalia of video cameras and social one-upmanship. Or the practice of 'drive-through' funerals in which mourners 'pay their respects' by observing the deceased on a video screen and recording their presence on a computer. How can tapping on a computer keyboard release pent-up grief? Better, undoubtedly, an old-fashioned wake when everyone sinks a few drinks and spends a day surrounded by family and friends talking about the deceased, reminiscing and celebrating that life, letting the tears flow when necessary, but recalling all the happy times as well. Surely therein lies healing and a growing acceptance of loss?

Good rituals are essential to our emotional, psychological and spiritual health. In a time when many of us live far from our family and don't even know our neighbours, rituals not only help us on a personal basis, but also give us a small sense of community, a sense of who we are and where we fit in the scheme of life. Without rituals, we drift. Today, however, we lack these essential rituals and ceremonies.

Rituals really can help us with difficult transitions such as puberty, menstruation and menopause; painful situations, such as divorce, death and illness; and even crises such as burglary, accidents and assault. Psychotherapists since the days of Jung have recognized the power of symbols, of age-old archetypes, of emotive ritual to cleanse the psyche and free the emotions. Say you have just recovered from a serious illness or come out of hospital, why not burn or bury a symbol of that time? Ritually discard your no-longer-needed medicines, burn your hospital bracelet. Alternatively, write a declaration celebrating your newfound health and vitality. It's a way of signalling to your unconscious mind that you are now well. Even the most ridiculous-sounding rituals can be effective. One couple who were always fighting agreed upon a ritual in which they put symbols of their quarrel 'on ice' in the freezer. They signed a pact to say that they could only fight about the issue after they had thawed the symbols out.

If you follow meaningful rituals, you will weather the inevitable changes of life far more easily.

bath rituals

Rituals do not need to be complex or elaborate, as we have seen. They can easily be part of everyday life, giving us a chance to stop and centre ourselves, even if only for a few minutes. One opportunity to introduce an element of ritual is our daily washing routine.

Water is extremely cleansing and purifying, so it makes sense to use your regular bath or shower as an excuse for

some deep, powerful cleansing. The purifying shower below is the perfect way to start your day, making you feel positive and upbeat about the day ahead. The bath is ideal for shedding the trials and tribulations of a stressful day.

purifying shower

Start your day with this invigorating shower, which will help you feel positive and confident about the day to come.

1 As you step into the shower, imagine you are stepping under the clean, pure waters of a beautiful waterfall in the wilderness. While you stand under the waters, visualize the magical water washing away any negativity, leaving you full of energy and vigour for the day to come.

2 Wash yourself with a sponge and some uplifting aromatherapy oils (citrus or pine fragrances work well).

3 Consciously let go of any worries, concerns or anxieties. Imagine they are being sloughed off you as the water cleanses your body. Breathe in deeply and believe that the day ahead will be positive and full of joy. Any problems are simply challenges which you will overcome with ease.

4. Step out of your shower and have a wonderful day!

deep-cleansing bath

This deep-cleansing bath is ideal as a 'winding-down' ritual at the end of the day.

1 Light candles all around your bath. If you like, you can also light an oil burner and put in a few drops of your favourite aromatherapy oils – sandalwood, camomile, geranium, lavender and ylang ylang are all good choices.

2 Your bath should be pleasantly warm, but not too hot. Add three drops each of your chosen aromatherapy oils (mixed in a little milk) and agitate the water to disperse them.

3 As you undress, imagine that you are dumping all your problems with your clothes. Start to let go of the stress, strain and any negativity of the day.

4 Sprinkle some sea salt on a damp face cloth. Gently scrub your entire body with small, circular movements. Work from the extremities of your body towards your heart. Imagine the purifying power of the salt loosening all the

psychic grime of the day. (NOTE: consult your doctor first if you have high blood pressure or heart disease and do not use salt if you have any irritated or broken skin.)

5 Relax in your bath and visualize the healing water gently drawing out all the negativity and unpleasantness of the day. Soak for at least 20 minutes.

6 As you step out of the bath, look back and see the water as containing all the anger, sorrow, frustration etc. of the day. Bless it, then let it go.

7 Having followed this ritual, you should find that you now sleep well and wake refreshed.

mealtime rituals

Bring ritual into your life by investing mealtimes with a sense of the sacred. All religions teach that food is a blessing from the Divine and should be treated with respect and gratitude. No Jewish, Christian, Hindu, Muslim or Buddhist family would dream of scoffing a meal without saying a blessing and giving thanks. In China, food is considered to be a physical link between humans and the Gods: beautifully prepared meals are given as a sacred offering on the family altars. As we've seen in Part 1, in the ayurvedic tradition of India, food is a spiritual science with precise prescriptions of how to prepare and eat food for physical, emotional and spiritual wellbeing.

Begin by considering the following questions.

• How do you eat? At table with family or friends? While working? On the run?

• What do you eat? Do you prepare your own food or do you buy ready-prepared processed food?

• Do you ever really taste your food?

• Are you mindful when you eat?

The simplest of rituals can turn even the humblest sandwich into a feast for the spirit. The principles of making mealtime sacred are very straightforward – and can easily be adapted to fit your circumstances and preferences. Preparing 'soul' food need not involve new recipes or expensive ingredients. Follow these simple principles to transform the food you eat.

• Take care when choosing food – pick the freshest, most local, seasonal, organic food you can find. If you eat meat, ensure that it has been farmed with care and consideration

OPPOSITE Even if you don't have time for any other rituals, make bathtime a small ceremony in itself. It's a chance to take 'time out', to relax completely and retreat quietly within.

for the animals. Perhaps think about perhaps growing some of your own food – even if it's just a window box with herbs.

- Say a prayer or blessing before you start to cook or prepare your food. Hold your hands over your ingredients and thank them for giving their life for you. Visualize the journey of your ingredients – how they grew, who tended them, how they came to be on your table. Ask them to help nourish you and family members, friends or guests with love.

- Prepare your food with love and attention. Concentrate on the task at hand – look on it as sacred meditation. Try not to distract yourself by watching television or listening to the radio as you cook. Take time to notice the textures, scents and look of the food you are cooking. Avoid gadgets and processors where possible – hand-chopping brings you closer into contact with the food.

- Think of your cooking as sacred alchemy. Remember you are using all the elements in your cookery – the earth from which your raw ingredients came; water to cook in; air you add as you stir or beat; and the fire of your stove.

- As you cook, pour in your hopes and wishes for the people who will eat your food. Focus your intention as you chop, stir, mix and blend. Cookery is a kind of spellmaking. If you add herbs and spices with their magical properties, you can increase the power.

- Lay your table with care – even the simplest meals can be made special by adding a small vase of flowers (a posy of wild flowers, buds or leaves is cheap but lovely) or perhaps a candle. You could also scatter petals or pine cones on the tablecloth. Don't eat in front of the television or on the run!

- Serve your meal so it looks inviting and appetizing. Choose colours which complement each other.

- Say grace or a blessing before eating.

- Eat your food mindfully. Smell the different fragrances before you start to eat. Notice how you choose your food – be aware of putting it on your fork and in your mouth. Don't just swallow – really taste the food, feel its texture. Make each mouthful mindful.

- If you are eating with others, allow time during your meal for conversation and a sense of community. Don't race off afterwards – sit and talk.

- Clean up with mindfulness and gratitude, too. Try adding a few drops of mandarin oil to your washing-up liquid to invigorate your senses.

blessings and graces

Blessings and graces have been said for millennia in many cultures and saying them is a simple ritual that makes a mealtime special. Every religion has its own varieties and, in the past, most families would have their favoured wordings. Nowadays, however, we rarely say grace – unless we happen to be at a large, formal occasion. Yet saying grace gives us the chance to think about all the blessings we enjoy and to offer thanks. Take the opportunity to bring this small but important ritual back into your everyday life.

1 Before you eat as a group, you might like to light several small candles around the table. Each person then says a few words of thanks, expressing pleasure at being together to share a meal.

2 Think about the processes which brought this food to your table. You might, for example, pick up a loaf of bread and think about the miraculous way it has come to you. It starts with a tiny seed which grows under the sun, nourished by the earth. It is harvested, threshed, milled into flour and then kneaded and baked into bread to feed you. Give everyone a piece of bread and invite them to give thanks in their own way for this gift of life.

3 Always try to be hospitable and welcoming to guests. Make some mealtimes special by inviting extended family, friends or neighbours. Is there someone needy who might appreciate an invitation – perhaps an elderly neighbour or someone who is new to the area and doesn't yet have friends who live close by?

4 Muslims often serve food in one large dish or on an immense platter. Everyone helps themselves from the same dish, choosing the portion of food closest to them. This symbolizes the sharing, caring aspect of the family or group – it draws people together. Try this, maybe by cooking something such as a large paella or experiment with Middle Eastern or African food, which lends itself well to this format.

5 Before you eat, pause a few moments for everyone to say their silent prayers of thanks and appreciation. Silent grace is a lovely idea, as it removes the need for what can become formulaic set graces and gives each person the chance to say whatever he or she wishes.

family rituals

Think about rituals that could bind your family more closely. How could you make Christmas more meaningful? What would make a birthday more special? Think about the meaning behind any religious rituals you observe – don't simply go through the motions. In addition, think of other events that could be reasons for inspiring family rituals. The following might provide a starting point.

- BIRTHDAYS These are a pivotal point in the year. Try to make them meaningful and special – however old you are! You might want to think about all that has happened in the past year (maybe sharing it with your friends or family). Give thanks for everything good that happened and let go all the bad. Ask yourself what lessons you have learnt. Think about what you would like from the year to come. You might want to smudge yourself and consciously let go of any negativity (see page 170). Be aware that this is a new start for you, a new year full of fresh opportunities.

- NEW YEAR This is a traditional time for a fresh start. Perhaps you could gather the family together and burn some special incense or aromatherapy oil – something fresh such as lemon or bergamot. Each of you could make a list of what you most want from the coming year, first for yourself and then for your family as a whole. Take turns to share your visions. You might also work together preparing a special meal, putting all your hopes for the year to come in the pot.

- A BIRTH The birth of a baby is a miraculous event, one worthy of celebration. Alongside any traditional religious ceremony, you might do something small and personal for the family and close friends. You may want to call down protection from guardian angels, spirit animals or other deities on your child. You may want to introduce the baby to your community in some way – either with a gathering or simply by walking him or her around your neighbourhood in his or her buggy. Dedicating a crystal for the baby is a nice idea (rose quartz is especially appropriate). You might also take a leaf from the fairy tale of Sleeping Beauty and have everyone present offer the baby a 'gift' such as courage, joy or confidence.

ABOVE BIRTHDAY CAKES AND PARTIES AREN'T JUST FOR CHILDREN. BIRTHDAYS ARE SPECIAL (HOWEVER OLD YOU ARE) AND OFFER A WONDERFUL OPPORTUNITY FOR A FAMILY RITUAL OR OTHER MEANINGFUL CELEBRATION.

- HOLIDAYS For most of us, getting ready for holidays can be a stressful time. Set aside a short space of time for everyone to gather and focus on what they want from the holiday. Light a candle and take it in turns to say what you need from your holiday and what you hope for. Think about activities you can do together (and pack the appropriate gear). Holidays are also an ideal opportunity to have time on your own for reflection, meditation or just vegging out with a good book, so agree beforehand how this will be achieved. Having clear, agreed expectations of each other will take away a lot of stress and irritation.

NATURE

WE HAVE A STRANGE RELATIONSHIP WITH NATURE. WE SEEM TO FEEL THAT WE ARE SEPARATE FROM IT, THAT NATURE IS SOMETHING TO GO AND SEE AS YOU MIGHT VISIT A ZOO OR A MUSEUM. LIVING IN OUR CENTRALLY HEATED, AIR-CONDITIONED HOUSES, WE BARELY NEED BE AWARE OF THE CHANGES IN THE WEATHER, THE PASSING SEASONS. STROLLING AROUND A SUPERMARKET FOR OUR FOOD, WE DON'T HAVE TO WORRY ABOUT HOW OUR CROPS ARE FARING OR WHETHER THERE ARE ANIMALS TO HUNT TO KEEP HUNGER AT BAY. IF WE GET SICK OF THE WEATHER AT HOME, WE HOP ON A PLANE AND GO ELSEWHERE, WHERE THE CLIMATE IS MORE TO OUR LIKING.

We want nature to be perfect and, when it doesn't behave as we want it to, we become irritated with it. We like to think we can control nature, to bend it to our will. We build our houses and factories where we wish; we tear down forests for development; we level mountains for roads or tunnel straight through them; and we pollute the seas, rivers, earth and air for the sake of modern, convenient chemicals.

Our ancestors would have been stunned by our attitude. They would have been terrified that the earth would retaliate – and maybe it has. For the truth is we cannot control nature, we cannot ever really 'rule' the earth. By trying to do so, we miss a vital soul lesson. Living in harmony with nature, accepting that we are no more and no less than another cog in the great wheel of life, is essential to our growth.

Some extreme ecologists say we need to get rid of our cars, abandon our houses and return to a life of hunter–gathering. We cannot, however, turn back the clock that far – it's impractical and a foolish pipe dream. We couldn't just drop our civilization like that, nor would most of us want to. It is possible to live more lightly on the earth, though, to stop interfering so grossly in its life, to prevent our egoism and greed from destroying our only home.

Taking responsibility for the earth, for our home, is a crucial part of the work of the soul. We modern soul-seekers cannot be hermits, burying our heads in the sand. We are part of the world and have to take responsibility for it. If we want our children and our children's children to feel their souls fill with the majesty of an ancient forest, with the fluting call of a lark, we have to take a stand. Once again, it need only be small gestures, small beginnings – but we do need to take these

steps. And taking steps like these, however small, gives us a sense that at least we're doing something. In a tiny way, it gives us back a little piece of personal power in what is an increasingly bureaucratic world.

how do you live on the earth?

Start to think about how you live on the earth. The earth is our only home – we physically need it. Beyond this primal power, our souls require a world that still has the ability to move and awe us. If all we have left is a world of concrete, plastic and fast food, what is left to nourish our souls? Think about what you could do to help, in your own small way.

- Start recycling household waste – separating glass, cans, papers and plastics. Organic waste (except potato peelings and meat) can become rich compost if you have a garden. You don't need a huge space to compost – there are now smart, speedy, smell-free composters on the market, so use one. Composting also saves gardeners money on expensive soil improvers.
- Think about leaving the car at home on some days and walking or cycling to work instead. If possible, work out a car-share with colleagues or friends.
- Make a commitment to eating organic food that has not been grown with harmful pesticides, herbicides, fungicides and hormones.
- Buy secondhand furniture (remember, antiques are basically fifth-or-more-hand!) or at least choose furniture that comes from sustainable sources.
- Support campaigns for better public transport so that we need fewer new roads and developments.
- Donate money to environmental groups that are trying to save the world's rainforests and other precious resources.
- Write to or lobby politicians until they open their eyes and realize that, beyond of industry and growth, profit and vested interests, the environment must be our prime concern.

exploring the elements

Few of us are really in touch with the elements. We tend to avoid them (keeping inside when it's raining or windy) or experience them in sanitized forms (such as swimming pools). These very simple exercises plug you in to elemental energy – they are especially important if you live in a city or built-up area.

STONE

Go to a place in nature (ideally wild, but, if not, a park or garden) and find 'your' stone, one that seems to speak to you in some way. Don't worry if you don't find it immediately (remember, patience is one of the key soul lessons of nature), and trust your intuition.

Pick up the stone and sit quietly with it. If it is too large, sit by it. Explore it with all your senses: really look at it, touch it, smell it. Now, perhaps hardest of all, listen to it. What has the stone seen in its long life? What lessons does it have for you? Imagine you are that stone. How does it feel to possess its energy? What would life be like as a stone? Where is your heart, your centre?

Spend some time each day meditating on stone. Think about the properties of stone that could be useful for you in your everyday life – and in your soul life.

WATER

Water feels so different from stone. You can't keep it and hold it, but you can explore it in its many different forms. If possible, spend some time by a spring or stream, investigating its exuberant energy. Once again, use all your senses. Think about its lessons. It's a fascinating process to follow a stream from its source to the place where it joins the sea if you can. Note the changes along the way. What parallels can you draw with your own life?

The ancients believed that every stream and river had its own spirits, the naiads: can you sense the spirit of the water? How would it appear?

Think about having a small water fountain in your home or outside in the garden. Use it as a place for contemplation and a chance to connect with the water spirit.

WOOD

Pick a tree and spend time observing it minutely. Look at its shape, how it grows, where it grows. Investigate its bark, roots, branches and leaves. Sit with your back against its trunk and quietly absorb its energy and share some of your own in return. Hugging is optional, but often irresistible (particularly if you are upset or confused). Employ all your senses and try to hear what the tree is saying. Again, every tree was believed to have a spirit, a dryad. What kind of spirit does your tree have? Can you talk to it? Compare the energy of different kinds of trees. Pick up a piece of dead wood and sense the difference to that of living trees.

Spend some time learning about trees so that you can then identify them and know their lore.

FIRE

If there is somewhere totally safe (with no chance of starting bush fires or causing damage), it can be inspiring to build and tend a small fire outdoors. Watch how a tiny spark glimmers into life. For a time it seems that it won't catch, but then it suddenly shoots away, crackling and sparking. Watch how the colours change in the flames, observe the shapes of the flames and see if you can see (or imagine) the salamanders, spirits of fire. See how hungrily the fire devours the wood, licking along its branches. Then, as the fire subsides, watch the embers glowing and, finally, the wood transforming into charcoal and ash. What would it be like to be fire? How would it feel?

Roast chestnuts or bake potatoes in the glowing embers as you reflect on the lessons of fire – how it can be so destructive yet also so helpful? Does its destructiveness have a purpose? Do we sometimes need to burn away our dross and start afresh? At home, light a candle to remind yourself of fire and its lessons.

AIR

Go to a high place – the top of a mountain, crest of a cliff or brow of a hill – to experience the element of air. Feel yourself on top of the world and breathe the fresh, clear and invigorating air deeply and fully. What would it be like to be the wind? How would it feel to be of air, able to enter any crack, however tiny? Imagine the air coming into your lungs, exchanging oxygen for carbon dioxide, then coming out again.

Next, go somewhere different – a low place, a forest, swamp or underground cave. How is the air different? Contrast it also to the air in a city, amid heavy traffic. What are we doing to our air?

It can be difficult to come to terms with air: we can't see it, we can barely feel it. Yet its lessons are important and it's worth trying to connect with this essential element. Remind yourself of air by lighting incense, burning aromatherapy oils or smudging, allowing the scent to rise on the air and up to the heavens.

linking ourselves with nature

Few of us spend time in nature. Even if we consider ourselves 'outdoor' people, few of us actually stop long enough to look and listen in a meaningful way. Set aside some time to go to a wild place – ideally not a park, but somewhere where you can be alone. First of all, just sit on the grass (or sand or stone). If it's wet, do sit on a groundsheet, but otherwise let your body connect with the earth. Close your eyes and let your other senses take over. What do you hear? At first, you will notice only obvious sounds (birdsong, the wind, far-off mechanical sounds perhaps), but as your listening becomes more attuned you may hear other, tinier sounds. Try to spend at least 20 minutes like this. You may find it disorientating, even a little scary (if you aren't used to being out in nature), so perhaps have a friend near by.

If you feel comfortable, repeat the exercise lying down on the earth. Feel your limbs sink into the earth, feel the ground supporting your head, your whole body. Work through your body, consciously relaxing each part – from your feet right up to your head. Now bring your awareness to your solar plexus and feel it becoming soft and warm. Visualize a golden cord of shimmering energy linking your solar plexus with the heart of the earth, grounding you and rooting you. Slowly stand up and feel your feet rooted to the ground, anchored and safe. The connection with the earth rises up through the ground, through your feet and up your legs into your torso. It pauses a moment at your solar plexus, then rises up again, through your heart, your throat, your head, and bursts through and rises up to the sky. You feel yourself standing, solidly grounded with the earth beneath, yet linked to the sky above. Know that this is your place – safely held between the earth and the heavens.

shamanism

While the so-called 'civilized' nations have mostly lost their relationship with nature, we can turn to those wise peoples who have kept alive the spirit of nature and the link between it and humankind. Many of the neo-pagan traditions (such as druidism, Wicca etc.) forge a strong link with nature and believe it central to their way of life. These all have a strong shamanic element and, if we want to learn how to come back into balance with nature, we need to look to the shamans. Shamans exist all over the world, in places where the tradition has been kept alive. A shaman is basically someone who can walk and talk with the spirits and who has maintained a close link with nature. It's a form of spirituality that reveres the earth as a sentient, living, vibrant entity.

Shamanism is undergoing a huge surge in popularity – it's as if people recognize, at some level, that we desperately need the shamanic wisdom to put us back in touch with our souls and nature.

There isn't the space in a book this size to delve deeply into the myriad practices of shamanism, but we can take a look at some of the most important principles.

medicine walking

In the shamanic view, there is no such thing as coincidence. Things happen because they are meant and because there is a lesson to be learnt. This can be seen in the broad picture of life – that sickness is a way for the body to insist on a much-needed rest; that losing a job might be a prelude to finding a better one; that the end of a relationship could be necessary for growth. But it can also be seen as a way of learning each and every day. Native Americans follow a practice known as the 'medicine walk', in which they go out into the wilderness and read, in every animal they see, every natural occurrence, a message. This can be a useful practice in everyday life. It helps us to become more aware of the natural world and also to appreciate that nature really can be our best teacher. Start to become aware of the world around you and ponder what messages it might have for you.

- What is the weather doing? What does it mean to you if it's raining, windy, snowing, hot and sunny? Think about your feelings and how they are reflected in the weather.
- What animals or birds do you see? Think about the associations any animals have for you personally. You might also like to look them up in books on symbolism or shamanic practice.
- What is the animal or bird doing? Is it behaving in a normal way or strangely? How does that resonate with you? Can you detect a lesson there? How are you like that animal in life, relationships, attitude?
- Pay attention to the plants, trees and flowers you see. Do any strike a particular chord? Perhaps a tree is growing

in a curious way (does it remind you of anything?). Maybe there is a flower blooming in an unlikely place – what lesson does that have for you?

- If an animal crosses your path, it is particularly important. Spend some time meditating on that animal – or asking it what message it has for you.
- You don't have to be out in the country to medicine walk. There are messages on every city street as well. Be aware not just of the natural world, but also of the movement of buses, trains, people.

spirit animals

Some animals have particular messages for you. Shamans believe that we all have special 'spirit animals' which can act as strong protectors and guides.

- Are there any animals which have always held a particular resonance for you? To which animals or birds are you drawn?
- Are there any animals or birds you really don't like? You may find you have a resistance because that particular animal has a tough lesson for you.
- Is there any animal you often dream about? If so, you could try getting in touch with it. When you next meet it in a dream, ask it whether it is 'your' animal (or you are 'its' human). If it agrees, you can ask it for advice or teaching.

In a similar way, you can take yourself into a deep meditative state (lie down and relax your body, then let your breathing become slow and regular). Imagine yourself in the kind of habitat your animal would inhabit (maybe a forest, a jungle, a mountain). Visualize it as clearly as you can and ask that, if the time is right, your spirit animal will come and meet you. If it does, again you should ask for its permission – and be willing to listen to any advice. Always be very respectful.

If you don't feel drawn to any animal in particular, you can still work with power animals. Perhaps the easiest way to do this is to start with the four great guardians of Native American belief. These are:

- BEAR Linked with the element of fire and the west, Bear's energy is strong, powerful and determined. Bear energy cleanses and gives energy.
- EAGLE Linked with the element of air and the east, Eagle's energy is inspirational, far-sighted and protective. Eagle energy clarifies.
- BUFFALO Linked with the element of earth and the north, Buffalo's energy is grounding and protective, and is said to give knowledge of life and death.
- COYOTE Linked with the element of water and the south, Coyote's energy is clever, quick-minded and swift. Coyote governs the emotions.

You can call on these powerful guardians for help at any time of need. Invoke Eagle when you need to keep your vision sharp and focused. Coyote can be very helpful in business meetings when you need to keep your wits about you. If you are in a situation when you feel uneasy or unsafe, Bear is a very comforting presence. Whenever you need some good, solid earthing, invoke Buffalo. Buffalo can also be a great friend if you cannot sleep – she ushers in sleep and bestows useful dreams.

invoking the guardians

1 Stand with your feet planted firmly on the earth. Close your eyes and imagine a piece of string is gently pulling your head up towards the sky.

2 As you stand firmly between Mother Earth and Father Sky, you gradually become aware of four mighty creatures standing around you.

3 At your back, you feel the power of an enormous she-bear rearing up behind you, supremely protective. Nothing can harm you while Bear protects your back.

4 Before you, you feel the beat of powerful wings. A vast eagle, wings outstretched, turns and fixes you with its sharp, all-seeing eye. With Eagle's eyes ahead of you, you will be prepared for all eventualities.

5 On your right-hand side, you feel the warm breath of Buffalo. She is a comforting and calming figure, and will ground you and give you wisdom and forbearance.

6 As your left hand rests by your side, you feel rough fur under your fingers. It's Coyote, master of clever speech and swift evasive action. With Coyote at your side, you should always have a ready answer and be quick-witted and smart. But watch out: Coyote can be a trickster – don't rely on his honeyed tongue alone!

7 Spend some time with these great creatures, allowing their power to seep into your body and soul. Recognize that you can call on them whenever you need their strength. Thank them for introducing themselves to you, then come back to waking reality.

RETREATING

SOMETIMES YOU DON'T JUST NEED A HOLIDAY, YOU NEED A RETREAT. IN THE PAST, GOING ON RETREAT WAS AN ACCEPTED PART OF LIFE. ANYONE WITH A RELIGIOUS TURN OF MIND WOULD SIMPLY TAKE HIMSELF OR HERSELF OFF TO A MONASTERY OR CONVENT (OR TEMPLE, SWEAT LODGE OR ASHRAM) AND SPEND SOME TIME IN CONTEMPLATION AND PRAYER, OFTEN FASTING AND KEEPING SILENT THROUGHOUT A PERIOD OF VIGIL. IT WAS A TIME TO SPEND WITH GOD; A TIME TO BE QUIET AND HEAR THE VOICE OF YOUR SOUL. IT WAS A TIME TO EVALUATE AND REASSESS YOUR LIFE.

Retreating is enjoying a huge resurgence in popularity. There are retreats to suit every religious belief system and, if you are not particularly religious, there are secular or non-denominational retreats to suit every soul. Stafford Whiteaker, author of a guide to retreats, explains: 'A retreat is an inward exploration that lets your feelings open out, and gives you access to both the light and dark corners of your deepest feelings and relationships. It is simply the deliberate attempt to step outside ordinary life and relationships and take time to reflect, rest and be still. It is a concentrated time in which to experience yourself and your relationship to others and, if you are fortunate, to feel a sense of the eternal.'

what do you need from your retreat?

Before you decide on your retreat, take some time to ask yourself what you really want and need from your 'time out'.

- Do you want a structured retreat? Some offer a programme of features, such as prayer, meditation, visualization and lectures. Others will leave you to your own devices.
- Do you want to be with others or on your own? In many retreat centres, you can arrange to go at a very quiet time or have isolated accommodation. If solitude is important, you might consider arranging your own accommodation (i.e. a rented cottage). If you don't want to be alone, there are also many retreats where you can be part of the community.
- Do you want to follow a particular path or belief system? Retreats can be a perfect opportunity to investigate

a religion and see what it offers you. Many religious retreats allow you to take part in community life to some extent (e.g. going to prayers or joining in communal meditation). Equally, others are not run according to any particular faith.
- Can you cope with the possibility of difficult feelings emerging? A lot of people find that the solitude and focus of a retreat can bring old or repressed emotions and memories to the fore. If you're not used to working with your emotions, it may be a good idea to choose a retreat that has skilled counsellors or wardens on hand.
- For how long do you want to retreat? If you're new to the concept, a weekend retreat might be the best option. Once you become used to the set-up, a week is usually the shortest recommended period. Some experienced retreaters will take themselves away for a month or even a year!

food for retreating

Food can set the tenor for a good retreat. It really doesn't matter what you eat when you're retreating, but, for many people, diet is an important part of the mix. Whatever your choice, be mindful of your sustenance. Look back at the suggestions on cooking and eating mindfully on pages 177–8.
- You might think about a detoxifying retreat – look at the ideas on page 67.
- Some people like to fast, but this should only be carried out under professional guidance. If you are in good health and the weather is warm, it's usually okay to try a juice fast of vegetable and fruit juices (but not for more than two days).
- Others see a retreat as a time for pampering and comfort: chocolate and a good bottle of wine might be the ticket.
- If self-catering, keep your food choices simple to prepare. You don't want to spend your entire retreat cooking! Often the most successful choices are easy soups, stews and

OPPOSITE RETREATING IS FAR MORE THAN A HOLIDAY – IT OFFERS A CHANCE TO REPLENISH YOURSELF IN MIND, BODY AND SOUL. TODAY, THERE ARE RETREATS TO SUIT EVERY INCLINATION AND BUDGET.

do-it-yourself retreating

Of course, you don't have to go anywhere in order to retreat. Although it is undoubtedly easier to put aside the detritus of everyday life when you are in a different environment, it's not impossible to retreat in the comfort of your own home.

Retreat weekend – Try a retreat weekend to get a feel for this kind of spiritual holiday. You will need to do some preparing, so allow yourself enough time to get ready.

- Warn people that you are going to be on retreat. If you'd rather keep the reason secret, you can make some other excuse, but make it clear that you are effectively out of touch. You might want to disconnect the telephone or put on the answerphone. Put a 'Do not disturb' sign on your door. If you have family or friends who live with you, try to pick a time when they will be away. Don't collect your mail, or leave it unopened.

- Get in all your provisions. Make sure you have all the food, drink, music, books, candles, incense ... whatever ... that you will need, so that you don't have to make sorties to the outside world for more. Find an attractive storage box in which to keep things, so you can use them whenever you retreat.

- Clean your space physically and cleanse it spiritually (see the space-cleansing exercises on page 169). You might want to dedicate the space for your retreat with a special ritual.

- Think about the energy you want for your retreat. Should it be vibrant and energizing, or calm and relaxing? Does it need to be nurturing and comforting? Bring in whatever you can to help provide the best possible atmosphere.

- Pick out suitable, comfortable clothes – particularly for any activities you are planning. Will you be warm enough if you are sitting meditating? Are your shoes comfortable for long walks? Do you have 'messy' clothes if you're going to paint?

Mini-retreat – Dedicate your retreat time as 'sacred time' with a ritual, such as lighting a candle or burning some aromatherapy oil, and saying a prayer or reciting a poem. You may like to do some smudging or space cleansing to make your space special.

This could be a time just to sit and think, do some painting or writing, or pray or meditate. It might be the time to carry out a long-term project (such as self-therapy). It doesn't matter how you structure it, but do make sure that, for that time, you aren't disturbed and can do as you wish.

casseroles (which can be prepared ahead and frozen), or salads, fruit, bread and cheese or cold meats.

- Always have plenty of fresh water. This could also be a good time to experiment with herbal teas or interesting juices. Have a large bowl of fresh fruit on hand for snacking.

- If you're planning to do a lot of exercise, make sure that you eat nutritious and satisfying food – think about some good protein choices.

- If you have problems related to food, be aware these may well intensify during a retreat. This isn't the time to go on a Draconian diet, but you may want to avoid the foods that you know 'block' your feelings – maybe bread, chocolate, sweets etc. The same applies to alcohol.

what to do on retreat?

There are 101 different ways of retreating and it's entirely up to you to decide what you need. Most people find that a retreat is an opportunity to connect in some way with their soul and we all have different ways to do this.

1 You may be a natural contemplative. Some people can easily sit in silence, meditating, praying or just contemplating. If this suits you, you may like to follow a pattern of prayers or times for meditation, perhaps interspersed with quiet reading or listening to music. Perhaps spend some time each day outside appreciating being in nature.

2 Other people are naturally energetic and find sitting still an impossibility. If this is you, focus your energy with a loose programme of yoga or dance (see pages 74–6 and 148–9). Go for long nature hikes. But do aim to spend at least a little time each day keeping still and trying to hear what your body tells you when you actually allow it to rest.

3 If you find it hard to focus, you may want to try activities such as painting, writing or dancing to bring you in touch with your inner self. Creativity can be a delightful way to open up the soul. Look back over the exercises and suggestions on pages 148–53 for ideas.

4 Many people manage not to think too deeply most of the time by immersing themselves in activities, even if it's just reading a book or listening to music. If you know you are avoiding issues, try to let yourself give up doing; instead, be quiet and contemplative for at least part of your retreat.

ABOVE DO-IT-YOURSELF RETREATS CAN BE WONDERFUL OPPORTUNITIES TO 'STOP THE WORLD'. USE YOUR RETREAT TO READ INSPIRATIONAL BOOKS, TAKE UP MEDITATION OR TRY NEW TECHNIQUES AND THERAPIES.

5 There may be a particular issue or event you want to focus on during your retreat. This could be a joyful event (conception, a relationship, a career shift) or a sad one (illness, separation or death). Think about the best ways to work with your issue.

6 This could be a good opportunity for trying out ritual or building a shrine, or any of the other ideas in this book.

7 You may want to do absolutely nothing. And that's fine.

mini-retreats

If you can, it's a great idea to incorporate 'mini-retreats' as a regular part of life. You might set aside an afternoon every weekend, or an hour at night, or even just 15 or 20 minutes once in a while. But make it a time that is just for you. Keep a box or drawer full of your retreat 'props': candles, incense, inspirational books and tapes, maybe the tarot or I Ching, drawing or writing materials (see the box opposite).

mental retreating

There are times when we all need to 'get away'. You could be in an unpleasant meeting, crammed on a train or stuck in a situation you really dislike. You can't physically get away, but you *can* take yourself off to a private mental retreat.

1 Take a few slow, deep breaths to calm yourself. Start to focus on your breathing and notice its rhythm.

2 Start breathing into your solar plexus area, visualizing it becoming soft and warm. This, in itself, is very calming.

3 Imagine that the energy in your solar plexus is bubbling up like a spring – it bubbles and bubbles until it bursts into a golden shower of light and energy. This spreads out all around you, settling into an encompassing golden bubble of light.

4 The bubble keeps you safe and relaxed, and protected from any negative impulses or energies around you. If you like, you can call on further images – use any that will help.

5 If you feel that someone wishes you harm, you can slightly modify the bubble. As it extends around you, imagine it forms into a big glass box, the sides of which are made up of gleaming mirrors. Any negative energy that is sent towards you will bounce off the mirrors and be sent back to your aggressor.

DEATH

We all die. It's the one certainty in life. Yet most of us steadfastly refuse to think about death. We shut it out from our consciousness and try to pretend it doesn't exist, that it won't happen if we don't think about it. Why does death frighten us so much?

Maybe it's because death is such an unknown quantity, or perhaps it's because we hate the idea that we could lose our identity, our self. It may be the thought that death means we will lose our material possessions, our loved ones, our consciousness. Some people, on the other hand, are terrified of pain. These are all very real and valid fears, which should not be lightly dismissed. Yet, by turning our backs on death, we do ourselves and our lives a disservice. By looking calmly and clearly at death and what it means, we can, paradoxically, learn a lot about living.

Pause right now and ask yourself what your thoughts are concerning death.

- Are you frightened of death? Are you frightened of your own death or that of others'?
- What do you find most frightening?
- Have you experienced the death of anyone close to you? What feelings did it bring up for you?
- Have you ever thought about your own death?
- What words would you use to describe death?
- Is death always a bad thing?
- Do you believe in an afterlife? In reincarnation? Or do you believe that death is the end?

It might be a useful exercise to write out your feelings about death as free-association, or as a poem or a story. Alternatively, you may feel drawn to the idea of painting death or modelling it out of clay. Imagine you were dancing with Death – what would that dance be like? What kind of figure would Death be: would it be the stock image of the Grim Reaper or something different? Spend some time looking at the various images of death in mythologies and religions from around the world. In some, Death is seen as kindly or compassionate, or stern and just. Think about how much your ideas of death are based on society's general avoidance and fear of it – and what you really feel about it when you remove that layer of fear.

death as a lesson for life

Ask almost anyone who has survived a serious illness or life-threatening accident, or had a near-death experience, and they will all say the same thing: coming close to death made them really appreciate the life that they have and made them determined to live each year, each day, each minute as if it really mattered. I have dear friends who have cancer and say it is the best thing that has ever happened to them, as it has made them realize how incredible life really is and how often and how foolishly we tend to waste it.

We can all learn from that for, if we choose to ignore death, there is nothing to remind us that life is precious. Truly none of us can tell when we will die. The first lesson of death is that we should live our lives as if every minute mattered. We should ensure that our lives have meaning – that, when we do come to die, we can look back over our lives with joy, satisfaction and peace, rather than with regret, anger and sadness.

Imagine that you have been told you have just one year to live then take some time to think about the following questions.

- What would you want to do with that year?
- Are there things that you have always wanted to do, but have put off?
- What job would you really love to have done?
- Are there people you love, but have lost touch with?
- With whom would you spend that year?
- Are there enemies you feel you would like to forgive?
- Is there any unfinished business to which you should attend before dying?

Spend time on this and really think about it. Why wait until you have only a year? Why not put some of your thoughts into practice right now?

OPPOSITE Are we really snuffed out like candles when we die? Or does a part of us always remain? Death is the ultimate mystery, possibly the most important of all rites of passage.

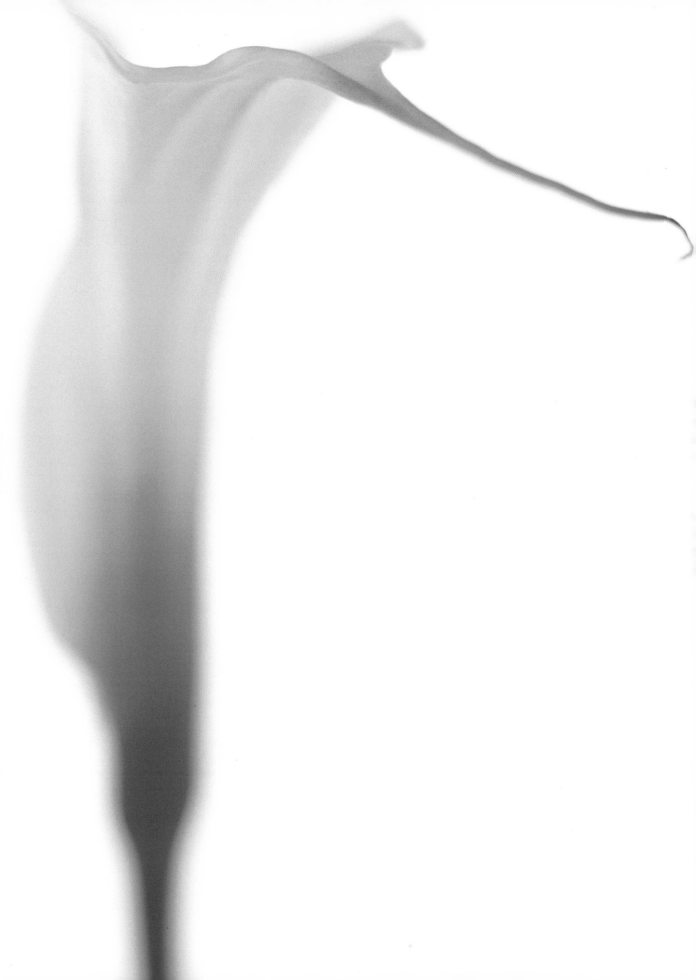

Do you hate your job? Change it! Do you have regrets about things you never tried? Try them. Are there people you should be in touch with? Write a letter or ring them. Don't leave any possibility of regret in your life. Forgive any old enemies – it's not worth the energy of holding on to hate.

If you like, you can take this exercise even further. Imagine that you had only a month, a week, a day, an hour: what would be your priorities? You may be surprised by your answers. Return to this exercise frequently, at the very least once a year, to make sure you keep on track. It's also a great exercise if you tend to project your hopes off into the future: 'I'll be happy when … I have that new job/ bigger house/ ideal relationship/perfect body etc.' We all do it, but focusing on the really important things that are in your life right now can put your life into perspective.

Are you spending too much time on your work and not enough with your children? Do you take your partner, your parents, your friends for granted? Are you resisting enjoying life because you're waiting to lose a few pounds? Don't wait too long – it may be too late.

what is death?

Do you remember the time before you were born? It's highly unlikely. Death is simply a transition, like birth, from one existence to another. Tibetan Buddhism has charted the terrain of death to a degree unsurpassed by any other religion and it has a lot to teach us. According to the Tibetans, there are actually six principal *bardos*, or transition periods:

- life
- sleep and dreaming
- meditation
- dying
- intrinsic radiance
- becoming or rebirth

In fact, we spend our entire lives moving through transitions. If you think about it, there are constant small births and deaths: the start or end of a relationship; leaving an old job and starting a new one; the welcoming into the family of a child or pet; the onset and end of illness; and so on. Nature provides us with the perfect

model: the year moves through change from fresh beginnings to ripeness to decay and finally death. Then the whole wonderful cycle begins again. If we see that life is an endless cycle of birth, maturation, death and rebirth, it gives us the sense that our lives are not finite.

It pays to look on the bardos as moments of opportunity and potential – at every point of transition we have the precious opportunity of change. We can transform ourselves as often as we wish. Every night you go to sleep as one person and wake up another: take advantage of that.

who are you?

The one vital lesson we all need to learn is to discover our true selves, to balance our inner natures. You will, I hope, be far closer to an understanding of yourself if you have worked through many of the exercises in this book. In particular, take time to look deeply at your relationships and heal any that are painful or unpleasant. If you find this hard, it might be worth looking into some form of psychotherapy or practising the empty-chair technique (see page 119) to understand the other person's point of view. Let go of any old grievances. Perhaps write letters to people – you don't even have to post them (you may want to have a ritual in which you burn them and release the negativity). On the other hand, it might be very healing to send them!

Meditation is an incredibly useful tool in gaining self-understanding and acceptance: notice that it is one of the Tibetan bardos in its own right. Make the time to practise the meditation exercises on page 109. In addition, you may like to introduce a life-enhancing practice known as *Tonglen*.

Tonglen is a Buddhist meditation practice that can have remarkable effects on your relationships and your entire life. It is a powerful way to rid yourself of any negative and toxic emotions that may be clogging your soul – such as anger, jealousy, hate and fear.

- Sit comfortably either on a chair or on the floor with your back straight (you may wish to sit on a small cushion so that your back naturally becomes aligned).
- Allow yourself to become aware of your breathing. Sit just observing your breath for about five minutes or try counting 21 out breaths.

- Now visualize someone you love dearly in front of you. As you breathe in, breathe into yourself any pain, upset and anger they might be feeling. Allow yourself to open up to them totally and without stinting.
- As you breathe out, breathe all that is good in you into them. Imagine their pain and suffering being transformed inside you into healing light – you are not holding their suffering, but instead transforming it.
- Repeat this for around 5 minutes.
- You can repeat this with as many people as you like. Keep practising until you are really proficient and can feel the healing energy inside you at will.

When you have perfected this exercise, you are ready for the next step. Instead of someone you love, imagine someone you dislike or even hate in front of you. Now transform their pain and anger, and give them back the pure, healing light of love. You may baulk at this, but stick

ABOVE FLOWERS BLOOM AND THEN DIE BACK, THEIR ENERGY RETURNING TO THE EARTH TO BE REPLENISHED FOR THE NEXT FLOWERING. MANY RELIGIONS TEACH THAT WE ARE THE SAME: WE LIVE, DIE AND ARE REBORN.

with it. Once you can perform Tonglen in this way for your greatest enemies, you will have taken a huge step forwards in your soul development. You may also notice that this exercise will have a noticeable effect on the disliked person or people. Expect surprises!

Once you have reached the end of this book, you will, I hope, hold fresh insights and be a different person from the one who started it. You might choose to go back and work more with the material or you may be ready to read another book and learn more in a different way. I think the same is true of life and death. You may come back and learn more here in this world – or you may go elsewhere. But the journey remains and I hope yours is filled with wonder and deep joy.

5 the therapies

There are literally countless different natural therapies on offer nowadays. Some, such as aromatherapy and reflexology, have become so popular and well known that almost everyone has heard of them. Others, such as watsu, chavutti thirumal and chua ka, are less well known.

We have already covered many therapies in the other sections of this book: this section outlines the rest of the best. The list is not exhaustive: new therapies spring up virtually every other week. It does, however, give you the lowdown on the therapies which you are most likely to come across and which, to my mind, are the most effective and interesting.

The vast majority of the therapies described here involve some form of bodywork – whether it's the deep touch of Rolfing, the gentle stretching of shiatsu or the almost imperceptible stroke of manual lymphatic drainage (MLD). Touch is something which is often missing from many people's lives and it can be remarkably therapeutic. We actively need to be touched – for our emotional health. This need is more than simply a desire. It is a physiological urge that, if unsatisfied, can have profound psychological effects. In fact, research has shown that even a 30-minute neck and back massage can reduce depression. It can lower levels of stress-related hormones and make people more alert, less restless and able to enjoy deeper, more restful sleep.

Equally, we are not just skin and bones, organs and muscles. We are more, far more, than mere flesh and blood. We are not just physical beings, but energetic ones, too. As you will have realized by now, our energy bodies are just as real as our mechanical ones. Most forms of natural therapies accept the role of energy, but some will work solely on the energy body. They believe the energy body is the linchpin for health – that, if you get the energy flowing freely, easily and smoothly, the physical frame will then fall naturally into good health. Many of the therapies in the 'Energy' section (pages 233–51) can appear rather strange if you are unfamiliar with this kind of work, but don't let that put you off: you may be surprised at the results.

With the growing interest in natural therapies, you may well find that many of these therapies are available in your area. Do investigate your local natural health centre to see what is on offer: it may have just the therapy you need.

THE SKELETAL STRUCTURE

osteopathy

Osteopathy is a system of massage and manipulation which aims to bring the structure of the body back into balance. Although considered a 'spine' therapy, it can achieve excellent results with a wide variety of conditions.

While many people think of osteopaths as simple bone-crunchers, that's a long way from the full story. Osteopathy was developed in the American Midwest in the nineteenth century, by a medical doctor and Methodist minister, Dr Andrew Taylor Still. He believed that by adjusting the structure, the framework of the body, its internal systems would be relieved and the body could then function properly and restore itself to health.

The philosophy underpinning osteopathy is that, if the anatomy and physiology are working well, the person is well. Sadly, we have a design problem working against us. In terms of human evolution, we have only recently made the transition onto two feet. Standing upright causes stresses and strains that our bodies have not yet adapted to: the discs between vertebrae have become weight-carrying and the continual strain can cause back pain and related problems.

The spine protects the major part of the nervous system, which, in turn, controls movement and registers sensations throughout the whole body. If the spine is badly aligned, symptoms might appear in any number of far-flung corners of the body. However, osteopaths don't focus just on the spine – muscular tension also needs to be relieved, as tension here can slow down the circulatory and lymphatic systems, inhibit heart function and worsen respiratory conditions.

Modern osteopathy uses a wide variety of techniques: manipulation and stretching, massage and gentle touch. In addition to these, your osteopath will often advise you on posture, diet and exercise.

what can osteopathy help?

- Osteopathy has good results with muscular and joint pain; frozen shoulders and all musculoskeletal problems.
- It is excellent for sports injuries and repetitive strain injury (RSI).
- Arthritic and rheumatic conditions respond well.
- Headaches and migraine can be helped.
- Chronic conditions such as asthma and bronchitis can respond well to osteopathy.
- Developmental problems can often be helped. So, too, can postural problems.
- It can be very valuable for the elderly.
- It can prove very useful both during and after pregnancy by helping a woman's body adapt to the considerable strains placed on it by pregnancy and birth.
- Some quite surprising ailments can be improved – including digestive problems such as irritable bowel syndrome (IBS) and colitis, and menstrual problems such as premenstrual syndrome (PMS) and painful periods.

what can I expect from a session?

WHERE WILL I HAVE THE TREATMENT?

You will sit down to discuss your case with the osteopath, and then be asked to stand and walk around the room. The majority of the treatment will be conducted on the osteopath's couch, either sitting or lying.

WILL I BE CLOTHED?

Most osteopaths will ask you to strip down to underwear. You may be given a gown to wear.

WHAT HAPPENS?

You will be asked for a case history (precise details of your past and present health; any accidents, operations, and medication or remedies currently being taken; your life at home and work; your present problem and how it started, and what makes it feel better or worse). You will then usually be asked to demonstrate your mobility and posture – standing, sitting, walking up and down the room, leaning in all directions. Next, the osteopath will ask you either to sit or to lie down on the couch while he or she works on you.

Although massage may form part of the treatment, osteopathy is definitely not a pampering remedy and everything is performed swiftly and functionally. Often massage, deep stretching and pressure-point work (pressing deeply into the muscles and connective tissue) is enough to solve the problem.

You may also have to have your spine manipulated, a treatment in which the vertebrae are swiftly cracked to allow them to return to their correct alignment.

WILL IT HURT?

It depends very much on the osteopath! Some are very gentle and only use manipulation as a last resort; others really do crack

and crunch your vertebrae, which can be a rather uncomfortable and unpleasant process. However, the sense of relief you will feel when a joint is returned to its correct alignment can be immense and it is well worth any slight discomfort.

WILL ANYTHING STRANGE HAPPEN?

You may well experience a feeling of flushing as the blood rushes into an area that has been constricted. Occasionally (although less so than in other bodywork therapies), you may also find that old memories resurface.

WILL I BE GIVEN ANYTHING TO TAKE?

No, medication is not part of the osteopathic treatment.

IS THERE ANY HOMEWORK?

Some osteopaths will give you exercises to perform at home to improve your posture or to help your problem. They may also advise you on diet.

home back class

Osteopathy is a precise science and you should not attempt it at home. You can, however, use this simple back-stretching routine to help keep your spine supple. If you suffer from back or neck problems, check with your doctor before stretching.

You should feel a gentle stretch while doing these exercises, but not pain. Stop immediately if you feel any pain at all. Don't continue with the exercises; instead, consult a qualified osteopath, as you may have a back problem.

1 Lie on your back on the floor. Bring your knees up to your chest and clasp them with your hands. Then, keeping your whole body as relaxed as possible, pull your knees in towards your chest slowly. Hold for about 10 seconds, then release.

2 Position yourself on all fours with your hands directly under your shoulders and your knees directly under your hips. Your back should be straight. Now gently arch your back, as if you were a cat. Let your head drop and feel your pelvis tuck in. Hold for about 20 seconds and release. Repeat this process several times.

3 Sit on the edge of an upright chair with your feet placed firmly on the floor, quite widely apart. Slowly begin to bend forwards, until your hands drop to the floor and your head is positioned between your knees. Make sure your movements are very slow and smooth – you should feel a gentle stretch (if you do feel any pain, stop). Hold for about 10 seconds. This is an ideal exercise to practise throughout the day, especially if you have a sedentary job.

cranial osteopathy & cranio-sacral therapy

The key to health and happiness may actually lie hidden in your head – not in your mind, but in the tiny joints that make up your skull. Cranial osteopaths and cranio-sacral therapists use the gentlest of touches to achieve remarkable results on these minute joints, called *sutures*.

There are two schools of cranial work: one practised by some osteopaths as part of their wider repertoire (see osteopathy on pages 194–5) and the other a sideshoot known as cranio-sacral therapy, which is either performed as a therapy on its own or incorporated into other forms of bodywork such as shiatsu, massage and reflexology.

Both forms originate from the same source – the work of William Garner Sutherland. Sutherland trained as an osteopath in the early part of the twentieth century when osteopathy taught that the bones of the skull were firmly fixed together and immovable. Sutherland found, however, that the cranium was actually a moving structure. Its movements were certainly minute, but, like any other joint, the sutures of the skull ran the risk of becoming traumatized, restricted or stiff. Equally, also like any other joint, they could be manipulated back into balance.

Sutherland also discovered that there are certain rhythms in the cranium – a pulse that echoes the fluctuation of the cerebrospinal fluid (the watery liquid that bathes the tissues of the brain and spinal cord). When there is a problem in the body, or illness, this pulse stops beating at its optimum level of 10–14 beats a minute. Very gentle manipulation of the head and lower spine (the sacrum) can, however, correct the pulse and cure the problem.

Cranio-sacral therapy developed out of cranial osteopathy and is now a discipline in its own right. Unlike cranial osteopathy, its practitioners do not require any training in osteopathy or chiropractic. It was founded by Dr John Upledger, an American osteopath and physician who found that a large amount of cranial work could be taught easily and effectively to people with no background in osteopathy. He also become increasingly fascinated by the psychological and emotional aspects of cranial work and came to the

conclusion that, for true healing, there had to be some form of psychological, as well as physical, release. Consequently, many practitioners combine their work with regression therapy, counselling, guided imagery or visualization.

what can cranial osteopathy and cranio-sacral therapy help?

- A wide variety of conditions respond well to these therapies.
- They are superlative for babies, as they are so gentle and are particularly indicated when birth was traumatic in any way (i.e. very swift, very protracted, with forceps or venteuse, or C-section). They can help a variety of problems from colic to feeding difficulties, poor sleeping to constant crying.
- They are also very useful for mothers after childbirth.
- Children respond particularly well – learning difficulties, poor coordination and hyperactivity can often be helped.
- Migraine, chronic headaches and sinus problems respond well.
- There has been success with cases of osteoporosis and tinnitus.
- Some digestive and gynaecological conditions respond well.
- Intriguingly, there has been considerable success in treating phobias with cranial osteopathy and cranio-sacral therapy.

LEFT CRANIAL WORK IS ONE OF THE MOST GENTLE FORMS OF NATURAL MEDICINE – BUT ITS EFFECTS CAN BE INCREDIBLY POWERFUL. BEST KNOWN FOR ITS EXCELLENT RESULTS WITH BABIES AND YOUNG CHILDREN, CRANIAL THERAPY IS ALSO USEFUL FOR TREATING A WIDE VARIETY OF ADULT PROBLEMS, FROM PHOBIAS TO OSTEOPOROSIS AND TINNITUS.

what can I expect from a session?

WHERE WILL I HAVE THE TREATMENT?

You will be lying on the therapist's couch.

WILL I BE CLOTHED?

Cranio-sacral therapists will ask you to remain fully clothed. Cranial osteopaths may well want you to strip to underwear, so as to be able to observe the entire spine.

WHAT HAPPENS?

Sessions start with a full case history, with particular emphasis on any injuries or illnesses. A cranial osteopath will ask you to strip down to your underwear and then observe your posture before asking you to lie on the couch. The touch is very gentle and the manipulations minimal – a slight twist here, a gentle pull there. Most of the work is performed on the sutures of the skull while the osteopath cradles the head. The base of the spine (the sacrum) is also held. The therapist's touch is so minimal that it is often hard to detect that anything is being done at all.

Cranio-sacral therapists use the same techniques, but usually keep you fully clothed. They often combine the treatment with guided visualization, colour therapy or, on occasion, holistic foot massage. Sessions are much longer than those with cranial osteopaths and generally more emotional and psychological (sometimes even mystical) in approach.

WILL IT HURT?

No, it doesn't hurt at all. In fact, you will feel only the tiniest, most gentle of touches. It is incredibly relaxing and soothing.

WILL ANYTHING STRANGE HAPPEN?

Some people find that images or colours 'pop' into their heads while on the couch. It's not uncommon to remember past events or relive old and sometimes painful emotions.

WILL I BE GIVEN ANYTHING TO TAKE?

No, medication is not part of the treatment, although some cranio-sacral therapists may include flower remedies in their practice if they feel these will be beneficial.

IS THERE ANY HOMEWORK?

It may be that the therapist will teach you some techniques to practise at home.

chiropractic

Chiropractors like to say that they practise bloodless surgery. Their aim is to maintain the spine and the nervous system (and hence the whole body) in good health and harmony, without recourse to surgery or drugs. Sometimes the results can seem like miracles – the chiropractor cracks a joint in the spine and a pain somewhere quite different simply vanishes. Although the name *chiropractic* sounds exotic, it simply means 'done by hand'.

The chiropractor is looking for a balanced spine that moves and functions harmoniously. If any of the individual joints move less or more than they should, or move in an abnormal way, the spine as a whole will fall out of its equilibrium and not work correctly.

Adjustments and manipulations help the mechanical function of the spine, which in turn helps muscles, nerves, joints and ligaments to work better. Chiropractors don't 'put bones back', as many people think; a bone only 'comes out' if it is dislocated. They prefer the word *subluxation*, meaning that a bone is out of alignment relative to the one below.

The first treatment using chiropractic in its present form took place in 1895 and was carried out by Daniel David (D. D.) Palmer, a Canadian schoolmaster-turned-storekeeper-turned-healer. Like many healers, he was driven to discover the true cause of sickness, as he believed that there is a fundamental reason why we become ill.

The start of chiropractic was quite dramatic. Palmer found that a man who had been deaf for 17 years also had a displaced vertebra. He put the vertebra back into position and the man's hearing returned instantly. Another case followed shortly: this time, once the displaced vertebra was replaced, Palmer found he had miraculously cured heart trouble. Palmer was fascinated. He began to theorize that all disease could be caused by an imbalance of tension in the nerves running through the spine.

Now, alongside osteopathy, chiropractic is probably the form of natural medicine most accepted by the orthodox medical world. Medical doctors quite happily refer patients to both osteopaths and chiropractors, recognizing that they have methods of treating the root causes of pain that doctors can only numb with drugs.

what can chiropractic help?

- Chiropractic is especially successful in treating mechanical problems of the spine, which can cause lumbago, sciatica, headaches etc.
- It is helpful in some cases of arthritis and rheumatism.
- Chiropractic promotes ease of movement in the chest and so can help asthma.
- It can be helpful in cases of Parkinson's disease, multiple sclerosis and some cancers.
- It can ease back problems and aches and pains in pregnancy.

what can I expect from a session?

WHERE WILL I HAVE THE TREATMENT?

You will start off the consultation sitting, while you talk to the chiropractor. You will then be asked to stand for observation. The actual chiropractic work is carried out with you lying or sitting on the practitioner's couch.

WILL I BE CLOTHED?

You will usually be asked to strip down to underwear. You may be given an open-backed gown to wear throughout the treatment.

WHAT HAPPENS?

A full case history will be taken – you will be asked about your medical history, any past illnesses and in particular any injuries to joints or bones. You will also be quizzed on your present problem – your symptoms, when it's better and when it's worse, how long you've had it. You will then be asked to stand and sit, so your spine can be examined, after which you will usually lie on the couch. Here, the chiropractor will test the mobility of your legs and will feel your spine to see if any joints or vertebrae are impaired. X-rays may be taken and possibly blood or urine tests.

The major work consists of adjusting the joints, using pressure and manipulation. You will feel a sharp click or crunch as the problematic joint is thrust back into position, or you may have to twist or turn your body into the correct position.

Chiropractic is a very pragmatic, down-to-earth therapy – ideal if you like a solid medical approach. It is well recognized and respected by most doctors.

WILL IT HURT?

It depends very much on the chiropractor and on your own personality. Some people enjoy the cracks and crunches; others hate them. The treatment is not really painful – more uncomfortable and a bit of a shock to the system!

WILL ANYTHING STRANGE HAPPEN?

You may experience a rush of blood as a joint is released. Very occasionally chiropractic can spark old memories. Some people find the results nigh-on miraculous – they walk in in agony and walk out pain free.

WILL I BE GIVEN ANYTHING TO TAKE?

No, medication is not part of the treatment. Some chiropractors, however, do work alongside medical doctors, who may prescribe drugs.

IS THERE ANY HOMEWORK?

You may be given advice on preventative measures to stop your problem recurring. You may also be taught postural exercises and stretches to do to help your spine.

how to soothe a bad back

1 Exercise if you possibly can: this will help mobilize the back and strengthen the muscles that support it. However, if you do suffer severe pain, you will need to consult an experienced physiotherapist or exercise therapist. Don't overdo the exercise and, if you experience pain (as opposed to a gentle stretch), *stop*!

2 Try gentle systems such as Pilates and yoga. There is a branch of yoga known as yoga therapy which can help bad backs specifically. Always see a well-qualified teacher, rather than trying to learn it yourself from books or videos.

3 Make sure your posture is good. Invest in a special 'back' chair from a specialist store if you have to sit down all day for work. A good example is the kind of chair that entails a kneeling position, so encouraging the healthy spinal curve, rather than a slump.

4 Check your mattress. Many people suffer from bad backs because they are sleeping on the wrong type of bed. Your mattress should be firm enough to support you, without being too hard (many orthopaedic beds are too hard for comfort). Also ensure you change your mattress every four or five years.

OPPOSITE IF YOU SUFFER FROM A BAD BACK IT'S WORTH LOOKING AT YOUR BED. DON'T AUTOMATICALLY ASSUME A HARD ORTHOPAEDIC MATTRESS IS BEST – IT MAY BE TOO FIRM. BUY THE BEST MATTRESS YOU CAN AFFORD AND TEST IT OUT THOROUGHLY BEFORE INVESTING.

mctimoney chiropractic

Although many chiropractors work very gently, there really is only one sure-fire way to be certain that your chiropractic treatment will never hurt and that's to find a McTimoney chiropractor. The McTimoney method seems to offer all the benefits of traditional osteopathy and chiropractic with none of the trauma. This holistic form of manipulative treatment uses a gentle technique to achieve harmony in the body.

John McTimoney, the originator of the system, was impressed by standard chiropractic, but felt that the system could be better still. First, he was convinced that the whole person should be treated, not just the part causing the problems. Secondly, he didn't see why the treatment should be uncomfortable or stressful. By experimenting, he found he could get the same, if not better, results by using very gentle techniques. In 1972, he started teaching his form of chiropractic. Although John McTimoney died in 1980, his students took up the baton and, in 1982, opened their own school to teach his work.

Many of us walk around with curves in our spines (caused by bad posture, carrying heavy bags, etc.). They are slight, but sufficient to cause twinges and pain. The McTimoney chiropractor aims to release these old patterns of holding, to wipe out bad habits overlaid on our ideal structure, so that our bodies can return to their original healthy blueprint.

The main technique used is called the *toggle recoil*. Basically, this involves the practitioner using one hand as a nail and the other as a hammer. The hands are held over the precise spot that needs treating and the 'hammer' is brought down sharply on the 'nail' with a slight twist. This action is rather like spinning a top and flicking it at the same time to set it moving. The effect is to change the tension surrounding the joint that has been 'toggled'. In a split second, the joint is freed: the adjustment is so rapid that it outwits the surrounding muscle, which does not have time to clamp fast into a protective spasm. The muscles are then able to relax and take up a more normal tension.

Because most of our holding patterns have been in place for years, most people tend to see McTimoney practitioners for around six sessions, in order to coax the joints to settle back into their natural position completely.

what can mctimoney chiropractic help?

- Most of the conditions that standard chiropractic alleviates – particularly joint and back pain – can be treated.
- Headaches, period pains and digestive pains often clear up.
- McTimoney chiropractic is wonderful both during and after pregnancy, as its manipulations can be safely used throughout – unlike standard chiropractic and osteopathy.
- Sports injuries respond well.
- There are special techniques to treat repetitive strain injury (RSI), carpal tunnel syndrome and tennis elbow.
- Many McTimoney chiropractors also treat animals with great success (under the auspices of a veterinarian).

what can I expect from a session?

WHERE WILL I HAVE THE TREATMENT?

You will be both sitting and lying on the therapist's couch.

WILL I BE CLOTHED?

You will be asked to strip down to underwear for the treatment.

WHAT HAPPENS?

You will be asked for a full case history, including the contact telephone number of your medical doctor. Expect to be asked about your medical history and current problem, as well as stress levels, sleep patterns, working conditions etc.

You will be asked to sit on the edge of the couch while the practitioner scans your spine. You then lie down, as the neck and pelvis are worked first. Small manipulations are then made to the knees, ankles and toes. The arms and hands are next to be treated, followed by the collarbone, face and skull.

McTimoney treatment always ends with a swift rubbing down, to bring you back to earth, as it were. As you sit up, your spine will be appraised again and it is possible the practitioner may feel it is necessary to make a couple more adjustments.

WILL IT HURT?

No, not at all. McTimoney is incredibly gentle.

WILL ANYTHING STRANGE HAPPEN?

It's not likely. The light 'swatting' feels a little strange to begin with, but it's not unpleasant.

WILL I BE GIVEN ANYTHING TO TAKE?

No, there is no medication, although some practitioners will refer patients to nutritional therapists if they think diet is a factor.

IS THERE ANY HOMEWORK?

You may be given postural exercises and stretches to do, and recommendations on how to keep your body properly aligned.

other forms of gentle chiropractic

Network chiropractic is a synthesis of all the varying forms of manipulation therapy. It is very gentle: nothing is ever forced. However much the practitioner might see the need to 'reset' a vertebra, he or she will not touch it until the body is absolutely ready, so relaxed that the adjustment causes no trauma whatsoever. Network chiropractors always look at the whole body, the whole person, rather than at individual vertebrae or bad knees. They seek to bring the entire body back into balance.

A study carried out at the University of California observed people who had undergone long-term network chiropractic. The subjects talked not just of physical improvements and pain relief, but also of more intangible benefits: greater self-esteem; more enjoyment at work and better family relationships. They reported feeling more motivated and felt more positive about the future. While such results are hard to prove scientifically, they seemed significant to the researchers.

BEST (bio-energetic synchronization technique) is another form of chiropractic. The job of the BEST practitioner is to update the neurology of the body. This is achieved by your lying fully clothed on the couch as the practitioner presses certain points while you hold your breath. Holding your breath means the brain cannot concentrate on anything except the need for oxygen so, as the point is pressed, the 'memory' held there is released. As you breathe out, the body updates its neurological information – the old trauma is left behind.

WHAT DOES YOUR PAIN MEAN?

BEST chiropractic teaches that where we hold our pain can indicate the emotional problems we have.

Lower back pain concerns trust, confidence and security, or worries over your job, money or household environment. It also often relates to your relationship with your mother.

Middle-dorsal pain has to do with emotional/love relationships or low self-esteem.

Tense shoulders reflect on self-expression – how you express yourself or how you deal with what people say.

Sciatica tends to affect people who can't stick by their decisions.

A stiff neck means you find it hard to listen to others.

zero balancing

Zero balancing is a therapy that aims not merely to soothe and relax your physical frame, but also to stretch and balance your energetic body. It's a hands-on treatment which works physically at the deepest level of the body – the bone structure – and then moves deeper still, influencing the body's innermost energy systems.

Many therapies rely simply on bodywork, others focus solely on the energy part of the equation, but zero balancing (ZB) is based on the idea that better, faster, deeper healing can take place when the two are treated in tandem. It was developed by Dr Fritz Smith, an American physician, acupuncturist and osteopath who investigated a wide range of bodywork therapies and ancient energy systems before concluding that, in order to bring people from sickness to health, from imbalance to balance, he needed to combine the two approaches. The result was zero balancing, which first came into being around 1973. Smith calls it a 'blending of Eastern and Western ideas in terms of body and structure. It brings energy concepts into touch, or body handling.'

In zero balancing, energy is seen with clear precision. Three distinct types of energy surrounding the body are recognized, and a further three circulating within the body. Apparently, almost anything, from physical accidents to emotional traumas, can affect our 'energy' body. A blow to the knee can cause physical damage, but, long after the bruising has gone, the energy could remain twisted or stuck. Equally, an emotional shock such as bereavement or a relationship breakdown can remain caught in the energy web, causing not just psychological stress, but possibly physical stress and strain as well.

Zero balancers are all professional, highly trained bodyworkers. Before being accepted for training, they must already hold recognized qualifications in other forms of healthcare such as osteopathy, acupuncture, physiotherapy, chiropractic or Rolfing.

In many ways, zero balancing is the ideal therapy for people who feel nervous or uncomfortable about having to reveal too much of themselves. You won't have to take your clothes off, nor will you be expected to divulge your innermost secrets in painful soul baring.

sensing energy

As part of its teaching, zero balancing holds that the consciousness, or energy, of the practitioner can have a distinct effect on the person being treated. This exercise demonstrates how important this energy link is.

You will need a partner with whom to experiment to carry out this exercise.

1 Ask your partner to sit down in a chair and make himself or herself comfortable. Ask him or her to spend a few moments just quietly becoming aware of breathing calmly.

2 Now stand behind and rest one hand on his or her shoulder.

3 Both of you should bring your attention to the hand resting on the shoulder. How does it feel? Be aware of the pressure, the temperature, the 'sense' of touch.

4 After a few minutes, keep your hand in exactly the same position, but take your awareness away from your hand (you might look around the room or focus your thoughts on something entirely different). Tell your partner when you do this.

5 Now switch places – you sit down and ask your partner to repeat the exercise in exactly the same way.

6 Tell each other what you experienced, comparing sensations and feelings.

This exercise is incredibly simple to do, but most people who try it are astonished by the results. When the awareness is taken away, there is often a feeling that the pressure lightens, that a sense of coolness replaces warmth (or vice versa).

what can zero balancing help?

- Zero balancing is often successful in curing headaches, and neck and shoulder pain.
- It is superb for alleviating back problems.
- Many sportspeople and performers rate zero balancing very highly.
- Although practitioners are cautious and won't make wild claims, many physical ailments clear up as a result of treatment.
- It has wide-reaching emotional effects – people often find they have more clarity and are able to make better decisions.
- Zero balancing has been described as akin to deep meditation: it takes people very deep into themselves so that the minor chitchat of the mind is silenced.
- It has good results on old injuries and any emotional troubles that have come about through past traumas and accidents. Emotional wounds – such as bereavement or great disappointments – can often be healed quite easily.

what can I expect from a session?

WHERE WILL I HAVE THE TREATMENT?
You will be lying on the zero balancer's couch.

WILL I BE CLOTHED?
Yes. You need to take off only shoes and jewellery.

WHAT HAPPENS?
The zero balancer may ask if there is anything in particular that needs attention, and if you are suffering from any pain or stress. You then simply take off your shoes and any jewellery, and lie on your back on a couch. The practitioner works from the lower back down the legs to the feet, then to the upper back and finally towards the feet again. The touch sometimes feels like acupressure, shiatsu or osteopathy; at others, it is akin to Rolfing or Hellerwork. But it is unique.

The aim of the zero balancer is to get in touch with your energy system so that you can both work together on the problem. This approach is often known as the *donkey-donkey touch* because it's like two donkeys walking up a hill. If the donkeys are on a steep slope, they will lean into each other to help them get up the hill. Similarly, the practice of zero balancing is seen very much as a collaboration between therapist and client, rather than a treatment that a person passively 'receives'.

WILL IT HURT?
This all depends on your pain threshold. The touch used for zero balancing is pretty deep, but it is generally not painful. Although you may feel a little stiff after a session, this sensation swiftly passes.

WILL ANYTHING STRANGE HAPPEN?
You may feel curious sensations in the body or remember old incidents. Some people 'see' colours or experience a buzzing in their heads.

WILL I BE GIVEN ANYTHING TO TAKE?
No, medication is not part of the treatment.

IS THERE ANY HOMEWORK?
You may be given postural exercises to do at home.

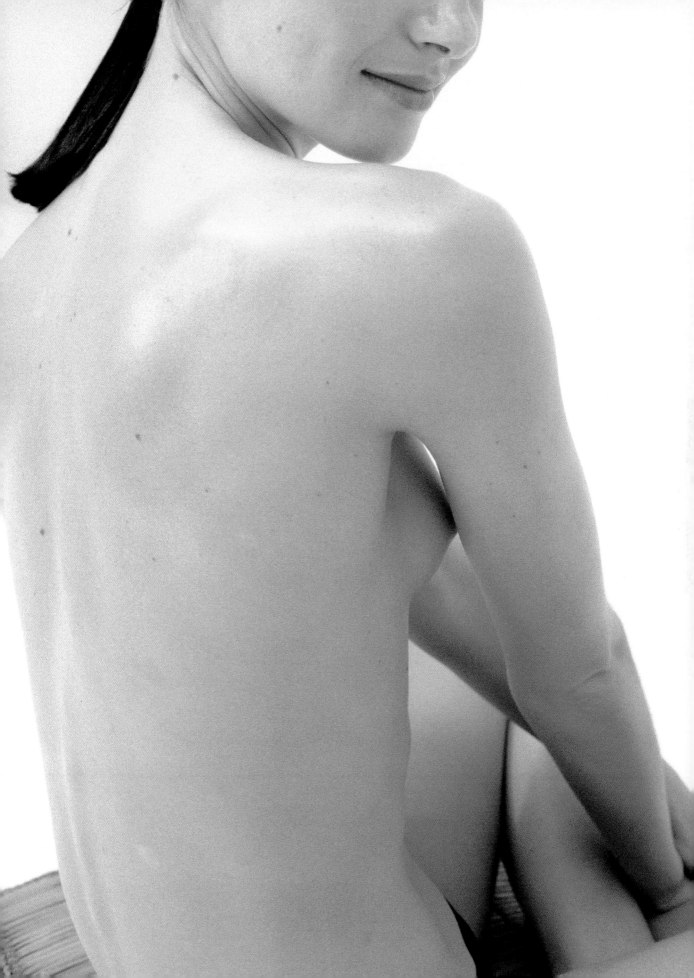

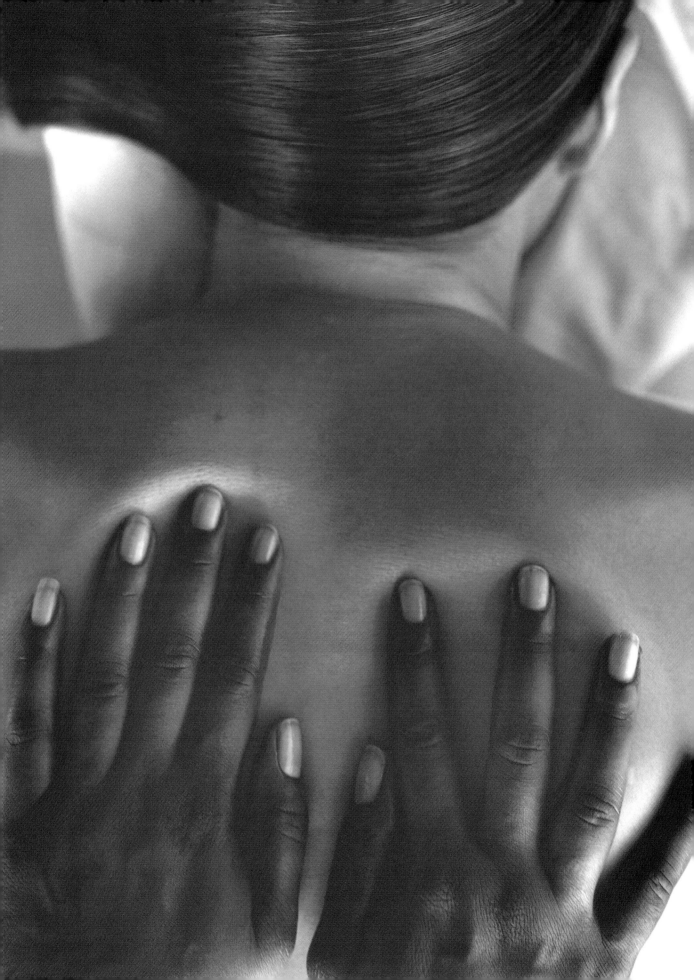

THE FASCIA

rolfing & hellerwork

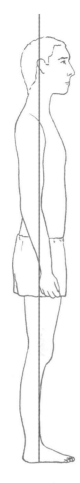

A session with a Rolfer or Hellerworker will transform the way you stand and alter the way you move. It could change patterns you have held for years, even since childhood. More incredible still, it could shift your whole emotional being. After a course of treatment (Rolfing has a standard 10 sessions; Hellerwork, 11), people's bodies quite literally look different – more upright, more centred, more relaxed.

At first sight, these treatments appear to be little more than a form of deep massage. So how do their practitioners achieve such dramatic results? The answer lies in the fascia, the connective tissue that encases every muscle and forms our tendons and ligaments. It keeps our whole structure, muscle and bone, in place.

Yet the fascial system had been generally ignored until the late 1940s when American biochemist Dr Ida Rolf discovered that the fascia would adapt to support whatever patterns of movement and posture the body adopted. If you put more weight on one leg than the other, the fascia will bunch and shorten to compensate. If you hunch your shoulders, the fascia will knot to accommodate and hold your posture. If we put our bodies into imbalance, the fascia will change to hold us in that position.

If they can change once, however, the fascia can change again. By manipulating and stretching the fascia back into their original positions, Rolf found she could reprogramme neurological pathways and return her patients to alignment. The benefit did not stop there. Rolf also found that, when she changed the body on a physiological level, her patients shifted on mental and emotional levels as well.

The other major deep-tissue technique is Hellerwork. Its founder, Joseph Heller, initially trained with Ida Rolf, but wanted to concentrate more on movement and the emotional side of treatment. As most Hellerworkers and Rolfers will admit, however, nowadays the differences between these two bodywork systems are minimal and you will get equally good results with either one.

ABOVE MOST OF US START LIFE AS CHILDREN POSSESSED WITH IDEAL ALIGNMENT. EMOTIONAL AND PHYSICAL TRAUMAS, HOWEVER, CAN EASILY COMBINE TO KNOCK THE BODY OUT OF SHAPE. ROLFING AND HELLERWORK COAX THE BODY BACK INTO BALANCE THROUGH STRONG MANIPULATION OF THE FASCIAL AND MUSCULAR SYSTEMS.

what can rolfing and hellerwork help?

- Postural problems respond best to Rolfing and Hellerwork.
- Long-term aches and pains often disappear.
- Chronic headaches can respond well to these treatments.
- Neck and back pains are usually alleviated.
- Energy levels are generally improved.
- Rolfing and Hellerwork can help improve athletic performance and general ease of movement.
- There are usually psychological benefits, such as increased confidence, the ability to deal with stressful situations and more honest relationships.
- Many people use Rolfing and Hellerwork to help them achieve personal growth.

what can I expect from a session?

WHERE WILL I HAVE THE TREATMENT?

You will be lying on a couch. Hellerworkers will ask you to move around as well.

WILL I BE CLOTHED?

You will be asked to strip down to your underwear.

WHAT HAPPENS?

The bodyworker will first scrutinize your body and posture as you stand in your underwear. You may be photographed or perhaps videoed so that you will be able to see the difference at the end of your sessions. Hellerworkers will also spend time teaching you how to sit, stand and walk in a more balanced way. Each Hellerwork session has a theme such as 'inspiration' and, while the therapist is working, he or she will ask you questions such as: 'What inspires you?'

Both therapies are performed on a couch and the touch is virtually identical. It's insistent and sometimes it can make you feel quite tender, but not unbearably so. It can feel wonderfully releasing, as old strains and stresses are stretched and straightened.

In the course of your 10 or 11 sessions, each part of the body is worked systematically – a different part is worked at each session. With Hellerwork, each session also deals with a different emotional problem.

WILL IT HURT?

Of all the natural therapies, these have the reputation for being the most painful. The touch is deep and can thus hurt, but nowadays most deep-tissue bodyworkers will try to work within your pain threshold.

WILL ANYTHING STRANGE HAPPEN?

It's not uncommon suddenly to recall old memories, or for past incidents to come into your mind, both during and in the days following your session. You may well find you experience a surge of energy after treatment.

Physically, people say that they notice a change in their posture and their skin tone. More subtly, there can be distinct changes in the way people present themselves, their vitality, their confidence and their overall energy levels. If you have a high level of toxicity, you may find yourself feeling worse to begin with, as the treatment can release toxins held in the muscles and joints.

WILL I BE GIVEN ANYTHING TO TAKE?

No, medication is not part of the treatment.

IS THERE ANY HOMEWORK?

You may be given some postural exercises to do at home.

rebalance your body

Try these simple exercises that will help to free your body:

- We often develop tensions because we are stuck in bad patterns. Try to break out of your habitual patterns by doing everyday things in a different way: try carrying your bag on the opposite shoulder from usual; throw or kick a ball with the opposite foot than normal; take your first step up stairs with the 'other' foot; brush your hair with the opposite hand. Although trying this strategy will undoubtedly feel strange, it will help to balance your body.

- Practise squatting whenever you can. Squatting is truly wonderful for the lower back and also helps to cure the scourge of modern life – constipation. Start gently and use a table or chair for support as you lower into a squat. Getting up from a squat may be even more difficult than getting down: push into the ground with your weight over your feet, so that you don't strain your back.
- Give yourself at least 10 minutes of 'real rest' a day. Lie on your back on a mat or thin cushions on the floor. Your knees should be bent and your arms folded across your chest. Gently become aware of your breathing – don't try to alter it, just become aware. Feel it quieten, then focus on the out breath. Lie there, aware of your breathing and body. Roll over slowly onto each side before rolling over onto your front, onto all fours and then slowly getting up.

bowen technique

There's no need to wind your head around any complex philosophy with the Bowen technique; no call for mystic mumblings or deep emotional encounters; no need to devote time to a drawn-out course of treatment. Quick, cheap and effective, it manipulates the muscles and connective tissue, leaving you walking tall and feeling relaxed, free and supple.

Bowen hails from the clean-living, no-nonsense, bright and breezy reaches of Australia. Its originator, Tom Bowen, studied medicine before the Second World War. By the 1950s, he was practising as a therapist, having developed a system of very precise, highly specific moves mingled with a liberal smattering of home remedies and almost folkloric advice. He allowed Oswald Rentsch to study his technique; after Bowen's death in 1982, Rentsch began to train other therapists.

The Bowen technique can be used on anyone, from the newborn to the elderly and immobile. A session takes just 20 minutes and you don't even have to take off your clothes.

Like Rolfers and Hellerworkers (see pages 205–6), Bowen practitioners work on the fascia, the connective tissue that covers the muscles, but with a quite different technique. It involves taking the slack across the muscle and moving over it. The touch is firm, but not painful. Around eight or ten prescribed moves are given in the first session, on the back and around the neck. Other moves can be used in later sessions. It may be simple, but Bowen is claimed to be highly effective: practitioners promise that 80–90 per cent of people need only one or two sessions to sort out their problems.

what can the bowen technique help?

- It is very useful for sports injuries in particular.
- Sportspeople also say it improves their performance.
- Lower back injuries and pain respond well.
- Chronic tension headaches often disappear after treatment.
- Problems such as asthma and bedwetting can be treated.

what can I expect from a session?

WHERE WILL I HAVE THE TREATMENT?
You will be lying on the therapist's couch.

WILL I BE CLOTHED?
Yes, you will be fully clothed.

WHAT HAPPENS?
You tell the practitioner your problem and then are asked to lie face-down on the couch. The therapist will start by working on your neck and back; you will feel a subtle resistance and then a sense of 'giving way', as each muscle is 'rolled over'. It's a deeply satisfying therapy – you really feel it has 'hit the spot' but it's also very gentle. You may feel marginally worse after a treatment, but therapists prefer that you feel some change, whether good or bad. Most people experience a distinct sense of relief either immediately or in the day or two after treatment.

WILL IT HURT?
No, it doesn't hurt at all.

WILL ANYTHING STRANGE HAPPEN?
No, Bowen doesn't usually have any strange effects.

WILL I BE GIVEN ANYTHING TO TAKE?
No, although you may be advised on home remedies.

IS THERE ANY HOMEWORK?
You may be given exercises to do or suggestions for home cures.

do-it-yourself bowen technique

The Bowen technique has a host of weird and wonderful home remedies. These include:

For bunions – soak your feet in warm water containing about 3 tablespoons of Epsom salts every night for 3 weeks. The salts apparently break down the calcification that causes bunions.

For swollen knees or other joints – put crushed washing soda in a handkerchief, wrap it in a cloth and fasten this to the joint with a stocking before going to bed. The washing soda should draw out the fluid and the swelling should go down.

For bruises – apple cider vinegar applied to bruises or sprained wrists should take away the pain and tenderness.

For bladder problems and dizziness – take two slices (no more than 50 g/2 oz) of raw beetroot daily, in juice form.

For bedwetting – often the problem is psychological, but children who bedwet should avoid dairy produce, apples and apple juice and go on an 80 per cent alkaline/20 per cent acid diet. Bowen believed that apple juice weakens the bladder.

For arthritis – Epsom salts in the bath water can help.

For rheumatism – regular doses of honey mixed with cider vinegar can ease symptoms.

PRESSURE POINTS

acupressure & shiatsu

Acupressure is generally known as acupuncture without the needles. So, it's perfect for anyone who wants the benefits of traditional Chinese medicine, but is wary of needles. The theory is that vital energy, qi, runs through the body via channels called meridians. If the energy becomes stuck or sluggish, or races too fast, ill health will ensue. The aim of acupressure and shiatsu (the Japanese version) is to restore equilibrium to the energy flow.

Acupressure is old – very old. A form of it has been practised for perhaps more than 5,000 years. It is thought to have originated in India, then spread to Central Asia, Egypt and China, but it was the Chinese who took the system and made acupressure their own. For thousands of years, it was part of the practice of the folk healers known as 'barefoot practitioners' who travelled from village to village offering basic medical knowledge and the power of acupressure. The practice of shiatsu began in Japan around the sixth century AD; although very similar to Chinese acupressure, it has its own special characteristics.

These pressure-point therapies all work by stimulating the acupoints (*tsubos* in shiatsu) and so inducing the correct flow of qi or ki through the body. Physiologically, therapists say that they are shifting and diffusing the lactic acid and carbon monoxide that tend to accumulate in muscle tissue. These, they say, can cause stiffness and sluggishness in the blood which, in turn, affect every system of the body. Most therapists prefer to talk purely in terms of energy – allow the qi to flow smoothly and all manner of ailments will clear up.

what can acupressure and shiatsu help?

- These therapies are superb for stressbusting.
- Emotional and psychological problems respond well.
- Chronic conditions such as back pain, migraine, rheumatism and arthritis can be helped.
- Asthma, constipation, insomnia and sciatica can benefit.
- Acupressure and shiatsu often have success with impotence.

what can I expect from a session?
WHERE WILL I HAVE THE TREATMENT?

Shiatsu is always performed on a mat on the floor. Therapists who use acupressure as part of other treatments will use a couch.

BELOW SHIATSU USES PRESSURE AND GENTLE STRETCHING TO BRING EASE TO THE BODY, MIND AND SPIRIT. IT BALANCES VITAL ENERGY FLOW ALONG THE MERIDIANS AND BOTH RELAXES AND ENERGIZES.

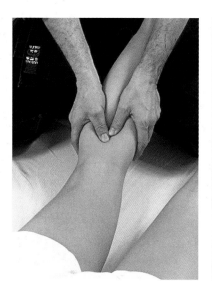  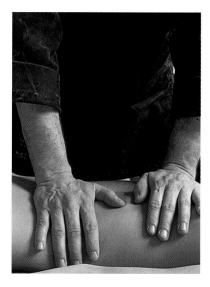

do-it-yourself shiatsu

Self-administered shiatsu is known as *do-in* and can be wonderfully energizing. Use this simple version whenever you feel tired or lethargic – it should give your batteries a good boost.

1 Tap all over the top of your head with your fingers. If you allow your wrists to become loose, you will find you are able to tap quite firmly. Use whatever rhythm suits you best.

2 Now place your hands on your forehead, with your fingertips meeting in the centre above your nose. Your elbows will be sticking out. Bring your fingers outwards to the edge of your forehead in a firm stroking movement. Repeat several times.

3 Using your fingertips, make little circles around your temples. Squeeze all along your eyebrows.

4 Next press firmly all around your eye sockets, but don't pull the skin.

5 Briskly rub your cheeks, then rub the end of your nose.

6 Press the points on either side of your nostrils (just under the nostrils there will be points that feel slightly tender). Press around your cheekbones with your thumbs, starting from the nostrils and moving round to your ears.

7 Pinch all around your ears. Gently tug your lobes. Rub all over the ears.

8 Pinch all along your lower jawline, from below the ears to your chin.

WILL I BE CLOTHED?

Shiatsu is always performed with the patient fully clothed (wear comfortable, loose-fitting clothes, ideally cotton). Other treatments may require you to strip down to your underwear.

WHAT HAPPENS?

Sessions start with a detailed case history. You will then be asked to lie on the couch or floor on your back. An acupressure practitioner may read your pulses. A shiatsu practitioner will perform hara diagnosis – gently pressing your abdominal area to detect which meridians (channels of energy) are blocked and which organs might be under stress. Both techniques enable the practitioner to decide how to treat you. Specific points and series of points will be pressed – sometimes gently, sometimes quite firmly. In shiatsu, there may also be some stretching, in which your body will be gently pulled into position by the practitioner. At the end of the session, your pulses may

be taken or your hara palpated again and you will finally be left on your own for a few minutes to 'come to'.

WILL IT HURT?

Some points can be quite tender – these are known as *ahsi* or 'ouch' points because people often say 'ouch' when they are pressed. Generally, however, these therapies are not painful.

WILL ANYTHING STRANGE HAPPEN?

It's not uncommon to feel a tingling or flushing effect as energy is released. You may find yourself 'seeing' images as if dreaming, or having flashbacks to events in the past.

WILL I BE GIVEN ANYTHING TO TAKE?

No, medication is not part of these therapies.

IS THERE ANY HOMEWORK?

It's quite likely you will be given suggestions of things to carry out at home such as changes to your diet, postural exercises, breathing techniques or accupressure or shiatsu points to press.

seiki soho

Seiki soho is a form of bodywork that almost defies the imagination. It treats stress and strain, and has the uncanny power to 'read' your body, unravelling aches, pains and emotional traumas you barely knew you had. Practitioners of seiki soho describe it as 'a new technique using massage as meditation to enhance youthfulness, beauty and spontaneity', and explain that it helps you get in touch with your body and mind, clearing out the dross and leaving you free to feel good – in every way. This sounds a bit vague and seiki practitioners are the first to admit that seiki soho is short on theory and dogma. In fact, it actively avoids stringent philosophies and prescribed techniques.

Seiki soho was originated by a Japanese shiatsu practitioner, Akinobu Kishi (known as Kishi). He felt that shiatsu was too controlling – it sought to change the person's body, whether it wanted to change or not. His solution was to learn, though precise observation, exactly what the client's body wanted him to do. This observation is a skilled art and appears highly mysterious to the outsider. Practitioners say they can actually 'see' the point where a body wants to be touched. The belief is that all the troubling feelings and irritations of life become lodged inside us – about everything from traffic jams to unpaid bills, from unemployment to difficult relationships. While we can analyse them mentally, unless we bodily process and eliminate those feelings, they won't go away and eventually turn into physical ailments. Seiki clears the blockages, breaking old patterns of holding in muscle, bone and fascia.

what can seiki soho help?

- Seiki doesn't seek to cure; it aims to do what the body wants, so there are no particular conditions it can help, but equally none it cannot treat.
- It is almost universally relaxing and destressing, and seems to promote a deep cleansing effect on both body and mind.
- Many people find that, after a session, they feel both calm and energized, relaxed yet alert. They sleep better and feel better able to cope with the demands of modern life.
- It is especially suited for pregnant women. It fosters an even deeper bond between mother and unborn baby.

ABOVE Although seiki soho is short on philosophy, it is very clear on its aims. The main focus is to detoxify – on both physical and emotional levels – through its unique massage.

what can I expect from a session?

WHERE WILL I HAVE THE TREATMENT?

You will be lying on a large mat on the floor.

WILL I BE CLOTHED?

Yes, you remain fully clothed.

WHAT HAPPENS?

A case history is not taken, as particular problems are not treated. You simply lie down on the mat. The practitioner pauses for a moment, looking for problems areas, and then plunges in, working swiftly and assuredly. Many of the moves feel similar to the deep stretching of shiatsu, but there is no rigid system or pattern to the touch. You should become very relaxed. After an hour, you are left alone for a few minutes to 'come to' gently and then asked to sit quietly for a while sipping a glass of water.

WILL IT HURT?

The touch is firm and often quite deep, but not usually painful.

WILL ANYTHING STRANGE HAPPEN?

As with all bodywork, you may 'see' images or past events.

WILL I BE GIVEN ANYTHING TO TAKE?

No, medication is not part of the therapy.

IS THERE ANY HOMEWORK?

No, homework isn't part of the treatment.

jin shin jyutsu

Jin shin jyutsu is an ancient Japanese therapy which works by balancing and harmonizing the body's vital energy, qi, through a series of 'safety energy locks'. The locks, of which there are 26 on each side of the body, are unseen regulators of our body's energy – they act almost like gears in a car. When the body is under strain, the locks can become congested and sore. Jin shin jyutsu aims to clear the locks so the energy can flow freely and the body helped back to optimum health.

You do not need long training or any experience for success. Many methods are so easy and unobtrusive that you can use them in a crowded bus – lots of jin shin jyutsu movements involve holds on the fingers and thumbs of the hand. Each of our fingers and thumbs can regulate 14,400 functions in the body, as they are connected by unseen paths of subtle energy to the rest of the body. By holding your fingers, you can affect any number of organs and bodily systems.

what can jin shin jyutsu help?

- A wide range of physical and psychological problems – headaches, menstrual pain, back tension, anxiety, depression, insomnia and even tantrums in children – can be helped.
- Some people say jin shin jyutsu can increase fertility.
- do-it-yourself jin shin jyutsu can alleviate jet lag and it can help in many first-aid situations.
- Common ailments such as constipation, cramps and even bunions respond well.
- Practitioners don't aim to 'cure' anything – they simply harmonize the body into healing.

what can I expect from a session?

WHERE WILL I HAVE THE TREATMENT?

You will be lying on a couch.

WILL I BE CLOTHED?

Yes, you will be fully clothed, except for your shoes and watch.

WHAT HAPPENS?

Your qi pulses are taken to detect which locks are out of balance. The practitioner then lays one hand on a certain point of the body and the other on another point. The effect is like that of jump leads on a car battery – the practitioner acts as a cable for the circuit to clear.

WILL IT HURT?

When out-of-balance points on your body are held, you may feel distinct tenderness.

WILL ANYTHING STRANGE HAPPEN?

Some people find they start twitching or jerking under treatment, or that they start to smile or laugh as the locks are released.

WILL I BE GIVEN ANYTHING TO TAKE?

No, medication is not part of the treatment.

IS THERE ANY HOMEWORK?

Practitioners often supply a self-help programme to practise each day. They encourage patients to back up jin shin jyutsu with good diet, regular exercise and lymphatic drainage.

self-jin shin jyutsu

This basic exercise will help bring your internal organs into balance. It can also help prevent jet lag – practise it during the flight whenever you fly.

1 Hold the thumb of your left hand with the fingers of your right and wait until you feel a steady pulse. This is your qi pulse, not the blood pulse.

2 Once you feel the pulse, do the same thing, but this time holding on to the index finger of your left hand. Again, stop once you feel the pulse.

3 Keep going, working your way through all the fingers of your left hand. Then swap over and do the same thing with your right hand.

4 You'll find that, as you practise, you will get quicker and quicker. Ideally, do this exercise every day in order to gain the maximum benefit.

If you're tense or irritable, this simple exercise can be performed discreetly.

1 Take the middle joint of your left middle finger lightly between your right thumb and fingers. Hold gently for a few minutes.

2 Swap hands, holding the middle joint of your right middle finger between your left thumb and fingers.

reflexology

Reflexology is much more than just a foot massage. This ancient technique can bring your whole body back into balance and, practised properly, can have deep, effective results on a large range of health problems.

The theory is that every part of your body is mapped out on the feet. It may sound a strange idea, but it's certainly not a new concept. More than 5,000 years ago, the Indians and Chinese were using a similar technique, and evidence suggests that the skill goes back still further to ancient Egypt and even beyond. Pictographs found in a tomb of an Egyptian physician dating back to 2500–2330 BC show a man being treated with a form of reflexology. It is also a strong tradition in many African tribes and Native American peoples.

However, it was left to Dr William Fitzgerald, an American ear, nose and throat specialist, to popularize a 'new' therapy, which he called zone therapy, in the Western world in 1902. Fitzgerald first realized the importance of pressure on parts of the body when watching how pain could be relieved during surgical operations through pressure being applied to certain areas of the body. His work was developed still more by a fellow American, Eunice Ingham, who concentrated almost entirely on the feet and turned zone therapy into what we recognize today as reflexology.

Reflexologists realized that different areas of the feet and toes corresponded to different body systems: for example, the big toe relates to the head and brain; the rest of the toes represent sinuses; the lungs spread across the ball of the foot; and the lower back is down near the heel. By massaging the relevant point on the foot, the reflexologist is loosening tension and relieving blockages in the flow of energy to the corresponding part of the system.

On a more general level, the massage works to stimulate blood circulation and the lymphatic system, increasing energy and helping with the process of elimination of toxins. A more recent form of reflexology is the Morrell system, which was developed by Patricia Morrell, a UK reflexologist. She discovered that it was not necessary to press hard on the points: in fact, she found that a very gentle touch could have as good, if not better, results.

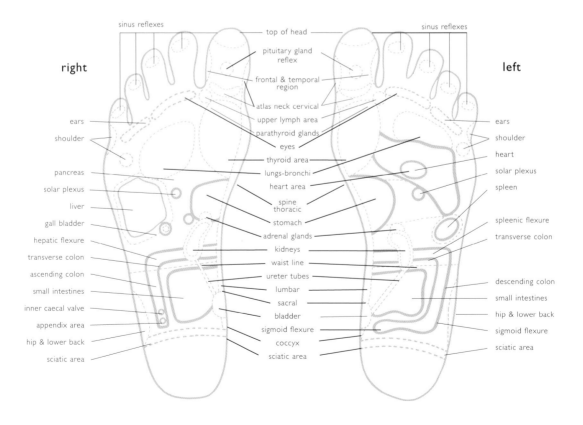

right · left

sinus reflexes · top of head · sinus reflexes
pituitary gland reflex
frontal & temporal region
atlas neck cervical
upper lymph area
parathyroid glands
ears · eyes · ears
shoulder · thyroid area · shoulder
heart
pancreas · lungs-bronchi · solar plexus
solar plexus · heart area · spleen
liver · spine thoracic
gall bladder · stomach · spleenic flexure
hepatic flexure · adrenal glands · transverse colon
transverse colon · kidneys
ascending colon · waist line
small intestines · ureter tubes · descending colon
inner caecal valve · lumbar · small intestines
appendix area · sacral · hip & lower back
hip & lower back · bladder · sigmoid flexure
sciatic area · sigmoid flexure · sciatic area
coccyx
sciatic area

self-reflexology

I am very cautious about self-reflexology. However, treating someone to this routine at home is generally quite safe (although do not give to a pregnant woman) and very soothing. Try it before bedtime for a wonderful night's sleep.

1 Gently warm some (plain, not roasted) sesame oil in a bowl.

2 Massage the right foot first. Pour some oil into the palm of your hand and then gently massage it into the foot. Use large movements to spread the oil evenly and well.

3 Now cover the foot in more detail, making small circling movements with your thumb. Work over the sole (firmly, if the person is ticklish), the heels and up to the ankles.

4 Sandwich the foot between your two hands and then massage with each hand moving in the opposite direction to the other – like the pistons on a train.

5 Circle gently but firmly all over the top of the foot.

6 Now pay attention to the toes – gently pull each one and massage.

7 Next work the following reflex points: the head, the solar plexus, the diaphragm and the heart. These lie across the tips of the toes and in a band across the widest part of the sole of the foot (see the diagram opposite). Use your thumb to hook firmly into each point, using the rest of your fingers behind the foot to balance your hand. If any point is tender, work carefully and within the person's pain threshold.

8 To finish, gently massage the centre of the forehead with sesame oil.

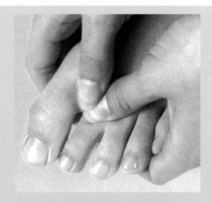

what can reflexology help?

- Reflexology can be remarkably powerful – in the right hands, it can affect almost all conditions.
- It is particularly effective for digestive disorders and constipation.
- Menstrual and menopausal problems respond well.
- Stress and fatigue can be helped.
- Migraines and skin conditions seem to respond.

what can I expect from a session?

WHERE WILL I HAVE THE TREATMENT?

You will be lying on a couch or, more usually, in a special chair.

WILL I BE CLOTHED?

Yes. You will be asked to take off only your shoes and socks.

WHAT HAPPENS?

A full case history will be taken before treatment. You then take off your shoes and socks, and lie down on the couch or chair, often covered with a blanket. You are asked to shut your eyes and relax. The practitioner will examine your feet, feeling for any tenderness and looking for visual signs such as bunions, areas of hard skin and callouses, all of which tell a story.

The practitioner's thumb is mostly used to apply pressure. Reflexology can be a very strong therapy; you should always make sure your therapist is properly qualified (unfortunately, as with aromatherapy, many people practise without proper training). If you are pregnant, never trust your feet to anyone other than a very experienced practitioner – and only in later pregnancy.

At the end of your session, you will be left for a few moments to 'come to' and will then probably be given a drink of water and told to take it easy for the next few hours.

WILL IT HURT?

It is not generally painful, although some practitioners can be overly forceful. If you have a congested area, it will feel sensitive.

WILL ANYTHING STRANGE HAPPEN?

Afterwards, you may want to urinate far more than usual, or you may erupt in spots or perspire more (all signs of elimination).

WILL I BE GIVEN ANYTHING TO TAKE?

No, medication is not part of the treatment.

IS THERE ANY HOMEWORK?

You may be given some simple techniques to carry out at home, but usually you should leave reflexology in the hands of experts.

watsu

Watsu is a deep, powerful and fascinating form of bodywork. A long, intense, intimate session of massage and manipulation techniques, carried out while you float in (or even under the surface of) a warm pool, watsu promises to heal you in mind, body and spirit. Fans claim it has remarkable regenerative qualities; that it can release stress, muscle tension and pain like no other treatment. They also say that it can equally release emotional anguish, giving you back a sense of childhood innocence and joy.

Watsu was the brainchild of Harold Dull, an American poet who became fascinated with shiatsu, the Japanese acupressure massage and stretching therapy. Having studied in San Francisco and Japan in the 1970s, Dull wanted to combine the therapeutic effects of shiatsu with the healing properties of water. He soon realized that he could achieve wonderful effects by floating his client in water, working on his or her body while cradling the head above water.

Several of Dull's students added their own twist to his idea. Jahara technique is performed much more slowly than watsu, with the client held further away from the practitioner. Floats are also used, making the whole experience less intimate. WaterDance was developed in 1987; like watsu, it begins with the client held above the water to be cradled, stretched and relaxed, but you are then given nose clips and gradually and gently taken entirely under the water. WaterDance is quite incredible to watch – the client moves underwater more like a dolphin or a mermaid than a human, somersaulting, rolling and undulating in complete freedom.

what can watsu help?
- Watsu takes the weight off the vertebrae and relaxes the muscles, giving greater freedom and mobility in the body.
- Watsu decreases muscular tension, increases superficial circulation and lymphatic function, strengthens the immune system and can aid digestion and respiratory difficulties.
- It is excellent for the later stages of pregnancy because it's so relaxing and water is so supportive.
- Many people find watsu helps insomnia and anxiety, and that it can release deeply held stress and improve posture.
- Watsu has achieved great success with sufferers of abuse.

- In California, it has been used successfully to help people with addictions and, paradoxically, it can even help people overcome a fear of water.
- It has profound effects on an emotional level, particularly with people who find intimacy difficult.
- The therapy is wonderful for children who have physical or mental disabilities.

what can I expect from a session?
WHERE WILL I HAVE THE TREATMENT?
You will be treated in a heated pool.
WILL I BE CLOTHED?
You will usually wear a swimsuit, although some people prefer to be naked.
WHAT HAPPENS?
The practitioner will ask you a series of questions. You then get into the pool, where the practitioner takes your head in his or her hands and asks you to lie back, relax and float. Throughout a watsu session, you are encouraged to breathe deeply and evenly, using only your mouth, and to keep your eyes gently closed. The breathing can feel a little unnatural to begin with; some people also find it strange and perhaps a little embarrassing to be cradled in the water by a virtual stranger. This feeling generally passes, however, and many people lose all sense of time.

ABOVE WATSU LOOKS SOMEWHAT LIKE A WONDERFUL FORM OF WATER DANCE — THE BODY BECOMES FAR MORE FLUID AND FLEXIBLE IN THE WATER. THIS THERAPY ALSO FEELS LIBERATING — AS IF YOU ARE BEING TRANSFORMED FOR A WHILE INTO A WATER CREATURE.

As the water is so supportive, your body can be stretched much further than would be possible on dry land. There is a wonderful sense of release which comes over you as you are stretched, rocked and manipulated.

WILL IT HURT?

Watsu can sometimes be quite painful as stubborn tension is unknotted and leaves your body.

WILL ANYTHING STRANGE HAPPEN?

Many people find that when they leave the pool they are far more flexible and can bend far further than normal. It's also quite common to feel emotionally moved and even quite tearful. Being held so closely, particularly by a stranger, is simply not part of our culture and can be quite confronting.

WILL I BE GIVEN ANYTHING TO TAKE?

No, medication is not part of the treatment.

IS THERE ANY HOMEWORK?

No, homework is not usual, although some practitioners may suggest you adapt your diet or offer breathing techniques or exercises for you to practise.

do-it-yourself water therapy

You cannot really practise watsu yourself – it takes a skilled practitioner – but you may find it interesting to lie in a warm bath and ponder the following questions. Just be aware of the water supporting your body and let your mind roam freely.

- Do you feel supported by the people around you?
- What does intimacy mean to you? With whom are you intimate?
- Are you held and touched enough in your life?
- Were you cuddled and held as a child?
- Has inappropriate touch ever been given?
- Where in your body do you hold tension? If you could imagine an emotion in that tension, what would it be? What colour would it be? What shape? What may it want to say to you?

Take time to write down any thoughts, emotions and insights you had while pondering these questions. If you find it hard to write, you might prefer to paint or draw to express your feelings.

NOTE: If you have experienced abuse, you may find it very helpful to consult a skilled counsellor. Watsu could also help.

MASSAGE

aromatherapy

Aromatherapy is probably the best-known natural therapy on offer and virtually every beauty salon will offer a version of this sweet-smelling therapy. Yet, true aromatherapy is much more than a sybaritic beauty treat – it's a powerful and far-reaching therapeutic tool.

Essential oils have a long and respected history dating back at least as far as ancient Egypt. Pots of scented unguents were found in Tutankhamen's tomb. Modern aromatherapy was 'born' in France in the early part of the twentieth century when René Maurice Gattefoss, a chemist, burned himself and discovered, by accident, that pure lavender oil could prevent scarring and infection.

About 300-plus essential oils are in use today. They are extracted from a wide variety of trees, shrubs, herbs and flowers. The oils work directly on the chemistry of the body: an essential oil contains on average 100 chemical components and chemists now know that they have myriad functions (for example, antibacterial, antifungal, antiseptic, deodorizing, digestive, antidepressant etc.). They are able to be effective therapeutically because they enter and leave the body with great efficiency, leaving no toxins behind.

Although it is clear that essential oils work in a direct way on the body's physiology, they also have more subtle effects. Scent works powerfully on mood – olfactory nerves connect to the limbic system of the brain, which regulates our sexual urge and our emotional behaviour. It also affects memory – in France, there are psychoanalysts who use fragrance to bring out the hidden memories of their patients.

what can aromatherapy help?

- Results are often most swift with any illness with a strong stress component. Aromatherapy is deeply relaxing.
- Skin conditions respond well.
- It can strengthen the immune system and is useful for muscular pains and rheumatism.
- High and low blood pressure can often be regulated.
- Psychological problems can be eased; it has good results with depression, anxiety, stress and insomnia.
- It can be very relaxing in the later stages of pregnancy, but pregnant women must only be treated by a very well qualified and experienced aromatherapist.

what can I expect from a session?

WHERE WILL I HAVE THE TREATMENT?

You will be lying on the therapist's couch.

WILL I BE CLOTHED?

You will usually be asked to strip down to underwear or just briefs, but will be well covered with towels.

WHAT HAPPENS?

The aromatherapist will take a full case history – some oils cannot be used on people with high or low blood pressure or epilepsy. Others should not be used on pregnant women or those who are breastfeeding. You will then be left to undress and lie on the couch. The aromatherapist will decide on a mix of oils and make up a massage blend. Some aromatherapists will ask you to sniff a variety of oils, believing that the ones to which you are drawn are those that you most need.

The massage itself is usually very gentle – the aim is not so much to affect the musculature as to apply the oils over the largest area of skin for maximum penetration. Most people find they become deeply relaxed and it's far from uncommon to doze off while you are lying on the couch.

WILL IT HURT?

No, aromatherapy massage is usually very gentle.

WILL ANYTHING STRANGE HAPPEN?

It's highly unlikely. You should just feel incredibly relaxed and may even drift off to sleep.

WILL I BE GIVEN ANYTHING TO TAKE?

No. Very few aromatherapists use essential oils internally, as they can be dangerous if taken in this way. If your aromatherapist suggests this, ask if they are medically qualified.

IS THERE ANY HOMEWORK

You may be given some of the oil blend so that you can use it on yourself at home. You may also be given suggestions of oils to use in massage or in the bath.

essential oils for home use

Always treat essential oils with great respect; if you're not sure of their effects, don't use them. That being said, these oils should be part of every home medicine cabinet. Always dilute oils: for a massage or bath oil, put eight drops of your chosen oil or oils in 4 teaspoons (15–20 ml) of a base oil such as sweet almond or walnut oil.

Geranium is a good-mood oil. Geranium lifts the spirits and can also alleviate insomnia and stress. It also helps to balance hormones and is useful for premenstrual syndrome. It can stimulate the lymphatic system and helps rid the body of toxins. Use as a massage oil or in the bath, or burn the oil in a diffuser.

Lavender is a natural antiseptic; it's also wonderful for soothing burns. It acts as an antidepressant if you're feeling low and can soothe stress and insomnia. This is one of the few oils that can be used undiluted.

Lemon is bright, fresh and tangy, and can help to shift cellulite and keep wrinkles at bay (or so they say!). It's a powerful bactericide and can help to stop bleeding, so use a drop or two of essential lemon oil in warm water on cuts.

Peppermint is a wonderful digestive tonic; if you're suffering from a stomach upset, massage your stomach with a peppermint blend. It's also useful in cases of shock – put a few drops on a tissue and sniff. A peppermint-blend bath oil will stimulate the brain and help you think more clearly – it's very energizing.

Rosemary is an excellent tonic for the heart, liver and gall bladder; it also helps to lower cholesterol levels. Use it to ease colds, catarrh and sinusitis. It can help to soothe rheumatism and arthritis, or overworked or strained muscles – rub the diluted oil into the affected area.

Tea tree is a powerful antiseptic, antiviral and antibacterial oil – use it in your bath and in massage blends if you feel a cold coming on. It's useful for catarrh and sinusitis (put a few drops in a bowl of boiling hot water and inhale the fumes, with a towel over your head and the bowl). If you have an operation coming up, use it in your bath in the weeks prior to surgery – it will encourage swift healing.

Ylang ylang is a powerful aphrodisiac; use this oil in blends for a sensual massage. Ylang ylang is also a wonderful relaxant and antidepressant; and it helps reduce high blood pressure.

hawaiian massage

Hawaiian massage has been practised in the Polynesian islands for centuries and promises to touch the part most massages fail to reach – your very soul. Practitioners say it can release hidden memories and spark change in your body, mind and soul. This massage can alter the way you think, feel, move and breathe.

Hawaiian massage (also known as huna massage or lomi lomi) is recognized in the USA as a byword for total pampering. Hosts of people (including many Hollywood stars) flock to Hawaii to put themselves in the hands of the kahunas. These are the native priests, acknowledged not only as great spiritual leaders, but also as superlative healers. They are taught that, in order to achieve perfect health and true happiness, you need to align yourself with the universal life force, to become one with creation. The massage acts as a gentle nudge, a reminder of how it is possible to feel at one with our bodies and, by extension, at one with creation.

The massage is known in Hawaii as the 'loving hands massage' and one of its key concepts is that the practitioner, often known as a performer, has to remain totally focused on the clients, feeling deep, unconditional love and compassion for them, rather than treating them as 'objects' to be 'fixed'.

The training of a kahuna is arduous, long and steeped in mystery – few outside Hawaii have completed it. Now the kahunas are allowing elements of their work to be taken beyond the islands, however, and teaching outer aspects, such as the massage, to enlightened Westerners. Although the massage is but the simplest manifestation of the Huna philosophy, its effects can be deceptively powerful.

what can hawaiian massage help?

- Hawaiian massage affects the lymphatic, immune, digestive, circulatory and respiratory systems. It helps a wide variety of ailments, from irritable bowel syndrome to headaches and colds.
- It works deeply on the muscles, tendons and ligaments of the body, relieving aches and pains, and neck and back tension.
- On an emotional level, it can release old memories and hurts, relieving stress, anxiety, depression, anger and fear.
- Many people find it helps them on an indefinable, spiritual level. They feel better about themselves, more peaceful and relaxed.

what can I expect from a session?

WHERE WILL I HAVE THE TREATMENT?

You will be lying on a couch.

WILL I BE CLOTHED?

It depends on the therapist. Some ask you to strip entirely; others will ask you to keep on your briefs and will cover you with towels.

WHAT HAPPENS?

Practitioners or performers practise in slightly different ways. Some will have the room temperature very high so that you can lie naked on the couch (as you would in Hawaii). Others tailor their work to a more traditional Western massage style – you can wear briefs and the parts not being worked are discreetly covered.

Some practitioners like to use volcanic stones placed down the spine to start the massage. Others will ask people to gaze at themselves in a mirror before the massage, trying to feel unconditional love for themselves.

The massage, however, always follows the same principles. Using light scented oils, the practitioner starts by massaging the back, sweeping down from your head right through to your legs in long, fluid strokes. The movement is rhythmic and repetitive and, after a few minutes, it becomes hard to sense where one stroke ends and the next begins. Practitioners throw their whole bodies into the work, often using not just their hands, but also the whole length of their forearm. As they pull, twist and stretch you, it feels as if you are partners in some strange dance.

At times, it feels like shiatsu and acupressure; at others, there's the firm but gentle feel of therapeutic massage, but the whole is far more than the sum of its parts. Almost every area of the body is covered, from the tips of your toes to the top of your head.

WILL IT HURT?

It can be quite deep and some points can be tender, but usually it's quite bearable.

WILL ANYTHING STRANGE HAPPEN?

It's easy to drift into a sense of total timelessness. Many people find that they shift from feelings of discomfort and embarrassment to ones of acceptance and connectedness. Some people have flashbacks to early experiences and it's not uncommon to feel intense emotions – people frequently report finding themselves either crying or laughing.

WILL I BE GIVEN ANYTHING TO TAKE?

No, medication is not part of the treatment.

IS THERE ANY HOMEWORK?

You may be asked to assess your lifestyle, diet and exercise.

thai massage

Traditional Thai massage stretches you to the limit. Often called 'lazy man's yoga' or 'passive yoga', it lets you reap the benefits of stringent yoga postures without doing all the hard work – the practitioner flexes you into positions you would never have dreamed of reaching on your own. During a one-and-a-half-hour session, your body will be bent and pulled, stretched and soothed. You will walk out feeling taller and looser, more open and expansive – as if every part of your body had been unlocked, allowing you to move and even breathe more easily, more freely.

Although still relatively new to the West, Thai massage has a long and venerable history. In the training schools in Thailand, they say it was developed more than 2,500 years ago in India by Jivaka Kumar Bhaccha, physician to the Buddha. Arriving in Thailand in the third century BC, the massage has been handed down from teacher to pupil ever since.

Like many Eastern massage systems, the Thai method works not just on the physical body, on unleashing tension in muscles and soft tissue, but also on the body's energy lines, the meridians. As an acupuncturist works with needles, so the Thai masseur works with his or her hands, feet and elbows to release blockages in the energy flow and to allow vital life force, qi, to run smoothly around the body once more. The result, they say, is improved flexibility, better circulation of blood and lymph, and an exhilarating dose of vitality.

what can thai massage help?

- Many people report that it has helped them considerably with headaches and sinus conditions.
- Stress and exhaustion caused by overwork respond well.
- Thai massage alleviates anxiety and depression, and a whole host of emotional problems.
- The massage loosens the body, ameliorating deep-seated aches and pains.
- It seems to help people become more open and better able to communicate.

what can I expect from a session?

WHERE WILL I HAVE THE TREATMENT?

You will be lying on a mat on the floor.

WILL I BE CLOTHED?

You will be asked to take off your shoes, socks and any jewellery, but otherwise stay fully clothed (ideally, wearing loose-fitting, comfortable clothes).

WHAT HAPPENS?

You will be asked if you are pregnant, or have a severe back problem or high blood pressure: if so, the massage can be adapted to suit your condition. The treatment starts at your feet, with your toes being bent back repeatedly. After the feet have been thoroughly stretched, the practitioner moves up the legs, round the hips and on to the stomach, using a pushing motion with his or her fingers.

Next come spinal stretches. With your knees bent one way and the practitioner pushing your shoulder in the opposite direction, you may well find your vertebrae starting to crack and crunch. Because the practitioner's body weight is gently rocking you into exactly the right position, the stretch goes much further than you could ever achieve on your own.

No part of the body is ignored in Thai massage – it really is a top-to-toe affair. Your hands, arms and shoulders receive the stretching treatment, and tension in the face and head is soothed by gently but firmly pressing on the pressure points. You are then pulled into a sitting position and the serious stress points in the neck and shoulders are addressed.

Some practitioners end with a special technique known as 'massage without touching', in which they sit behind you and, breathing swiftly and deeply, move their hands up and down the spine, without actually touching the body. Mysteriously, you feel an incredible tingle running throughout the body, a little like being hosed down with a powerful shower of water.

WILL IT HURT?

Sometimes the practitioner hits sore or particularly tense spots, which can feel a little tender, but generally the experience proves a very relaxing one.

WILL ANYTHING STRANGE HAPPEN?

At times it feels as if you are being stretched and manipulated by two or three people, but it's just that the practitioner is using his or her feet or elbows, as well as hands, to lend extra stretching power to the treatment.

WILL I BE GIVEN ANYTHING TO TAKE?

No, medication is not part of the treatment.

IS THERE ANY HOMEWORK?

No, you will not have any homework.

chavutti thirumal

Chavutti thirumal (often known as the Indian rope massage) is practised with the feet, rather than the hands. While the idea may sound strange and even unpleasant, the reality is quite different. This is one of the deepest and yet most subtle of massage therapies: it feels heavenly and bestows prodigious health benefits.

Chavutti thirumal originated in South India and was developed primarily to keep practitioners of both the local martial arts and dance supple and flexible. Dancers and fighters would be given a 10-day intensive course of the massage before performances to enable them to perform in peak condition. It generally prevented injuries and strains, but, if anything did go wrong, a further course would equally coax them back to health.

The massage affects people in different ways. Some find the effects are all physical, while others find it affects them psychologically as well. Some people bounce away feeling on top of the world; others feel calm and centred. Some people actually feel worse before they feel better. This, say practitioners, is because the therapy draws things out. It can help eliminate toxins, too, which means people can sometimes suffer sore throats or headaches. But these side effects are short-lived.

Chavutti reaches every external muscle and ligament in the body, while stimulating the circulation and the lymphatic system. Stimulating the lymphatic system inevitably helps push toxins to the lymph nodes to be eliminated. It is this elimination that leads people to say that chavutti thirumal can be a factor in successful weight loss and even rejuvenation. In addition, the deep, kneading action is said to promote the breakdown of cellulite.

Today, chavutti thirumal has a small but fervent band of Western devotees. Because the massage is long (at least one-and-a-half hours), it is incredibly satisfying. The feet are, surprisingly, not clumsy at all and can do all that hands can do – and more. As the practitioner is standing (balancing his or her weight on a rope slung across the room), he or she can use much greater pressure if need be and really attack deep-seated tension and stress. The massage is much loved by overworked businesspeople, sportspeople and performers.

what can chavutti thirumal help?

- It is very helpful for muscle spasm or back tension.
- It's ideal for sportspeople, dancers, martial-arts practitioners and performers who need to keep their bodies supple and in tiptop condition.
- Practitioners say that the massage can help improve body image and encourages you to foster a sense of acceptance of your body, however imperfect.
- It can help troublesome emotions to clear and can sometimes relieve psychological blocks.
- It stretches every external muscle and ligament in the body while stimulating the circulation and the lymphatic system, helping toxins to be transported to the lymph nodes for elimination. This has led many people to claim the massage has helped them lose weight and feel rejuvenated.
- The deep, kneading action is said to promote the breakdown of cellulite.
- It can help alleviate the ill effects of overexercising and strained and sprained muscles.
- It is deeply stress relieving and can help any condition that has a stress-related background.

what can I expect from a session?
WHERE WILL I HAVE THE TREATMENT?
You will be lying on a line of rush mats on the floor with a large towel down the middle. Strung across the room, at head height, will be a thick red rope.
WILL I BE CLOTHED?
Usually, you will be asked to strip entirely. Some practitioners will give you a loincloth to wear. This may feel strange at first, but, once the treatments starts, you will forget about anything so mundane! The room is kept very warm, so you will not get cold.
WHAT HAPPENS?
The practitioner asks a few questions about any health problems, then prepares himself or herself. Practitioners regard chavutti thirumal as a spiritual exercise, so spend a few moments in prayer and meditation before the session. Throughout the massage, they breathe deeply to keep their energy channels open.

Your body is liberally doused with warm sesame oil and then, using the rope for balance and to modulate his or her weight, the practitioner starts to massage. The feeling is wonderful – strong, deep, yet highly sensitive. The feet are used expertly to knead, probe, stretch and soothe every muscle and ligament in the

body – from the shoulders down to the toes, before ending up with your face and head. By the time the massage is finished, you will feel totally refreshed and yet relaxed.

WILL IT HURT?

The massage is very strong and tense muscles can feel quite sore. On the whole, however, it is a delicious experience.

WILL ANYTHING STRANGE HAPPEN?

You may find the breathing of the practitioner (which is fairly loud) rather strange to initially. At the end of the session, the practitioner usually spends a few moments working with your energy, with his or her hands off the body, something which can feel slightly odd after such an intense body workout.

WILL I BE GIVEN ANYTHING TO TAKE?

No, medication is not part of the treatment.

IS THERE ANY HOMEWORK?

No, you won't be given any homework.

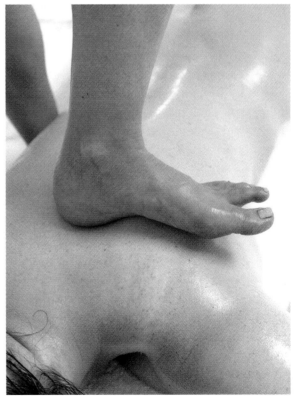

ABOVE AND RIGHT Chavutti thirumal looks quite extraordinary. We might well imagine that being trodden on would feel clumsy or uncomfortable; however, in practice, this is one of the most powerful and delightful forms of bodywork available.

indian head massage

Indian head massage has been practised in India for thousands of years. Children are massaged from birth by their mothers and learn early how to give massages to the rest of the family. By the time they reach adulthood, they know it as a well-established family ritual.

Women have head massages to keep their hair beautiful and glossy; the men have it to prevent them from going bald. Everyone enjoys it as a supreme stressbuster and particular techniques can help prevent headaches and treat insomnia. Above all, because this massage can easily be learnt and shared, it has the valuable capacity of being able to bring both partners and families closer together. As Indian head massage expert Narendra Mehta explains: 'Touching makes us feel nurtured, cared for and relaxed. If husbands and wives could massage each other, even just on the top of the head, it would bring them closer.'

Originally, head massage was part of the system of ayurveda and was practised therapeutically; however, over the years the techniques were watered down and altered. Before the advent of barbers' and hairdressers' shops, barbers used to visit the homes of Indian families. Among their techniques, they introduced head massage, which not only improved the quality of their clients' hair, but also made them deeply relaxed. Sometimes the barbers took advantage of this deeply relaxed state and some were even renowned as spies who extracted secrets from their clients when they were utterly at ease after the massage!

The tradition of head massage has continued up to this day in India. It's quite common to find masseurs offering head massages on the beach, on street corners and even in busy markets. Quite apart from its cosmetic benefits, head massage is uniquely powerful as a stressbuster. The head, neck and shoulders (which are also included in a massage) are classic places in which we hold stress and so massage can be an easy, swift and effective way of preventing tension from building up in your body.

Almost anyone can benefit, from the very young to the elderly. The only people who are not advised to have Indian head massage are those with weeping eczema or head injuries, the psychotic or those with epilepsy.

what can indian head massage help?

- The massage improves blood flow to the brain – many businesspeople swear that it helps their performance, making them more alert and better able to concentrate.
- It alleviates anxiety and improves mood.
- Tension headaches and eye strain respond well.
- Indian head massage can help insomnia.
- The oil and massage improve the texture of your hair, giving a wonderful shine. Regular massage is said to help stop hair falling out and prevent it turning grey!
- It deeply relaxes the face muscles, making you look healthier and happier.

what can I expect from a session?

WHERE WILL I HAVE THE TREATMENT?
You will be sitting in a comfortable chair.

WILL I BE CLOTHED?
Yes, although some people prefer to take off their top or shirt in case the oil stains clothing.

WHAT HAPPENS?
Treatment starts with a deep kneading and probing of the neck and shoulder muscles. Sometimes the treatment seems almost akin to osteopathy. but there is no crunching or cracking.

The therapist then moves on to the head. The scalp is squeezed, rubbed, tapped and prodded; your hair is tugged and then 'combed' with the therapist's fingernails. The jawline is worked and ears are pulled, tugged and pressed.

Finally, the therapist moves to the face, pressing acupressure points to relieve sinus pressure, stimulate blood circulation and increase alertness. The face is then gently stroked.

WILL IT HURT?
Some points may be tender or sore, but generally the treatment feels divine.

WILL ANYTHING STRANGE HAPPEN?
The touch is so gentle that it can seem almost too intimate for some people. Some find it releases feelings of past hurt and a grieving for lost childhood.

WILL I BE GIVEN ANYTHING TO TAKE?
No, medication is not part of the treatment.

IS THERE ANY HOMEWORK?
Not specifically, although you may be taught massage techniques to practise at home; many people in fact go on to learn how to practise on friends and family.

getting a head start at home

Indian head massage is one of the simplest techniques of massage to learn. You can easily give a highly effective treatment. Use either sesame or coconut oil. It should be warm but not hot – stand it on or near a heater for around half an hour, or place it in a microwave for a minute.
NOTE: Do not perform head massages if your subject has a skin condition such as weeping eczema or psoriasis, or there are open cuts or sores on the head.

1 Have your subject sit upright in a straight-backed chair. Gently lay your hands on the crown of his or her head; hold them there for about 30 seconds. Slowly begin to massage the scalp with the pads of your fingertips. If using oil, apply it now. Don't drench the hair: use just enough to lubricate the scalp. This gives a connection between you and your subject, putting you both at ease.

2 Progress to a technique known as 'windscreen wiper'. Support the head with one hand. Using the palm of your other hand, employ a swift rubbing motion, as if you were buffing a window. Start behind the ear, going around it and then away. Repeat on the other side of the head. This relaxes and warms the muscles.

3 Next support the head with one hand while the other gently strokes the top of the head. Use long, sweeping motions first, then 'comb' the hair, running your fingernails through the hair in long strokes. Work all the way around the head, swapping hands where necessary. This stimulates blood flow through the scalp, giving a lovely tingly feeling to the head.

4 Take the weight of your partner's head on your arm. Starting at the top of the neck (where it joins the cranium), massage down either side of the spine, using small circling movements of the thumb and middle finger. Go carefully and be aware of how your subject reacts – don't press too deeply. This stroke soothes and calms the brain itself.

5 Massage the temples using gentle circular movements – use the tips of the index fingers. Then support the back of the head with your hands and employ a firmer but still soft pressure, massaging the temples with your thumbs.

6 Now concentrate on the neck and shoulders. Imagine you are ironing the shoulders, using the heel of your hand to roll forwards over the shoulder from the back to the front. Start from the outside edge of the shoulder and move in towards the collarbone. If you are performing the massage on someone much taller than you, use your forearm to press across the shoulder, deploying your body weight for pressure. This is wonderful for releasing tension in the shoulders and neck.

7 Put both hands around the head to form a cap. Squeeze, lift and let go several times. You can use this movement alone to combat headaches.

8 Now stroke the face lightly with the whole of your hands (palm against the face), moving gently down from the forehead to the chin. Repeat as much as you like. Cover the eyes with your palms, then press very gently on the eyeballs. If performing the massage before bedtime, it is best place to end here as it will send your subject gently off to sleep. This step done on its own can help treat insomnia.

9 If your subject wants to feel energized, finish with a brisk rubbing motion back and forth across the scalp. Vary this with a fast scratching action, using your fingernails. Both can be firm and deep. Finish by pressing firmly but carefully on the crown, as at the beginning.

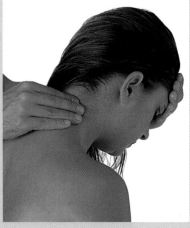

manual lymphatic drainage

Manual lymphatic drainage (MLD) combines pure bliss with deep healing. It's a gentle massage technique that encourages the elimination of toxins and the stimulation of the lymphatic system. MLD is now being recognized as an essential part of treating oedema (swelling); it is highly effective at bringing down oedema after surgery and after radiotherapy and chemotherapy for cancer. However, it's not just a medical treatment: MLD is also one of the best-kept secrets on the beauty scene.

Dr Emil Vodder and his wife Estrid developed MLD in France in the 1930s. Vodder noticed how people suffering from chronic catarrhal and sinus infections tended to have swollen lymph glands and, going against medical practice at the time, started to work with the lymph nodes. The massage the Vodders developed has a circular, pumping effect which increases the efficiency of the body's lymphatic system (which acts as the body's garbage disposal system). By helping to clear the body of debris and old toxic waste, MLD makes your skin look brighter and healthier on the

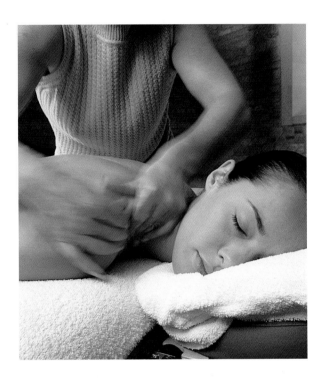

outside, while inside your immune system is given the chance to function at optimal levels, offering your body protection against colds, flu and other illnesses.

The medical establishment is beginning to take MLD very seriously. If a massage is given to burns victims soon after the accident, it can rapidly reduce the burn. Scar tissue can be encouraged to build up only where needed, preventing large, unsightly scars. The therapy is often used on cancer patients, post-operatively, to limit the oedema that can arise.

People also visit MLD therapists for cosmetic reasons – MLD draws the skin in and tightens it. While it won't actually make you thinner, it will certainly make your face *look* thinner by tightening up all the little saggy, baggy bits, all the unsightly puffiness. It's rather like a mini facelift without surgery.

what can manual lymphatic drainage help?

- It can stop a cold in its tracks in many cases, or certainly reduce the symptoms. Sinus problems respond very well.
- MLD can improve your immune system in general, making you less susceptible to infections.

ABOVE AND LEFT MANUAL LYMPHATIC DRAINAGE, WHICH EMPLOYS A VERY LIGHT TOUCH TO ENCOURAGE TOXINS TO BE TAKEN TO THE LYMPH NODES AND THEN ELIMINATED, IT IS ALSO A USEFUL TREATMENT FOR OEDEMA.

- Oedema (swelling) comes down dramatically. MLD is very useful in treating lymphoedema, which often develops after mastectomy or surgical removal of the lymph nodes, or following radiotherapy treatment.
- This therapy has wonderful effects on scar tissue and burns. Stretch marks and acne scarring can be cleared or diminished with commitment.
- Some people say it can reduce cellulite. MLD is also sought as a quasi-beauty treatment to firm facial tissue.

what can I expect from a session?

WHERE WILL I HAVE THE TREATMENT?

You will be lying on the therapist's couch.

WILL I BE CLOTHED?

You will be asked to strip down to your underwear, but will be covered by towels throughout the session.

WHAT HAPPENS?

A full case history will be taken and the therapist will check that you haven't had tuberculosis and don't have heart problems (the massage is contraindicated in these instances). You will be quizzed not just on your medical history, but also on your lifestyle. Then you will be left alone to undress and get on the couch.

The MLD touch is unique – it is a very gentle touch, rather like having your skin stroked by a child's gentle fingers. It involves a light, repetitive movement that has an almost hypnotic effect and does, in fact, switch the body's nervous system to its relaxed 'night-time' mode.

After the massage, you will be left on the couch to relax for 5 minutes or so, before being given a glass of water to drink.

WILL IT HURT?

Absolutely not. This is about the most gentle kind of massage you could ever experience.

WILL ANYTHING STRANGE HAPPEN?

After the treatment, you may find your glands feel slightly swollen or uncomfortable – a sign that toxins are moving to the lymph nodes. You may be surprised at how much brighter and tighter your skin looks and feels. Any sniffles or stuffiness may vanish.

WILL I BE GIVEN ANYTHING TO TAKE?

No, medication is not part of this treatment

IS THERE ANY HOMEWORK?

You may well be given guidelines on healthy eating and exercise. For the best results, you should practise MLD on yourself regularly – the therapist will show you how to do it.

ways to ease the load on your lymphatic system

You need to be shown MLD by a trained therapist, but there are lots of other things you can do to help your lymphatic system detoxify.

Walk and swim – exercise acts as a powerful pump for the lymphatic system, but high-powered aerobics may be counterproductive as it can overuse the muscles, creating more waste products. Swimming and walking are both superb.

Bounce – perhaps the best way to get your lymph moving is by bouncing on a small trampoline (a rebounder). Just 5 minutes a day will make a significant difference.

Eat well – high-fat diets (particularly dairy produce and red meat) encourage a build-up of toxins. Make sure your diet is rich in green vegetables, fresh fruits and sprouted seeds.

Drink water – make sure you drink at least 2 litres (2 quarts) of fresh spring water every day. Warm water can be helpful, too (keep a flask near to hand).

Skin brush – skin brushing moves the lymph and softens any impacted lymph mucus in the nodes. Use a natural-bristle brush and brush smoothly, always moving towards your heart.

Try yoga – yoga positions, combined with deep breathing, help the lymphatic system. Headstands and other inverted positions are particularly good. If you find it tough to stand on your head or shoulders, lie down with your legs up the wall.

Use rosemary (right) – put a couple of drops of rosemary oil (in a base oil) in a warm bath and relax. Gradually add cool water until the water is quite cold – this change of temperature helps to stimulate the lymphatic system.

chua ka

Chua ka is a form of deep-tissue bodywork with effects similar to those of therapies such as Rolfing and Hellerwork – although it achieves its results without quite so much discomfort. Chua ka is rumoured to have originated from a ritual used by ancient Mongolian warriors before battle to cleanse their bodies physically and prepare their minds for the mental and spiritual ordeal ahead. It's a great story, but one which, sadly, can't be proven. What is certain, however, is that, in its current form, chua ka was developed by an American, Oscar Ichazo, in the 1960s, as a result of his research into physiology and psychology. What is also crystal-clear is that, whatever its origins, chua ka is a highly effective massage technique. Better still, you can learn how to perform chua ka on yourself so that you can reap the benefits at any time.

Chua ka is a deep, detoxifying therapy. Ichazo believes that we were born as smooth and supple human beings. With age and the stress of life, however, we lose this elasticity and start to build up deposits on both the physical and emotional level. Physically, these are made up of metabolic waste products. Equally, if not more, toxic, however, are memories of pain – whether physical, emotional, mental or even spiritual. Say, for example, you fell off a bicycle as a child, you might simply suffer a physical bruise and forget about it. But if you were surrounded by a crowd of children laughing at you, you could develop a 'psychic bruise' and store the memory in the muscle and connective tissue. Hence it's not uncommon when receiving deep-tissue massage such as chua ka to find old memories resurfacing quite unexpectedly.

what can chua ka help?

- Chua ka can be highly effective in treating back pain.
- Stress-related problems such as insomnia respond well.
- It is useful for digestive problems.
- Some people swear that it has helped reduce cellulite.
- Some chua ka practitioners have been able to help people with ailments as varied as rheumatoid arthritis, foot injuries, acne and bowel problems.

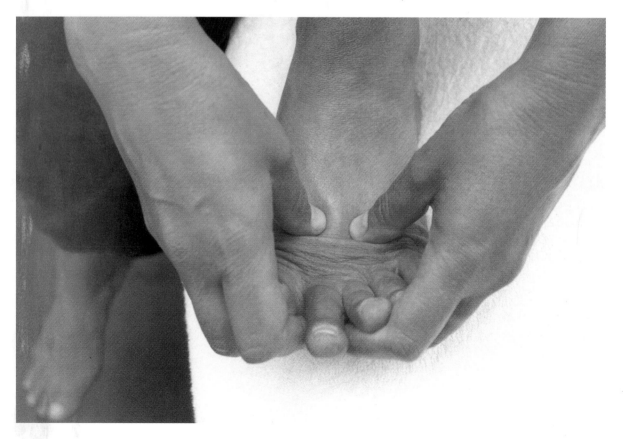

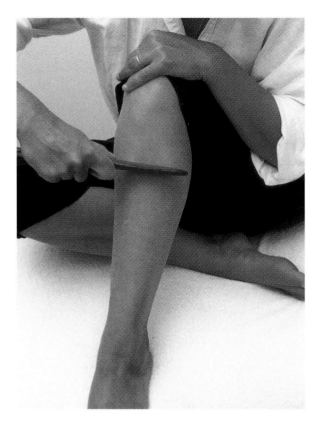

OPPOSITE, LEFT AND BELOW CHUA KA IS A DEEP DETOXIFYING TREATMENT WHICH REPUTEDLY HAS ITS ORIGINS IN ANCIENT MONGOLIA.

IT USES VARIOUS DEEP-PRESSURE TECHNIQUES ALL OVER THE BODY TO TREAT PHYSICAL TENSION AND OLD EMOTIONAL TRAUMAS.

body' – it feels as though the therapist is hitting every acupressure point in turn. Typically, you could expect the therapist to work on your back, shoulders, arms and legs, ending with some deep work on your neck and some powerful pressure on your scalp and face.

WILL IT HURT?

At times it can be almost painful, but the pain is forgotten as your body releases its tension – it's that weird kind of 'good hurt'. If you are very sensitive to strong pressure, however, this may not be the best form of bodywork for you.

WILL ANYTHING STRANGE HAPPEN?

You may relive old hurts or find buried memories surfacing.

WILL I BE GIVEN ANYTHING TO TAKE?

No, medication is not part of the treatment

IS THERE ANY HOMEWORK?

You may be asked to adust your lifestyle, diet and exercise habits.

- In New York, politicians and models often have chua ka on their faces before television slots or photographic shoots, as it reduces puffiness and gives a form of 'instant facelift'.
- It also has a strong psychological effect, working to heal emotional wounds and helping people deal with fear.
- Many people use it as a self-help tool for greater self-awareness.

what can I expect from a session?

WHERE WILL I HAVE THE TREATMENT?

You will be lying on a couch.

WILL I BE CLOTHED?

You wear just briefs, but are well covered with towels.

WHAT HAPPENS?

On the first visit, time is spent taking a history of your health, diet and lifestyle. Treatment can then be tailored to suit your needs or medical condition. The technique is unusual: long, slow, fluid strokes that probe deeply into the body, stimulating the circulatory system and helping the body regain some of its original elasticity. Strong pressure movements with the thumbs are also used to work into the deep tissue, releasing physical tension and stored trauma. Chua ka has aptly been described as 'reflexology for the

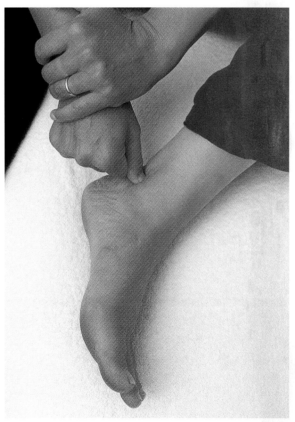

trager®

Trager® or Trager Psychophysical Integration (to give it its full name) is a gentle system of bodywork, the predominant goal of which is to make life easier, more comfortable and more pleasurable. It helps you build up deep stores of energy and vitality, and yet keeps you calm and centred. In a typical session, you receive several thousand light, rhythmical touches and get up off the couch feeling like a child who has been rocked in its mother's arms.

The history of this deeper-than-deep relaxation treatment started back in the 1930s. Milton Trager was a young boxer and acrobat in Miami, Florida, intent upon training his super-athletic body. He was always pushing himself to the limits, aiming to jump the highest, the farthest, to be the best. One day, he suddenly had a completely new thought. 'How can I land softer?' he pondered. Then: 'How could I land the softest?' His whole philosophy changed overnight – from aiming for maximum effort, he sought instead to achieve maximum effortlessness, to become ever lighter, easier, softer and freer. Trager discovered he could introduce the same feeling of ease and comfort to others by means of gentle rocking and stretching, and this became his life's work.

Over the next 40 years, he perfected Trager. Keen to put his ideas on a firm scientific footing, he trained and qualified as a medical doctor. However, throughout his training, Trager continued to treat people and he was given his own clinic, where he helped those with polio and other neuromuscular problems, with near-miraculous results.

Basically, the therapy of Trager is a form of bodywork that involves gentle stretching, rocking, rolling, bouncing and 'shimmering' (a swift but soft stroking movement over the body). It is extremely soothing for the central

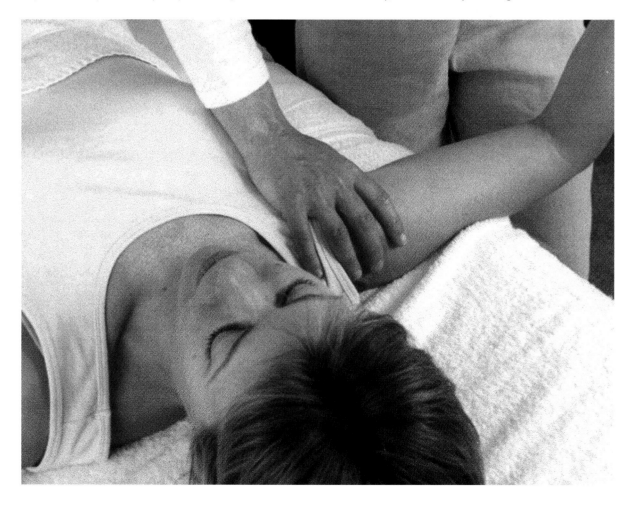

nervous system, as the rocking movements take people into a comfort zone, into a very deep state of relaxation.

Nothing is forced with Trager, nothing hurts, nothing is remotely uncomfortable or embarrassing. Rather than aiming to go in and fix problems, practitioners try to show the body how it could be more comfortable, more flexible, more easy.

what can trager help?

- It can ease pain and often help to eliminate headaches.
- It promotes greater joint flexibility. The reverberations of the rocking movements echo right through the body and actually massage the internal organs and deep muscles.
- It can help digestion because it tones the abdominal muscles.
- Equally beneficial is Trager's effect on blood circulation, lymphatic drainage and the respiratory system.
- On an emotional level, it battles against stress, eases insomnia and can help you to cope with the strains of modern living.
- Devotees say that Trager gives them a sense of ease and peace, combined with a charge of energy and vitality.

what can I expect from a session?

WHERE WILL I HAVE THE TREATMENT?
You will be lying on a couch.

WILL I BE CLOTHED?
You can wear whatever makes you feel comfortable. Most people eventually end up in underwear, but practitioners will happily work with you fully clothed.

WHAT HAPPENS?
The therapist will first ask a few questions and then ask you to get on the couch. The first movements cradle your head and neck, gently rocking, stretching and flexing. Within minutes, you might find the vertebrae of your neck popping themselves into position quite naturally and painlessly. The session generally floats by like an enchanting dream.

Trager is very different from any other form of bodywork. It does not use the oils or long strokes of conventional massage, nor does it press into the connective tissue as Rolfing, Hellerwork and Looyenwork do; it does not manipulate the skeletal system

as do osteopathy and chiropractic. Although Trager is so very soft and gentle, it is not simply about healing, either.

WILL IT HURT?
If an area is painful, the last thing a Trager practitioner would do would be to press or prod. Instead, they would back off and try another approach.

WILL ANYTHING STRANGE HAPPEN?
No, you will just experience a delightful feeling of total relaxation.

WILL I BE GIVEN ANYTHING TO TAKE?
No, medication is not part of the treatment.

IS THERE ANY HOMEWORK?
Once you get off the couch, you will be taught a few simple 'exercises', or 'mentastics', as they are known. Not at all arduous nor in any way remotely resembling physical jerks, these exercises are simply little reminders of how to sit, stand and move with ease – ways to continue your Trager session in everyday life. You will be advised to practise these every day for optimum results.

trager® body awareness

It's nigh-on impossible to duplicate the Trager touch at home. These exercises, however, will help you get a feeling for the Trager philosophy.

- Think about softening, widening, lengthening and expanding. Think about light, lighter and lighter still. Think about a dancing cloud. Now, pause a to notice how your body feels as you just think about these things.
- Let one arm drop softly by your side, gently waggle the fingers of your hand and think about feeling the bones. How much does that hand weigh? Now, do the same on the other side. You will probably find that your arms visibly lengthen as you relax.
- Sitting down, imagine that your head is attached to the ceiling by a large rubber band. Feel how that affects your posture – making you straighter, but not bolt upright. Feel your shoulders softly come down, as your head bobs on the rubber band.
- Now imagine that you have a paintbrush fixed to the top of your head and that you are gently painting the ceiling with it. Allow your head to wobble from side to side with slight movements.

OPPOSITE THE TRAGER TOUCH IS UNIQUE AND COMPRISES A BATTERY OF UNUSUAL TECHNIQUES. MANY PEOPLE HAVE SESSIONS PURELY TO ENJOY THE DEEP RELAXATION OF THIS DELIGHTFUL THERAPY. THEY ALSO SWEAR IT GIVES THEM EXTRA VITALITY, AND A SENSE OF CALM AND PEACE.

ENERGY

colour therapy

Researchers into the amazing world of colour have found that the colours we encounter – in our homes and our workplaces, in the clothes we wear and even in the foods we eat – can have enormous effects on our lives. Colour can affect health and happiness, success and our sex lives. Red walls in a pub or bar could mean more fights at closing time, while pink walls in a prison appear to make inmates quieter and less aggressive. People who wear a lot of blue may be on a constant diet yet never lose weight, while royal blue in a custody cell might urge criminals to come clean.

There is no doubt that colour sends out messages. 'It has been noted that 60 per cent of an individuals' reaction to any situation is based on colour (surroundings, clothes etc.),' says colour therapist Marie Louise Lacy, 'so it is important to have the right colours in our environment, whether at home or at work.'

Psychologists have used colour as a form of personality testing for years; the colours we choose can give a very clear indication of our current state of mind. In 'chromatotherapy', colour therapists use lamps with different coloured filters which flood the body with colour; some prescribe 'colour diets' or advise clients to dress in certain colours or decorate their houses in particular hues to heal an array of physical and emotional conditions. Practitioners of 'colourpuncture' beam coloured light onto precise points on the body.

A growing mass of solid scientific research seems to back the claims. Carlton Wagner, director of the Wagner Institute for Color Research in California, has shown that viewing certain colours triggers physical changes. Dr David Rainey, of John Carroll University in Ohio, agrees. He has found that seeing red can stimulate the glandular system and increase heart rate, blood pressure and respiration.

OPPOSITE THESE BEAUTIFUL JEWEL-LIKE BOTTLES ARE THE TOOLS OF AN AURA-SOMA COLOUR THERAPIST. IN THIS THERAPY, EACH BOTTLE IS DESIGNED TO HEAL A PARTICULAR EMOTION OR SPIRITUAL PROBLEM.

do-it-yourself colour breathing

Lie down or sit in a comfortable chair and allow yourself to relax. Breathe comfortably and deeply, but keep the rhythm of your breathing natural and relaxed.

Now imagine yourself bathed in the colour you choose. As you breathe in, imagine the colour entering your body through your solar plexus (just above your abdomen) and spreading throughout your body. As you breathe out, visualize the complementary colour suffusing and leaving your body. **Blue** relaxes and brings peace. Visualize blue when you can't go to sleep – it's great for insomnia. Use blue also when you can't stop to think calmly. Its complement is **orange**.

Green is the great healer. Use it to cleanse, to balance and to purify your system. It is useful if you continually take your work home with you or take your home worries to work. Green helps to keep thoughts in balance. Its complement is **magenta**.

Magenta is the great releaser. Breathe magenta when you need to let go of the past, of old thoughts and obsessions. It's wonderful as an aid during change, of whatever kind. It also brings out your spiritual energies. Its complement is **green**.

Orange is for fun, happiness and sheer joy. If you are feeling dull and gloomy, or fed up with your work, choose orange. Its complement is **blue**.

Red gives energy and vitality; it increases your strength and your sexuality. Use red when you lack energy, when you're so exhausted you can barely think. Its complement is **turquoise**.

Turquoise calms and soothes; it strengthens the immune system and can help feverish conditions and inflammations. Use turquoise if you feel dominated by other people or always give in to their thoughts and ideas. Its complement is **red**.

Violet is the colour of dignity and self-respect. Breathe it in when you feel lacking in self-esteem. Use it also when you find you are putting yourself down or start to feel that, no matter how hard you try, you will never do as well as others. Its complement is **yellow**.

Yellow is a wonderful colour for studying and concentrating, as it stimulates your intellectual and mental powers and increases your ability to be objective. It increases detachment and helps if you are feeling oversensitive or controlled by other people, or when you can't let go. Its complement is **violet**.

what can colour therapy help?

- Colour therapy is useful for centring people; it is helpful in difficult situations such as bereavement, shock and dependency.
- It eases stress-related conditions and can soothe anxiety, depression and insomnia.
- Research into colourpuncture has shown it to be effective in treating children's insomnia, bronchitis and migraine.
- Practitioners of colourpuncture say it can help virtually any complaint and even help people overcome psychological trauma.

what can I expect from a session?

WHERE WILL I HAVE THE TREATMENT?
You will usually be lying on a couch in the therapist's room.

WILL I BE CLOTHED?
Yes, you will be fully clothed.

WHAT HAPPENS?
A colourpuncture session can last from 10 minutes to an hour, depending on the problem. Before treatment, the practitioner will take a full case history and also a Kirlian photograph to gain an impression of the person's energy. On the basis of this, he or she will decide which points or areas to target, and which colours to use out of the 200 or so in the colourpuncture repertory. You will then lie on a couch, and points (often on the face, back and feet) will be targeted with the colourpuncture tool for between 30 and 60 seconds at a time. It's pleasant and deeply relaxing.

Chromatotherapists will beam a precise intensity of colour at the patient using large lamps or small torches; some employ a computer-controlled instrument called a colour-form-rhythm beamer which transmits finely tuned intensities of colour. Some may use coloured oils. Clients usually pick the oil that most appeals to them – a basic tenet of colour healing is that we intrinsically know what we need. The oil is then generally spritzed around the aura or at specific chakras. You may also be asked to visualize particular colours (see the exercise on the left).

WILL IT HURT?
No, it doesn't hurt at all.

WILL ANYTHING STRANGE HAPPEN?
It is usually just very relaxing.

WILL I BE GIVEN ANYTHING TO TAKE?
No, but you may be asked to spritz yourself with coloured oils.

IS THERE ANY HOMEWORK?
You may be advised to wear certain colours or alter your surroundings to include different colours.

electro-crystal therapy

Electro-crystal therapy doesn't just talk about meridians and chakras; it lets you actually see them. Harry Oldfield, the originator of this remarkable system, is an ex-science teacher who doesn't just tell you about your inner secret-energy self; he lets you see it with your own eyes. Oldfield developed a means of filming the body's subtle energies. While you are scanned with a camera, a multicoloured image of your body appears on a computer screen. On it you can see what mystics have known for years but scientists have refused to admit: energy points (the acupuncture points), energy channels (the meridians), energy centres (the chakras) and the cocooning egg-like field of energy that surrounds us (the aura).

The system is called a poly contrast interface, or PIP, and it is being touted as the X-ray of the future. The camera records very high frequencies of light not normally detected by the human eye. A computer program identifies the waves of light and gives each a different colour reading so that you can literally see the shape of your energy.

Once the problem has been diagnosed, electro-crystal therapy takes over: electromagnetic fields are beamed at the patient, using crystals to amplify the energy. Oldfield found that, if disease showed up as a disturbance in the body's forcefield, directing a correcting vibratory pattern back into the body would correct the imbalance. However, as he points out, how long the 'cure' lasts depends on the patient.

Oldfield began his healing journey more than 30 years ago with Kirlian photography, when he discovered he could detect illnesses and diseases from the patterns of energy exposed by the photograph. Doctors and scientists were impressed with his findings. But when he began to develop more precise diagnostic tools and then to treat – and heal – people, the orthodox community turned away almost en masse. Patients, on the other hand, descended in hordes, their numbers swelling by word-of-mouth. Oldfield and his disciples do what very few practitioners of alternative medicine would ever dare do: they talk about remissions and cures for even the most serious and terminal of diseases. To be fair, they don't promise cures and they admit that there are times when people simply don't get well. Even so, they will freely discuss what most people would term miracles.

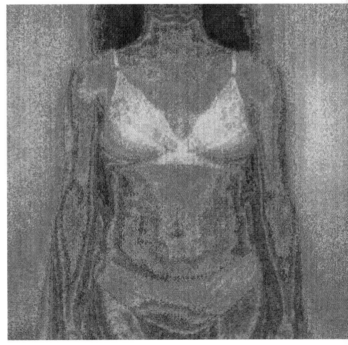

ABOVE THESE PHOTOGRAPHS REVEAL WHAT THE NAKED EYE CANNOT SEE: THE BODY'S ENERGY SYSTEMS (MERIDIANS, CHAKRAS AND THE AURA). IN ELECTRO-CRYSTAL THERAPY, A PRACTITIONER IS ABLE TO SHOW YOU YOUR ENERGY FIELDS ON A COMPUTER SCREEN, AS YOUR BODY IS SCANNED WITH A SPECIAL FORM OF CAMERA.

what can electro-crystal therapy help?

- Practitioners claim it can balance (and hence heal) virtually any disease – some patients have reported nigh-on 'miraculous' recoveries from a wide range of conditions.
- People claim to have been cured of eye diseases, degeneration of the optical nerve, glaucoma and retinitis pigmentosa.
- Some people say mechanical problems with the body have been helped with electro-crystal therapy.
- Children and the elderly seem to respond well.
- Many people use it as a 'last-chance' therapy.

what can I expect from a session?

WHERE WILL I HAVE THE TREATMENT?
You will be standing, then sitting, in the practitioner's room.

WILL I BE CLOTHED?
You will be asked to strip to underwear for the examination. You will be fully clothed for treatment.

WHAT HAPPENS?
The practitioner will move a meter that reads sound waves in the body around you, noting any imbalances. You will then be asked to strip to your underwear while the PIP scanner is pointed at you. You will see yourself on a small computer screen, your body shape clearly visible, but covered in swirling bands of colour. The practitioner will point out your meridians and chakras, and check your organs and all other parts of your body. A few calculations are then made to work out what frequencies you need for optimum balance. You are next plugged into a small machine while seated in a chair, with a kind of rod pinned under your collarbone and a headband of flexible plastic filled with crystals placed over your head. You sit like this for the whole session.

WILL IT HURT?
Treatment is totally painless – in fact, you don't feel a thing.

WILL ANYTHING STRANGE HAPPEN?
It can be quite strange to see the energy system of your body in such a graphic way. The PIP scanner can pick up imbalances even before they manifest, so you may be given warning of a cold or a sore throat!

WILL I BE GIVEN ANYTHING TO TAKE?
Some practitioners use flower or gem essences in combination with the treatment.

IS THERE ANY HOMEWORK?
Some people buy their own machines for home use, or you may be allowed to borrow one if you need intensive treatment.

flower & gem therapies

Flower and gem remedies are among the most remarkable healers known. They treat not physical symptoms as such, but the emotional states that underlie much illness and disharmony. They are gentle enough to use on tiny babies, yet powerful enough to produce profound shifts. Dr Edward Bach, a pioneer in the field, even brought people out of unconsciousness by using the remedies.

Numerous ancient cultures employed flowers to treat emotional states; some people even go so far as to claim that flower and gem essences were the ultimate healing systems in the highly evolved mythical cultures of Atlantis and Lemuria. Around 70 years ago, the British physician Dr Edward Bach established 38 remedies based on common trees and plants such as oak, walnut, clematis and mustard. Bach believed that the healing power of plants lies in their energy, an energy that can restore ailing bodies and souls. In order to tap that energy, he discovered, it was not necessary to ingest the whole plant (as in herbalism), but merely to take in the essence of the plant, captured by putting the flowers in a glass bowl of pure spring water and letting them steep in the sunlight for a few hours.

Practitioners believe that the remedies work by vibration. Apparently, the essences of flowers and gems vibrate at a very high level and so affect our bodies at the most subtle level. Rather than dealing with the dense matter of flesh and blood, the remedies go straight to the core of our being, working from the epicentre out to the denser fabric of the emotional and physical body.

In the past decade or so, other people have expanded the Bach system and now there are a host of various flower, tree and gem remedies. People over the world over have discovered their native flowers and plants' healing properties: there are around 30 ranges of flower and gem essences from places as far afield as Australia, Alaska and the Himalayas.

OPPOSITE Dr Edward Bach placed flower heads in a glass container full of fresh spring water. The glass was then placed near the parent plant and exposed to direct sunlight for a few hours. Alternatively, the plant can be simmered in spring water for around half an hour.

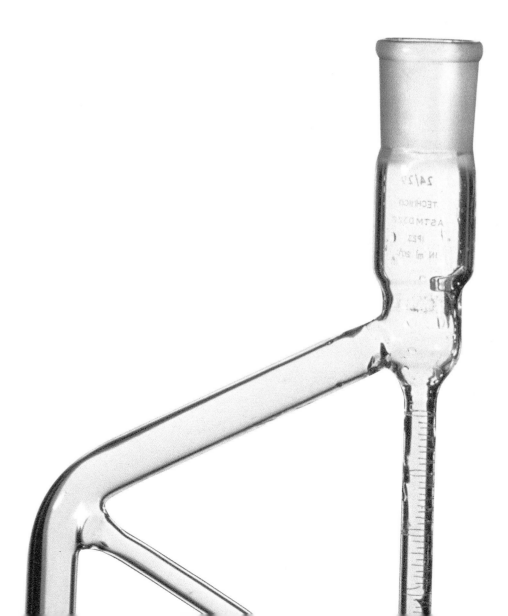

what can flower & gem therapies help?

- Flower and gem essences will help any problem that has an emotional element.
- They have been used in conjunction with nutritional therapy to help people lose weight.
- They work wonderfully with children – helping to combat nightmares, fears, anxiety and exam nerves.
- Chronic depression responds well to these therapies, as do most psychological disorders.
- They can help with problems such as fears and phobias, uncertainty, doubt and anxiety.
- Some remedies help with life shifts such as moving, marriage, having children, menopause, retirement and death of a loved one.

what can I expect from a session?

WHERE WILL I HAVE THE TREATMENT?

You will be sitting in a chair in the therapist's room.

WILL I BE CLOTHED?

Yes, you will be fully clothed.

WHAT HAPPENS?

Expect to be asked a lot of questions. It can be a lengthy process to find precisely the right remedies; a skilled practitioner will be looking for the underlying emotional blockages. Don't be surprised if the practitioner asks about any fears and concerns; about how you view yourself, the world and the people around you; or if you have any negative emotions; and so on.

Some practitioners combine these essences with other therapies, such as hypnotherapy, cranio-sacral therapy or more general psychotherapy. At the end of your session, the therapist will make up a bottle of remedies for you to take away with you.

WILL IT HURT?

No, it won't hurt physically. However, some people find the close questioning may bring up painful realizations.

WILL ANYTHING STRANGE HAPPEN?

It's unlikely that anything strange will happen during the session, but you may find quite sudden shifts occurring once you start taking the remedy.

WILL I BE GIVEN ANYTHING TO TAKE?

Yes, you will be given a bottle containing your remedies diluted in water and with a little brandy as preservative. You will take them (usually in water or other drinks) several times a day.

IS THERE ANY HOMEWORK?

No, you don't usually have anything else to do.

the bach remedies at a glance

The Bach flower remedies are totally safe to self-administer. Simply add one or two drops of the remedy you feel you need to a glass of water and sip it throughout the day. Alternatively, you can make up a stock bottle containing several essences. Fill a 30 ml (1 fl oz) bottle three-quarters full with natural spring water. Add 2 drops each of your chosen remedies (you can use up to 5). Top up the bottle with a little brandy or cider vinegar for preservation. Shake well. Take at least 4 drops four times daily until the bottle is finished. These are the main personality traits associated with the 38 Bach flower remedies.

For fear – aspen (vague, undefined fears); mimulus (fear of known things – heights, spiders etc); cherry plum (irrational thoughts and fears); red chestnut (overanxiety and fear for others); rock rose (sheer terror, sudden shocks and alarm).

For uncertainty – cerato (doubting your judgment); gorse (hopelessness, pessimism); gentian (despondency, discouragement); hornbeam (lack of energy, listlessness); scleranthus (indecisiveness), wild oat (lack of direction in life, uncertainty about career).

For loneliness – impatiens (impatience); heather (self-obsession), water violet (aloofness, disdain).

For oversensitivity – agrimony (tortured thoughts hidden behind a cheerful façade); centaury (timidness, subservience); holly (envy, jealousy, hatred); walnut (difficulty adapting to change).

For despondency or despair – crab apple (self-disgust); elm (overwhelmed by responsibility); larch (lack of confidence); oak (struggling on against the odds); pine (guilt, self-blame), sweet chestnut (extreme despair); star of Bethlehem (after-effects of severe shock); willow (resentment).

For overconcern for others – beech (intolerance, need always to be right); chicory (selfishness, possessiveness); vervain (overenthusiastic, fanatical); vine (domineering); rock water (self-repression).

For insufficient interest in the present – chestnut bud (keep repeating same mistakes); clematis (daydreaming); honeysuckle (nostalgia); mustard (depression); olive (exhaustion, 'burn-out'); white chestnut (persistent worries); wild rose (resignation, apathy).

health kinesiology

Health kinesiologists talk to bodies. They bypass the rational mind, preferring to address their questions to the body itself. Give a practitioner of this extraordinary therapy an hour with your body and it will tell him or her exactly what it's allergic to and precisely what is wrong with it, then proceed even to dictate the prescription it requires.

Health kinesiology (HK) was originated by a Canadian scientist, Dr Jimmy Scott. He started out working primarily with allergies. Irritated that most forms of allergy testing were not really accurate, he stumbled upon a system of muscle testing called kinesiology which appeared to be swift, sensitive and reliable. Its principle is that the body, at some deep, unconscious level, knows precisely what it needs. By asking the body directly, the practitioner bypasses the conscious mind, which might *think* that it knows what is best, but which has really lost touch with the body.

The kinesiologist asks questions by applying light pressure to the patient's outstretched arm while the patient is trying to keep the arm still. If the body answers yes, the arm will resist the pressure and remain strong. If the answer is no, the muscle weakens slightly and the arm will drop. It's rather like dowsing, using the body instead of a pendulum.

Health kinesiology looks at the person as a whole, taking into account their psychological state, their environment, the needs of the physical body and also the interplay between the subtle energy bodies and the chakras (centres of subtle energy in the body). The practitioner will bring the meridian system (lines of subtle energy in the body) into a state of temporary balance before commencing work. Only then, practitioners believe, will muscle testing produce reliable and consistent results. The practitioner then asks the body for permission to continue – to ensure that only appropriate work is done, rather than imposing work on the body. Health kinesiology also uses a variety of highly unusual, and seemingly esoteric, methods for healing the body's imbalances. While the vast majority of scientists and doctors would scoff with cynicism, health kinesiology is not ridiculed in Germany and Switzerland. In these countries, an increasing number of doctors, pharmacists and veterinarians are using this extraordinary therapy as an additional diagnostic tool.

what can health kinesiology help?

- Health kinesiology has helped a seemingly endless array of ailments, including many that have proved immune to other forms of medicine, both orthodox and complementary.
- Practitioners report success with asthma, eczema, migraine, arthritis, acne, menstrual and menopausal problems, irritable bowel syndrome and food allergies.
- Psychological troubles respond well: panic attacks, phobias, stammering, stress, lack of confidence, shyness and grief.
- As practitioners believe they are working with the body's own healing mechanisms, virtually any complaint is theoretically curable.
- Health kinesiology can be very useful for people with severe emotional trauma because feelings can be released without having to delve into the past or dwell on painful thoughts.

what can I expect from a session?

WHERE WILL I HAVE THE TREATMENT?
You will be sitting in the practitioner's therapy room.

WILL I BE CLOTHED?
Yes, you will be fully clothed.

WHAT HAPPENS?
You sit with one arm outstretched while the practitioner talks to your body, asking a long string of questions. They pause almost imperceptibly between each to gauge your arm's response. Once the practitioner has ascertained the problem, as your body perceives it, he or she will ask the body what cures it requires.

Health kinesiology also includes highly unusual techniques for healing, including tapping – touching the body with little tapping movements supposedly clears the body of intolerances and allergies. Sometimes magnets or crystals are placed on the body; homeopathic remedies and essential oils are also held against the body. You might be asked to think of a certain word or phrase while the practitioner holds you.

WILL IT HURT?
No, it's not at all painful.

WILL ANYTHING STRANGE HAPPEN?
Not specifically, but the whole experience feels quite strange.

WILL I BE GIVEN ANYTHING TO TAKE?
Generally, you will just be given the remedy, crystal or oil to hold while the practitioner is working on you, rather than having to take it.

IS THERE ANY HOMEWORK?
Adjustments in lifestyle and diet may be suggested.

light therapy

One dose of spring sunshine and the whole world seems to smile. Since time immemorial, people have valued the healing energy of light. From the earliest writings, we know that, among others, the Egyptians, the Greeks, the Romans and the Arabs all recognized the healing powers of sunlight. The modern history of light therapy as such starts in the nineteenth century, when natural sunlight was used as a cure for all kinds of ailments, from paralysis to tuberculosis. Modern research shows demonstrably that the pure sunlight of spring can have measurable, highly beneficial, effects on our health, both physiological and psychological.

Unfortunately, few of us take enough of this essential 'medicine'. Light therapists say that changes in our working lives mean that most of us are now seriously light deprived. In the past, we used to work on the land: now we work mainly indoors. An office may be warmer, drier and more comfortable than the average field, but it is also darker. Our offices are lit at between 200 and 1,000 lux (the measurement for light) when, in reality, we need levels around ten times brighter. The most common result is the well-documented syndrome of seasonal affective disorder (SAD), but light therapists reckon this is the tip of the iceberg: around 60 per cent of the population suffer in a less dramatic way. Lack of light can lead to

RIGHT SUNLIGHT IS VITAL TO HEALTH AND WELLBEING: WITHOUT IT, WE FALL ILL OR BECOME DEPRESSED. THIS IS WHERE LIGHT THERAPY COMES IN.

depression and lethargy, disturbed sleep patterns and plummeting energy levels. Our metabolism can suffer; so, too, can our hormone levels. Even conditions such as osteoporosis and asthma worsen without regular doses of sunlight.

If we can't go out into the light, we have to bring the light in to us. SAD sufferers have used light boxes for some years now to help their symptoms, but recently a new brand of light therapy has been developed which promises benefits for virtually everyone. This new light reproduces as closely as possible the pure spring light of the northern hemisphere, the clear, soft gleam that so revitalizes us, body and soul. In practical terms, it's a combination of fluorescent tubes that gives out the whole spectrum of wavelengths in natural daylight, except the harmful ultraviolet (UVB) rays that can cause burning and skin cancer.

what can light therapy help?

- Light therapy increases energy levels.
- It can help with many types of depression.
- A mere 20 minutes of light therapy can apparently lower blood pressure for up to a week and will also lower blood cholesterol levels.
- Light therapy balances hormones, so it can be used as an alternative to hormone replacement therapy (HRT) and also to increase fertility.
- Full-spectrum light can kill bacteria and accelerate wound healing.
- Exposure to the lights increases the production of vitamin D in the body, which in turn improves the absorption of calcium, phosphorus and magnesium, making light therapy useful in cases of arthritis, osteoporosis and dental caries.
- As daylight suppresses the production of melatonin (which helps send us to sleep), light therapy can be used to treat sleep disorders and jet lag with great success.

what can I expect from a session?

WHERE WILL I HAVE THE TREATMENT?
You will be lying on a comfortable couch.

WILL I BE CLOTHED?
You can wear as much or little clothing as you like.

WHAT HAPPENS?
First, a detailed medical history will be taken. You will then be asked to take off your shoes and as much clothing as you wish, and to lie on the couch. Any glasses or contact lenses

must be removed because the light can only reach the pineal gland (essential for hormonal balance) through the eyes.

The lights are mounted in a panel above the couch several feet above your body – they look much like a sunbed, except that the centre tubes are a beautiful shade of blue. For the best effects, you keep your eyes open (although you don't have to look directly at the light) for the first 20 minutes.

WILL IT HURT
No, it's absolutely painless – in fact, you won't feel anything at all except pleasantly warm and relaxed.

WILL ANYTHING STRANGE HAPPEN?
No, nothing strange occurs with this therapy.

WILL I BE GIVEN ANYTHING TO TAKE?
No, medication is not a part of the treatment.

IS THERE ANY HOMEWORK?
No, there's no need to do anything at home.

bright ideas to bring sunlight into your life

Lightbathing, say light therapists, stimulates the circulation, tones up muscles, detoxifies the body and boosts production of vitamin D and hormones. Here are some tips on simple ways to maximize your light exposure.

- At times of the year when the danger of burning is very low, get as much natural daylight as you can. There is no need to lie exposed to the sun – gardening, dog-walking or even just walking outside in your lunch hour can help.
- As the sun gets brighter, you need to adjust the amount of sun you take to suit your skin type. Light therapists insist that it is burning that causes skin cancer, not sensible exposure. As a rough guide, you need to stay out for half the amount of time that you can safely be in the sun before burning; that will be around 10 minutes in very bright sunlight for very fair skins, through to an hour for people with very dark-toned skins.
- The more of your skin that is exposed to the light the better.
- Glasses, sunglasses and contact lenses all filter out the light. Wearing dark glasses all the time, say light therapists, will tend to make you depressed or irritable – use a hat instead to shield you from glare.

magnetic therapy/ alpha pulse therapy

In Japan, magnetic therapy is as mainstream as aspirin. Even the humblest corner store will boast a range of magnetic products – from insoles to car cushions, from back massagers to mattresses. Magnetic therapy may be a multibillion dollar industry, but it's one based on solid scientific research, rather than marketing hype. Clinical trials and studies have shown that using magnetism can have wide-reaching beneficial effects.

The idea that magnets have remarkable properties is nothing new: Cleopatra is said to have worn one on her forehead to keep her beautiful and young. It is only in the past 20 years, however, that the mythology has been proven as medical fact. NASA found that its astronauts were returning to earth feeling sick and debilitated. Intensive research revealed they were suffering withdrawal symptoms from the earth's magnetosphere, which allows the blood to circulate properly and be thoroughly oxygenated. NASA promptly placed static magnets in spacesuits and within the spacecraft, and the problem was overcome. This is known as the Hall Effect – blood flow is stimulated by magnetic pads attracting electrically charged particles (positive and negative ions) in the bloodstream. Even though we generally travel no further than to work and back, many of us suffer a similar problem, albeit on a lesser level. Living in concrete cities, travelling in steel cars, buses, trains and aeroplanes, we are missing out on the health-giving benefits of natural magnetism and so our circulation (and as a consequence, our entire body) is working under par.

Another type of magnetictherapy is called alpha pulse therapy or pulsed magnetic field (PMF) therapy. This sends very low pulsed fields to the person and has proved extremely effective, particularly for sports injuries and broken bones.

what can magnetic therapy/alpha pulse therapy help?

- Magnets can help boost your general wellbeing, improving sleep and concentration and energy levels, while alleviating stress and tension.
- They are very useful for injuries (aiding recovery of torn muscles, ligaments and tendons, accelerating the healing of bone fractures, and reducing swelling and bruising).
- Alpha pulse therapy, in particular, has had great success with treating osteoporosis.
- They can also ameliorate serious medical conditions (improving mobility in rheumatic and arthritic conditions, easing migraine, correcting hormonal imbalances and treating chronic fatigue).
- Jet lag seems to be diminished and hangovers have been found to disappear after magnetic therapy.
- Some people have discovered that they have mysteriously lost the desire to smoke, while many others have reported that magnetic therapy does wonders for their sex life.
- Alpha pulse therapy seems to be able to treat phobias.

what can I expect from a session?
WHERE WILL I HAVE THE TREATMENT?
You will be lying on a special 'bed' (rather like a sunbed) or, in the case of alpha pulse therapy, on a couch with an arc that transmits the pulsed field over the part requiring treatment.

WILL I BE CLOTHED?
Yes, you will be fully clothed except for shoes and jewellery.

WHAT HAPPENS?
You will be asked if you are pregnant, or have a pacemaker or active cancer (the bed is not suitable for you if any of these apply). You should avoid treatment if you are menstruating or have thrombosis, as it increases blood flow. You then remove shoes and jewellery, and lie down. After a few minutes, you may notice some tingling and, after about 15 minutes, the machine tends to become quite warm. Ideally, you would have treatment every day for 10 days. Alpha pulse therapy treatment is similar, but you feel absolutely nothing.

WILL IT HURT?
No, it is totally painless.

WILL ANYTHING STRANGE HAPPEN?
No, although the machine tends to make strange noises and you may notice some tingling. With alpha pulse therapy, you will notice nothing strange.

WILL I BE GIVEN ANYTHING TO TAKE?
No, medication is not part of the treatment.

IS THERE ANY HOMEWORK?
Not specifically, although some people buy equipment (pillows, mattresses, car seats, insoles, bands etc.) for home use.

metamorphic technique

The metamorphic technique is neither a therapy nor a massage. It's not healing and nor, its practitioners insist, is it even a treatment. Of all the practices in complementary medicine, this is perhaps the most mystical and unexplained. Yet, nebulous though it may appear, thousands of people who have experienced the technique affirm that life is never the same once you step onto the metamorphic path.

The metamorphic technique was developed in the 1960s while naturopath and reflexologist Robert St John was working in a school for mentally challenged children. Although his work did seem to be helping the children, the changes were, to his mind, not deep or lasting enough. He wanted something that would change the children for the better permanently. While practising reflexology, he came to the conclusion that not only are all the parts of the body represented in the foot (as reflexology teaches), but also that our passage through the womb, from conception to birth, is mapped out on the side of the foot, along the points reflexologists call the spinal reflexes. His finding, in itself, would be merely a curiosity were it not for the fact that St John also came to believe that the ailments we suffer and the characteristics we carry through life are established during the gestation period, in our mothers' wombs. By working on the feet with a particular light touch, he found he could release blocks and facilitate 'transformations' on both a physical and an emotional level.

In 1979, the Metamorphic Association was set up as a registered charity to promote the theory worldwide. Despite testimonials from both orthodox doctors and complementary practitioners, clinics, schools and institutions, practitioners claim it is not the technique itself nor the practitioner which brings about such results: it is the life force working inside the person. It's hard to see how such a simple technique can instigate profound changes, but people swear it has transformed their lives. Some find new relationships or end outdated ones; some move house or change their jobs; others are prompted to pursue a healthier lifestyle or to seek medical advice.

Although the philosophy of metamorphosis is esoteric, the practice is remarkably simple. It can be done by anyone and there is no need to go into deep meditation — you can talk or watch television while you are doing it.

what can metamorphic technique help?

- People attest that metamorphosis has helped them change their lives — it provides the impetus to make profound shifts.
- If given during pregnancy and labour, it can ease labour; many midwives are now learning the technique.
- Babies and young children react very well — it calms and soothes them.
- It can help families bond and to become more of a unit.
- It has been given to people with HIV and AIDS, and taught to their friends and family.
- Metamorphic technique is used a lot with children who are physically or mentally challenged, or have learning difficulties.
- Some people have introduced the metamorphic technique into use in hospitals, hospices and jails.

what can I expect from a session?

WHERE WILL I HAVE THE TREATMENT?

You will be sitting in or lying on a comfortable chair or couch.

WILL I BE CLOTHED?

Yes, you just take off your shoes and socks.

WHAT HAPPENS?

You won't be asked for any details about your life. You are simply invited to remove your shoes and socks, and sit in or lie on a relaxing chair or couch. The practitioner then takes your foot and starts to work. The touch is light and fluid; sometimes it feels as if your foot is being gently polished; at others, it is as if the practitioner were searching for something. Occasionally, he or she may yawn, sneeze or even burp — this is caused by blockages passing through the practitioner's hands into his or her body. Yawning, sneezing or even burping apparently allows the blocks to disappear harmlessly into the air.

After working on both feet, the practitioner works on your hands and then finally on your head, leaving you feeling very relaxed yet surprisingly energized.

WILL IT HURT?

No, it's totally painless and very pleasant.

WILL ANYTHING STRANGE HAPPEN?

Not usually, but some people report that, during a session,

RIGHT THE LIGHT TOUCH OF THE METAMORPHIC TECHNIQUE IS VERY SOOTHING AND RELAXING. PRACTITIONERS INSIST THAT THEY DO NOT 'CURE' OR 'HEAL' ANYTHING: THEY JUST PROVIDE A CATALYST FOR POTENTIAL CHANGE IN THE BODY, MINDS, EMOTIONS AND SOUL.

they 'see' scenes from their lives or that they re-experience emotions that they felt when they were in the womb.

WILL I BE GIVEN ANYTHING TO TAKE?

No, medication is not part of the treatment.

IS THERE ANY HOMEWORK?

There is not any specific homework, although many people learn the technique for use on family and friends. Even though the philosophy of metamorphic technique is a rather esoteric one, the actual practice is remarkably simple. It can be learned over a weekend (the basic touch can be taught in just 5 minutes). Absolutely anyone can learn to practise the metamorphic technique and you can even talk or watch television while doing it. The Metamorphic Association is particularly keen to teach parents this technique, as it believes it can help to bond families together and allow them to move and transform as a unit, a functioning whole, rather than as individuals.

polarity therapy

According to polarity therapy, the human body is a living magnet. Just like a magnet, we have electromagnetic currents of energy flowing constantly backwards and forwards within us between positive and negative poles. Polarity therapy teaches that, if we could only regulate an even flow of energy, we would all enjoy rude good health. It's a well-balanced form of natural healthcare, combining nutrition, exercise, bodywork and counselling: a neat synthesis of Eastern and Western therapeutic techniques, a potted, 'best of' complementary therapy.

The founder of polarity therapy was an extraordinary human being called Randolph Stone. Born in 1890, Stone studied a bewildering array of religious philosophies and natural forms of healthcare. He trained as a physician and also learnt osteopathy, chiropractic and naturopathy. Sensing that there was still something missing, he then studied Eastern systems of medicine such as ayurveda.

The result of his studies was his conviction that the basis of good health lay purely in energy. Blocked energy was, to his mind, the root cause of all unhappiness and physical illness. It took him 50 years to assemble the comprehensive package that finally became polarity therapy.

Stone taught that energy flows from the centre of any system to its circumference, and then returns by magnetic pull. It will flow from the top downwards, from within the system to without.

A polarity therapist is looking for imbalances in the energy flow which he or she will try to correct using exercise, bodywork, nutrition and counselling.

what can polarity therapy help?

- Polarity therapy usually manages to improve most conditions.
- It has consistently good results with migraine, digestive problems and allergies.
- Myalgic encephalomyelitis (ME) and other debilitating illnesses respond well, as do all stress-related illnesses.
- Back pain and sciatica generally improve or are cured with polarity therapy.
- It's excellent if you feel you need to get back in touch with your body and need an overall grounding in healthy living.

what can I expect from a session?

WHERE WILL I HAVE THE TREATMENT?

You will be in the therapist's room: lying on a couch for bodywork; sitting in chairs for nutritional guidance and counselling; on the floor for polarity yoga.

WHAT HAPPENS?

You will be asked to monitor your diet for 5 days before your first session, simply writing down everything you eat and drink. You will then spend some time in the first session talking about your life, health and any problems. If bodywork is deemed necessary (it usually forms a part of every session), you will be asked to sit on a chair or lie on a couch. The touch is firm and focused, pressing deeply into points of tension and manipulating stiff joints. You may also find yourself being rocked or shaken to stimulate energy flow.

Afterwards, you will be given dietary guidelines, often cleansing diets or juice fasts. Time is set aside just to talk – emotional wellbeing is seen as essential.

Finally, you will be taught some polarity yoga exercises – simple poses which are held either statically or while gently rocking.

WILL I BE CLOTHED?

Yes, unless you have a structural problem that is clearer with you undressed.

WILL IT HURT?

Some points can feel quite tender, but generally it doesn't hurt and is very relaxing.

WILL I BE GIVEN ANYTHING TO TAKE?

Medication is not a part of the treatment, but you will probably be given dietary guidelines (see right).

IS THERE ANY HOMEWORK?

Yes, lots. Expect to be asked to shift your eating habits and also to practice polarity yoga. You may be advised to go on a juice fast or cleansing diet.

do-it-yourself polarity therapy

THE PURIFYING DIET

This diet is said to help constipation, high blood pressure, arthritis and rheumatism, congestion and general toxicity. Try it for a weekend to begin with. While on this regime, cut out all dairy produce, tea and coffee, alcohol, carbohydrates and starchy foods. Water can be drunk freely. If you have any health concerns, check with your doctor before carrying out this diet.

First thing – two or more cups of hot herbal tea made from equal amounts of liquorice root, anise or fennel, peppermint and fenugreek. Add fresh ginger, lemon juice and honey to taste.

Breakfast – liver-flush juice: 3–4 tablespoons of pure cold-pressed olive or almond oil with twice the amount of fresh lemon juice. Add 3–6 cloves crushed garlic, plus fresh ginger to taste.

Mid-morning (two hours after breakfast) – 225 ml/8 fl oz of fresh vegetable juice, made from cabbage, lettuce, carrot and beetroot. Add radish or onion if you like and ginger, lemon, honey and garlic to taste.

Lunch (noon) – raw salad of fresh radish, lettuce, cabbage, grated carrot, onion, cucumber, tomato and sprouts. You may use a little dressing of almond, olive or sesame oil with lemon, garlic, onion and ginger. Fresh fruit for dessert.

Mid-afternoon – as for mid-morning.

Evening meal (around 6 pm) – fruit: choose from apples, pears, grapes, pomegranate and papaya. Herbal tea. If you are very hungry, you may repeat the lunchtime salad.

JUICING FOR HEALTH

Polarity therapy strongly advocates the use of fresh, organic fruit and vegetable juices to help the healing process. Try out the combinations given below (equal quantities of each ingredient, taken freely) for the following common conditions:

Anxiety and nervous tension – lemon and lime

Arthritis – carrot, celery and cabbage

High blood pressure – celery, beetroot and carrot

Asthma and catarrh – carrot and radish

Low blood pressure – carrot, beetroot and dandelion

Blocked sinuses – horseradish and lemon (use 100 g/4 oz horseradish and 50 ml/2 fl oz lemon juice, combined with a teaspoon of garlic juice and a tablespoon of honey – take a teaspoon four times daily)

Constipation – cabbage, spinach, celery and lemon

Insomnia – celery

Skin conditions – carrot, beetroot and celery

Sore throats and colds – lemon, lime and pineapple

OPPOSITE JUICING IS AN IMPORTANT PART OF POLARITY THERAPY. THE THERAPY'S FOUNDER, RANDOLPH STONE, BELIEVED THAT RAW FRUIT AND VEGETABLES, WHEN JUICED, COULD PROVIDE CURES FOR A WIDE VARIETY OF AILMENTS. FROM ARTHRITIS TO INSOMNIA.

radionics

Radionics has been dubbed the medicine of the future and, at first glance, it seems like nothing more than science fiction. Say you need to consult your doctor, but you are in Australia on business while your doctor is in the UK. You simply ring him, explain your symptoms, put down the telephone and wait. Back in the UK, your doctor takes out your file and scans a sample of hair you provided several years ago. Popping it in a machine, he directs a light beam through a series of cards for a few minutes. End of treatment. Some 17,000 km (10,000 miles) away, you start to feel better. Wishful thinking? Apparently not.

Radionic systems of healing have been in use since the early part of the twentieth century. Practitioners worked with a pendulum to find their diagnosis and remedy, by means of a process of dowsing. In addition, they employed curious 'black boxes' which measured what they then believed were simply electromagnetic forces. Until recently, however, they were generally dismissed as quacks, with diagnosis and cures summoned seemingly by the practitioner's supposed psychic powers influencing the pendulum.

Radionics, however, has lately taken on a fresh lease of life, having been given credibility with new advances in physics. Quantum physicists perceive nothing odd or alien about a system of medicine that takes no notice of time or place; that ignores physical examination and doesn't need to treat you with pills or potions.

Illness, according to the radionic consultant, occurs when there is a disturbance to our energetic frequency. It's rather as though we were radio stations – the signal sometimes gets a little confused and you need to twiddle the radio dial a bit. The causes for such disturbances are pretty basic: mechanical injury to the body; environmental stress (pollution, poisons, toxins etc.); trauma; mental or emotional anxiety; and hereditary and genetic factors. However, the most important factors of all are our personalities and understanding our purpose and role in life. If a person is at peace mentally, emotionally and energetically, it is very difficult for the body to be sick. Your body's immune system will be working well and you will simply fend off all sorts of diseases and deal with all kinds of environmental pollutants.

what can radionics help?

- Satisfied customers claim they have been cured of a wide variety of ailments, including asthma, eczema, irritable bowel syndrome and chronic fatigue, to name but a few.
- People find the effect of their treatment goes way beyond the physical: they develop new interests, start new careers, generally become happier as well as healthier.
- Some doctors, dentists and specialists refer cases that orthodox techniques can't help.

what can I expect from a session?

WHERE WILL I HAVE THE SESSION?

Initial sessions are usually held at the therapist's consulting room. You will be seated in a chair.

WILL I BE CLOTHED

Yes, you will be fully clothed.

WHAT HAPPENS?

A radionics case history will include not only questions about past illnesses and operations, but also about your hobbies and pastimes, and even your temperament. You will be asked for a small piece of hair, which acts as a 'witness', a way of tuning in to your vibration. Your hair will remain in energetic equilibrium with its source and its energetic characteristics will vary from moment to moment according to your own energetic patterns. If you can accept this (and it does take a radical shift in thinking), it becomes logical (if not perhaps understandable) that correcting imbalances of energy within the hair witness will set up a ripple effect and bring the rest of the patient back into balance.

Radionics practitioners don't rely solely on such subtle means of energetic healing. Sometimes they send people back to their doctors with an accurate diagnosis, or they refer to dentistry, as radionics theory recognizes is a firm link between general health and the teeth. There may be dietary solutions or the person may be referred to an osteopath because of a mechanical problem.

WILL IT HURT?

No, not at all.

WILL ANYTHING STRANGE HAPPEN?

Frankly, the whole radionics experience is strange!

WILL I BE GIVEN ANYTHING TO TAKE?

You may be referred to a homeopath or given flower remedies.

IS THERE ANY HOMEWORK?

You may need to have further consultations with other specialists, once a firm diagnosis has been obtained.

reiki

Reiki, the Japanese art of spiritual healing, is mysterious and inscrutable. Contradictions abound as to its purpose and practice. Some practitioners call reiki 'relaxation therapy'; others insist it can be far from relaxing. Although it is known as 'healing', its exponents freely admit that sometimes reiki chooses not to heal. Reiki, in its truest form, is far more than just a system of healing – it is a profound spiritual path. The word *reiki* is made up of two words: *ki* is the life force (the Japanese equivalent of the Chinese qi or chi that flows through the meridians), while the word *rei* means spiritually guided.

Reiki was 'discovered' by a Japanese man called Mikao Usui around the beginning of the twentieth century. After a 14-year search for the secret of physical healing, Usui found the 'answer' in an ancient sutra or sacred text in a Zen monastery. In the manner of all the best yarns, no one since then has been able to rediscover the precise text, but it led him to meditate on a mountain where he was shown a vision of four symbols which could be used for healing. Coming down the mountain, Usui stumbled and hurt his toe. When he placed his hand on the foot, the injury healed – and he realized his quest was over.

The physical part of the reiki system is very simple. Consisting of 20 'holds', it can be learnt in a weekend. There is no need to learn anatomy or physiology; students aren't expected to study even basic psychology. The key is in the spiritual symbols which are 'transmitted' to the trainee healer. Then, it seems, the healing force is free to flow through. Practitioners insist it is not *they* who are healing; it is not even the reiki which heals. Rather, it is the individual who is being treated who decides how much of the healing energy to take and use.

Currently, reiki is big business. There are countless workshops promising to transform you into a reiki 'master' in a weekend or two. Frankly, they smack a little of pyramid selling and I would urge you to find someone who has followed the reiki way of life for many years and slowly gained their attunement.

what can reiki help?

- Practitioners do not promise to heal anything through reiki – rather, the body will choose what to do with the energy and may heal itself or may not.
- Many people have it simply for deep relaxation and stress relief.
- It is often used as a tool for self-development and spiritual questing.
- Studies have shown that can hasten healing after injuries.
- There have been cases of 'miraculous' cures – tumours disappearing, wounds healing, illnesses vanishing, long-term depression lifting. Practitioners are adamant, however, that they can make no claims.
- Reiki is practised extensively in hospices, especially with cancer patients. Sometimes people go into remission; sometimes they die, but in peace – without fear and feeling calm and accepting.

do-it-yourself reiki

The heart of reiki is spiritual. Although the actual holds are easily learned, you need to have the spiritual symbols 'transmitted' to you before true reiki healing energy can flow. However, this breathing and touching exercise gives a taste of the reiki touch. You will feel more calm, centred and relaxed. Find a time when you won't be disturbed to practise this exercise for best results.

1 Lie on your back, make yourself comfortable and close your eyes. Start paying attention to your breath and follow its rhythm, noticing how it flows in and out.

2 Now put your hands on your body wherever you feel drawn to or where you feel tension. Drawn on your intuition to locate the spot in your body that needs relaxation the most.

3 Now direct your breath to this place. Imagine you are breathing into that place. Visualize your breath as universal life energy that is flowing through you. Imagine it collecting and expanding under your hands. Notice the feeling of relaxation and peace as it gradually spreads from that place beneath your hands throughout your entire body.

4 After about 5 minutes, place your hands on another part of your body and repeat step 3. You may find that your breathing changes with this place. If so, just notice it and continue.

5 Now move on to two further places in your body and charge them with revitalizing energy.

6 Slowly open your eyes, stretch and return to normal consciousness.

what can I expect from a session?

WHERE WILL I HAVE THE TREATMENT?

You will be lying on a couch.

WILL I BE CLOTHED?

Yes, you will remain fully clothed throughout.

WHAT HAPPENS?

It's up to you whether you talk to the practitioner or not – you can tell them any problems or simply keep your counsel. However, you will be asked if you are on any medication, particularly insulin. The reason is that diabetics need to be carefully monitored after reiki because sometimes the amounts of insulin they need decline sharply. The same can be true for dosages of other medication.

You lie fully clothed on a massage table, with soft Oriental music playing in the background. The practitioner begins by gently but firmly touching your head with his or her fingers. After several minutes, he or she will lift one hand and touch another part of your head, then the other hand follows. So it continues as the practitioner works down your body.

You will find yourself becoming more and more relaxed, and probably quite drowsy. It's not uncommon to fall fast asleep while lying on the couch. Time becomes quite fluid and it can be hard to tell whether 5 minutes or 50 have passed. After an hour (the usual length of most sessions), you will be gently 'brought to' by the practitioner, who will usually leave you alone for a while to bring yourself back to full waking awareness.

Don't be surprised if you find you feel emotional after a session: it's not uncommon to feel sadness, anger or intense joy. Many practitioners will sit and talk with you about your experiences (often over a cup of herbal tea).

WILL IT HURT?

No, it is completely painless.

WILL ANYTHING STRANGE HAPPEN?

You may well 'see' past scenes from your life. Your limbs may spontaneously convulse or twitch. You may also find that, after a while, you can't feel the practitioners hands on you or you don't know exactly where they are. Some people see brilliant colours or feel a burning sensation from the hands during a reiki session. Others feel nothing at all.

WILL I BE GIVEN ANYTHING TO TAKE?

No, medication is not part of the treatment

IS THERE ANY HOMEWORK?

No, although a lot of people do go on to learn reiki so that they can practise it on their family and friends.

sound therapy

A soprano can break a glass by matching its vibration. You can bring down a bridge by stamping over it in rhythm. So, the reasoning goes that, if you can destroy with sound, then there is no reason why you can't heal with sound.

Simply making different sounds can affect your mood in minutes. Listening to powerful chants can affect both body and mind. Sound researchers believe that sound could be the medicine of the future.

'Disease is simply part of our body vibrating out of tune,' says pioneering sound therapist Jonathan Goldman. He explains that, 'Every organ, bone, tissue and other part of the body has a healthy resonant frequency. When that frequency alters, that part of the body vibrates out of harmony and that is what is termed disease. If it were possible to determine the correct frequency for a healthy organ and then project it into that part which is diseased, the organ should return to its normal frequency and a healing should occur.'

By creating sounds which are harmonious with the 'correct' frequency of our organs, we could all learn how to heal ourselves. Goldman and other sound researchers have been focusing most of their attention on the sacred chants of varying traditions, believing that the incredible harmonics which most of them share could have profound effects on body and mind.

Dr Alfred Tomatis, a French physician and researcher, found that Gregorian chants can have a neurophysical effect which charges the brain and stimulates the central nervous system. American researchers found that harmonic sounds reduced respiration and heart rate, relaxing the entire body and mind.

Apparently when sound healing is taking place, a process called 'entrainment' occurs: everything within the body that has a rhythm (heartbeat, respiration, brainwaves, movement in the intestine, etc.) starts to change in order to synchronize with the rhythm of a more powerful body – the healer.

what can sound therapy help?

- Sound therapy can increase confidence.
- It can alleviate stress and help stress-related illnesses.
- It increases energy and wellbeing, and can be deeply relaxing.
- It can help dissipate headaches and prevent migraine.
- Many people use it as a tool for personal or spiritual growth.

what can I expect from a session?

WHERE WILL I HAVE THE TREATMENT?

You will be treated in the sound therapist's room.

WILL I BE CLOTHED?

Yes, you will be fully clothed.

WHAT HAPPENS?

An experienced sound therapist directs sounds at your body – either working through the major chakras or focusing on specific organs or parts of the body. You simply stand still with your eyes shut while he or she projects the sound at you. This can feel incredible, like being doused with a cool shower of sound. You may also be taught how to make healing sounds, or toning, yourself.

The aim is not to make perfect sounds – in fact, it doesn't even matter if you are tone deaf. Many people go on to learn sound healing at workshops, where participants are taken through simple exercises as part of a group.

WILL IT HURT?

No, it doesn't hurt at all.

WILL ANYTHING STRANGE HAPPEN?

When sound is directed at you, it's not uncommon to feel surges of energy through your body. Some people say they feel a hum in their bones and explosions in their heads.

WILL I BE GIVEN ANYTHING TO TAKE?

No, medication is not part of the treatment.

IS THERE ANY HOMEWORK?

Yes, ideally you should practise making sounds and toning at home.

do-it-yourself sound techniques

- Humming is a great way to calm yourself. If you're feeling anxious, stressed or nervous, just sit quietly and hum very gently. Feel the hum resonating through your body. Where can you feel it? Does it change if you alter the note of the hum?

- Exaggerated yawning is ideal if you're feeling tired. We hold a lot of tension in our jaws and mouths, so stretching the mouth therefore reduces tension.

Give your body as good stretch as well to wake it up.

- If you're feeling irritable and tense, try an elongated, noisy sigh. Groaning, too, can help release negative emotions. Forget about being polite – really let go.

- Take every opportunity to sing. Sing along with the radio, while you're doing housework, in the bath (of course!) and while you're driving in the car. Don't worry about what your voice sounds like – just belt it out.

- Try toning the different vowel sounds – ah, eh, iii, oh, uh. Where can you feel them in your body? How do these sounds make you feel?

- Play with mantras. They don't have to be 'ohm' or anything spiritual – simply try singing positive statements, repeating them with different tunes. If you're feeling tense, try singing: 'I'm calm, I'm calm, I'm really, really calm.'

- Experiment with listening to different kinds of music and work out what effect each one has on your mood. Try listening to some of the sacred chants – Gregorian, Tibetan, Mongolian overtone chanting etc.

FURTHER READING

PART ONE
AYURVEDA
Morningstar, Amadea and Desai, Urmilla, *The Ayurvedic Cookbook*, Wilmot WI, Lotus Light, 1991
Morrison, Judith H, *The Book of Ayurveda*, London, Gaia, 1995
CHINESE MEDICINE
Harper, Jennifer, *Body Wisdom*, London and California, Thorsons, 1997
Hicks, Angela, *Chinese Medicine*, London and California, Thorsons, 1996
Mercati, Maria, *Step-by-Step Tui Na*, London, Gaia, 1997
ENERGY HEALING
Alexander, Jane, *The Energy Secret*, London, Thorsons, 2000
HEALING
Cowens, Deborah with Monte, Tom, *A Gift for Healing*, New York, Crown Trade Paperbacks, 1996
HOMEOPATHY
Lockie, Dr Andrew, *The Family Guide to Homeopathy*, London, Elm Tree, 1989
PSYCHONEURIMMUNOLOGY
Shapiro, Debbie, *Your Body Speaks your Mind*, London, Piatkus, 1996
TIBETAN MEDICINE
Donden, Dr Yeshi, *Health Through Balance*, New York, Snow Lion Publications, 1986

PART TWO
ALEXANDER TECHNIQUE
Brennan, Richard, *The Alexander Technique Workbook*, Shaftesbury, Element, 1992
BREATHING
Weller, Stella, *The Breath Book*, London, Thorsons, 1999
DETOXING
Alexander, Jane, *The Detox Plan*, London, Gaia, 1998
FELDENKRAIS
Shafarman, Steven, *Practical Feldenkrais for Dynamic Health*, London, Thorsons, 1998
FENG SHUI
Kingston, Karen, *Clear your Clutter with Feng Shui*, London, Piatkus, 1998
Rossbach, Sarah, *Interior Design with Feng Shui*, London, Rider, 1987
Spear, William, *Feng Shui made Easy*, London, Thorsons, 1995
HERBALISM
Oddy, Penelope, *The Herb Society's Complete Medicinal Herbal*, London, Dorling Kindersley, 1993
NATUROPATHY
Hartvig, Kirsten and Rowley, Dr Nic, *You are What you Eat*, London, Piatkus, 1996
Newman Turner, Roger, *Naturopathic Medicine*, London, Thorsons, 1984
NUTRITION
Holford, Patrick, *The Optimum Nutrition Bible*, London, Piatkus, 1997
Lazarides, Linda, *The Nutritional Health Bible*, London, Thorsons, 1997
PILATES
Ackland, Lesley, *10-Step Pilates*, London, Thorsons, 1999
QI QONG
Reid, Daniel, *Chi-Gung*, London, Simon & Schuster, 1998
SLEEP
Lavery, Sheila, *The Healing Power of Sleep*, London, Gaia, 1997
VASTU SHASTRA
Niranjan Babu, B., *Handbook of Vastu*, New Delhi, UBSPD, 1997
YOGA
Sturgess, Stephen, *The Yoga Book*, Rockport, Element, 1997

PART THREE
ART THERAPY
Brown, Daniel, *Art Therapies*, London, Thorsons, 1997
BODYWORK
Caldwell, Christine (ed) *Getting in Touch*, Wheaton IL, Quest, 1997
Webb, Marcus and Maria, *Healing Touch*, New Alresford, Godsfield, 1999
DREAMS
Weiss, Lillie, *Practical Dreaming*, Oakland CA, New Harbinger Publications, 1999
FAMILY
Bryan, Mark, *Codes of Love*, London, Simon & Schuster, 1999
FLOATING
Hutchison, Michael, *The Book of Floating*, New York, Quill, 1984
MEDITATION
Strand, Clark, *The Wooden Bowl*, Dublin, Newleaf, 1999
MINDFULNESS
Kabat-Zinn, Jon, *Mindfulness Meditation for Everyday Life*, London, Piatkus, 1994
NLP
O'Connor, Joseph and McDermott, Ian, *NLP*, London, Thorsons, 1996
RELATIONSHIPS
Davies, Dr Brenda, *Affairs of the Heart*, London, Hodder & Stoughton, 2000
SEXUALITY
Richardson, Diana, *The Love Keys*, Shaftesbury, Element, 1999
SOUND HEALING
D'Angelo, James, *Healing with the Voice*, London, Thorsons, 2000
Goldman, Jonathan, *Healing Sounds*, Shaftesbury, Element, 1992
STRESS
Adams, Jenni, *Stress a Friend for Life*, Saffron Walden, C W Daniel, 1998
TALKING THERAPIES
Avery, Brice, *Psychotherapy*, London, Thorsons, 1996
WORK
Williams, Nick, *The Work we were Born to Do*, Shaftesbury, Element, 1999
WRITING
Schneider, Myra and Killick, John, *Writing for Self-Discovery*, Shaftesbury, Element, 1998

PART FOUR
DEATH
Levine, Stephen, *A Year to Live*, London, Thorsons, 1997
PRAYER
Weston, Walter, *How Prayer Heals*, Charlottesville, Hampton Roads, 1998
RETREATING
Louden, Jennifer, *The Woman's Retreat Book*, New York, HarperSanFrancisco, 1997
RITUAL
Alexander, Jane, *Sacred Rituals at Home*, New York, Sterling, 2000
SACRED SPACE
Alexander, Jane, *Spirit of the Home*, London, Thorsons, 1998
SHAMANISM
Rutherford, Leo, *Shamanism*, London, Thorsons, 1996
SHRINES AND ALTARS
Linn, Denise, *Altars*, London, Ebury Press, 1999
Streep, Peg, *Altars Made Easy*, New York, HarperCollins, 1997
SPACE CLEARING
Linn, Denise, *Space Clearing*, London, Ebury Press, 2000
SMUDGING
Alexander, Jane, *The Smudge Pack*, London, Thorsons, 1999
SPIRITUAL TRADITIONS
Freke, Timothy, *Encyclopedia of Spirituality*, New Alresford, Godsfield, 2000

PART FIVE
AROMATHERAPY
Worwood, Valerie Ann, *The Fragrant Pharmacy*, London, Bantam, 1990
CHIROPRACTIC
Howitt Wilson, Dr Michael B, *Introductory Guide to Chiropractic*, London, Thorsons, 1987
COLOUR THERAPY
Gimbel, Theo, *Healing with Colour*, London, Gaia, 1994
FLOWER AND GEM THERAPY
Harvey, Clare G and Cochrane, Amanda, *The Encyclopaedia of Flower Remedies*, London, Thorsons, 1995
HELLERWORK
Golten, Roger, *The Owner's Guide to the Body*, London, Thorsons, 1999
HUNA
Hoffman, Enid, *Huna*, Rockport, Para Research, 1976
JIN SHIN JYUTSU
Burmeister, Alice, *Practical Jin Shin Jyutsu*, London, Thorsons, 1997
KINESIOLOGY
Holdway, Ann, *Kinesiology*, Shaftesbury, Element, 1995
LIGHT THERAPY
Liberman, Jacob, *Light – Medicine of the Future*, Santa Fé, Bear & Company, 1991
MCTIMONEY CHIROPRACTIC
Andrews, Elizabeth and Courtenay, Anthea, *The Essentials of McTimoney Chiropractic*, London, Thorsons, 1999
METAMORPHIC TECHNIQUE
Saint-Pierre, Gaston and Shapiro, Debbie, *The Metamorphic Technique*, Shaftesbury, Element, 1982
POLARITY THERAPY
Stone, Dr Randolph, *Health Building*, Sebastopol, CRCS Publications, 1985
RADIONICS
Mason, Keith, *The Radionics Handbook*, London, Piatkus, 2001
REFLEXOLOGY
Gillanders, Ann, *Reflexology*, London, Gaia, 1995
REIKI
Hall, Mari, *Reiki*, London, Thorsons, 2000
SHIATSU
Ferguson, Pamela, *The Self-Shiatsu Handbook*, London, Newleaf, 1996
THAI MASSAGE
Mercati, Maria, *Thai Massage*, London, Marshall, 1998
ZERO BALANCING
Smith, Dr Fritz Frederick, *Inner Bridges*, Atlanta, Humanics, 1986

RESOURCES

When writing to organizations please include a large SAE. Many websites now have on-line registers of practitioners, so checking the website first. All information is correct at the time of going to print but organizations do change address so our apologies if any become out of date.

UK
PART ONE
AYURVEDA
Ayurvedic Living, PO Box 188, Exeter EX4 5AB
Information on all aspects of ayurveda plus guidelines for finding a practitioner. Send SAE with four second-class stamps.
CHINESE MEDICINE
The British Acupuncture Counci, 63 Jeddo Road, London W12 9HX (020 8735 0440)
www.acupunyure.org.uk
Information on all aspects of traditional Chinese medicine.
HEALING
The National Federation of Spiritual Healers, Old Manor Farm Studio, Church Street, Sunbury-on-Thames, Middlesex TW16 6RG
(01932 783164) www.nfsh.org.uk
HOMEOPATHY
The Society of Homoeopaths, 2 Artizan Road, Northampton, NN1 4HU
(01604 621400) www.homeopathy-soh.org
NEUROTHERAPY
International Federation of Neurotherapy, PO Box 30419, London NW6 1GA
www.ifn-nadivigyan.com
TIBETAN MEDICINE
The Kailash Centre, 7 Newcourt Street, London NW8 7AA (020 7722 3939)
www.orientalhealing.co.uk
Kate Roddick teaches preventative Tibetan healthcare in workshops and consultations around the UK. For details send SAE to Tibetan Healing, Burnside, Kinnel Bridge, Lochmaben, Dunfriesshire, DG11 1TB

PART TWO
ALEXANDER TECHNIQUE
Society of Teachers of the Alexander Technique (STAT), 129 Camden Mews, London NW1 9AH (020 7284 3338)
www.stat.org.uk
CHI KUNG
Sue Weston runs introductory workshops: (01435 866215)
ENVIRONMENT
The Healthy House, Cold Harbour, Ruscombe, Stroud, Gloucestershire GL6 6DA (01453 752216)
Mail-order company for people with allergies, selling light boxes, water-purifying equipment, ecologically friendly paint, etc.
www.healthy-house.co.uk

FELDENKRAIS
Feldenkrais Guild UK, PO Box 370, London N10 3XA (07000 785506)
www.feldenkrais.co.uk
FENG SHUI
The Feng Shui Company, 15 The Regency, Esterbrooke Street, London SW1P 4NL.(07000 781 901)
Consultations and workshops.
The Feng Shui Network International, PO Box 2133, London W1A 1RL (07000 336474) Email Feng1@aol.com
Consultations and workshops.
The Lucky Feng Shui Company Sunshine Cottage, Chedzoy, Somerset TA7 8RW (01278 433523) www.fengshuisite.com
Mail-order feng shui 'cures'.
GEOPATHIC STRESS
British Society of Dowsers, Sycamore Barn, Hastingleigh, Ashford, Kent TN25 5HW (01233 750253)
Can advise on dowsers able to detect geopathic stress.
HERBALISM
National Institute of Medical Herbalists, 56 Longbrook Street, Exeter, Devon EX4 6AH (01392 426022)
www.btinternet.com/~nimh
For details send a 44p stamp.
MÉZIÈRES METHOD
Joel Carbonnel, 4a Berrymede Road, London W4 5JF (020 8747 8583)
The only UK practitioner at present.
NATUROPATHY
General Council and Register of Naturopaths, 2 Goswell Road, Street, Somerset BA16 0JG (01458 840072)
www.naturopathy.org.uk
NUTRITIONAL THERAPY
The Institute for Optimum Nutrition, 13 Blades Court, Deodar Road, London SW15 2NU (020 8877 9993)
www.ion.ac.uk
PILATES
Body Control Pilates Association, 14 Neal's Yard, Covent Garden, London WC2H 9DP (020 7379 3734)
www.bodycontrol.co.uk/association
YOGA
The British Wheel of Yoga, 1 Hamilton Place, Boston Road, Sleaford, Lincolnshire NG34 7ES (01529 306851) www.bwy.org.uk

PART THREE
ART THERAPY
British Association of Art Therapists, Mary Ward House, 5 Tavistock Place, London W1H 9SN (020 7383 3774)
www.baat.co.uk
AUTOGENIC TRAINING
British Autogenic Society (BAS), Royal London Homoeopathic Hospital, Great Ormond Street, London WC1N 3HR
www.autogenic-therapy.org.uk
BIODYNAMIC THERAPY
The Association of Holistic Biodynamic Massage Therapists (AHBMT), 42 Catherine Street, Cambridge

CB1 3AW (01223 240814)
www.ahbmt.demon.co.uk
The London School for Biodynamic Psychotherapy, Willow Cottage, off Wokingham Road, Hurst, Berkshire RG10 0RU (07000 794725)
www.isbp.org.uk
DANCE THERAPY
Biodanza UK, 48 Clifford Avenue, London SW14 7BP (020 8392 1433)
Email martello@biodanza.demon.co.uk
DREAMS
Many Jungian psychotherapists use dreams as part of their work.
The Association of Jungian Analysts, 7 Eton Avenue, London NW3 3EL (020 7794 8711)
FLOATING
The Floatation Tank Association, PO Box 11024, London SW4 7ZF (020 7627 4962)
www.floatationtankassociation.net
MEDITATION
There are around 60 UK centers teaching Transcendental Meditation. For details contact 0990 143733
www.transcendental-meditation.org.uk
NLP
Association of Neuro-Linguistic Programming, PO Box 78, Stourbridge, DY8 4ZJ (01785 660665) www.anlp.org
SHEN®
The London SHEN® Centre, PO Box 115, Beckenham BR3 4ZF (020 8658 6505)
The SHEN Therapy Centre, PO Box 13034, Edinburgh EH13 9YD (0131 478 4780)
SOLUTION-FOCUSED THERAPY
see *United Kingdom Council for Psychotherapy* (Talking therapies, below)
TALKING THERAPIES
United Kingdom Council for Psychotherapy, 167–9 Great Portland Street, London W1W 5PF (020 7436 3002)
www.psychotherapy.org.uk
TIMELINE THERAPY
The Institute of Human Development, Freepost, Tonbridge, Kent TN11 8BR (01732 834354).

PART FOUR
RETREATING
The Retreat Company, The Manor House, Kings Norton, Leicestershire, LE7 9BA (0116 2599211)
www.retreat-co.co.uk
SHAMANISM
Eagle's Wing, 58 Westbere Road, London NW2 3RU (020 7435 8174)
www.shamanism.co.uk
The Sacred Trust, PO Box 16, Uckfield, East Sussex TN22 5WD (01825 840574)
www.sacredtrust.org
SMUDGING
see Shamanism, above
SPACE CLEARING
Karen Kingston, Suite 401, Langham House, 24 Margaret Street, London W1N 7LB (07000 772232)

www.spaceclearing.com
Workshops and products.

PART FIVE
AROMATHERAPY
The Aromatherapy Organisations Council, The Secretary, AOC, PO Box 19834, London SE25 6WF (020 8251 7912)
www.aromatherapy-uk.org
Represents 13 professional associations.
BOWEN TECHNIQUE
The Bowen Association, PO Box 4358, Dorchester, Dorset DT2 7XX (0700 269 8324) www.bowen-technique.co.uk
CHAVUTTI THIRUMAL
The Soma Institute, 17 Condray Place, London SW11 3PE (020 8699 5066)
CHIROPRACTIC
British Chiropractic Association, Blagrave House, 17 Blagrave Street, Reading, Berkshire RG1 1QB (0118 950 5950)
www.chiropractic-uk.co.uk
CHUA KA
MetaFitness, Squires Hill House, Squires Hill Lane, Tilford, Surrey, GU10 2AD (01252 782661)
COLOUR THERAPY
International Association of Colour, 46 Cottenham Road, Histon, Cambridge, CB4 9ES (01223 563403)
www.internationalassociationofcolour.com
CRANIAL OSTEOPATHY
The Sutherland Society, c/o 15a Church Street, Bradford-upon-Avon, Wiltshire BA15 1NL (01225 868282)
www.cranial.org.uk
CRANIO-SACRAL THERAPY
The Cranio-Sacral Therapy Association of the UK, Monomark House, 27 Old Gloucester Street, London WC1N 3XX (07000 784735) www.craniosacral.co.uk
ELECTRO-CRYSTAL THERAPY
School of Electro-Crystal Therapy, 117 Long Drive, South Ruislip, Middlesex HA4 0HL (020 8841 1716)
www.electrocrystal.com
FLOWER AND GEM THERAPY
The Bach Flower Centre, Mount Vernon, Sotwell, Wallingford, Oxfordshire OX10 0PZ (01491 834678).
International Flower Essence Repertoire, The Living Tree, Milland, near Liphook, Hampshire, GU30 7JS (01428 741572) Email flower@atlas.co.uk
Wide range of essences by mail order.
HELLERWORK
www.hellerwork.com
HUNA
Rosalie Samet (07974 083432)
For details of the few UK practioners of this form of massage.
INDIAN HEAD MASSAGE
The London Centre of Indian Champissage, 136 Holloway Road, London N7 8DD (020 7609 3590)
www.indianchampissage.com
JIN SHIN JYUTSU
Jin Shin Jyutsu, 40 Archers Road, Eastleigh, SO50 9AY
UK coordinator.

KINESIOLOGY
Health Kinesiology UK, Sea View House, Long Rock, Penzance, Cornwall, TR20 8JF (01736 719030)
www.healthk.co.uk
Kinesiology Federation, PO Box 17153, Edinburgh EH11 3WQ (08700 113545)
www.kinesiologyfederation.org
MASSAGE
British Massage Therapy Council (BMTC), 17 Rymers Lane, Oxford OX4 3JU (01865 774123) www.bmtc.co.uk
MCTIMONEY CHIROPRACTIC
McTimoney Chiropractic Association, 21 High Street, Eynsham, Oxon OX8 1HE (01865 880974) www.mctimoney.org.uk
METAMORPHIC TECHNIQUE
The Metamorphic Association, 67 Ritherdon Road, Tooting, London SW17 8QE (020 8672 5951)
www.geocities.com/~metam
MLD
MLD UK, PO Box 14491, Glenrothes, Fife, KY6 3YE (01592 840799)
www.mlduk.org.uk
OSTEOPATHY
General Osteopathic Council, Osteopathy House, 176 Tower Bridge Road, London SE1 3LU (020 7357 6655)
www.osteopathy.org.uk
POLARITY THERAPY
International School of Polarity Therapy, 7 Nunney Close, Golden Valley, Cheltenham, Gloucestershire GL51 0TU (01242 522352)
RADIONICS
The Radionic Association, Baerlein House, Goose Green, Deddington, Oxfordshire OX15 0SZ (01869 338852)
www.radionic.co.uk
REFLEXOLOGY
The British Reflexology Association, Monks Orchard, Whitbourne, Worcester WR6 5RB (01886 821207)
www.britreflex.co.uk
REIKI
The Reiki Alliance, 27 Lavington Road, London W13 9NN (020 8579 3813)
www.reikialliance.org.uk
ROLFING
Contact 020 7834 1493 or www.rolf.org for details of nearest practitioner.
SHIATSU
The Shiatsu Society (UK), Eastlands Court, St Peters Road, Rugby, Warwickshire CV21 3QP (01788 555051) www.shiatsu.org
SOUND THERAPY
Sound Therapy, Harmony, 1a Railway Cottages, Pinchinthorpe, near Guisborough TS14 8HH (01287 636350)
THAI MASSAGE
Bodyharmonics Centre, 54 Flecker's Drive, Hatherley, Cheltenham GL51 3BD (01242 582168)
www.bodyharmonics.co.uk
TRAGER®
Trager® Association UK, c/o 20 Summerdale Road, Hove, East Sussex BN3 8LG www.trager.com

WATSU

For details of UK practitioners contact
www.waba.edu

ZERO BALANCING

ZBA UK, 10 Victoria Grove, Bridport,
Dorset DT6 3AA (01308 420325)
www.zerobalancing.com
US site but has UK section with
register of practitioners.

Jane Alexander's website
www.smudging.com provides
information on a wide range of
mind, body, spirit topics. It also
provides links and an opportunity
to buy Jane's other books.

USA

PART ONE

ACUPUNCTURE

National Acupuncture and Oriental
Medicine Alliance (NAOMA),
14637 Starr Road, Southeast Olalla,
WA, 98359 (253 851 6896;
fax 253 851 6883) www.acuall.org
General information on acupuncture,
conferences and workshops, herbal
safety and advice for potential students
as well as referrals for state-licensed or
nationally certified practitioners.

AYURVEDA

The Ayurvedic Center, 4100 Westheimer,
Suite 235, Houston, TX 77027 (tel./fax
713 436 2525) www.holheal.com
Holistic health resources – services
and classes, steps for better health,
order herbs on-line.

HEALING

Spiritual Healing, Rebecca Kurtz,
101 First Street, Suite 212 Los Altos,
CA 94022-1157 (650 948 7265)
www.spiritheals.com
Individual sessions, private workshops,
healing products, mailing list.

HOMEOPATHY

Homeopathy Home
www.homeopathyhome.com
Directory, reference library, services and
supplies, recommended books, discussion
forums, chatroom, listing of non-
commercial sites and societies.

TIBETAN MEDICINE

Tibetan medicine
www.tibetanmedicine.com
Information, articles and clinical resources.
Tibetan Medicine World Wide Web
Virtual Library
www.unituebingen.de/psi/yuthog/
frameset/vl_htm
Listing of Tibetan medicine resources –
newsletters, healers, consultants, colleges
and related environmental organizations.

PART TWO

ALEXANDER TECHNIQUE

The Alexander Technique Center, Email
info@alexandercenter.com
www.alexandercenter.com
Learn the technique, lessons and

workshops, recommended reading,
and list of certified teachers.

CHI KUNG

National Qigong (Chi Kung) Association
USA, PO Box 540, Ely, MN 55731
(218 365 6330; fax 218 365 6933)
Email info@nqa.org www.nqa.org

ENVIRONMENT

All Allergy
www.allallergy.net
Allergy gateway site, articles,
organizations, publications, events,
products, databases.
Environmental Health Network (EHN)
PO Box 1155, Larkspur, CA 94977-0074
Advocacy organization and resource site.
For information call 415 541 5075
National Institute of Environmental
Health Sciences Library (NIEHS)
POBox 12233 Research Triangle Park
NC 27709. General information,
scientific research, community
outreach, grants and contracts,
National Toxicology Program.
Natural Choice Directory
www.naturalchoice.net/sec1/geopath.htm
Fitness and beauty, natural food
markets and restaurants, natural remedies,
bookstores, counselling, Education

FELDENKRAIS

Feldenkrais Guild of North America,
3611 SW Hood Avenue, Suite 100,
Portland, OR 97201
(800 775 2118 or 503 221 6612; fax
503 221 6616) www.feldenkrais.com

FENG SHUI

Applied Feng Shui, Patricia Shetley,
Seattle, Washington (206 523 8855)
Psychic clearing, home, office and land
consulting. Geopathic stress, analysis
and treatment.
Feng Shui Help.com
www.fengshuihelp.com
Glossary, history, book club, FAQ, links,
tip of the week.
Western School of Feng Shui, 437 South
Hwy 101, Suite 752, Solana Beach,
CA 92075 (toll free 800 300 6785
or 858 793 0945) www.wsfs.com
Practitioner training, workshops,
products, design services.
The Feng Shui Directory of Consultants,
PO Box 6701, Charlottesville VA 22906
(1 804 974 1726) Email
info@fsdirectory.com
www.fengshuidirectory.com
Consultant listings, schools, seminars,
articles, books, objects and materials.

NATUROPATHY

Medical Herbalism, on-line magazine
from the journal of herbal medicine
published by Bergner Communications,
PO Box 20512, Boulder, CO 80308
Email web@medherb.com
www.medherb.com
History, photographs, bookstore, folk
uses, medical journals, organizations,
clinical nutrition, schools, therapeutics,
newsletter, distance learning.
American Naturopathic Medical

Association, PO Box 96273, Las Vegas,
NV 89193 (702 897 7053; Fax 702
897 7140) www.anma.com
Nonprofit scientific and
educational organization.
The Wellspring, (toll free 888 551 1207
or 530 926 6036) Email
services@healingretreat.com
www.healingretreat.com
Learn about toxins and nutrition, the
importance of mind and spirit to
health, and alternative healing
techniques. Healing and wellness
programmes, consultation,
supplements, and lodging at the
Wellspring Life Enhancing Center.

PILATES

The Pilates Center, 4800 Baseline Road,
Suite D206, Boulder, CO 80303
(303 494 3400; fax 303 494 5151)
Email info@thepilatescenter.com
www.thepilatescenter.com

YOGA

Berkeley Yoga Center, 1250 Addison
Street, Suite 209 Berkeley, CA 94702
(510 843 8784) www.berkeleyyoga.com

PART THREE

ART THERAPY

American Art Therapy Association,
1202 Allanson Road, Mundelein,
IL 60060 (1 888 290 0878 or
847 949 6064; fax 847 566 4580)
Email arttherapy@ntr.net
www.arttherapy.org/ss

CRANIO-SACRAL THERAPY

International Schools for Biodynamic
Craniosacral Therapy, 13878 Oleander
Avenue, Juno Beach, FL 33408
(561 627 7327; fax 561 625 3775)
Email info@sheacranial.com
www.sheacranial.com
Public Orgonomic Research Exchange,
www.orgone.org

DANCE THERAPY

American Dance Therapy Association,
TDTA National Office, business hours
8:30am–4:00pm (410 997 4040; fax
410 997 4048) Email info@adta.org
www.adta.org

DREAM THERAPY

The Association for the Study of
Dreams, PO Box 1166, Orinda,
CA 94563 (925 258 1822; fax 925
258 1821) Email asdreams@aol.com
www.asdreams.org

MEDITATION

Holistic-online.com,
Email info@holisticonline.com
www.holistic-online.com/stress/stress
_autogenic-training.htm
International Meditation Center, 4920
Rose Drive, Westminster MD 21158
(410 346 7889; fax 410 346 7133)
ccpl.carr.org/~imcusa/
A practical guide to autogenetic training
On-line course published by published
by HSCTI, PO Box 1298, Woodstock,
GA 30188 www.magitech.com/autogenic

NEUROTHERAPY

The Neuro-Linguistic Programming
Information Center, www.nlpinfo.com
The Society of Neuro-Linguistic
Programming, John La Valle, President,
Box 424, Hopatcong, NJ 07843
(201 770 3600; fax 201 770 0314)

PHYSICAL THERAPY

Quality Physical Therapy, Inc.,
Sturbridge Office Center, 48 Main
Street, Sturbridge, MA 01566
(508 347 8141; fax 508 347 7576)
www.qualityphysicaltherapy.com
Specialize in manual therapy,
biodynamic balancing and
myofascial release techniques.

SOLUTION-FOCUSED THERAPY

American Counseling Association,
5999 Stevenson Avenue, Alexandria,
VA 22304 (703 823 9800; fax 703
823 0252) www.counseling.org

SPA THERAPY

Floatspa.com, Lighthouse Point, Florida
(954 899 6182) Email info@floatspa.com
www.floatspa.com

PART FOUR

RETREATS

Body/Mind Restoration Retreats, 56 Lieb
Road, Spencer, NY 14883 (607 272 0694)
www.bodymindretreats.com

PART FIVE

CHIROPRACTIC

American Chiropractic Association, (703
276 8800) www.amerchiro.org
International Institute of Reflexology Inc.
5650 First Avenue North, PO Box
12642, St Petersburg FL 33733-2642
(727 3434811; fax 727 381 2807)
Email ftreflex@concentric.net
www.reflexology-usa.net

FLOWER THERAPY

Flower Essence Society, PO Box 459,
Nevada City, CA 95959 (800 736 9222
or 530 265 9163; fax 530 265 0584)
www.flowersociety.org

OSTEOPATHY

American Osteopathic Association, 142
East Ontario Street, Chicago, IL 60611
(800 621 1773; fax 312 202 8200)
Email info@aoa-net.org
www.aoa-net.org

SOUND THERAPY

Sound Feelings Publishing, 7616 Lindley
Avenue, Reseda, CA 91335 (818 757
0600; fax 818 757 0834)
www.soundfeelings.com

THAI MASSAGE

The Thai Massage Center
17383 Peace Lane Bow, WA 98232
(360 724 4673)

TRAGER®

The Trager Institute, 3800 Park East Drive,
Suite 100, Room 1, Beachwood,
OH 44122 (216 896 9383) Email
admin@trager.com www.trager.com

WATSU

The Watsu Oasis, Desert Hot Springs,
Palm Springs, Los Angeles, San Diego, CA
(760 329 1214) www.watsuoasis.com

The publishers would like to thank
the following sources for their kind
permission to reproduce the pictures
in this book:

Hugh Arnold: 65, 108, 214r, 215l,
215r, 226bl, 226br, /Elemis: 36, 59,
72, 203, Graham Atkins-Hughes: 15,
198, Atlantic Syndication: 230b,
Carlton Books Ltd: 95r, 218, /Sue
Atkinson: 225, /Graham Atkins-
Hughes: 18, 19, 55, 95l, 144, 151,
176, /Jason Bell: 141, /Michael
Clarke: 22, 29, 74/75, 78, 195, 205,
206, 209, 211, /Janine Hosegood:
179, /Howard Shooter: 63, 248,
/Polly Wreford: 31t, 56, 99, 146,
167, 182, /Mel Yates: 94, The
Complemetary Group/Polly
Borland: 88, 89, Neil Cooper: 210,
DK Photo Library/Marc Henrie: 86,
Donna Francesca: 44, 60, 221,
Ebury Press: 93, /Jonathan Root:
196tr, Elemis Press: 238, Garden
Picture Library/Chris Burrows: 117,
Getty Images Stone: 1, 10, 26, 47,
77, 104, 110, 111, 127, 128, 137,
138, 142, 148, 152, 168r, 168cr,
168l, 187, 244, John Hicks: 4, 16,
34, 71, 80, Barry J Holmes: 241,
The Image Bank: 31b, /Rita Maas:
66, 68, IPC Syndication: 213t, 213b,
/Caroline Arber: 237, /Chris
Craymer/Marie Claire Health
& Beauty: 107, Mainstream/Ray
Main: 48, 96, 91 (Architect Simon
Condor),133, James Mitchell: 175,
Trish Morrissey: 21, Narratives/Jan
Baldwin: 10, /Tamsyn Hill: 157,
/Polly Wreford: 168cl, 101, The
National Magazine Co./Zest/Mark
Read: 232/3, Fleur Olby: 2, 189,
191, Photonica/Neo Vision: 83,
129, 130, Lucy Pope: 171, Alex
Sarginson: 185, 205, 251, Science
Photo Library: 38, 208l, 208c, 208r,
Society of Neuropathy: 25tl, 25tr,
25br, Jane Solomon: 235t, 235b,
Kate Stewart: 228b, 229tl, 229br,
Rosie Walford: 223tl, 223tr, 223br.

Every effort has been made to
acknowledge correctly and contact
the source and/or copyright holder
of each picture, and Carlton Books
Limited apologizes for any
unintentional errors or omissions
which will be corrected in future
editions of this book.

ACKNOWLEDGEMENTS

This is a big book and certainly not
one I could ever have written
single-handedly – so I would like to
give heartfelt thanks to the many
Mind, Body and Spirit experts who
have given so generously their time
and knowledge to me. They include:
Angela Hope-Murray, Judith
Morrison, Doja Purkitt, Dr Rajendra
Sharma, Andrew Johnson, Ruth
Delman and Kenneth Gibbons, Dr
Tamara Voronina, Roger Newman
Turner, Dr Andrew Lockie, Roger
Savage, Penelope Ritchie, Keith and
Chrissie Mason, Kate Roddick,
Rosalie Samet, Dr Natsagdorj, Karin
Weisensel, Dr Mohammad Salim
Khan, Linda Lazarides, Patrick
Holford, Dr Marilyn Glenville, Fiona
Arrigo, Nicola Griffin, Andrew
Chevalier, Christine Steward,
Godfrey Devereux, Sebastian Pole,
Charlotte Katz, Sue Weston,
Malcolm Kirsch, Joel Carbonnel,
Kate Kelly, Gail Barlow, Barbara
McCrea, Julie Crocker, Jane
Thurnell-Read, Geraint and Sylvia
Jones-David, Wilma Tait, Tom
Williams, Sarah Shurety, Liz
Williams, Simon Brown, William
Spear, Karen Kingston, Denise Linn,
Gina Lazenby, Kajal Sheth, Lynne
Crawford, Rob Russell, Kati Cottrell-
Blanc, Jane Mayers, Richard Lanham,
Ron Wilgosh, Dave Hawkes, Jo
Hogg, Kieran Foley, Jennie
Crewdson, Terry Peterson, Allan
Rudolf, Carol Logan, Tony Bailey,
Angela Renton, Gillie Gilbert, Sarah
Dening, Patricia Martello, Gabrielle
Roth, Caroline Born, Shan, Leo
Rutherford, Kenneth Meadows,
Howard Charing, William Bloom,
Will Parfitt, Vera Diamond, Maria
Mercati, Julian Baker, Monica
Anthony, Phil Parker, Jon Mason, Jeff
Leonard, Peter Bartlett, Corina
Petter, Sue Ricks, Pat Morrell,
Rosalyn Journeaux, Elaine Arthey,
Pim de Gryff, Sara Hooley, Eileen
Fairbane, Dee Jones, Jessica Loeb,
Emma Field, Narendra Mehta, Jill
Dunley, Agni Eckroyd, Harry
Oldfield, Rosamund Webster,
Margaret-Anne Pauffley and Paul
Dennis, Natalie Handley, Chris
James, Susan Lever, Angelika
Hochadel, Gaston Saint-Pierre.

Lots of love to the original Williams
family who started me off on this
curious path and to the many
friends and fellow seekers who
have guided me along the way.

A large debt of gratitude to Bonnie
Estridge who introduced me to
Carlton and to everyone there
(with special thanks to Zia
Mattocks, Venetia Penfold, Abi
Dillon, Siobhán O'Connor and
Barbara Zuñiga).

A big hug as always to über-agent
Judy Chilcote.

INDEX

Figures in italics indicate captions.